GLOBAL MELTDOWN AND INDIAN ECONOMY

GLOBAL MELTDOWN AND INDIAN ECONOMY

Edited by

ANIL KUMAR THAKUR *and* **PARAMANAND SINGH**

Published on behalf of
THE INDIAN ECONOMIC ASSOCIATION

DEEP & DEEP PUBLICATIONS PVT. LTD.
F-159, Rajouri Garden, New Delhi-110027

GLOBAL MELTDOWN AND INDIAN ECONOMY

ISBN 978-81-8450-354-8

Typeset by S.S. COMPOSERS
3190, Mohindra Park, Shakur Basti, Delhi-110034.

Printed in India at MAYUR ENTERPRISES
WZ Plot No. 3, Gujjar Market, Tihar Village, New Delhi-110018.

Published by DEEP & DEEP PUBLICATIONS PVT. LTD.
F-159, Rajouri Garden, New Delhi-110027.
Phones: 25435369, 25440916
E-mail: ddpbooks@yahoo.co.in • ddpubs@gmail.com
Showroom:
2/13, Ansari Road, Daryaganj, New Delhi-110002 • Telefax: 23245122

Contents

PART II

GLOBAL MELTDOWN: POLICY DECISIONS AND REGULATORY MEASURES AND ITS VARIOUS FACETS

PART III

GLOBAL RECESSION—REGIONAL AND SECTORAL VARIATIONS AND VULNERABLE STATES

PART IV

GLOBAL FINANCIAL CRISIS AND INDIAN ECONOMY

Preface

The Global Meltdown and its impact on Indian Economy is a current debate among the economists of the country. That is why it was discussed as one of the theme issue in the first technical session of the three days Indian Economic Association 92nd Annual Conference at KIIT, Bhubaneswar during 27–29 December, 2009.

The problem of crisis originated due to faulty credit policy of U.S. banking system and its mishandling by private investment U.S. corporates led by Lehman Brothers Inc. The flawed credit system created real estate bubbles and hence this crisis and the whole capitalist world seemed to be in the cobweb of U.S. depression. The economists of world were astonished to see this failure of capitalism and there was wide range of debate in Amercian academic world led by Paul M. Sweezy and Harry Magdoff, that it is the result of the inherent weakness of capitalist system which concentrates more on saving via profit and less on investment. So the strong will power to save and weak potential to invest is the real cause of this crisis. The post-Keynesian economist later on inventing Keynes revolution much earlier in the writings of Marx, Michael Kalaecki, said in 1968 that it is weak will power to utilize capitalist equipment to its full that led to weak power to invest and mad rush for profit in capitalism.

The interesting debate on crisis management was discussed in the remedial and regulatory measures in different parts of the world in Part III of this volume.

The last part discusses its impact on Indian Economy which seems to be more resilient in facing this crisis. The ten articles explain the various facets of its impact on the economy.

This conference technical session concluded that any

financial crisis in capitalism can only be averted when there is an expanding opportunity for the use of its men, material and natural resources of the economy. Then only gainful long-run employment opportunity be created and a sustained avenues of income generation with its sustainable growth potential will come in existence.

ANIL KUMAR THAKUR
PARAMANAND SINGH

List of Contributors

A. Venkateswarlu, Centre for Economic and Social Studies, Hyderabad.

Abhay Narayan Rai, Research Scholar, Department of Economics, University of Allahabad, Allahabad, U.P.

Amrita Nandi, Professor, General Management (Economics), Chanakya Institute of Management Studies and Research, Mumbai.

Arindam Das, Sr. Lecturer, Department of Business Administration, The University of Burdwan, West Bengal.

Ashwani Kumar Srivastaba, Reader in Economics, Mahila College, Dalmianagar, VSK University, Ara.

Asim K. Karmakar, Senior Lecturer, Department of Economics, Jadavpur University, Kolkata.

B.G. Lobo, Lecturer of Economics, Sinhgad Institute, N.B. Navale College of Commerce, Kusgaon (Bk), Lonavala, Pune.

Bharti Kapur, Research Scholar, Punjabi University, Patiala.

Bhavik M. Panchasara, Lecturer of Accountancy and Finance in R.K. College of Business Management, Kasturbadham, Rajkot, Gujarat.

Ch. Paramaiah, Department of Economics, Faculty of Social Sciences, National University of Lesotho, Southern Africa.

Channabasavan Goudap, Department of Economics, Gulbarga University, Gulbarga, Karnataka.

Duresh Kumar Singh, Research Scholar, Department of Economics, University of Allahabad, Allahabad, U.P.

G.P. Tripathi, Ph.D. Scholar, Department of Economics, Rani Durgavati University, Jabalpur (M.P.)

Harvinder Kaur, Reader in Economics, Punjabi University, Patiala, Punjab.

Heena S. Bharadiya, Scholar of M.Phil. Economics at Krantiguru Shyamji Krishna Verma Kachchha University, Bhuj, Gujarat.

Hena Nisar, Department of Economics, Aligarh, Muslim University, Aligarh (U.P.).

K.A. Rasure, SGL in Economics, Nrupatunga Arts, Commerce and Management Degree College, Sdam, Dist. Gulbarga, Karnataka.

M. Sundara Rao, Department of Economics, Andhra University, Visakhapatnam, A.P.

Mandakini Mahore, Reader, Jawaharlal Nehru College, Wadi, Nagpur, Maharashtra.

Manjit Singh, Lecturer, Punjab School of Economics, Guru Nanak Dev University, Amritsar (Punjab).

Manmohan Krishna, Department of Economics, University of Allahabad, Allahabad, U.P.

Mithilesh Kumar Sinha, Associate Professor, Department of Economics, Nagaland University, Lumami, Mokokchung, Nagaland.

Mohammad Asif, Associate Professor, Department of Economics, Aligarh Muslim University, Aligarh. (U.P.)

Mohua Mazumder, Sr. Lecturer, Faculty of Management Studies, Dr. B.C. Roy Engineering College, Durgapur, West Bengal.

P. Ramu, Research Scholar, Department of Economics, Andhra University, Visakhapatnam, A.P.

P.S. Kamble, Reader, Department of Economics, Shivaji University, Kolhapur, Maharashtra.

Paramanand Singh, H.O.D., Department of Economics, B.N.M. College, Barhiya, T.M.B.U., Bhagalpur, Bihar.

Pradhyumna Tripathy, Sr. Lecturer, Department of Business Administration, The University of Burdwan, Burdwan, West Bengal.

Prahlad Kumar, Department of Economics, University of Allahabad, Allahabad, U.P.

R.S. Bawa, Professor, Punjab School of Economics, Guru Nanak Dev University, Amritsar, (Punjab).

R.Y. Mahore, Prof. and Head, Department of Economics, RTM Nagpur University, Nagpur.

Rakesh Kumar Singh, Department of Economics, R.D.S. College, Muzaffarpur, Bihar.

S.K. Choubey, Professor and Chairman BOS in Economics, Rani Durgavati University, Jabalpur (M.P.)

S.K. Dhage, Reader and H.O.D. of Economics, Baburaoji Gholap College, Sangvi, Pune.

Samit Mahore, Kavikulguru Institute of Technology and Science, Ramtek, Maharashtra.

Shashi Bhushan Prasad Singh, Principal, A.P.S.M. College, Barauni, Begusarai, Bihar.

Suraj Kumar, Research Scholar, T.M. Bhagalpur University, Bhagalpur.

Tapan Kumar Shandilya, Principal, R.C.S. College, Manjhaul, Begusarai (Bihar).

Vipla Chopra, Professor of Economics, Department of Distance Education, Punjabi University, Patiala.

Introduction

I.I. Origin and Nature

Market centered economy used to be financial crisis ridden. Every country is likely to face it sometime or other. One IMF study counts 113 episodes of financial crisis after world war II and sixty of them originated from banking sector. The current global financial crisis began with U.S. sub-prime mortgage problem in 2007. Since the crisis originated in the heart of world economy, its contagion effect spread very quickly, first to Europe and then to the rest of the world economy. By the end of 2008, it was evident that almost the entire world was affected one way or the other. As events unfolded and severity of the crisis exceeded the worst earlier apprehensions, it became common in public discussions to compare the current crisis with great depression of 1930's. Counter measures, which broadly followed Keynesian prescriptions, have been initiated in various countries since late 2008.

I.II. Why this Crisis?

Several factors have contributed to the building up of the crisis. The primary structural factors have been the prevalence of large and persistent global macroeconomic imbalances across major economic powers characterized by large heterogeneity. U.S. trade deficit running over two decades reached a peak of 6.1% of gross domestic product (GDP) in 2006. On the other hand, some of the Asian economies had large current account surpluses, U.S. spent more than its income while China muted much less compared to its savings rate which varied between 40%-50% of its GDP. The basic fact behind the crisis was U.S. citizens consumed too much and saved very little a few years ago. An influential section in the U.S. put forth the "**Global**

savings glut hypothesis" and held the view that U.S. consumed too much because rest of the world consumed too little. After all, world income and expenditure balance must be maintained expost. This approach treats U.S. consumption as a residual and echoes a Johansenian type of macro-closure. The savings glut hypothesis located the cause for the problems faced by the U.S. outside the country and implicitly indicated that the large trade and fiscal deficits in the U.S. was essentially because it was acting as "consumer of the best resort" and bearing the burden of imbalances caused by foreigners. This obviously is in tradition of making a virtue of own mistakes.

Other analysis had expressed concern about danger of global imbalances without adequate action at the national and international level. Some authors, however, viewed the imbalances as **natural but transitory consequence of globalization** of the financial market. Several others were, however worried about the emerging global imbalances and its implications.

Cline (2005) for example viewed the U.S. macroeconomic trajectory as unsustainable and advocated **Coordinated exchange rate realignment by G-20 countries** in a manner similar to 1985 "Plaza Agreement", Eichengreen (2006) reviewed four different perspectives on global imbalances and argued that "uncertainty about whether a disorderly correction is imminent doesn't justify inaction." He suggested progressively tightening of fiscal policy for the U.S. and loosening fiscal policy for China and East Asia to stimulate domestic demand.

It is against this backdrop, the emergence of U.S. sub-prime crisis became the immediate cause of the global economic crisis. Availability of easy loan at low interest rates led to a housing boom in the U.S. with soaring property prices, banks were happy to provide sub-prime loans to customers of doubtful repaying capacity, assuming that mortgaged property could any way be sold to recover the loan. The Housing bubble burst eventually resulted. The structured financial market spread of the contagion to European Union.

Reddy (2009) has characterized the current crisis as **"synchronized extensive excesses"** of several factors. Some underlying causes responsible for these developments, apart from above are: (a) Innovation of new complex products by the financial sector and using them to redistribute wealth in its favour, (b) inadequate regulation and supervision, and (c) inability of policy-makers to appreciate the potential externalities of failure of financial sector on the belief that market would correct itself.

I.III. Understanding the Crisis: Some Revealing Facts

The crisis, thus originated from U.S. sub-prime mortgage market in August 2007 soon spread to markets for other securities in both the U.S. and else where it caused in few months a string of bankruptcies and a sharp slow down in all the industrial world. Initially the economists believed that the emerging Asian countries, i.e. China and India will remain "decoupled from the crisis but soon they proved to be wrong."

The crisis originated from the financial sector which has become a very important part of the economic framework of any country. A well functional financial system is the pre-requisite of the process of growth with stability. Schumpeter (1971) propounded that financial intermediaries are essential drivers for innovation and growth. Mckinnon Shaw also supported Schumpeter's argument.

With revolution of ICT several innovations have accrued in the financial system to reap the economies of scale on the hand and on the other they have increased the complexity and vulnerability of the financial system.

Hyman Minsky, a follower of Keynes has very elaborately dealt with the financial side of the business cycles. In his theory finance is regarded as the cause of the instability of capitalism. Keynes, on the other hand believed that finance can only amplify the fluctuations.

Minsky pointed out that stability is paradoxically destabilizing, good times encourage experimentation and excessive risk taking ending up in a mess. Minsky stated that a prolonged period of stability would induce some units to migrate from hedge to speculative to Ponzi finance. A Ponzi finance is one when a unit has to constantly borrow more to meet its debt servicing commitments.

The present financial crisis originated from complex financial pyramid created through financial innovations. It erupted in U.S. sub-prime mortgage market with interest rate rising and prices falling. There was sharp jump in defaults and more closures. However, there could have remained a mortgage crisis. But for the fact that these mortgages were securitized and packaged into products that were rated as investment grade. Once doubt about these assets arose, they turned illiquid making it hard to price them. This affected a number of institutions which had invested in these products. The international financial system being highly integrated, the crisis spread to almost all countries of the world. The crisis in financial sector has now moved to the real sector resulting in slump in growth and employment worldwide.

I.IV. Dealing with the Crisis: Keynesian Propositions

Many of the Keynesian prescriptions have once again became relevant in dealing with the situation created by this crisis. Keynes was a supporter of active macroeconomic policy involving Government intervention, in contrast to the free play of market forces as advocated by classicals. Keyne's influence in macroeconomic policy continued till 1970's called the Development decade. But in the decade of 1970's doubts were raised against Keynesian economics. Mckinnon Shaw Hypothesis, which condemned the intervention of the government in the financial sector (termed it as financial repression) supported the idea of deregulation with fall of Berlin wall and disintegration of the Soviet Union in late 1980's, popularized as End of history by Francis Fuknyama. The world again moved towards free market fundamentalism and *laissez-faire* ideology of the classical era. The idea of Keynes were sidelined in over optimism that the market is the most efficient when left to itself.

The conditions under which Smithian invisible hands worked as laid down by Gerold Debreu and Kenneth Arrow are unrealistic and don't exist in the real world. Jo'sheph Stigliz in his research have shown that the conditions like perfect competition and symmetric information do not exist in the real world which is one of the reason why Adam Smith's invisible hands do not work. Keynes believed that government intervention and regulation can often play an important role in making them work better and in limiting the scope of the conflict of interest that repeatedly appeared in accounting business and finance.

IMF February 2009 analysis reflect the same idea in describing the root cause of the crisis. "In market failure....bred by a long period of high growth, low real interest rates and volatility and policy failures in financial regulation which are not equipped to see the risk of concentration and flawed incentive behind the financial innovation boom; macroeconomic policies which did not take into account systemic risks in the financial system and in housing markets and global architecture where a fragmented surveillance system compounded the inability to see growing vulnerabilities and links.

The policy prescription which derives from the current experience and supported by Keynesian theory is that of efficient regulator of the financial system. But here one must not forget fact that Keynes prescription came in the circumstances of insuffient demand situation which he called back of effective demand situation and for that he advocated public investment programme via financial institution. In the present crisis, the cause of crisis is over consumption or management of demand. It is because of private or public casino and other investment. It is because of investment in gamble and other assumed area and amusement important for financial sectors, which is more fragile and influenced by expectations. The exogamous and spontaneous shift in the needs "optimism or pissiumismis at the heart of fluctuations in stock prices." Keynes called it as animal spirits in the general theory.

He argues that "Even apart from the instability due to speculation there is instability due to the characteristic of human nature that a large proposition of our positive activities depend on spontaneous optimism rather than on mathematical expectation, whether. moral or hedonic or economic, most probably of our decisions to do something of our decisions to do something positive the full consequences of which will be drawn out over many obeys to come can only be taken as a result of animal spirits of spontaneous urge to action rather than in action and not as the outcome of weighted average of quantitative benefits multiplied by quantitative probabilities."

Thus it becomes important that the government should intervene and there should be an efficient and transparent regulatory system to check the market inefficiencies and failures.

I.V. Crisis and Regulatory Reform

The world economic crisis has glaringly made it clear that there are flaws in the regulatory framework. The Geneva report has highlighted two crippling weaknesses in the system of regulation. First, it is excessively micro prudential containing not a hint of recognition that the major problem arises due to the correlation of risks.

Second, it concentrates entirely on the composition of a bank's assets and neglects completely whether those assets are financed in inherently stable ways or by borrowing short-term loans in the inter-bank market.

Geneva report proposed a system of macro-prudential regulation to the existing system of micro-regulation. This would increase bank's capital asset ratios during boom and reduce them in the period of crisis, providing a deterrent to increasing credit when there is an abundance of credit available and an incentive to lend more at times when the system as a whole is short of lending.

The second fundamental charge to the regulatory system, it proposes addresses the observation that banks and other financial intermediaries engaged in risky practice of borrowing short and lending long. The answer to this is to penalize the maturity mismatches through increased CAR's

Y.V. Reddy, Governor of R.B.I. in 2009 ('India and Global Crisis: Managing Money and Finances' Orient Blackswan) has proposed some resilience measure to Global financial system as follows:

(a) Risk management framework including governance arrangement in banks and financial institutions required a review by management.

(b) Supervisors need to play a more active role in scrutinizing the risk management practices including stress testing and governance arrangements, off balance sheet entities and structured products.

(c) Supervisors should encourage institutions to develop more robust models that use more prudent and reliable assumptions and stress testing methodology and monitor more closely the internal processes and controls for managing risks.

(d) There is need to rationalize the regulatory and supervisory prescription with a view to reducing the scope for arbitrating.
(e) Greater Transparency is needed so as to make the markets more efficient and optimize the allocation of capital.
(f) There is a need to review and resolve the element of pro cyclicality in prudential regulation, accounting rules and attitude of the authorities that tend to apply there.
(g) The supervisors should be given the clear authority to intervene at the first signs of weaknesses preferably much before the institutions net worth become negative.
(h) The deposit insurance systems should aim to limit the likelihood of retail depositors runs in the troubled banks through adequate coverage and have the ability to pay the depositors quickly.

All these above measures suggested by Y.V. Reddy require global cooperation in this direction. Keynes himself was a supporter of international cooperation for proper functioning of global economy and in this spirit he recommended the formation of international institutions (I.M.F., World Bank) Bank of international settlement. The Bank of international settlement is also an important super national institution advocated by Keynes requiring a coordination among difference intuitions regulating trade and finance across borders.

I.VI. The Fiscal Stimulus Packages, adopted by Governments of Countries, throughout the World

In the wake of growth rate down swing, increasing under employment to unprecedented level, severe stress faced by financial institutions compelled to take a cue from Keynesian theory. All stimulus packages aimed to stimulate the aggregate demand, which I thinks a raw deal, because the crisis originated from ostentatious consumption fuelled by Casino private and public investment. As a result of it whole package provided little cure to basic illness and it is still continuing in major modern capitalist world. The crisis cold has catched the entire industrial capitalist world, they are still sneezing.

The model of stimulus prepared by national institute of economic and social research, suggested that such a coordinated developed country stimulus could lead to a GDP rise of around 1 to 1.5% in 2009-10. I.M.F. suggested a stimulus of 2% of G.D.P. for developed world. **Robert Zoelick,** President World Bank, advocated that all developed countries should pledge 0.7% of its stimulus packages to assists vuluerability fund for assisting the developing countries. The targeted transfers announced by governments across the world is expected by have considerable multiplier effect on the economy and would help reverse the negative expectations. In an ideal scenario where fiscal stimulus is both global and supported by monetary accommodation, and where financial sectors that are under pressure and being supported by facts, every dollar spent or government investment can increase GDP by about $3, while every dollar of targeted transfers can increase GDP by $1. In countries in which fiscal space is limited, it will be essentially important to focus fiscal stimulus on those measures that will have largest on aggregate demand-targeted transfers and government's investment where possible. The discretionary fiscal stimulus around the Globe sluggers that China, Russia, Japan, Korea provide above 2 per cent to 3.7 percent of GDP as fiscal packages both targeted as well via government investment. Many studies (Studies by Valerie A, Ramey and Mathew Shapir, 1998, Oliver Blandchand and Robert Perotti, 2002, Burnside, Eichenbaum and Jones, D.M., Fisher (2004), Valerie A. Ramey, 2008, have shown that both tax cuts and government expenditure variables and fiscal stimuli if designed as per need of the economy will work. Where both targeted transfers public investment should work side by side based on need of the system. The crisis virtually cropped from the failure of the regulatory system in U.S. and other Eropean countries.

I.VII. Economic Crisis—A Systemic Reappraisal

The crisis that appeared in 2007-08, in U.S. and soon catched the entire world, were in fact, not merely a credit meltdown effect. It was in fact a systemic crisis inherent in basic characteristic of the capitalist system which market propelled and greed-based profit earning naturally produce. So this crisis originated from the mismatch between a system managed by money and credit, while the basic rational behind any system's ruling is that it should be ruled by social needs. If any system concentrates on profit managed by financial players of money and credit, ignoring social needs, the crisis will crop up and prolonged leading to the collapse of the system.

Marx once wrote the famous lines in his third volume of Das Capital: "The illusions concerning miraculous power of the credit and banking system as nursed by some socialists, arise from the complete lack of familiarity with the capitalist mode of production and credit system as one of its form".

Capitalism is market centric system subject to fluctuations. These fluctuations are the resultant effect of market forces on which the system operates. The fluctuations as an aggregate economic activity is called business cycles or trade cycles. Economic literature is replete with these trade cycles analysis.

Pigou, Howtray, Kaldor, Hicks have interpreted these fluctuations in terms of their trade cycle interpretations. Likewise, we have a bulk of theories analyzing the capitalist system fluctuations. The psychological theory of Pigou was replaced by monetary theory of Hawtray. We have climate theory or under consumption theory propounded by Keynes. The Schumpeterian Innovation of trade cycle theory and Keynesian general theory of trade cycles are very popular and followed favours by policy designers. Samuelson, also followed Keynesian lines and evolved his super multiplier trade cycle theory. The basic facts in all these interpretation of capitalists fluctuation is that capitalism is not a coherent system and is subject to discrepancies and ultimately leading towards a collapse or crisis in the system.

Paul M. Sweezy, Harvard Club lecture (March 22/1982) is important landmark in this debate wherein he compared 1929 depression with present financial crisis from various angles and propounded there from a new version of the analysis of the present global meltdown.

The great depression crisis depicted unemployment rate of 23.6 percent (1929) of the labour force, it reached to its high 24.9% in 1933 and remained double digit throughout the decade till 1938-39. During the time of recovery which was at its peak in 1937, the unemployment rate was 14.3% in U.S. The year 1937 is important in capitalistic history because in that year Paul M. Sweezy propounded in his Ph.D. thesis that the real problem of capitalism or market centric economy is not fluctuations or cyclical ups and downs of business activity but secular stagnation (Prolonged Recession).

Referring Hanson–Schumpter debate—their debate in 1937-39 forms important corollary to focus on the real rythem behind the crisis.

The Harvard top in 1930, Hanson's book in 1938—"Full Recovery and Stagnation" and Schumpeter's agreement on that crystalized on the issues in his two volume treatise "The Business Cycles in 1939."

Schumpeter labeled in his business cycles analysis Hanson's theory of stagnation as the theory of vanishing investment opportunities in his stagnation analysis, which is but an apt characterization of the phenomena which Hanson analyzed.

According to Hanson proposition—"Modern developed capitalist world has an enormous capacity to save, both because of its corporate structure and because of its very unequal distribution of income. But, if adequate profitable investment opportunities are lacking this saving potential translates into real capital formation and sustained growth, results into lowered income and mass unemployment and depression of a chronic nature a condition often summed up in stagnation.

Hanson derivation of this framework of analysis directly stem from Keynesian general theory published in 1936. He was the best known champion of Keynes at Harvard.

Schumpeter called 1929 crisis of depression as world crisis. Therefore, unlike Hanson, asking what caused stagnation of 1930's and interpreting in simplifying terms, Schumpeter began with his explanation of why cyclical upspring began in 1933 and cause to an end in 1938, in so short off. What he and others on his side assumed to be the normal situation of the end of prosperity phase of cycle full employment, rising prices and tight credit.

Schumpeter, further classified business cycles into three, each named after earlier investigator of these phenomena, i.e. as very short cycles as Kitchen's cycles, inventory cycles by Jugler's cycles, Long cycle by Kondratief's cycles of some fifty years duration.

To Schumpeter the experiences of 1930's depression is

disappointing as it is disappointing Juglers of inventory nature, which remained for a very short period. The present Global financial crisis is disappointing and dismaying in the perception of Schumpeter and in Paul M. Sweezy vocabulary. Schumpeter interprets Hanson's vanishing investment opportunity as anti-business climate, which essentially is the byproduct of capitalist development.

The anti-business climate created by present capitalist growth is the genesis of the present crisis in Schumpeterian incidental thinking. He thus, created a platform for a new deal theory of stagnation. In one form or another it was shared by most political conservatives of the time (Roosevelt Administration).

The Government should by corrective regular modification of the system create positive climate for new opportunities of investment. Very recently Prof. Pulin B. Nayak has presented an "Anatomy the financial crisis between Keynes and Schumpeter" (*EPW*, March 2009). In his analysis he emphasized the fact that state public investment must be directed towards using the increasing capability of resource use in the system be it nature, human or economic. Unless this is done in a targeted way with prolonged interest in sight and with a mission by government, agencies. Any slackness on this part will create abnormal anti-business climate. The postwar economic boon, the energy created by it, instead of lying dormant have increasingly been channelled into a variety of wasteful expenditure, parasitic and generally unproductive uses. This is being done by an enormously complex process via value addition and standardization of the product and by not increasing its value in real terms. This lag in society's utilization of productive resources is creating problems in the system. This process is still very imperfectly understood by present mainstream economic analyst and they even does not recognize its existence. The debt structure of the U.S. Economy, the government, the corporate and individual function arise at pace far exceeding the sluggish expansion of the underlying real economy. The present emergence of an unprecedented large and fragile financial super structure subject to stresses and strains that increasing is threatening the stability of the economy as whole. So, a systemic view will provide an alternative way to come out of to prevent financial morass the whole world economy is facing now.

I.VIII. Global Financial Crisis and Indian Economy

India is no exception to the adverse effects of the financial crisis of U.S. particularly after opening up of the economy and financial integration with trade and FDI. During the last two decades market-friendly reforms have created a favourable economic environment for integration of the Indian Economy with the world economy. The break from the stagnant Hindu rate of growth of 3.5 percent witnessed after independence occurred around 1980 when economy recorded a growth rate of 5.5 percent per annum. Further acceleration of the economy to a medium run growth path of above 8% in recent years could be clearly seen.

India's GDP stands at about US $ 1.2 trillion in nominal terms and $ 3.2 trillion in ppp terms. India is not a major player in world trade as adjudged by its share of 1.2% in world merchandise trade value, though it plays a larger role in service trade with a share of 2.7% of world transactions. But, trade and capital flows have been major driving focus in bringing about structural changes in recent years in the economy. The share of exports goods and services in GDP increased substantially from 11.7% in 1999-2000 to 22.1% in 2006-07. Imports too rose from 13.6% to 25.1% during the same period. The share of current account transaction in GDP currently at above 45% is comparable to other large countries.

Foreign investment which was only $ 13-15 billion till 2006-07 suddenly rose to $ 45 billion (a third of which was FDI) in 2007-08. India was getting considerably integrated with the global economy in the decade prior to the crisis. With a long-term average GDP growth rate close to 7 percent per annum (6.5% over a 16 year period 1992-2008), India was seen to be among the fastest growing economies in the world. It recently entered the group of lower middle income countries as per the classification of the world bank. The recent high growth phase of 8-9% during 2003-07 looked to be sustainable in the medium run given that the economy had withstood several shocks like East Asian crisis, boarder tension, the Iraq war, oil price fluctuations and major drought without major disruptions. Policy-makers were, in fact looking forward to accelerate the process further. The 11th Five Year Plan (2007-12) thus targeted a GDP growth rate of 9 per cent per annum. The first year of the plan did achieve this growth rate, the second year also achieved 7.5% growth rate. Global crisis in U.S., E.U., emerged in 2006-07. Then came the Global crisis. Initially it was thought that the magnitude of the crisis would be small and its impact would be limited to U.S. and E.U. given their restricted operation abroad. It happened in mid 2006. There was also crisis in East Asia, that occurred in mid-1990's, i.e. 1994-95-96. The problem that accrued in East Asia has its fore runner in Latin American nations too in the year 1980 and then in Mexico in 1994, followed by crisis in Norway and Sweden in early 1990s. In these nations there was problem of currency depreciation and speculative attacks coupled with large outflows. The crisis that broke out in Thailand spread to Malayasia, Indonesia, Philipines and then to South Korea. The G-7 nations attributed the crisis to domestic ills in the East Asian economies. According to them improper judgment of Banks and financial institution, over speculation in real estate and the share market the collusion between governments and a business bad policy of having fixed exchange rates the dollar and rather high current account deficits. They avoided blaming financial markets and currency speculation and the behaviour of large international investors.

On the other hand another view attributed it to the global financial system the combination of financial deregulation and liberalization across the world, the increasing inter-connection of markets and speed of transactions through computer technology and the development of large institutional financial players namely the **Speculative hedge funds,** the investment banks, the huge mutual and pension funds.

A large amount to the tune of US $ 184 billion entered developing Asian countries as net private capital flows in 1994-96 as per the bank of international settlements. In 1996, US $ 94 billion entered in and in the first half of 1997 another 70 billion flowed in. As the crisis gained momentum $ 102 billion went out in the second half of 1997 and the large outflows continued since then. One can understand, based on large magnitude of the flows of funds, how much volatile they were and how capital flows can be subjected to the tremendous effect of herd instinct which Keynes said animal's spirit.

The crisis situation in Thailand was attributed to the action of financial speculation and hedge funds. The Thai Government used up over US $ 20 billion of foreign reserves to ward-off speculative attacks. The speculaters seem to have borrowed and sold Thai **Baht** receiving the U.S $ in exchange. When the Baht fell, the speculators needed much less dollars to repay the Baht loans, thus making huge profits. According to *Business Week*, the hedge funds made around **10.7 percent net profits** on an average for the period Jan. to June 1997. But the average profit rate soared to 19.1 percent between Jan. to July 1997. Thus, there was tremendous windfall of profit in the month of July 1997. So the main causes of crisis for the East Asian Giants be summarized as financial liberalization, currency depreciation, and debt crisis and liberalization and debt, the case of Malaysia. In the process of financial liberalization the nations followed total convertibility both in the current and capital account of the balance of payments. This obviously facilitated large inflows of funds in the form of international bank loans to local banks and corporate purchase of bonds and portfolio investment in the local stock markets. The alarming increase in short-run debt, the sudden deprecation of the currencies of Thailand, Malaysia and South Korea accounted for the crisis. This resulted in huge servicing obligations of their debt.

The global meltdown with its widespread impact happened because of sub-prime lending in U.S. economy and it's widespread sneezes in European Union. So, this was a crisis which compelled the world economy to collapse due to excessive securitization leading to cash crunch.

Indian economy has limited impact of this world economic crisis because Indian banks were nationalized and had limited exposure to structured financial market involving sub-prime loans. But as the crisis intensified its severity became clear. It was not confined to banking sector alone. As the effect considerably spread to the real sectors in U.S. and E.U. it was realized that the "decoupled" hypothesis did not hold. The India economy also to some extent felt the burn of the crisis.

The overall impact may be judged in terms of the fall in GDP growth to 6.7% in 2008-09 from 9% in the previous year. It looked as if the crisis put the Indian Economy back on the June 2003 growth trajectory. However, the whole of the fall of 2.3 percentage points should not be attributed to the global crisis.

There was other factors responsible for this fall in India. During the period there was slow growth in agricultural sector. Agricultural income grew by only 1.6% in 2008-09 as against 4.9% in 2007-08.

I.IX. World Financial Crisis and Indian Capital Flows Scenario

In the initial phase of the crisis, when the "decoupled" hypothesis was debated, India was thought to be a relatively attractive destination. As a result foreign institutional investment (PII) increased till January, 2008. As the crisis in U.S. and EU grew, the flows reduced and considerably reversed later to meet cash commitments and cover losses in the home countries.

During the year 2008-09 as a whole, there was net outflow of $ 14 billion as against a peak inflow of $ 29 billion in the previous year. This has strong impact on the stock market index which witnessed sharp fluctuations and fell sharply from about 21,000 in Jan. 2008 to about 9000 by March 2008. Stock market certainly went through turbulence and settled for some orderly behaviour at low level of the index. Recently FIIs have returned back to India with positive inflows.

The rising trend in net foreign direct investment (FDI) witnessed for several years prior to the crisis slowed down considerably during 2008-09. It stood at $ 17.5 billion in 2008-09 compared to $ 15.4 in 2007-08 [Ghose, Jayati and C.P. Chandrashekhar (2009)]. The costs of coupling the global crisis and Indian Economy. *Cambridge Journal of Economics*, 33, pp. 725-36. The net commercial borrowings came down substantially from 22.7 billion to 6.9 billion.

All these developments meant that overall balance of payments turned negative of $ 20 billion leading to decrease in foreign exchange reserves. The reserves fell by $ 40 billion due to revolution, thus leading to total fall by as much as $ 60 billion during 2008-09 additionally. No doubt comfortable levels of foreign exchange reserves bolt up over the years which peaked 316 billion on mid-2008, helped India to tide over this as well as several other problems by precutting flexibility on trade policy decisions without resorting to restrictive measures.

The trade and capital flows thus, put pressure on exchange rate of the rupee. It depreciated by more 25% with respect to U.S. Dollar and Japanese year, though changes with respect to Ero and Pound sterling was similar to previous year. Depreciation of the rupee in dollar terms had raised the cost of imports and of commercial borrowings.

The above are the effects of global economic crisis on Indian Economy via balance of payment deficiencies in terms of trade flows, capital flows, exchange rate depreciation in terms of Dollars and Yen, GDP real effect via slow agricultural sector growth, oil prices rate and increasing cost effect, etc.

I.X. World Economic Crisis and India's Policy Responses

Policy response adopted by Govt. of India to avert this crisis includes fiscal and monetary counter measures to limit the adverse effects.

This involved increased government expenditure on infrastructure and other projects. [Kimbeing, Han, Hong Ghi Min and Young (2009)].

A Kumar, Ganesh and Manoj Panda, 2009 have extensively elaborated these policy responses. The policy response involves increased government expenditure on infrastructure and other projects, reduction in indirect taxes, reducing interest rates, easing the liquidity available with the Banks. How much these policy responses have been effective in countering the bad effects of crisis in India. This question has been adversed by A. Kumar and Panda (2009) by carrying out a series of simulations using a computable general equilibrium model of the Indian economy. The CGE framework determines only relative prices and does not incorporate monetary variables. Hence, Prof. Panda and Kumar exhausted only "Real shocks and fiscal counter-measures" leaving out effects of monetary policy responses such as increased access to credit and reduced interest rate. Specifically they looked at the impacts of (a) fall in exports due to changes in the world economy, (b) a reduction in the foreign inflows into India, and (c) the fall in global oil prices that happened in the second half of fiscal 2008-09 on the response side, they (A. Kumar and Panda) examined effects of two fiscal measures: (i) a rise in government consumption and (ii) a cut in indirect taxes undertaken to mitigate crisis effect.

Effects of Crisis and Counter Measures on Real GDP (percent change from base)

A ten percent fall in export of goods and services course a real GDP loss of 3.3%. The total effects capture the direct effect due to exports change and the induced effects due to charges in all other endogenous variables model. Given the current share of exports of goods and services in GDP, a 10% fall in exports could have a direct effect on GDP by about 2.0% and the rest might be considered as indirect multiplier effect. Since export in India have low import content and the indirect effects are not insignificant. The GDP effect have is due to export fall alone (partial effects) and not trade flows which also involved sharp contraction in imports whose "Competitive" component would have favourable impact on GDP.

The second simulation refers to fall in capital flows in the form of 10% fall in remittances and 15% fall in foreign savings. The effect on GDP operating through consumption and investment demand elements amounts to 1.87 percentage point decline. Simulation corresponds to fall in international oil and gas price observed in the second half of the last fiscal which turn out to be about 10% on yearly average data over the previous year. As expected oil price decline had a favourable effect on overall GDP Growth of 0.9 percent. The adverse effects on GDP of the first three scenario due to global developments turn out to 4.2 percentage points. The actual fall in GDP growth rate in 2008-09 was not as sharp in practice, balance observed change is the resultant of all factors operating in that year including counter measures. Yet it is educative to note the various potential effects under "Controlled Conditions" for policy formulation.

So far policy measures undertaken to counter the effects involving scenario D, E, F, i.e. government consumption rise, indirect tax cut and NREGS (Full demand of bottom 70 percent of rural population combined) consumption in real term by 5% from base helps to raise GDP by 0.7 percent, which means GDP fall due to global meltdown is arrested to this extent due to government expenditure.

On indirect tax front, government had announced an average reduction of about 4 percentage points in indirect tax rates in goods and services (except for petroleum products) in the middle of the financial year. Prof. Panda tried to incorporate this aspect by reducing the indirect tax rates by a quarter of the base value to get a tax rate reduction of about 2 percentage point for the whole year. Simulation E indicates that indirect reduction might have helped the economy by raising the aggregate income by 0.8 percent. These results indicate that the **Fiscal stimulus** undertaken by the government, thus, possibly helped to counter GDP fall by about 1.5 percentage point.

On the income distribution front, their results showed that all income classes are infavourably affected by the crisis and fiscal measures provide only partial relief to all sections. While the richer classes might somehow, cope with the income loss, the poor might find it extremely difficult to do so. Hence, A. Kumar and Panda, in experiment attempt to expand the rural employment guarantee scheme to full cover all those unemployed among the present 70% of the rural population in the last stimulus experiment. It is interesting to note that nearly 19 million additional jobs are needed to undertake such a target at a cost of 1.4% of GDP. By design, such a programme significantly increases the welfare of the targeted group. With unemployed resources in the reverences case, it increased GDP by 0.5 and provides marginal income gains to other income cases too.

Kumar, A. Ganesh and Manoj Panda (2009) "Global Economic Shocks and Indian Policy Response: An Analysis (GE Model" in Kirit, S. Parikh (ed.) Macro (Common Government Expend).

Modeling for the Eleventh Five Year Plan of India. (Published by Academic Foundation and Planning Commission, New Delhi).

I.XI. World Economic Crisis: The Task Ahead

The global economic crisis is still continuing sometimes above streams and many times within it. The recent turmoil in Dubai Real Estate crisis indicates that contagion effect very much perish. The debt service crisis of Greece economy recently engaged entire main land European economy including Germany. So far Indian economy is concerned a silver line is seen in the turn around of economic growth during 2009-10. GDP Growth was 6.1% in the first quarter of 2009-10, but it picked up considerably to 7.9% in the second quarter.

More importantly the manufacturing sector which contracted in absolute terms with a negative growth (-1.4%) in the last quarter of 2008-9 is showing indications of revival. It has recorded 3.4% and 9.2% growth in the first and second quarters of 2009-10 respectively.

We would be mistaken if we consider early exist of the stimulus package despite the fiscal strain. The withdrawal of packages may be initiated. When growth continues for a few quarters and be carried out in stages hopefully, policy measures need to be calibrated taking into consideration the emerging changes in the structure of the economy in favour of non-tradable sectors such as infrastructure and construction.

Cost of coupling is a natural corollary of benefits of coupling. Minimum cost and maximum benefits of globalization requires careful calibration of policies to suit national interest. The present economic crisis should not lead to severing policies capital flows, though international financial markets are intrinsically highly volatile and regulations need to be in place due to the externalities of these markets. Policy goods should support long-term capital flows (FDI and equity) whereas short-terms capital movements should be liberalized in a gradually limited manner. McKinnon and Pill (1996) noted critical role of sequencing of financial reforms: first put in place of well functioning domestic capital system before allowing capital convertibility. Fortunately, this advice is well recognized in India.

I.XII. World Financial Crisis and Proactive Role for India

India should be ready for pro-active role in the new international initiative to connect global imbalances. Safeguarding national imports necessarily calls for understanding the implications of policy initiatives at the international level. Critical to this process is a complex question: Who bears how much cost of global rebalancing. Alternative scenarios can have very different implications for developed and emerging market economies.

Using CGE model, Von Arnim Rudigar (2009) Recession and Rebalancing—How the housing and credit crisis will impact U.S. real activity. Journal of Policy-making show some interesting results on recovery process. First if U.S. reduces its consumption by 5% and Asia continues to accumulate reserves, global macroeconomic imbalances are likely to rise. Such a scenario would require that Europe acts as consumer of last resort. EU exchange rates appreciates giving rise to small current account deficit and fall in GDP.

Second, adjustments induced by large relative prices possible exchange rate adjustments to correct global imbalances tend to be very volatile and places the burden of adjustment mostly on Asia.

Third, acceptable solutions involve 5% reduction in U.S. consumption and increase in private savings and $ 1.25 trillion increase in government spending across the world involving switch in demand from traded to non-traded goods, however, Von Armin results does not indicate smooth reduction in global imbalances.

So, whatever exercises on various simulations of crisis effect is done, the basic fact is unless labour and capital is set free to exploit and use the natural resources to its maximum use prosperity every where and for every one can't be possible and economic crisis, this and that way will prevail and poor and depressed lot somewhere have to bear it.

Thus, our economy, like many others, had to suffer from the consequences of this crisis, although, we are least concerned with its origins. We have been protected from the severity of its impact primarily because of the prudent management of our financial sector by R.B.I. As the crisis was brewing abroad, and in the face of pressures for more rapid liberalization of financial markets in the interest of higher growth credit also goes to the gradual pace of reforms introduced in post-reform period and institution building and policies including nationalization of major commercial banks in the pre-reform period, which enabled harmonizing of reforms in the financial and external sectors with in progress in fiscal and real sectors.

The fundamental issues concerning global financial crisis, architectural changes deserve proper attention in the field of financing. Since we do not have much influence in this regard, we should be prepared to live with several uncertainties on this front. So policy option open to Indian Economy are largely on the domestic policy front to cope with the emerging challenges. The government and the RBI responded promptly with measures to minimize the impact of this crisis on the domestic economy. The government by putting fiscal stimulus packages designed to tone up domestic demand by strengthening infrastructure and raising purchasing power, particularly in rural areas. As a result, Indian Economy seems to be recovering steadily despite draught hitting agriculture.

The long-term lessons or long-term perspective point of view the present crisis assume great relevance. First, the market fundamentalism has now been called into question as never before, after great depression of 1930s. The important factor behind the financial global meltdown was serious under estimation of the potential for market failures.

Second, there is also glaring state failures. Y.V. Reddy prefers to call it "Regulatory Capture" Financial markets developed far more rapidly than the real economy and the process fostered considerable linkages with the political economy, that drove the actions and inactions of both central banks and governments, leading to the failures of both the market and the state, morally and intellectually.

Dr. Robert A. Johnson, member of the U.N. commission on reforms of the international monetary and financial system (2009) says, "the incentives faced by Public officials, regulators and elected officials and the role of the money in politics are important antidotes to romantic notions of the efficiency of regulation to correct the market failures."

In addition to this the role of expertise, and the incentives of experts who themselves are incentivised by considerations of power, prestigious awards and compensation should be thoroughly examined (R. Johnson, 2009), U.N. Reforms Commission regarding international financial and monetary institutions.

Third, and the most important one, the crisis has given a policy lesson to both developed and developing economies that the rising inequalities in income level have led to insufficiencies of global aggregate demand exacerbating the present crisis. Hence emphasis on inclusive growth, measures for social protection and financial inclusion are a must. For large economies like India and China an inclusive strategy for raising domestic demand could provide safety net against vagaries of global markets. China, a hardly hit economy than India by this global crisis, because of its exposure to globalization seems to be already moving in this direction.

Leaving the question of survival of capitalism apart, and Schumpeterian pessimism on that way, thanks goes to Keynesianism and its powerful impact on growth models of both developed and developing economies, capitalism has managed its survival so far. The present crisis professes the dictum we need a growth pattern that could tame both the market and the state through the governance of financial and economic sectors that is inclusive and widely participatory and so accountable both at national and international level.

The present volume on Global Meltdown and Indian Economy analyses altogether twenty-two articles on various dimensions of the issue and its impact on Indian Economy.

The article focusing on concept, content and theoretical explanation of the crisis have been written by Dr. Paramanand Singh and Shashi Bhushan Prasad Singh, Duresh Kumar Singh and Prahlad Kumar, G.P. Tripathi, S.K. Choubey and Amrita Nandi.

Dr. Paramanand Singh and Dr. Shashi Bhushan Prasad Singh have highlighted the genesis of the crisis and analyse the issue from systemic angle. They were of the view that market centered capitalist world has always been a victim of such a crisis because of its endemic failures and its very nature to save more and invest less. Dr. Duresh Kumar Singh and Prahlad Kumar explain the causes, consequences and its contagion effects.

G.P. Tripathi and S.K. Choubey have questioned the Keynesian way of analyzing the crisis and highlighted a remedial path beyond that Amrita Nandi explains the decoupling theory as its way out and examines the ground realities concerning the crisis on that basis.

We have four articles concerning the policy dimensions and regulatory measures adopted in the wake of global meltdown. In this concern, articles by A. Venkateswarlu, Mithilesh Kumar Sinha, Ashwani Kumar Srivastaba, Abhay Narayan Rai, Rakesh Kumar Singh and Manmohan Krishna are important.

The issue concerning Global Recession regional and sectoral variations and vulnerable states is important. The four articles covered in this section discuss the issues in its regional and sectoral dimensions. The article by Tapan Kumar Shandilya and Suraj Kumar, Harvinder Kaur explain the crisis impact on Real Estate in Indian Economy. While Choudhary Paramaiah explans the global meltdown in the South Asian Context. Pradhyumna Tripathy, Arindam Das and Mohua Mazumder explain the crisis impact service sector context.

Section four of the content discusses in detail the impact of global financial crisis on Indian Economy. In this section there are altogether ten articles discussing the various dimensions of the crisis and its impact on Indian Economy. In this section articles by S.K. Dhage and B.G. Lobo, R.S. Bawa, Manjit Singh and Asim K. Karmakar are important.

The volumes thus presents a comprehensive detail of the cause of crisis, its consequences, regional and sectoral ramifications and the all encompassing impact on Indian Economy, propounding the thesis that unless resources natural, material and human at the disposal of the economy are best utilized, expanding opportunities for employment and income generation in various regions and different sectors of the economy can't be created. So we should attempt to halt the operation of negative multiplier effect arising out of excessive saving in the profit-biased and market centered capitalist system. So the need of the hour is to make a real balance between propensity to save an increasing potential to invest and for this a new entrepreneurial class be created with cohesive entrepreneurial society wherein innovation and motivation is the rule and not dependence on destiny and exigency of favours or prop.

References

Amit Bhaduri (2009), Understanding the financial crisis, E.P.W. 2001 (XLIV), No. 13, March 25 April 3, p. 123.

Anger Maddison (2001), The World Economy: A Millennium Perspective OECD, Paris.

Arun Kumar (2009), "Tackling the Current Global Economic and Financial Crisis: Beyond Management", *E.P.W.*, Vol. XLIV, No. 13, March 28-April 3, p. 151.

Bernanke, Ben S. (2005), "The Global Saving Glut and the U.S. Current Account Deficit", Sandridge Lecture, Virginia Association of Economics, Richmond, Virginia.

Cline William R. (2005), "The Case for New Plaza Agreement, Policy Briefs in International Economics", Institute for International Economics.

Dudley Dillard, "Marx and Keynes: A Centenary Appraisal, "Commemorating Hundredth Anniversary of Marx's Death and Keynes Birth", Published in the Journal of Post-Keynesian Economics, Spring 1984.

Eichengreen, Barry (2006), "Global Imbalances: the New Economy, the Dark Matter the Savey Investor and the Standard Analysis", Univ. of Califorina, Berkeley.

Ghosh, M. Jaati and C. P. Chandrashekher (2009), "The Costs of Coupling: The Global Crisis and Indian Economy", *Cambridge Journal of Economics*, 33, pp. 725-39.

Heonard Silk, Editor Newyork Times, "What is Happening is not Depression". It is a Chronic State of Unemployment and Industrial Slackness also Business Slackness, Sunday, March 14, 1985. "The Root of the Problem go a long way".

Hanson Alvin H., "Full Recovery and Stagnation", Harvard University Press, 1938.

Johansen (1961), Multi-sectoral Growth Models, North Holland.

Kalaecki Michael (1968), "Determinants of Investment Decision", Social Science Information Index, Dec. 1968.

Marx Karl, *Das Capital*, Vol. III.

Ozlem Onaran (2009), "A Crisis of Distribution", *EPW*, Vol. XLIV, No. 13, March 28-April 3, p. 171.

Pulin, B. Nayak (2009), "Anatomy of Financial Crisis: Between Keynes and Schumpeter", *EPW*, Vol. XLIV, March 28-April 13, p. 158.

Reddy, Y.V. (2009a), India and the Global Financial Crisis: Managing Money and Finances, Orient Blackswan.

Reddy, Y.V. (2009b), "Global Financial Crisis and Asia", Justice Konda Madhava Reddy Memorial Lecture.

Roy, Rothein, Keynes Monetary of Value, appeared in *Journal of Post-Keynesian Economics*, Summer, 1981.

Schumpeter, A. Joseph, "The Business Cycle", 1938.

Sweezy Paul, M., Why Stagnation?, Talk by the author at Harward Economic Club, March 22, 1982, June 1982, Monthly Review.

This Polish Economist is credited with inventing Keynesian Revolution before Keynes, analysing Keynes' affinity with Marx. He quoted Keynes as saying at the time of his death. " Long run growth of national income involves satisfactory utilization of equipment is far from obvious."

Tesedore Shamins, (ed.) Late Marx and Russian Road: Marx and the Peripheries of Capital, Monthly Review Press, 1984.

1

The Global Economic Crisis: The Genesis and the Wayout of the Conundrum: An Analysis

PARAMANAND SINGH AND SHASHI BHUSHAN PRASAD SINGH

SOME REFLECTIONS

The illusions concerning the miraculous power of the credit and banking system, as nursed by some socialists, arise from a complete lack of familiarity with the capitalist mode of production and credit system as one of its forms."—Karl Marx

Falstaff: I can get no remedy against the consumption of the purse; borrowing only lingers and linger it out, but the disease is incurable—King Henry.

> "Money is a good servant and a bad master". An outline of money.—G. Crowther , 1958"
>
> "In the long run, we are all dead."—J.M. Keynes in the general theory, 1936.

These reflexions of great architect of two alternative economic systems give a common issue, i.e. money if managed in a fallacious way creates illusion and capitalism uses this as a tool via the fructuous power of credit and banking system to expand its area of profit. But excessive consumption leading to ostentatious direction results in the consumption of the purse, thus subverting the system and it results in the lingering of borrowing, and which is an incurable disease of the capitalist system.

The article is an attempt to analyse these facts keeping in mind the above reflexions of great authors on economic systems managed by money and the system ruled by social Needs. G. Crowther, in 1958, writing on the outline of money says, "Money is a good servant and a bad master. Money was devised to best serve the business community and in order to avoid periodic shortages of money credit functions of bank got expanded. Thus the main creators of money in modern capitalist economies are the banks. It is the expansion and contraction of credit issued by banks that determines the money supply. The central banks role in this game is essentially secondary. Its operations are directed to accommodating the need of the banking system and thus presenting the collapse of the financial market. With these inter and intralinkages between the credit markets and financial market *vis-à-vis* the supply of money by monetary institutions or banks, this article is an analysis of the flow of excessive doses of credit led to outstretching of the known sources of incomes, resulting in lingering of borrowing and lingering it out for long. The volume of transaction thus has boomed far beyond anything needed to support the economy. Borrowing, politely called leverage, is getting out of hand. And futures trading enabled people to play in the capital market without owning a share of stock. Thus, the present economic resultant effect is crisis with global impact. It arose because of its titling from investment to speculation, thus making a bigger gap between credit created and liquidity support thus, a cash crunch and the Global financial meltdown.

The article thus runs into four parts discussing the whole issue of global crisis, its gensis, the conundrum it created and a systemic wayout. Part I deals with introduction and background of the crisis mentioning its broad frontiers Part II discuss its genesis. Part III the conundrum it created and Part IV How to come out of it—the alternative ways out of this economic puzzle.

INTRODUCTION AND THE THEORETICAL BACKGROUND

Capitalism is a market centric system subject to fluctuations. These fluctuations are the resultant effects of market forces as on which the system operates. These fluctuations as an aggregate economic activity is called Business cycle or trade cycle. The economic literate is replete with this trade cycle analysis.

Pigou, Howtray, Keynes, Kaldor, Hicks have interpreted these fluctuations in terms of their trade cycle interpretations. Likewise we have a bulk of theories analyzing the capitalist system fluctuations. The psychological theory of Pigou was replaced by monetary theory of Hawtray. We have climatic theory or under consumption theory propounded by Keynes. The Schumpeterian Innovation theory of trade cycle and Keynesian general employment theory of trade cycles are very popular and followed favour by policy designers. Samuelson also followed Keynesian lines and evolved his super multiplier trade cycle theory. The basic facts in all these interpretations of capitalists fluctuation is that capitalism is not a Coherent system and is subject to discrepancies causing disequilibrium leading to up and down swing of trade activities and ultimately leading towards a collapse or crisis in the system.

Paul M. Sweezy delivering in Harvard club, on March 22, 1982 has presented a comparative analysis of 1929 depression raged crisis with present financial crisis from various angles and propounded therefrom a new version of the analysis of the present global crisis.

The great depression crisis depicted unemployment rate at 23.6% level of the labour force. It reached to the high point of 24.9% in 1933 remained double digit throughout the decade till 1938-39. During the time of recovery, which was at its peak in 1937, the unemployment rate was 14.3%. The year 1937 is important in capitalistis history, because in that year Paul M. Sweezy, propounded in his Ph.D. In his thesis he propounded that the real problem of capitalism or market centred economy is not fluctuations or cyclical ups and downs of business activity but secular stagnation.

I would like here in this context to make a brief reference to the debate between in this context between two great visionary proponents of present day capitalism in Harvard-Josoph Schempeter and H.W. Hanson. These two prominent protagonists of capitalism and their debate in 1937-39 forms an important corollary to focus on the real rythem behind this crisis.

Harvard top in 1930's H.L. Hanson's book in 1938, "Full recovery or stagnation", and Schumpeter's argument came and got crystalised on the issue in his two volume treatise—"The business cycles in 1939."

Schumpeter labeled in his business cycles analysis Hanson's theory of stagnation as the theory of vanishing investment opportunities in his stagnation analysis. Which is but an apt characterization of the phenomena, which Hanson analysed.

According to Hanson's theory modern developed capitalist economy has an enormous capacity to save, both because of its corporate structure and because of its very unequal distribution of income. But if adequate profitable investment opportunities are lacking, this saving potential translates into real capital formation and sustained growth, results into lowered income and mass unemployment and depression of a chronic nature—a condition often summed in the stagnation.

Hanson's derivation of this frame work of analysis directly stem from keyne's general theory published in 1936, and Hanson was best known interpreter and champion of Keynes at Harvard.

Schumpeter refuted Hanson's interpretation and called the great depression crisis of 1929 as a world crisis. Therefore, unlike Hanson, asking what caused stagnation of 1930's and interpreting it in terms of simplifying assumption, Schumpeter began with his explanation of why cyclical upswing began in 1933 and cause to an end in 1938 in so far short-off. What he and others on his side assumed to be the normal situation of the end of prosperity phase of cycle—full employment, rising prices, and tight credit.

Schumpeter further elaborating the business cycles classed it into three, each named after earlier investigator of these phenomena, i.e. as very short cycles by Kitchen's cycles, Inventary cycles by Juglers cycles and long cycles by Kondratief's long cycles of some fifty years duration. The reality of which schempeter belived in.

Schumpeter was very disappointed by experiences of 1930's depression as it is like disappointing juglars of inventory nature which remained for a short period. The present global crisis is disappointing and dismaying in the perception of Schempeter and in Paul M. Swezy's vocabulary: Schumpeter interpretes Hanson's vanishing investment opportunity as antibusiness climate which is essentially the by-product of capitalist development.

The anti-business climate created by capitalist growth is the gensis of capitalist crisis in Schumpeterian incidental thinking. He thus, created a platform for new deal theory of stagnation. In one form or another it was shared by most political conservatives of the time.

The heart of Schumpeterian analysis is that it is not the content of new deal legislation which he considers as being compatible with normal functioning of capitalism, but personnel, who administered the legislation and the way he acted, all went anti-business. It had a dampening and repressive effect on entrepreneurs. Confidence and hopes, optimism blighting their hopes of future is lacking and it all inhibit investment activities in the present.

This theoretical debate on stagnation with Hanson on one side advocates Keynesian tools in the context of vanishing investment opportunity a positive tool for making a booster dose via public investment method or by fiscal stimuli. Schumpeter interpreted in his new deal theory of stagnation that capitalist growth has an inherent anti-business climatic tilt and the way new deal stagnation theory worked had a dampening and repressive impact on entrepreneurs. Thus, the content of new deal theory of stagnation seems compatible but the personnel who administered it and the way stimuli works goes anti-business shaking the confidence of the people in future.

The upswing which continued as a result of new deal in 1933 faced sharp cyclical decline in 1937-38 resulting in this type of interpretation by Schumpeter. The down-turn of 1937-38 came as a rude shock with unemployment jumped from 14.7 to 19% in 1938 and remained over 17% in 1939. Thus, anti-business climate created by new deal can no longer be denied. Thus, Hanson's and Schumpeter debate on the functioning of capitalism and its capitalist centric modern growth approach, forms the background of the present crisis.

II

THE PRESENT GLOBAL ECONOMIC CRISIS: ITS GENESIS

The present global economic crisis is not stagnation of the first type (1929-32 depression) but a prelude, it is linked as prelude to the wide economic conundrum.

Present capitalism got an external fillip with the outbreak of Second World War in 1939. The increased demand for armaments hoping a push factor for industrial growth resulted in expanded ranges of profits. This hopeful trend created by war externalities continued for a long period. But it could not continued for long and became ever lasing and the system felt breakdown of its profit scale with the energy crisis escalation in the wake of OPEC formation in early 1970's and both rate and range of profit started after that a declining trend. The excess capacity building and internal motive of saving in the system led to further weakening of the system and the capitalist system tried to maintain its previous profit growth rate via funding the OPEC world and the third world with oil-based modernisation game both in automobile industry, manufacturing and even agriculture and trade. How these funding acted in OPEC and third world opens an another issue of debate, but one thing is clear that these phenomenal change of capitalist expansion strategies from war, military intervention to funding development gave rise to another form of capitalist expansion popularly known as financial capitalism.

Leonard Silk editor of *New York Times* called this growth of capitalism as "Middle of the Road Economics." He deals at length the basic roots of the present economic crisis. He says that five consequitive U.S. Administration since 1965 has caused this global crisis. Silk says what is happening is not depression, but a chronic state of unemployment and industrial slackness and U.S. Administration has caused it. So the present global crisis is a tale of how U.S. economy failed as a controller of the world economy. So Leonard Silk's interpretation of the crisis, is the best serious study of stagnation after war. Criticizing Reagan Administration, suggesting ways to do better in business, his explanation till now seems realistic.

Josef Steindle earlier work on "Maturity and Stagnation in

American capitalism in 1982, went unnoticed by scholars in U.S.A. and abroad. However, it was a scholarly and intuitively penetrating on the problem of stagnation.

The character of present phase of capitalist world is same where H.L. Hanson began in 1930s.

"The structure of the economy in both its corporate form or its individual dimensions is basically the same as it was half a century ago. If its savings potential is still enormous, what changes have taken place that has tended to make it greater rather smaller in the intervening period."

Because of the increase in the corporate concentration, the distribution of individual incomes remains highly unequal. Besides, the changed tax structure have been more and more favourable to corporates and the rich. As always under such conditions a strong and sustained investment performance is needed to prevent the economy from falling into stagnation and that is precisely, what has been missing for a longtime now since 1977 in mass-based agriculture, manufacturing, and sectors it speeded up since 1990 in the wake of rampant globalization game. So the immediate cause of stagnation in the present form of economic slowdown is the same as it was in 1930, that is vanishing investment, in Hanson's terminology. Both public as well as private investment is scanty in mass activities sectors, i.e. agriculture and industry including manufacturing all over the world economy. So a strong propensity to save and weak propensity to invest is the greater cause of concern, so far the genesis of present crisis is concerned and this is the inherent weakness of capitalism. They increase their investment in high profit generating area with shorter duration of time.

Since Reagan Administration in America and Thactcher Administration in Britain, this process intensified and led to stretching of income already generated and not further expansion of income generation due to limit to geography because of ICT boom and plateauing of technological advancement in new areas. All thus culminated into the slowing down of economic activities, reducing thereby rate of profit and a stage of secular stagnation. Previously strong incentive to invest was created by external forces of war. The World War II created gap between present and required investment through its ravages all over the world. These ravages produced a brust of investment, which in turn undermined the incentive to investment as an eternal propelling mechanism for sustained growth path. The secret of long post-war boom was also further intensified by Korean war in 1950-52 and Vietnam war in early 1960. These were not war intervals but war intervention to make the long post-war boom flourish and the Neo classical thinkers of capitalism, thought it to be a state of mature growth process. Believing in this long dogma they embarked on the new phase of financial capitalism via the mechanism of borrowing and vast credit creation. Ladden with this burden, capitalism started crediting in area where it was due and this process resulted in cash crunch in many leading financial institutions in U.S. and European world, converting the global economic system into meltdown syndrome. So the fundamental weakness of the system remained the same, what it witnessed in 1930's. We can't reap profit without investing in new areas and innovative technological advancement therefrom. So the genesis of the present crisis rests where it rested in 1930's as analysed by H.L. Hanson. The weak propensity to invest and strong propensity to save is the root. The deviation to trade and services benefits is not the rescue area of the system since these sectors have a weak potential earning compare to the core sectors of agriculture, industry including manufacturing. [T.S. Papola, 27 Dec., 2005 quotating U.S. Economy Study by Victor Fuchas in 1968] IEA Presidential speech. This also resulted in macroeconomic imbalances and affected macroeconomic stability adversely.

III

THE CONUNDRUM IT CREATED

The concurrent condition and direction of U.S. Economy and its handmaid the European world created the present economic puzzle. The movement of these economies in 1970's and 1980's makes the point that economic circumstances of both the crisis 1930's and 2007-08 resembles on the same footing, arising out of the inherent saving potential in the system thus resulting the present phase of debt driven crisis because of the shifting base of capitalism from industrial expansion and export to expanding lending in the third world development and enlarged institutional borrowing from inland and abroad, thus turning into explosion of the financial administration of the system itself.

Prof. Walker and Harold G. Vatter—"Stagnation performance and policy: a comparison of depression decades with 1973-84." Published in *post-Keynesian Economic Journal,* in summer, where they say:

> "There have been only ten years in which actual GNP has equalled or exceeded the potential. These ten years have been noteworthy for the presence of expansionary government. Unfortunately most of the expansion was war laden through these years were (1950-52) Korean war, the Vietnam war, with overlapped the activities. We have this as a result of Kennedy-Johnson, Keynesian and civilian regimes. Without the strong pull from government demand over the last half century, the civilian economy has achieved its potential only in 1956 and 1973. Even in those two years on the basis of utilization of human resources, i.e. unemployment creation were significantly inferior to 1929."

This is a persistent tendency of society's under utilization of productive resources, which is lagging behind its huge and growing potential.

In the earlier depression crisis of 1930's this tendency worked itself in a catastrophic collapse of production leading to unemployment at 23% level and capacity utilization averaged between 18 percent and 63 percent respectively, as worked out by Paul M. Sweezy in his Ph.D. dissertation in 1938.

The post-war economic boom, energies created instead of lying dormant, have increasingly been channeled into a variety of wasteful, parasitic and generally unproductive uses. This has been done by an enormously complex process via value addition and standardization of the product and not increasing its value in real terms. This lag in society's utilization of productive resources is creating problem in the system. This process is still very imperfectly understood by present mainstream economic analyst, they even does not recognize its existence.

The debt structure of U.S. Economy, the government, corporate and individual functionaries at pace are far exceeding the sluggish expansion of the underlying real economy. The result is the emergence of an unprecedented huge and fragile financial super structure subject to stresses and strains that increasingly threaten the stability of the economy as a whole. The update evidence make these development clearer following the Tables given below:

TABLE 1

($ in billion)

Years	*1960*	*1965*	*1970*	*1975*	*1980*	*1985*
Outstanding U.S. debt.	800	1000	1200	2500	4800	7000
GNP	500	800	700	1800	3800	3800

Source: U.S. Federal Reserve Board, Flow of Funds Accounts and Survey of Current Business, Feb. 1986.

TABLE 2

Borrower	*Outstanding debt.*		*Index 1965 = 100*		
	1965	*1970*	*1975*	*1980*	*1985*
1. Govt. (Feb. State, Local)	100	123.1	182.4	284.5	585.8
2. Households (personal trusts, Next profit foundations private schools, hospitals Labour, and various churches)	100	140.1	226.8	421.2	696.5
3. Non financial business	100	165.1	277.9	468.8	762.8
4. Financial Business	100	200.5	421.6	917.0	1920.2
Total	100	144.5	236.5	414.4	742.2

Source: U.S. Federal Reserve Board, Debt Burden, Accounts and Survey of Current Business, Feb. 1986.

(i) Line 4 of Table 2 is important where startling rate of growth in borrowing occurred in financial sector itself. To contain extent the numbers give an exaggerated impression of what actually happened. Since debt of financial firms are relatively small in the base year, the rate of increase shows up abnormally high when compared with sectors that already had a much more substantial debt at the outset. Yet transformation of firms that are at the core of the debt explosion to major borrower is itself significant. Traditionally most of these enterprises are intermediaries that receive otherwise idle funds, which are then lent out. But in the new financial environment, these firms (borrowing enterprises) has gone beyond the role of intermediaries. They have themselves become large borrowers thus stimulating a more rapid and intensive circulation of the economy's cash reserves. As a result of if in 1970's the outstanding consumer debt in U.S. amounted to 68 percent after tax of consumer income and in 1985, it was close to 85 percent.

(ii) The non-financial business as the line 3 in table represents also witnessed the feverish accumulation of debt. The dominant components in this category is corporations, some of which has taken debt obligation to keep alive and hence forced to keep on borrowing just to meet payments on the past of debt. Others in contrast have long been awash with idle cash and many of these joined the parade. Unable to find profitable investment in the face of excess capacity and flagging demand, they became lager participants in merger, take over and leverage buy out frenzy that has swept the country in recent years and they thus becomes in the process both lenders and borrowers on an enormous scale. For all these reasons non-financial cooporations as whole carry a debt load of $ 1.5 trillion which exceeds their total networth by 12 percent. Since 1982 debt service cost has been absorbing fifty percent of the entire corporate cash flow. By comparison, during 1975-79 recovery, this cash averaged only twenty-seven as reputed by Felix G. Rohatyn, before joint economic committee fortieth anniversary symposium, Washington, D.C., July 1986.

The abnormal borrowing let lossen by financial institutions and non financial business players during 1965-35. It increased from 917.0 to 1920.2 in 1985 and in financial business and in non-financial business borrowing from 468.6 to 762.8

billion dollars. The outstanding debt of financial firm more than doubled in united states. The self-expansion of financial sector firms, conversion of these financial firms from intermediary borrower to large borrowers, led to more rapid and intensive circulation of economy's cash reserves converting the system into out stretching of income generated *per se* and not its expansion.

This self-expansion of financial sector turned into a complex and enormously powerful process with most far reaching consequences.

A report by Federal Reserve Bank of Newyork, presented by its Vice-President Edward J. Fridle says in its 1985 annual reports says:

> "The votality of prices for the entire spectrum of financial assets has risen considerably. In step with this development new financial instruments such as futures, options, swaps that sub-prime lending sources that provide additional ways to transfer price risks among market participants flourished. The active trading of these new instruments and of conventional instruments underlying them has bourgeoned or make growing or flourishing the financial sector. The Volume of financial transaction accelerated at an alarming and unprecedented rate."

Competition has greatly increased the whole range of financial services. Commercial banks, thrift institutions, investment banks, insurance companies, all are expanding the range of their activities and crossing over into each others traditional business preserves. Non-financial businesses are directly entering financial services as well. Foreign financial institutions are increasing their involvement in markets. Competitive pressures have been compounded by the on going trend towards financial regulation of the terms that institutions can change or offer kinds of transaction in which they may engage and the geographical markets they may enter. This liberation in terms of regulation of institution and its increasing space increased the degree of competition which squeezed earning margins on many conventional financial activities accelerating the development via diffusion of financial innovations.

This process weakened economic and financial conditions of majors—energy, agriculture, commercial real estate in U.S., Europe and various developing countries dependent on U.S. borrowings. This resulted in diminished credit standing of many borrowers. One consequence of this has been that in recent years the costs of capital and funding for some bank lenders to those sectors have tended to rise relative to the costs for high quality commercial credit. At the same time direct credit market have become more accessible to business borrowers. Banks have a difficult time competing with commercial papers and securities for corporate credit demands specially those of the blue chip firms.

Indeed in many cases Banks have sought to profit from the trend towards market financing by generating loans and selling them off. Either directly or packaged as securities or by expanding their roles as guarantors and distributors of capital market instruments.

Thus, all forces—innovations, competition, deregulation, securitization and the growth of trading have thus combined to create a challenging environment, thus resulting to the present economic crisis of cash crunch via diffusion of excess credit and their securitization resulting into economic crisis of credit and liquidity resulting in slow down in major economic sector wreaking economic and financial conditions of nations—thus a global economic crisis of widespread nature.

This represents a case of failure of U.S. Economy as a regulator of world economy. It is a case of excess of financial firms product over real goods production as result of financial sector boom through diffusion of financial innovations raising the financial sector share as percentage of goods production in real sense, thus creating a credit bubble. All these became possible because of increasing gap between speculation and real production and as result of it increasing outstanding gap between outstanding debt and national production in real terms. The debt burden over the developing world increased and mechanism of reaping profit via increasing debt burden either by supply of undesirable technological capital input or via making it redundant through new technological upgradation, the increasing debt burden over poor nations and poors in general and went on increasing exploiting their resources both men and material, and reaping profit out of it. Thus making profit out of undesirable use of technological capital input created a case of undesirable lending thus pushing the entire system in unrealistic direction leading flow of easy credit to frivolous area and credit crunch in core area where majority of the poors live and eke out a living base.

Thus, the present crisis represents a case of failure of money to control future markets resulting in highest ever increase of finance contract trade that is 53.6 percent in U.S. economy in 1983 compared to commodity trade contract and precious metal contact. Thus combined trade contracts of financial instruments, foreign currency, stock rose in 53.6 and it has speeded up during succeeding periods till the melting of big brothers Lehman, and other giants. It is thus a case of mismastering of money which is considered as a good servant. The money went out of control creating a big gap between Federal resources and money supply. Hence the present crisis.

Tables 3 and 4 regarding growth of financial sector in U.S. and Gross National product since 1950 up to 1985 and the same trend onwards continued and Table 4 regarding future speculation trade trends in U.S. shows how sick shows U.S. economy and expanded all over the world economy depicting two things—U.S. Economy failed as a regulator of world economy and money as a managing tool of business. Short sighted entrepreneurial climate and diffusion of financial innovations automatically results in to such a financial catastrophies. It is case of money completely out of

TABLE 3

Growth of U.S. Financial Sector and G.N.P.

Year	*G.N.P. Good Production*	*Billion dollars Financial Product*	*Financial as Percentage of Goods*
1950	153.3	32.2	21.0
1960	250.5	72.8	29.1
1970	440.7	145.8	33.1
1980	1144.06	400.8	35.0
1985	1566.7	626.1	40.0

Source: National income and product accounts as reputed in survey of current business, various issues, United States.

TABLE 4

Speculative Markets, Future Trade in U.S.

No. of Contracts in (millions)

Itemes	1960	1976	1981	1982	1983
1. Commoditities	3.9	29.3	53.8	51.2	64.4
2. Precious metals	-	7.2	15.7	28.8	22.6
3. Financial instruments	-	.2	22.9	18.8	28.1
4. Foreign Currency	-	.2	6.1	8.7	11.9
5. Stock indexes	-	-	-	4.9	12.8
Total	3.9	36.9	98.5	112.4	140.0

Source: Releases of Future Industries Association, US.

control as Marx-prophecised to which Kalecki indicated much earlier in 1968.

Thus, the key to understanding present crisis rests on the base of understanding capitalism as the process of capital accumulation as Heilbrover called it.

Comparing capital with human organism we see M-C-M as the heart beat that pumps the systems monetary life blood through its arteries and views got eroded by future trading creating gap between commodity money commodity relation. In one case as in the other the health of the system depends on the proper functioning of the heart; irregularities or weaknesses causes systemic illness and in extreme cases threatens the life itself. Once the centrality of Marx's famous short hand truism is duely recognized, it hardly becomes an avoidable step. Seeing it not only convenient but economically viable conceptualization. Keynes recognized it not simply as the engine of the economy but the dominant force in shaping the system's political, ideological and cultural aspects. By public investment mode, he channelised the investment decision via infrastructural build up to commodity direction. Thus he bridged the gap between future production via futures trade through financial instruments in the system and via fiscal stimuli it makes fiscal multiplier to operate for the good of common people. Keynes thus showing affinity with Marx attempted to bridge the gap between future trade and real trade via fiscal stimuli, which when goes in undesirable direction by less foresighted administrators or left unused creates further crisis strengthens the chord of crisis.

Thus Helibroner takes this step with full awareness of its far reaching significant. Heilborner is as an unambiguous Marxist, in the sense that his enquiry of what is capitalism? explains in fact, the complex and many sided regime of capital. His explanation of stagnation and financial explosion is unique and unrivalled in many ways. He was helpful in changing the center of gravity in capitalist system from its developed to under developed part. The penetration in latter by the regime of capital created a mass suffering humanity confronting closely to Marx-Engles description of the fully developed proletariat, who is fully aware of those living conditions as representing the focal point of all human conditions in modern society. Thus, capitalism forbades the Holy Family emerge in this situation. (*The Holy Family,* written in 1843). Thus, the crisis goes on penetrating, if the fiscal stimuli does not go in right direction and the new proletariate class thus created by the regime of capital, will take revolution to occur on the system's weakest link, i.e., poor in the poor nations. Extremism, terrorism and wider links to large scale misuse of finance loot let loosen by fiscal authority or institutions in undesirable direction are cases to point this malady of the present capitalist regime.

Maichal Kalecki commented on the issue shortly before the Keynes death on the capitalist system—this way in 1947—"Why can't a capitalist system once it has deviated downward from the path of expanded reproduction (growth) and find itself in a position of long-term simple reproduction, "No growth or recession". Infact we are absolutely in the dark, concerning what will happen in such a situation, so long as we have not solved the problem of derterminants of investment dicissions. Neither Marx nor modern economists have developed such a theory. Some attemps have been made in this direction, while evolving a theory of cyclical fluctuations. However, even this has failed to explain the long-run trend and concentrated much more on explaining temporary business cycles. Long-run growth on income involves satisfactory utilization of equipment (capital) which is far from obvious in this system (quoated from Marx, Social Sciences Information, Dec. 1968) by Kalecki. As a result, we have this worldwide conundrum to face due to clumsy mode of future trading and interplay of inflation and interest rates in it leading the supply of money lose the ground of real production and turning towards recession and financial meltdown. Thus Kalecki is also glorified for inventing Keynesion revolution before Keynes commented on this issue much before Keynes commented on it 1936 in his general theory of employment interest and money.

TABLE 5

Explains the World Crisis Scenario this Way

Region Country	*Real GDP*				*Consumer Price inflation*		*Percent Short term interest*
	2007	*2008*	*2009*	*2010*	*2007*	*2008*	
1.	2.	3.	4.	5.	6.	7.	8.
World Economy	5.2	3.4	0.5	3.0	-	-	-
Advance Economies	2.7	1.0	(-2.0)	1.1	2.1	3.5	-
United States	2.0	1.1	(-1.6)	1.6	4.1	3.8	0.36
European Area	2.6	1.0	(-2.0)	0.2	3.2	3.1	2.05
Japan	2.4	(-0.3)	(-2.6)	0.6	0.7	1.4	0.61
Emerging Economies	8.3	6.3	3.3	5.6	6.4	9.2	-
Developing Asia	10.6	7.8	5.5	6.9	5.4	7.8	-
China	13.0	9.0	6.7	8.0	6.5	5.9	1.34
India***	9.3	7.3	5.1	6.5	5.5	8.2	4.78
South Korea	5.0	4.1	(-2.8)	-	3.9	4.9	2.93
Singapore	7.7	1.9	(-2.9)	-	4.4	6.6	0.56
Thailand	4.8	3.4	(-1.0)	-	4.3	5.5	2.22
Argentina	8.7	5.5	(-1.8)	-	8.5	8.6	15.13
Brazil	5.7	5.8	(1.8)	3.5	4.5	5.7	12.66
Mexico	3.2	1.8	(-0.3)	2.1	3.8	5.1	7.16
Central and Eastern Europe	5.4	3.2	(-0.4)	2.5	-	-	-
Russia	8.1	6.2	(-0.7)	1.3	12.6	14.1	13.0
Turkey	4.6	2.3	0.4	-	8.2	10.5	14.0

Updated from World Economic Outlook, Jan, 28, 2009s.

The Economist, Feb. 7, 2009.

Average Annual change in percent.

*** : For India Wholesale prices,

Note: Interst rate percent per annum.

Source: IMF, World Economic Outlook and the Economist.

R.B.I., India's and Financial Sector—As Assessment, Vol. III, Table 1.1, 2009.

IV

THE WAYOUT MECHANISM

The wayout from this conundrum is in the proper and balanced investment decision of capital. The open door policy of supply side monetarism and their misbegotten off spring the Reganomics, and Thatcherism put in practice led the system to crisis.

It is not income but quality of earning matters. It is not speculative profit but profit realized creates the base for further economic action. So it is not future trading but actual trade done delivers. Credit trade which realized profit is important and but to credit where credit is due is wrong. The M-C-M truism will not help economic growth simply to flourish. So fiscal stimuli will not help simply unless we are willing to lead it in proper direction with foresighted financial administrators.

Prof. Lester Thurow in his outspoken article in *Newyork Times*, on Oct. 17, 1982, depicted the present economic crisis and all which added up to this "The world economy is likely to continue sinking into quick sands. We are likely to have more of rising unemployment, increasing financial distress. We have been experiencing since the last one and half years. There is simply no indication that the western nations individually or jointly have any programme or any approach that is capable of turning this trade."

The talk of old fashioned Keynesian stimulus, if used and left in unpractising direction as Lester Thurow pointed out it becomes irrelevant as the Neoclassical chatter of the monetarist and supplysiders. This does not make Keynes irrelevant. Keynes, in fact put into reconsideration the whole theory of investment among twentieth century figures of economics. Only Schumpeter and Keynes qualify for inclusion as an economic analysist who has inbuilt social system with which they are concerned. They have vision that embraces social actors. The form and content of their interrelations, the dynamics of the system and its historical destiny. Classical political economy from Adam Smith, through John Stuart Mill had such a vision followed in twentieth century by Keynes and Schumpeter. The neoclassical school too has a vision but this vision is so totally dominated by apologetics (Logic for sake of logic) that it converts into a pale and lifeless caricature of the historical reality it purports to reflect. Instead of classes in collision and conflict, the actors of neoclassical analysis are powerless individual seeking to maximize their utilities, their medium of impersonal markets and in this fantasy world, they are all equal and have no inter-relations outside the market.

The dynamic of the market system is to move more or less smoothly and expeditiously towards a state of general equilibrium. The system's historical destiny is to reproduce the *status quo adfinitum*. Such a vision is against the ground situation and it may give rise to intriguing intellectual games, but it does not help any one to understand the world we live in and the problems we face.

It was Heibroner, who brought out economics from status *quo courtiers*, as a narrowly circumscribed science as was the tradition in Harward to treats it. Heibroner puts economics in the tradition of Adam Smith, Karl Marx by recognizing the affinity between Keynes and Marx, which later on came in as an interesting article by Dudley Dillard in spring 1984 "Max and Keynes: a centennial appraisal" published in the journal of Post-*Keynesian Economics*, 1984. Dillard says, "one of rare occasions in which Keynes praised Marx with the pregnant observation that the nature of production in the actual world is not as economists seem often to suppose a case of C-M-C that is exchanging commodities or effort for money in order to obtain another commodity or effort. That may be the stand point of private consumers, but it is not the attitude of business, which is a case of M-C-M that is a parting with money for commodities or effort in order to obtain more money." (Keynes's collected works No. 1.29, p. 81).

Unless *status quo* motive of capitalism change, old fashioned Keynesian stimules turs-out to be irrelevant as the neoclassical chatter of monetarist and supplysiders. Michal Kalecki, the Polish Economist, who has been justifiably be credited with inventing the Keynesian revolution, before Keynes commented on this subject shortly before his death in following terms:

"Why can't a capitalist system once it has deviated

downward from the path of expanded reproduction (Growth) find itself in a position of long-term simple reproduction (no growth)." In fact we are absolutely in the dark concerning what will happen in such a situation, so long as we have not solved the problems of the determinants of investment decisions. Marx did not develop such a theory. Nor this has been accomplished by Modern Economists. Some attempts has been made in the development of the theory of cyclical fluctuations. However, the problems of the determinants of investment decisions involving the long-run trend are much more difficult than the case of the pure business cycles. One thing is clear to me long-run growth of income involves satisfactory utilization of equipment is far from obvious." (*Source*: Social Sciences Information Dec., 1968.)

Recent developmental explanation of fast emerging nations of China and India by Lucas, Paul Streeton, Barrow, pointed out the fact that due to mass layers of skilled labour confronts the new rising capitalization in these new emerging economies the MRR (marginal rate of returns) to capital is greater in these economies compared to the rich economies. But due to ICT boom and other knowledge awareness these skilled labour layer penetrates into the deep even with little knowledge base. So long-run growth demand of capitalism lies at its weak ends in these economies with greater capability build up and their use and the use of fiscal stimuli in these hither to unnoticed areas. Otherwise, the nature of underlying crisis will have two faces—first is working out through upswings and downswings and another with more dire consequences of what Marx called "the absolute general law of capitalist accumulation and thus the deepening and expanding the crisis situation with absolute increase in mass of proletariat, unproductiveness of its labour and greater the reserve army". (Marx: *Capital*, Vol. I, Chapter XXIII, Sect. 4)

References

Anger Maddison, 2001. The World Economy: A millennium perspective OECD, Paris.

Arun Maria, "A matter of Trust, Accountability Inspres confience in Free market", *Times of India*, Feb. 2, 2009.

Central Cuts Key rates *Times of India*; Patna Jan. 3, 2009.

Dudley Dillard, "Marx and Keynes: A Centennial Appraisal-" Commemorating hundredth anniversary of Marx's death and Keynes' birth, Published in the Journal of *Post-Keynesian Economics*, Spring 1984, The volume depicted one of the rare occasion in which Keynes praised Marx occurred in 1933 draft of the general theory when it was called "The monetary theory of employment. Keynes credit Marx with Pregnant observation .... That the nature of production in the actual world is not as economists, seen often to suppose, a case of C-M-C, i.e. of exchanging commodity/effort for money in order to obtain another commodity or effort. That may be the stand point of private consumers, but it is not the attitude of business, which is a case of M-C-M, i.e., a parting with money for commodities/effort in order to obtain more money." (This quotation from Keynes from his collected works, Vol. 29, p. 81).

Keynes use of the Marxian formula C-M-C and M-C-M was first called to attention of Dudley Dillard by Roy Rotheim in Keynes's "monetary theory of value" appeared in *Journal of Post-Keynesian Economics*, Summer, 1981. Dillard wrote to Joan Robbinson (March 2, 1982) I was fascinated to learn from an article by Roy J. Rutheim that Keynes was influenced by Marx's C-M-C and M-C-M Schemas. From his published remarks about Marx—Consigning him to the underworld of Gesell and Major Douglas, etc. I had no idea of this link. Could he have picked up Marx's distinction between the two kinds of economy from discussion of the time of General theory was in gestation or did he get it from his own reading of Marx, which I had always assumed to have been minimal. Anyway, it shows that he had an eye for what is important in Marx far keener than any of the other bourgeoise economists.

In March 11, 1982, Joan Robbinson replied in her usual terse style, I was surprised of the note about Keynes and Marx. Keynes said to her that he used to try to get sraffa to explain to him the meaning of labour value, etc. and recommended pages and Passages to read, but that he could never make out, what it was about.

Subsequent enquiries have yielded no further information on how Keynes came to acquaint with Marxian formula since his reading of Marx was obviously casual, today the least, it seems possible that he may have come across them in a secondary source. In any case the fact that they made an impression on him (Keynes) is clear evidence of a certain similarity between his own and Marx's way of conceptualizing the capitalist economy."

Heonard Silk, Editor *New York Times*—What is happening is not depression. It is achronic State of unemployment and Industrial Stack, also Business Section, Sunday, March 14, 1965. The roots of the problem go a longway."

Hanson Alvin H., "Full recovery and Stagnation, 1938, Harvard University Press.

Heilbroner Rober L. (Holder of Norman Thomas Chair in Economics of New School) his writings enquiring into the human prespects (1974), Business civilization in decline (1976), Beyond Boom and Crash (1978), Marxism for and against (1980), The nature and logic of capitalism (1985). This last of his series is for more interesting from a marxist point of view: Heil brower is not Marxist but these books …….. him squarely within the Marxist universe of discourism.

Keynes J.M., General theory of Employment Interest and Money, 1936.

Karl Marx' *Das Capital,* Vol. I, Chapter XXIII, Section 4, referred to the quarrel between industrial capital and aristocratic landed property which entitled participation of England's outstanding economic thinkers in the decade of 1820.

Lester Thurow (Harvard, Professor of Economics) "The Great Stagnation," *Newyork Times,* Oct. 17, 1982.

Lalecki Michael (1968) Determinants of Investment Decision, "Social Science Information Index, Dec. 1968. This Polish Economist is credited with Inventing keycusian resolution before Keynes, analyzing Keynes affivity with Marx. He quoted Keynes as saying at the time of his death " Long run growth of national income involves satisfactory utilization of equipment is far from obvious".

Marx Kare, *Das Capital,* Vol. III.

Magdoff Harry, The world debt—Past and Present—article presented at Allied social Science Association Meetings, *Newyork City,* Dec. 1985, Feb. 1986 of monthly review.

Schumpeter, A. Joseph, *The Business Cycles,* 1938.

Sweezy, M. Paul, "Why Stagnation", Talk given by the author at Harvard Economic Club on March 22, 1982, June 1982, Monthly Review.

Sweezy, M. Paul, The Dynamics of U.S. Capitalism: Corporate structure, Inflation, credit, Gold and Dollar (1972), Credit, Gold and Dollar (1972), The End of American Prosperity in 1970 (1977).

Tesedore, Shamin (ed.), Late Marx and Russian Road: Marx and the Peripheries of Capital, Monthly review. Press, 1984.

2

Global Economic and Financial Crisis: Causes, Consequences, Channels of Contagion and India's Prospects

DURESH KUMAR SINGH AND PRAHLAD KUMAR

It is now evident that this is an unprecedented phase in the history of global capitalism. The still unfolding financial crisis has already moved well beyond the predictions of more pessimistic observers. Across the world real economics are being affected by the financial distress in direct and indirect way associated with sharply slowing economic activities and rising unemployment. Of course, this particular crisis reflects contradictions at the heart of the capitalist system, including those emanating from its dependence upon inelastic expectations about the value of money, which are inherent to the smooth functioning of capitalism (Patnaik, 2008).

Economists have offered theories about how financial crises develop and how they could be prevented, however, financial crises are still a regular occurrence around the world. Since 2000, the growth was driven to a large extent by strong consumer demand in the USA, stimulated by the easy credit and supported by a booming housing market coupled with a high rated of investment demand and strong export growth in some developing countries notable China. Increasing US deficits were financed by increasing trade surpluses by China, Japan and other countries that has accumulated large force reserves and were willing to by Dollar denominated assets. At the same time increasing financial deregulation along with a floury of new financial instruments and risk managements techniques such as mortgage backed securities, collateralized debt obligation credit default swap, etc. encouraged massive accumulation of financial assets. A growing level of debts in the household, corporate and public sectors sustained them. The massive explosion of debt inevitably resulted in collapse of many established financial institutions, evaporating the liquidity and several affecting the real economy.

The basic cause of the crisis was largely an unregulated environment mortgage lending to sup prime borrowers. Since the borrowers did not have adequate repaying capacity and also sub-prime borrowing has to pay two to three percentage points higher rate of interest and they have a history of default the situation became worse. But once the housing market collapsed the lender institution saw their balance sheets go motored. (Dutt, 2009)

The meltdown has also revealed the inability of the legal and regulatory frame works of today to respond to a global financial contagion. This warrants and honest discussion of the role and scope of the IMF and whether it could be converted in to a more democratic and participative 'Supra Regulator' that overseas the global financial systems. The fear is that in the absence of such a regulator, emerging economics would be loathe further liberalize and integrate their financial systems with the world and would therefore be deprived of access to low cost capital that their development agendas so urgently demand. Promises at the recent G-20 summit not with standing substantial progress is still needed for a securer and more regulated financial order (ORF, Issue Brief, 2009).

CHANNELS OF CONTAGION

A redeeming feature of the current crisis is that its magnitude is much lesser than that of the Great Depression of the 1930s when unemployment rate the United States exceeded 25 percent. Currently, it stands at 6.5 percent and is predicated to remain around eight percent in 2009.

The Channels of the contagion through which crisis affects developing countries include the financial contagion and the economic downturn in the developed countries. As a result of the financial contagion and spillovers for stock markets in the emerging markets. The Russian stock market had to stop trading twice, the India stock market dropped by 8% in one day at the same time as stock markets in the USA and Brazil plunged. Stock markets across the world developed and developing have all dropped substantially since May, 2008.

The first channel through which economic down turn impacts of developed countries on developing countries appears is trade and trade prices. In which the growth in China and India has increased imports and pushed up the demand for copper, oil and other natural recourses, which has led to greater exports and higher prices, including from African Countries. Eventually growth in China and India is likely to slow down, which will have knocked on effects on other foreign countries. The remittance to developing countries will decline and the foreign direct investment and equity investment will come under pressure. The year 2007 was a record year for FDI to developing countries. Banks under pressure in developed countries may not be able to lend as much as they have done in the past. Aid budgets are under pressures because of debt problems and weak fiscal positions and the capital adequacy ratios of development finance institutions will be under pressure. The impact on the response in developed countries to the financial crisis and the slowdown and the economic characteristics and policy responses, in developing countries. The deep and lingering crisis in global financial markets the extreme level of risk a version, the mounting losses of banks and banking institutions the elevated level of commodity prices (until the third quarter of 2008) and their subsequent collapse and the sharp correction in a range of assets process all combined have suddenly led to a sharp slowdown in growth momentum in the major advanced economics, especially since Lehman failure. Global growth for 2009, which was seen at a healthy 3.8 percent in April 2008, is now projected to contract by 1.3 percent (IMF, 2009c).

As a result of the financial crisis, the international trade is contracting. Between 1990 to 2006, the growth of world trade was six percent, which has outstripped the growth rate of world output of three percent. In 2008, the growth of merchandise trade decelerated to around four percent. The WTO has predicted that the volume of world merchandise trade would shrink by nine percent in 2009

TABLE I

Global Economic Outlook for 2009

(%)

	Months of Forecast											
	April 2008		*July 2008*		*October 2008*		*November 2008*		*January 2009*		*April 2009*	
Indicators	*2008*	*2009*	*2008*	*2009*	*2008*	*2009*	*2008*	*2009*	*2008*	*2009*	*2008*	*2009*
1. **Global Growth**	3.7	3.8	4.1	3.9	3.9	3.0	3.4	0.5	3.4	0.5	3.2	-1.3
(a) Advanced Economies	1.3	1.3	1.7	1.4	1.5	0.5	1.0	-2.0	1.0	-2.0	0.9	-3.8
(b) EMEs	6.7	6.6	6.9	6.7	6.9	6.1	6.3	3.3	6.3	3.3	6.1	1.6
2. **World Trade Volume***	3.7	3.8	4.1	3.9	3.9	3.0	4.1	-2.8	4.1	-2.8	3.3	-11.0
3. **Consumer Price Inflations**												
(a) Advanced Countries	2.6	2.0	3.4	2.3	3.6	2.0	3.5	0.3	3.5	0.3	3.4	-0.2
(b) EMEs	7.4	5.7	9.1	7.4	9.4	7.8	9.2	5.8	9.2	5.8	9.3	5.7

Source: World Economic Outlook, Various Issues, International Monetary Fund.
Volume growth in goods and services.

Major economics are in recession and the EMEs – which in the earlier part of 2008 were widely viewed as being decoupled from the major advanced economics – have also been engulfed by the financial crisis led-slow-down. Label trade volume (goods and services) is also expected to contract by 11 percent during 2009 as against the robust growth of 8.2 percent during 2006-07. Private capital flows (net) do the emerging market economics (EMEs) fell from the peak of US $ 617 billion in 2007 to US $ 109 billion in 2008 and are projected to record net outflows of US $

190 billion in 2009 will be mainly on account of act flows under bank lending and portfolio flows. Thus, both the slowdown in internal demand and the lack of external financing have dampened growth prospects for the EMEs much more than that was anticipated a year ago.

IMPACT ON INDIA WITH SPECIAL REFERENCE TO TRADE

Although at one time it was thought that this crisis wouldn't affect the Indian economy later it was found that the foreign direct investment started drying up and this affected investment in the Indian economy. It was therefore felt that the Indian economy will grow at six percent in 2009-10 (Dutt, 2009)

India is now facing another crisis, which unlike, 1991, has into origin abroad. The entire world is witnessing a finance turbulence fallowing the sub-prime mortgages crisis in the United States of America. While the exact reason are not yet know at the fundamental level, the crisis could be ascribed to the persistence to large global imbalances, which, in turn, is the outcome of long periods of excessively loose monetary policy in the major advanced economics during the early part of this decade. (Mohan, 2009).

The purport of the above references is to highlight the Indian experience. The tumultuous development in the past one year had a negative impact on the pace of economic activity in Indian eight do nine percent has slowed down. The tentative estimates expect the economy to have grown at around five percent through official estimates place it at more optimistic seven percent. The stock market has last 50 percent of its value. The rupee has lost some 208 percent of its value in terms of the dollar. There have been high losses in sectors of the economy with large export dependence such as textiles and diamond cutting and polishing. No fresh recruitment and job creation is taking place even in the high profile IT sector.

Our Honorable Prime Minister, Dr. Manmohan Singh, on a two day visit to France, said the crisis at the moment, can spread to the rest of world. He said, "We live in an interdependent world and the fate of all countries is related to the international financial system. Our value markets are opened to the world and if they are affected, this will affect our capacity to finance our development. If the financial crisis causes a recession in the main economics, this will comprise our exports.".

The unfolding global financial crisis is, however having major repercussions in India that are different from that witnessed during 1991. Although the magnitude of impact on India is still low, it could potentially weaken the economy though trade channels if not tackled properly, at a time when India is much more globalized than in the early 1990s. (Asharya, 2009; Rakshit, 2009)

TABLE 2

India's Merchandise Trade

(US $ billion)

Year	*Exports*	*Imports*	*Total*	*Trade in GDP (%)*	*EPC#(US$)*
1950-51	1.27	1.27	2.54		3.53
1960-61	1.35	2.35	3.70	11.77	3.10
1970-71	2.03	2.16	4.19	7.76	3.71
1980-81	8.49	15.87	24.36	15.56	12.34
1990-91	18.15	24.07	42.22	15.48	21.36
1995-96	31.80	36.68	68.48	23.13	34.11
2000-01	44.56	50.54	95.10	27.38	43.86
2001-02	43.83	51.41	95.25	26.38	42.45
2002-03	52.72	61.41	114.13	29.92	50.28
2003-04	63.84	78.15	141.99	30.70	59.98
2004-05	83.54	111.52	195.06	38.22	77.37
2005-06	103.09	149.17	252.26	43.61	94.18
2006-07	126.23	185.60	311.86	48.78	113.77
2007-08	163.13	251.65	414.78	49.38	146.86
2008-09	168.70	287.76	456.46		152.01

Source: Calculated based on (a) Economic Survey, 2008-09, (b) Press Release on India's foreign trade (date 1 April, 2009 and 1 May, 2009), New Delhi.

India's accelerated trade in the recent part has caught the world's attention. By any standard Indian trade performance has greatly improved; export per capita has increases much more rapidly in the post-reform period than in the earlier years. Although, with an import substitution policy in place India took two decades (1950/51 to 1960/70) to cross the US $ 2 billion export mark, with a much more liberal policy the country

FIGURE I

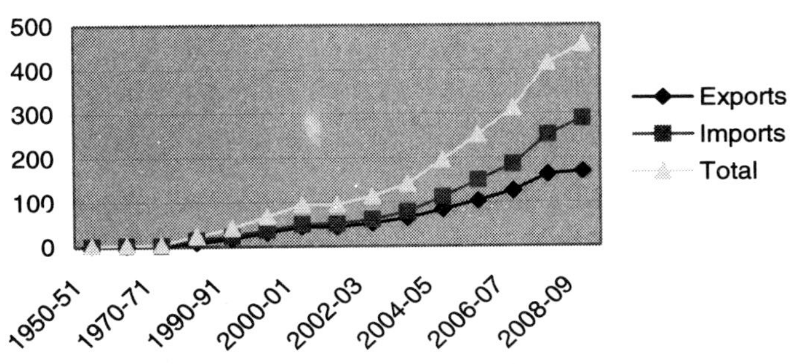

crossed the US $ 20 billion export over time, with greatly reduced barriers to international transactions, Indian participation in the international economy has improved rapidly. Today, with a 19 percent per annum growth rate, India's exports have passed US $ 169 billion (2008/09), while imports have increased to US $ 288 billion, having grown at about 25 percent per annum since 2000/01. India's trade growth rate in the present decade has thus been the highest of all the decades since the 1950s. Higher growth in the post-1991 period helped India not only to enlarge but to diversity its exports.

TABLE 3

Growth Rate of Exports and Imports

(US $ term)

	Exports	*Imports POL*	*Imports Non-POL*	*Imports Gold Silver*	*Non-POL Gold & Silver*	*Imports Total*	*Trade Balance*
2007-08							
April-Aug.	20.8	18.4	43.6	131.7	33.0	34.4	68.4
Sept-March	35.3	56.1	38.5	-30.3	49.2	44.0	63.7
2008-09							
April-Aug.	29.5	69.2	27.9	-13.7	36.7	40.9	61.2
Sept-March	-12.1	-12.8	4.0	3.2	2.9	-1.7	17.8

Source: Economic Survey, 2008-09.

India's share in the world merchandise exports after remaining unchanged at 1.0 percent between 2005 and 2006 reached 1.1 percent in 2007 and continued to remain at that level in 2008. However in 2008-09 (April-February) as a result of global recession, the overall growth of exports in US $ terms was only 6.6 percent compared to 29 percent compared to 29 percent in the corresponding period of the previous year. For the year 2008-09, an export target of US $ 200 billion was set earlier and later it was revised to US $ 175 billion. In 2008-09, the value of merchandise exports reached US $ 168.7 billion with a growth of 3.6 percent despite global recession, thus achieving 96.4 percent of the revised export target. While export growth was robust till August 2008, it became law in September and became negative from October 2008 to March 2009 due to the global recession. The negative trend continued in April 2009 with export growth at (-) 33.2 percent.

With respect to GDP, exports, which accounted for 22 percent of the GDP are expected to fall by 12 percent. The Government fiscal package provides an interest rate subsidy of two percent on exports for the labour-intensive sectors such as textiles, handicrafts, leather, gems and Jewellery, but the Federation of Indian Export Organization (FIEO) felt the measure are not enough as they will not make the export price—competitive and therefore will not boast exports. G.K. Pillai, the Commerce Secretary has estimated a loss of 1.5 million jobs in the export sector alone during 2008-09 on account of the $ 15 billion decline in the expected exports.

CONCLUSION AND SUGGESTIONS

Thus it can be concluded that international trade has a key role to play in the economic recovery during the current global crisis provided it is complemented by trade liberalization and trade facilitation and trade transaction costs have an equally strong catalytic role in enhancing India's trade.

So it is clear that many of the challenges for India and other EMEs do not arise from the crisis directly but are a result of the unilateral, nationalist and protectionist responses of nations first affected by the crisis. These responses are likely to harm the Indian economy and its growth more than the actual event itself. This in effect will make the political content of this crisis as large, if not larger, as the economic content. India and EMEs will need to engage politically with the world to safeguard their economic interests. This need for engagement also dilutes the "decoupling" hypothesis, which was dominated Indian economic discourses and which assumes India's growth far from that of the United States in particular and the west generally.

The combined impact of the reversal of portfolio equity flows, the reduced availability of international capital both debt and equity, the perceived increase in the price of equity with lower equity valuations, and pressure on the exchange rate, growth in the Indian corporate sector is likely to feel some impact of the global financial turmoil. On the other hand on a macro-basis, with external saving utilization having been low traditionally between one to two percent of GDP, and the sustained high domestic savings rate, this impact can be expected to be at the margin. Moreover the continued buoyancy of foreign direct investment suggests that confidence in Indian growth prospects remains healthy.

Securities and Exchange Board of India (SEBI) Chairman, C.B. Bhave says, there is no panic in market. He calmed the fears of the US financial crisis affecting Indian Markets, saying there was no panic as the capital market watch log was monitoring the situation very closely. He also added that the Indian stock market is resilient and the clearing system has proved its ability to deal with stock market fluctuations.

The Finance Minister P. Chidambaram assured that Public Sector Banks had virtually no exposure to Lehman Brother although the credit crunch globally will impact credit availability in the Indian market; there is no cause for any alarm that any Indian bank is vulnerable.

The Prime Minister of India, Dr. Manmohan Singh set-up a high-level panel to monitor the impact of the global financial crisis on domestic industry. The panel headed by Dr. Singh includes India's Central Reserve Bank chief and finance and trade ministers who will advise the premier on steps needed to reassure Indian Industry.

Now the main suggestions for policy implications are—

- Our Agriculture and industrial development policy

should be determined by the unique requirement of India's teeming millions and should not become a prisoner of default economic ideas.

- Government should give priority to public investment in infrastructure and social sector.
- Development should be done with a human face with the realization that people are both the means and end of development.
- Banks should ensure credit for private sector to enable participation in infrastructure and manufacturing sectors. This would generate employment and spur GDP growth.
- Public and private investments should be encouraged through tax and other incentives in Rural Development and Agriculture sectors. Supply chain infrastructure should be made a national mission.
- The alternative business models to 'SEZs' should be developed and policy should encourage 'rural business hubs' along with development of rural markets.
- Domestic BPOs and IT services markets should be developed and special emphasis on development of IT infrastructure should be in rural and semi-urban areas.
- The multilateral trading regime of GATT/WTO ,the most successful attempt since the Second World War at achieving a transparent, equitable and efficient rules-based world-wide trading system is the best solution to the ongoing crisis. Therefore, India should expand the geographical reach of the RTAs because multilateralizing RTAs would generate more exports for India.

References

Acharya, S. (2009), "India and Global Crisis", Academic Foundation, New Delhi.

Baldwin, R.E. and D. Taglioni (2007), "Trade Effects of the Euro: A Comparison of Estimators", *Journal of Economic Integration*, Vol. 22, No. 4, pp. 780-818.

Datt, Ruddar (2009) "Global Meltdown and its impact on the Indian Economy", *Mainstream*, Vol. XLVII, No. 15, pp. 1-9.

Economic Survey, Ministry of Finance, GoI, Various Issues.

http://www.hinduonnet.com/2008/09/16/stories/2008091656401600.htm

http://www.newstrackindia.com/newsdetails/29681.

International Monetary Fund, 2009a. Direction of Trade Statistics. Yearbook, CD-ROM, March 2009, Washington, D.C. MF, 2009b. World Economic Outlook Database April 2009, Released on 22 April 2009, Washington, D.C.

Jonatham, Lymn, (2009), "IMF says clean up banks to tackle dire world crisis", *Reuters*, March 23, 2009, Reuters.com.

Lamy, P., 2009, Retreating from market opening is not a solution to the economic crisis", speech delivered to the Peterson Institute for International Economics, 24 April, 2009, Washington D.C.

Mohan, R., 2008, "Global Financial Crisis and Key Risks: Impact on India and Asia", speech delivered at the IMF-FSF High-Level Meeting on the Recent Financial Turmoil and Policy Responses, 1 October, 2008, Washington, D.C.

Mohan, R., 2009, "Global Financial Crisis: Causes, Impact, Policy Responses and Lesson", Reserve Bank of India, Mumbai.

Nachane, D.M. (2007), "Liberalization of the Capital Account: Perils and Possible Safeguards", *Economic and Political Weekly*, Vol. XLII, No. 36, Sept. 8-14, pp. 3633-43.

Patnaik, Prabhat (2008), The Value of Money, Tulika Books, New Delhi.

Rakshit, M. 2009, "India amidst the global crisis", *Economic and Political Weekly*, Vol. 44, No. 13, pp. 94-106.

Research and Information System for Developing Countries (RIS), 2009, South Asia Cooperation and Development Report, 2008, Oxford University Press, New Delhi.

Reserve Bank of India, 2009, Annual Policy Statement, 2009-10, 21 April 2009, Mumbai.

Subbarao, D. (2009), "India—managing the impact of the global financial crisis", speech delivered at the 2009 National Conference and Annual Session, 26 March, 2009, Confederation of Indian Industry, New Delhi.

Taylor, John (2009), "The Financial Crisis and the Policy Responses: An Empirical Analysis of what went wrong", Working Paper 14631, January, National Bureau of Economic Research.

World Bank, 2009. World Development Report, 2009, Washington, D.C.

World Trade Organization, 2009a, "World Trade, 2008, prospects for 2009", press release No. 554, 23 March 2009, Geneva.

WTO (2009b), "Report of the TRPB from the Director General on the financial and economic crisis and trade-related development", 26 March, 2009, Geneva.

Financial Crisis: Is it Time to Think Beyond Keynes?

G.P. TRIPATHI AND S.K. CHOUBEY

The Global Economic Crisis that erupted in USA on 9th August 2007 has compelled the G8 and G20 Nations to have summit meetings four times so far, which have ended with lurking doubts and without any convincing clues or capitalistic remedy. World Economy has witnessed over 40 economic meltdowns, panics, recessions or depressions since 1797. From 1970s alone, four major economic meltdowns and global financial failures have taken place. These recessions wipe out the years of economic gains and prosperity almost instantly. The measures required to curb the effects of such financial crisis like: stimulus packages, etc. go against the grains of capitalism and free market principles. This crisis is more remarkable because it originated in the most sophisticated financial centers of the world, Wall Street and the City of London, rather than in emerging markets or developing countries, whereby, their underdeveloped financial markets, regulation and supervision can not be made out to be the scapegoat.

To prevent re-occurrence of such recessions or at least to reduce their severity and provide for quick recovery is the biggest challenge thrown at economists of today or else the entire Structure of Economic studies could risk getting discredited as a "Dismal Science". With economic bubbles bursting without giving any clue to the economists, the credibility of Economics as a subject of social science also bursts, discrediting the discipline as a whole. This systemic crisis has shaken confidence in the key rules and institutions expected to sustain financial stability; it has shattered the faith of many in the applicability to the financial sector of free market logic and self-regulation (Buiter, 2008). But, before Economics as a science is put onto cross-examination stand, the basic causes of Recession must be examined first.

CAUSES OF FINANCIAL CRISIS

The precise causes of recession are the subject of fierce debate among academics and policy-makers, although most would agree that the common denominator of all recessions are Rooted in nasty greed and excessive speculation. Factors at the epicenter of all the recessions, including that of the depression of 1929 have been:

1. The "bubble" in real estate, assets or in stocks
2. And subsequent to such bubble bust, the "systemic failure of banking"

A cursory skimming of literature on recessions and financial cycles reveals that the bubble in real estate or in stocks in Japan in the 1980s was the mother of all asset price bubbles. There were bubbles in real estate and stocks in Thailand, Indonesia, Malaysia, and their neighboring countries in the first half of the 1990s. A closer analysis of Great depression of 1929 by various economists leads to similar conclusion.

Causes of Economic Crisis of 2007

Gjerstad 2009, explains sub-prime crisis: the price decline started in 2006. Then policies designed to promote the American dream instead produced a nightmare. Trillions of dollars of mortgages, written to buyers with slender equity, started a wave of delinquencies and defaults. Borrowers' losses were limited to their small down payments; hence, the lion's share of the losses was transmitted into the financial system and it collapsed. Similarities in causes responsible for present economic crisis of 2007 is so striking as pointed out by Buiter, 2008.

1. Following the collapse of the tech bubble in late 2000, monetary policy in the US and, to a lesser extent also in the Euro Area, was too expansionary for too long starting around 2003, flooding the world with excess liquidity. For reasons not yet well understood, this excess liquidity went primarily into credit growth and asset price booms and bubbles, rather than into consumer price inflation.
2. The unsustainable current account deficit of the US was made to appear sustainable through the willingness of China and many other emerging markets to accumulate large stocks of US dollars, both as official foreign exchange reserves, it helps to be the issuer of the dominant global reserve currency. A fair number of countries that continued to peg to the US dollar (or to shadow the US dollar) experienced excessive domestic liquidity and credit creation, contributing to asset booms and bubbles.
3. Formation of asset bubble in the form of sub-prime housing mortgages that were further securitized, sold and resold through shadow banking instruments like debt swap, etc. which first manifested itself as regulatory and supervisory failure in the US home loan market, especially in its sub-prime segment.
4. While the Finance has become Global its regulation is still a National issue, allowing financial innovations based on myths that are away from the gauge of regulators.

TOO MUCH FINANCIAL INNOVATION

While there is no denying the fact that the root cause of all recessions has been human greed and excessive speculation on stock exchanges, yet this greed has always found a camouflage in some sort of financial or economic innovation. One example from present crisis could be said to be the brain child of Eugene Fama, of the University of Chicago, who postulated: that the price of a financial asset reflects all available information that is relevant to its value. Another example that house prices will never go down. To spot the consequences of such misplaced beliefs or myths was made difficult, until it was too late.

From such camouflaged ideas, powerful conclusions were drawn, not least on Wall Street. It also followed that bubbles could not form or, at any rate, could not last: some wise investor would spot them and pop them. Such hidden, less analyzed and over used financial innovation become the nemesis for Economic depressions. If prices reflect all information, then there is no gain from going to the trouble of gathering it, so no one will. As Krugman, 2007, says the bottom line is that policy-makers left the financial industry free to innovate and what it did was to innovate itself, and the rest of us, into a big, nasty mess.

The damage caused by financial sector excesses is way out of proportion to whatever gains from financial innovation may have accrued to the wider economy in the last couple of decades (Willem H. Buiter, 2008). Thus every economic crisis is preceded by flotation of a theory on which the instrument of greed are erected to sail through the willing sea waves of Wall Street, with tacit support of its select group of beneficiary who may be the shadow bankers, Politicians or bureaucrats, that created the $62 trillion market for credit-default swaps out side their balance sheets, but the economists are targeted to get the blame.

ECONOMICS BLAMED TO BE A DISMAL SCIENCE

The Economist, 2009C and 2009D, has vividly described how the usefulness of Macroeconomics is openly questioned by leading economists since the financial crisis. These internal critics argue that economists missed the origins of the crisis; failed to appreciate its worst symptoms; and cannot now agree about the cure. In other words, economists misread the economy on the way up, misread it on the way down and now mistake the right way out. To the uninitiated, economics has always been a dismal science. But all these attacks come from within the guild: from Brad DeLong of the University of California, Berkeley; Paul

Krugman of Princeton and the *New York Times;* and Willem Buiter of the London School of Economics (LSE), respectively.

Paul Krugman, winner of the Nobel prize in economics in 2008, argued that much of the past 30 years of macroeconomics was "spectacularly useless at best, and positively harmful at worst." And at other place he says: the past 30 years of macroeconomics training at American and British universities were a "costly waste of time". Barry Eichengreen, a prominent American economic historian, says the crisis has "cast into doubt much of what we thought we knew about economics." There are three main critiques: that macro and financial economists helped cause the crisis, that they failed to spot it, and that they have no idea how to fix it.

Even great advocate of macroeconomics, Robert Lucas' claim in The Economist 2009A, is tinged one: modern macroeconomics remains a useful science, albeit an inexact one. Overall he is correct to reject the view that a single crisis means we should toss out everything we once knew or at least thought we knew. To do that would be overreacting to short-term data, just as some of the guilty parties behind the financial crisis themselves overreacted to short-term price and profit signals. Nobel prized economist Scholes thinks much of the blame for the recent woe should be pinned not on economists' theories and models but on those on Wall Street and in the City who pushed them too far in practice. Buiter, 2008, emphasizes that capitalism, based on greed, private property rights and decentralized decision-making, is both volatile, cyclical and subject to bouts of financial manic-depressive illness. There is no economy-wide auctioneer, no enforcer of systemic 'transversality conditions' to rule out periodic explosive bubble behaviour of asset prices in speculative markets. It's unfortunate, but we have to live with it. New external control and regulation is especially important in the financial sector, because finance is trade in promises.

*The Economist, 2009B states that n*o other branch of social sciences suffers more stereo typing than that of economics. Economists have to come out of their silos and instead to shouting slogans of their specialty or raising the flags of isms they should begin to shoulder the responsibility of economic functioning in totality. Economists now are unable to agree on the best way to resolve the crisis. They mostly overestimated the power of routine monetary policy (i.e. central-bank purchases of government bills) to restore prosperity. Some now dismiss the power of fiscal policy (i.e. government sales of its securities) to do the same. Others advocate it with passionate intensity. The guild of economists at prestigious LSE has already admitted in writing to the British queen about their collective failure.

BRITISH ECONOMISTS SEND APOLOGY TO THE QUEEN

The British Queen (when she visited the LSE to open its £71 million New Academic Building in November 2008) said of the financial situation that caused the crisis: "Why did nobody notice it?" Prof. Luis Garicano, director of research at the London School of Economics' replied: "At every stage, someone was relying on somebody else and everyone thought they were doing the right thing." The Queen described it as "awful".

The Observer newspaper (27/11/09) reported that a letter has been sent to the Queen after she demanded, to know why nobody had anticipated the credit crunch. This letter says that "financial wizards" who believed that their plans to manage risky debts and protect the financial system were infallible were guilty of "wishful thinking combined with hubris." In summary, your majesty, "the failure to foresee the timing, extent and severity of the crisis and to head it off, while it had many causes, was principally a failure of the collective imagination of many bright people, both in this country and internationally, to understand the risks to the system as a whole." The contents were discussed during a seminar with a group of leading economists in June, including Nick MacPherson, a permanent secretary at Britain's Treasury, and Goldman Sachs chief economist Jim O'Neill and the signatories to this three-page letter included Tim Besley, a member of the Bank of England's monetary policy committee and historian Peter Hennessy.

FINANCE: MASTER OR SERVANT?

Buiter, 2008 points: it started as a crisis *in* the financial system, became a crisis *of* the financial system and has now reached the point at which most of the western cross-border financial system of the past 30 years has effectively been destroyed and the remnants socialized or put in a state of subsidized limbo. It is correct but unhelpful to characterize the crisis as the result of greed and excess or as a crisis of capitalism. Greed has always been with us and always will be. Greed can be constrained and need not lead to excess. Excess is just another word for greed combined with wrong incentives and defective regulation and supervision.

The shadow banking system was as important to the economy as the ordinary kind, but was far more vulnerable. Its collapse was the modern re-run of the bank failures of the 1930s, said Krugman 2007. Hence it is seen that finance becomes the master of the real economy rather than its servant which results in the economic crisis.

Finance is a veil, obscuring what really matters and when Finance becomes master the facts go blur. "Bags of wheat are more important than stacks of bonds" as claimed in *The Economist,* 2009D. As a poet once said, "promises of payment/is neither food nor raiment". In many macroeconomic models, therefore, insolvencies cannot occur. Financial intermediaries, like banks, often don't exist. Convenience, not conviction, often dictates the choices economists make while selecting the variables of the market.

TIME TO REVISIT KEYNES

Unlike the recent euphoria about blaming Macro-economics to be a dismal science (*The Economist*, 2009 B, C, D) or rejecting the contributions of John Maynard Keynes this paper fully respects and appreciates the insight offered by Keynes and the great contributions it has made and continues to make to international economics. However, at the same time, it proposes to revisit and look beyond Keynes in order to discover solutions to 21st century economic troubles that can not be fully supplied by concepts and theories that originated in 1930s, as proven by the crisis after crisis.

While there is no denial that intervention by government can help ward off slump in economy as witnessed even in present crisis and pointed out by Brad Delong's (2008) praise for Bernanke: (as by intervention Commercial-bank reserves grew from $50 billion at the time of the Lehman failure to something like $800 billion by the end of the year), as short-term fix is better than no fix, yet controversies erupt when such interventions are seen as socialistic approach. Injection of up to $2 trillion of liquidity has in a way repressed the depression II of 2009. If zero interest rates cannot get consumers to spend, then governments must spend instead. That remedy comes from economics so the discipline is not without merit. The trouble is, "the analysis we're using is decades old". It dates back to Keynes, one of the few economists whose reputation has been burnished by the crisis.

For Mr Krugman 2007, we are living through a "Dark Age of Macroeconomics", in which the wisdom of the ancients has been lost. What was this wisdom, and how was it forgotten? The history of macroeconomics begins in intellectual struggle. Keynes wrote the "General Theory of Employment, Interest and Money", which was published in 1936, in an "unnecessarily controversial tone", according to some readers. But it was a controversy the author had waged in his own mind. He saw the book as a "struggle of escape from habitual modes of thought" he had inherited from his classical predecessors.

Hitting at Economic Modeling the Economist 2009D laments: Modern macroeconomists worried about the prices of goods and services, but neglected the prices of assets. This was partly because they had too much faith in financial markets. If asset prices reflect economic fundamentals, why not just model the fundamentals, ignoring the shadow they cast on Wall Street? Why was the main factor that allowed the crisis to spread, the interconnectedness of financial markets, missed? Economists can become seduced by their models, fooling themselves that what the model leaves-out does not matter. It is, for example, often convenient to assume that markets are "complete" that a price exists today, for every good, at every date, in every contingency. In this world, you can always borrow as much as you want at the going rate, and you can always sell as much as you want at the going rate.

Shiller as pointed out by Rosenblum, 2009, portrays Keynes as the true "centrist," with actual socialists to his left arguing for the government to take over private enterprise and assign jobs to the unemployed. Meanwhile, critics on the right clung to Adam Smith's hallowed economic model: They insisted that through balanced budgets and limited government regulation "as if by an invisible hand" private markets would create a job for any worker willing to get paid less than he produced. Shiller, 2009 warns that capitalism is vulnerable to irrationality. People are not so keenly self-interested as free-market conservatives have assumed.

Schiller 2009 further questions: What had people been thinking? Why did they not notice until real events, the collapse of banks, the loss of jobs, mortgage foreclosures were already upon us? There is a simple answer. The public, the government, and most economists had been reassured by an economic theory that said that we were safe. It was all OK. Nothing dangerous could happen. But that theory was deficient. It had ignored the importance of "ideas" in the conduct of the economy. It had ignored the role of animal spirits. And it had also ignored the fact that people could be unaware of having boarded a rollercoaster. Insofar as animal spirits exist in the everyday economy, a description of how the economy really works must consider those animal spirits.

COMPULSIVE/SINISTER SOCIALISM WITHIN CAPITALISM

Recessions/Depressions and their rescue measures distort the fundamentals of capitalism to the extent it gets close to socialism or even immoral. One observation of situation during 1929 depression narrates: A feeling that the American economy was profoundly unfair emerged, leading to intense labour unrest and the specter of communism. Genuine socialism's only real chance in the United States came during this crisis. Measures taken to limit the damage of the current crisis have been designed to maximize bad incentives for future reckless lending and borrowing by the institutions affected by them. This was done without the extraction of any significant *quid-pro-quo* and without proportional pain for shareholders, creditors and top managers of the institutions that benefited.

For present financial crisis Brad Delong, 2008, vividly brings out the stimulus (compulsory dole-outs) as immoral but necessary in the broader interest of the economic recovery, as follows:

1. It's immoral because people have a right to be

treated like adults, which means that they have a right not to be rescued by the government from the consequences of their bad judgment, and we are violating that right.

2. It's unfair because feckless greedy financiers who caused the problem ought to lose money and aren't or aren't losing enough money, and because feckless greedy imprudent thriftless borrowers who caused the problem ought to lose money and aren't or aren't losing enough money.
3. It won't work at least not in the long-run.

Delong is not alone justifying the short-term need for this compulsive socialism within capitalism as Federal Reserve vice chair Don Kohn says: it is bad public policy to hold the jobs of tens of millions hostage in an attempt to teach a few feckless financiers (or even somewhat more thriftless borrowers) even a much-deserved lesson.

NEED AND OPPORTUNITY TO GO BEYOND KEYNES

Keynes himself is said to have appreciated the classical model's elegance and consistency, virtues economists still crave. But that did not stop him demolishing it. In his scheme, investment was governed by the animal spirits of entrepreneurs, facing an imponderable future. The thought experiment of Adam Smith correctly takes into account the fact that people rationally pursue their economic interests but it fails to take into account the extent to which they are irrational or misguided. It ignores the animal spirits. In contrast, John Maynard Keynes sought to explain departures from full employment, and he emphasized the importance of animal spirits. Hence in a way Keynes himself had shown the path to future economists and predicated going beyond his own theories by emulating him. This time economist may begin by exploring; Keynes' use of the term "animal spirits" a little further, may be this will lead to ever predominant "human greed" side of economic recessions.

A beginning of sorts may have already been made by behavioural economists, some inkling of which could be found in Shiller's (2009) latest book, "Animal Spirits". Where the title is taken from John Maynard Keynes's description of the quirky psychological forces shaping markets. It argues that macroeconomics, too, should draw lessons from psychology: When the public mood swings from exuberance to anxiety, or even fear, the effect on asset prices as well as on economic activity outside the financial sector can be large. The heady share prices that have caused many recessions are the result of investors' "irrational exuberance." As per Shiller, 2009, Keynes' followers dumbed down his theory of government spending to make it politically palatable and comprehensible. The neo-Keynesians de-emphasized the centrality of "animal spirits," transforming Keynes' mercurial and often irrational economic man into a rational, self-interested automaton. In fact by going beyond the cocoon of age-old Keynesian practices we may perhaps end up reviving the true Keynesian legacy.

Another way of looking at the need for renaissance would be comparing Economics to other disciplines like sciences as to many high-tech economists it is a bit undignified to keep referring to cult like old theories. Real scientists, after all, do not leaf through Newton's "Principia Mathematica" to solve contemporary problems in physics, nor do electrical engineers swear by the name of Michael Faraday. In the era of internet from queen to commoner, all can demand and access same level of precision of information gathering. These days even the forecasting of earth quakes, tornados and Tsunamis have found a scientific foundation, how long Economics would survive as a dismal science against expectations raised by contemporary developments in other disciplines of knowledge? As the commonality of knowledge spreads, it would be demanded of Economics to accurately forecast Economic recessions, which may require revisiting Keynes. Thus we observe four compelling reasons to reach beyond Keynes:

1. Keynes himself had gone beyond Adam Smith to offer remedies to economic issues of 1930s, hence emulation is in order and will not do away with the wisdom of the ancients.
2. Keynes mentions about "Animal Spirits" in *"The General Theory of Employment, Interest and Money"* but does not elaborate on it (devoting hardly a

paragraph to it), the issue needs attention as macroeconomics is not fully explaining the contemporary issues while behavioural economics is expanding its scope and may read irrational economic man, better.

3. In the era of rapid development and interconnected financial markets, Keynesian intervention to fight one recession may be laying foundations for another (as explained in "causes of economic crisis 2007" here). What is the guarantee that lax fiscal measures and slew of stimulus packages that may herald a new recovery will not cause another fall?
4. For how long Economists will keep offering a theory originated in 1930 as elixir to economic crisis of 21st century, falling back on antiquated Keynesian doctrines is akin to admitting as if nothing had been learned in the past 73 years.

CONCLUSION

Jacob Marschak in his 1945 article (as quoted in economist 2009D) reviewed the profession's growing understanding of the business cycle, making an analogy with other sciences. Seismology, for example, makes progress through better instruments, improved theories or more frequent earthquakes. In the case of economics, Marschak concluded, "the earthquakes did most of the job". Luckily for the Economists they were deprived of earthquakes for a quarter of a century. The Great Moderation, as this period was called, was not conducive to great macroeconomics. Thanks to the seismic events of the past two years, the prestige of macroeconomists is low, but the potential of their subject is much greater. The furious rows that divide them are a blow to their credibility, but may prove to be a spur to creativity. Creativity that answers the questions clearly and accurately as it is not sufficient to clean up after the bubble bursts, but essential to forecast and work against the formation of the bubble in the first place.

As Economist, 2009B mentions, this is not the first international banking crisis the world has seen. The previous ones occurred without credit default swaps, special investment vehicles, or even credit ratings. If crises keep repeating themselves, it seems reasonable to argue that policy-makers need to carefully consider what they are doing and not just "double up" by superficially reacting to the specific features of today's crisis. While we cannot hope to prevent crises, we can perhaps make them fewer and milder by adopting and implementing better regulation in particular, more macro-prudential regulations.

Shiller redefines the role of government thus: "The role of the parent is to create a *happy home,* which gives the child freedom but also protects him from his animal spirits." For economics not to get branded as dismal science, the economists have to think hard whether they will remain hooked to wisdom of 1930s or will raise the bar and think beyond Keynes? As *Rosenblum, 2009 states:* Macroeconomics is now everybody's business especially when the banks are playing with people's money.

References

Buiter Willem H., 2008, Lessons from the North Atlantic financial crisis, London School of Economics.

DeLong J. Bradford, 2008, Understanding the Three Ways of Dealing with Financial crises, *The Semi-Daily Journal of Economist Brad DeLong,* Department of Economics, U.C. Berkeley.

Fisher Irving, 1933, "The Debt-Deflation Theory of Great Depressions", *Econometrica,* Vol. 1(3): pp. 337–57, October 1933.

Gjerstad Steven and Vernon L. Smith, 2009, From Bubble to Depression?, *The Wall Street Journal,* April 6, 2009.

Keynes John M., 1936, The General Theory of Employment, Interest and Money, London: Macmillan.

Krugman Paul, 1998, Is the Economic Crisis a Crisis for Economics?, Or, where is macroeconomics when we need it?, The State Magazine: the dismal science: The search for better economic policy, Nov. 13, 1998.

Krugman Paul, 2007, Innovating Our Way to Financial Crisis, Op-Ed Columnist, *The New York Times,* Published: December 3, 2007.

Krugman Paul, 2008. "Partying Like It's 1929," *New York Times,* March 21.

Marschak Jacob, 1945, A Cross Section of Business Cycle Discussion, *The American Economic Review,* Vol. 35, No. 3 (Jun., 1945), pp. 368-81.

Prescott Edward C. and Timothy J. Kehoe, Ed. 2007, Great Depressions of the Twentieth Century, Federal Reserve Bank of Minneapolis, 1st edition (July 2, 2007).

Rosenblum Andrew, 2009, Citizens Keynes, *The New York Observer,* February 17,

2009 (A review of Animal Spirits: How Human Psychology Drives the Economy, and Why It Matters for Global Capitalism By George A. Akerlof and Robert J. Shiller)

Rothbard Murray N., 2002, A History of Money and Banking in the United States: The Colonial Era to World War II, Ludwig Von Mises Inst.

Roubini Nouriel, 2006, "Why Central Banks Should Burst Bubbles," *International Finance*, Volume 9, Number 1, pp. 87-107 (16).

Shiller Robert J. and George A. Akerlof, 2009, Animal Spirits: How Human Psychology Drives the Economy, and Why It Matters for Global Capitalism, Princeton University Press (February 18, 2009)

Stiglitz Joseph, 2008. Unfettered Markets Do Not Lead to Societal Well-Being, economistsview.typepad.com/economistsview 2008/02/joseph-stiglitz.html

The Economist, 2009A, In defense of the dismal science, The Economist print edition, Aug. 6th, 2009.

The Economist, 2009B, What went wrong with economics, The Economist print edition, July 16th, 2009.

The Economist, 2009C, Dismal Science, Paul Krugman's London Lectures, The Economist print edition, June 11th, 2009

The Economist, 2009D, The other-worldly philosophers, The state of economics, The Economist print edition, July 16th, 2009.

Decoupling Theory—A Myth or a Reality

Amrita Nandi

INTRODUCTION

The pendulum of global economic power started swinging back from West to East during the latter half of the 20th century, reversing a westward shift with the emergence of the miracle economies of East and S.E Asia, followed by the rise of China and India. We are going through what is by all accounts the deepest economic crisis of our time. The global financial crisis which moves into its third year now, is truly a momentous crisis of the network economy and globalization. The current crisis which first surfaced in the US sub-prime mortgage market in August 2007 soon spread to markets for other securities in both the US and elsewhere, and in the process caused, a huge financial meltdown and a synchronized recession in practically all industrialized countries. Every country in every part of the world has been affected by the crisis, although through different channels and to different degrees. The United States and Europe which had become dependent on the financial sector as their engine of growth were at the very epicenter of the crisis. Export growth led Asia, which managed its external sector cautiously after the crisis of a decade ago, saw its growth plummet through a sharp decline in demand for exports. The global GDP is projected to contract for the first time since the World War II anywhere between 0.5 and 1.0 percent, according to the March 2009 forecast of the IMF.

Since the outbreak of the crisis, it appeared that the emerging Asian economies, especially the leading ones like China and India, would not only remain relatively insulated from the crisis, but also play role in moderating the global downturn and paving way for a worldwide recovery in a year or so. The basis of this robust optimism was located in the 'decoupling theory.' However, with a marked deterioration in the conditions of both advanced and emerging economies since September 2008, the so-called 'decoupling hypothesis' has proved seriously wrong. It was the Lehman collapse that changed the situation dramatically. Until then, it was reasonable to expect that the downturn in the US economy would not be too prolonged and the impact on the global economy would not be too great.

Against this background, the paper tries to analyse the situation of how far other countries can 'decouple' from the US economy and sustain strong growth in the face of a US slowdown and examine the impact of financial crisis on emerging markets. The main object is to pinpoint what factors would likely determine the magnitude of the spillovers—the effects on the output of other countries from weaker US growth—in present circumstances.

DECOUPLING THEORY

The starting point of a discussion is to define 'decoupling' as a global macroeconomic theory and not a stock market theory. Wikipedia defines decoupling as 'lessening of correlation or dependency between variables'.

Akin to globalization, the decoupling theory of late has caught the fancies of the policy-makers and investors across the globe. The theory simply asserted that growth in Asia was driven mainly by domestic factors, that these factors were decoupled from trends in the West and that the growth engines in Asia (ASEAN-5, China and India) will not only continue to chug along, (even in case of a US recession which is indeed a local problem , an outcome of the widespread default in the sub-prime mortgage market) but would also serve as shock absorbers for the Western economies and might even help to pull them out of the recession. The strength of the Asian economies was seen to stem from their recent (the last two decades) shift to market-oriented policies in a big way, their regional consolidation via trade and investment relationships, and the benefits they derived from global inflows of capital.

Decoupling proponents believe that the rest of the world will continually become less dependent on the United States and some day may even enjoy growth and prosperity while the US stagnates or declines. They base their theory on the idea that consumption in the rest of the world will eventually rise to a level where it can replace any consumption fall off from the US Thus, it is the theory that the rest of the world can shrug off US domestic weakness as other economies can sustain their growth levels in backdrop of strong domestic macroeconomic conditions. As early as even last year, economists and analysts argued that the engine of global growth has shifted. The world has according to them decoupled from the US economy. Asia is seen as the engine of growth that could drive the global economy out of the recession with China, India and other emerging market economies starting to provide a consumer base for the world that can stave-off any problems emanating from the economic slowdown in the US. According to the IMF's PPP, collectively India and China account for 21% of the world's GDP. Japan's share is 6%. It is believed that the down shift in America's GDP which is 20% of total world would be neutralized by Asian growth machine. Asian countries' dependence on the US consumer has declined 'dramatically', since the technology bubble burst. Exports of consumer goods to the United States declined to 6% of total Asian exports in 2006 from 8% in 2001.

Decoupling theorists had drawn strength from the fact that until last summer the slowdown in the United States had little effect on growth in most other countries and that trade linkages with the US has become less important "An enormous shift has occurred in the global economy away from the developed world to emerging markets according to Antone Van Agtmael, the chairman of emerging markets management LLC in Arlington, Virginia who is credited with coining the term "emerging markets". John Arthurs described, in the *Financial Times* of Feb. 29, 2008, decoupling as 'the notion that demand for raw materials in the developing world will allow emerging markets to grow even if there is a US recession'.

China is viewed as a major engine powering the next global recovery. The country's financial system is amazingly healthy, flush with funds and is mostly exporting low-priced consumer goods to the US because, the slowdown in US was not concentrated in private consumption rather housing. India on the other hand appears to be less vulnerable to the global downturn because it is much more dependent on domestic demand for growth. It is argued that the domestic market in Asia is very large and would provide ample room to grow and avoid any kind of slow down as they are able to expand domestic demand substantially. Emerging markets now account for about one quarter of global GDP about the same as the US contribution.

The followers of this theory believe that because of the strong GDP growth of many developing countries especially of China and India, their markets will remain bullish even during US 'recession'. China is the only country where growth has returned to its underlying trend rate of 8% following last year's economic meltdown. The demand impulse from China is now buoying exports and sentiment in several other economies. The global economy too needs the developed world to start contributing to world growth again for a broad based recovery to materialize and that in turn requires the US consumer to spend at least a small part of the stimulus funds. Even China is betting on the US consumer making some sort of a comeback. While Chinese policy-makers are indeed attempting to reorient the economy by encouraging more domestic consumption, such structural changes take a long time to pan out. Boosting infrastructure spending is the quickest way to shore up demand in the short-term and that's what China has done over the past few months.

China essentially remains the world's main manufacturing base and herein lies the problem with the global economic recovery story. It will be very difficult for China to maintain its 8% expansion pace if its export growth does not pick up by the end of the year as there's a limit as to how much investment it can add to its already large and increasingly idle manufacturing base. The rise in economic optimism since March this year has largely been due to a turnaround in the manufacturing sectors in many countries, starting with China. Manufacturing activity that declined across the world by more than 15% in the year to March 2009 began to stabilize in the first quarter of 2009 with Asian countries taking the lead. In the long-run, final demand trends of the developed world will play a less significant role and the growth leadership has to be provided by the emerging market consumer.

REASONS FOR DECOUPLING

In the initial stages of the crisis, several reasons were put forward as to why the emerging markets might hope to get "decoupled" from the US and other advanced economies:

1. The US slowdown was driven mainly by its specific sectoral corrections in housing and manufacturing sectors rather than to broader global factors such as an oil shock or adverse equity market developments.
2. Implications for global demand has diminished as trade linkages with US has become progressively less important for the leading emerging economies.
3. Growth in some of the leading emerging markets was driven overwhelmingly by domestic demand.
4. The emerging markets were net savers in the world economy, not borrowers.
5. Over the past decade, the emerging markets had effected several economic reforms, as a result of which they had become more stable and efficient.

Nevertheless, the IMF did distinguish between the effects of a moderate slowdown in the US and a sharp slowdown or recession.

"Overall, these factors suggest that most countries should be in a position to 'decouple' from the US and sustain strong growth if the

slowdown remains as moderate as expected. However, if the US experienced a sharper slowdown, the spillover effects into other economies would be larger, and decoupling would be more difficult.

The prize question is why should the severity of a slowdown in the US determine whether emerging market economies should 'decouple' from US or not? The IMF provides an explanation that appears plausible. In a modest US slowdown, emerging markets are affected mainly through the trade channel. However, when the US economy runs into serious problems, the asset price channel gets activated. Financial flows to emerging markets are severely affected during a serious US recession and equity prices also tend to become highly correlated with those in the US market. Besides, there is a broader impact through undermining of confidence among consumers and investors. This would explain why emerging markets, particularly India and China remained 'decoupled' from the US almost through 2008. The Lehman episode in September 2008 dramatically changed the outlook for the US economy and, in consequence, for emerging markets, including India and China. Both economies have a high degree of 'openness 'as measured by trade and financial flows put together.

THE LIMITS TO DECOUPLING

In the initial stages, there was a fairly high degree of optimism about the capacity of at least some of the emerging markets, particularly the large ones such as China and India, to insulate themselves substantially from the crisis. Such optimism has since worn thin. Decoupling is an incremental process and given the trade and capital flow linkages, developing countries cannot pull away from the developed world too far, too quickly. The decoupling theme staged some sort of a come back this year after being derailed by the economic crisis in 2008. This is reflected in the relative performance of emerging markets *versus* developed markets: the gap between the indices of the two blocs is back at the levels last seen at the peak of the decoupling mania in late 2007. Though China's policy-makers have already succeeded in stimulating their economy but beyond a point, it too needs the largest buyer of its goods—the US consumer—to start spending again. If that doesn't happen soon enough, then the global economy faces the prospect a relapse. Most Asian markets are now on big recession. The most pessimistic claim being that 'it makes no sense to talk about decoupling in an era of globalization' as economies have become more intertwined through trade and finance consequently, no market can remain completely insulated from global shocks.

However, recent data stemming from sources such as the IMF and other international organizations as well as national sources, is seriously at variance with the decoupling thesis. Growth estimates for 2008 and projections for 2009 and 2010 have been scaled down considerably *vis-à-vis* the November update.

Countries	*2008*	*2009*	*2010*
Advanced economies	1.0 %	- 2.0 %	1.1 %
ASEAN-EME	5.4 %	2.7 %	4.1 %
China	9 %	6.7 %	6 %
India	7.3 %	5.1 %	6.5 %

GROWTH ESTIMATES FOR 2008 AND PROJECTIONS FOR 2009 AND 2010

The potential size of Spillovers are most important for countries with close trade and financial ties with the US and particularly the industrial nations. They tend to be larger during recessions, when import growth turns sharply negative. What seems to have happened currently is that the channels of contagion have been substantially underestimated. As is well known from the literature there are atleast four major potential channels of contagion, *vis-a-vis*:

1. Trade channel, 2. Foreign channel, 3. Contamination of Financial Assets, 4. Interdependence of Asset Markets. The major drawback of the theory is that it has not considered the multiple economic relations and globalization trends. Despite the formation of Euroarea and performance of emerging economies, the US economy is still the largest economy in the world on most parameters and has always been a net importer for many years thereby, helping other economies prosper.

THE CASE OF ASIA

In May 2008 Asia seemed to be in an enviable position, with its economies continuing to boom even as the United states was becoming mired in recession. At that time, many analysts argued that this situation would continue, since Asia would 'decouple' from the West. Things turned out quite differently. Instead of decoupling, some of Asia's key economies, including Japan, are experiencing recessions more severe than those at the epicenter of the crisis. The prize question is how did this happen? At the time, the arguments for decoupling seemed plausible to many. After all, Asia was far from the centre of the crisis, in the sense that it had not engaged in the financial practices that led to such problems elsewhere. Its corporate and financial institutions were in robust financial health, and it had accumulated fiscal surpluses and high buffers of international reserves. So, if any region of the world seemed in a position to decouple from the United States, Asia was that place. In reality, as the IMF pointed out a year ago in its Asia-pacific Regional Economic Outlook (REO), decoupling from the rest of the world was always an unlikely scenario. That's because Asia has long depended on exports as its engine of growth. As the new May 2009 REO shows, whenever exports have slumped Asia has typically gone into recession and has not recovered until exports have started to revive. Asia has suffered from an accelerator effect, because its exports are concentrated on technologically sophisticated goods, such as IT products, for which worldwide demand has collapsed. As a result, GDP in Emerging Asia excluding China and India fell at an astonishing 15% annual rate in the fourth quarter of 2008, and a further decline most likely took place in the first quarter as well.

In a new variant of the decoupling argument, some analysts are claiming that Asia has already turned a corner, and is poised for recovery. They make two main arguments. First, they claim that China will be able to act as a locomotive for the region as its economy has begun to rebound. But this argument ignores the fact that the fiscal stimulus propelling China's growth has shifted the pattern of production towards infrastructure, which has relatively little import content. So, the benefits to the region are likely to remain small. The second argument is that Asia's domestic demand is likely to revive, because of the large stimulus that governments are providing. But by themselves they will not be able to regenerate sustained growth. Thus, as long as exports remain depressed, private investment will remain low. Meanwhile, consumption will be hampered by growing unemployment as firms retrench in order to restore profitability. So a sustained recovery will once again need to await an improvement in the global economy. This will take some time as IMF does not expect these economies to recover until the middle of 2010. Accordingly, growth in Asia is forecast to decelerate to just 1.3% this year, before rebounding to 4.2% in 2010, still well below the region's potential and the 5.1% rate recorded in 2008.

Policy-makers also face a more structural issue: the need to reduce Asia's dependence on an export driven model of growth. The past year has provided an ample demonstration of the dangers of relying solely on one growth engine. In short, Asia has not decoupled – and should not decouple from the rest of the world. But neither can it continue to rely exclusively on exports for growth; it needs to develop its own autonomous sources of demand. A return to sustained rapid growth may depend on it.

CONCLUSION

There is some merit in the 'decoupling' hypothesis but in the present circumstances, in the era of globalization the theory is proving to be a myth. Now, its proponents are being laughed at. They were both right and wrong. They were correct in stating that the emerging markets are substantially 'decoupled' from the US when the latter suffers a mild slowdown; but a serious recession in the advanced economies, however, tends to drag down emerging markets as well. This is because emerging markets get affected initially mainly through trade channel and as economic conditions in the advanced economies worsen, the financial channel also gets activated. India has not escaped unscathed in the present crisis rather it has suffered a more severe impact than supposed earlier.

However, in a globalized world it is difficult to imagine how emerging economies can remain isolated because, developments taking place in one part of the world have their repercussions on the other part of the world and capital markets are no exception. Hence, there is a need of multiple poles of growth as the global economy can no longer rely on the US consumer to sustain global growth. While the five largest emerging market economies now account for one-fourth of global GDP on a purchasing power parity basis, their role in global trade is not yet commensurate and it is difficult to argue whether they could entirely replace the US economy as an engine for global growth.

References

Agrawal, Amol (2008), 'Decoupling or Recoupling".

Bernard Lunn (Feb. 2009), 'The other decoupling theory'.

Kochchar Kalpana (May 2009), "Asia's recovery: what lies ahead."

Kunal Kumar Kundu (Sept.17, 2008), "Indian economy decoupled from US."

Li Hong, (2009) Decoupling theory and low wages".

Nachane, D.M. (2009), 'The fate of India Unincorporated' , *Economic and Political Weekly*.

Rakshit Mihir (2009), 'India amidst the Globa l Crisis', *Economic and Political Weekly*.

Ram Mohan, TT (2009), "The impact of the crisis on the Indian Economy", *Economic and Political Weekly*.

RBI (2009), '*Third Quarter Review*, January 2009', Reserve Bank of India.

Saima Rizvi (2008), 'Emerging Markets Decoupling Theory—A Myth."

Sanjai, D. and Barathi, Y.B. (March 2008), "Debunked for New", *Chartered Financial Analyst*, Vol.14, No. 3.

Sharma, Ruchir (2009), "The Limits to Decoupling."

Sheel, A. (April 2008), "Decoupled Globalization", *The Economic Times*.

Shinnick Richard (Feb. 10, 2008), "Decoupling Thesis Intact One Comment."

The Economist (March 2008), 'The Decoupling Debate", 6 March.

Venu, M.K. (March 2008), "The Decoupling Formula."

World Bank (2009), "Swimming against the Tide: How Developing Countries are Coping with the Global Crisis.

5

Home-owning Democracy to Housing Bubble: Recent Financial and Economic Crisis in USA

A. VENKATESWARLU

The world is suffering through the worst financial crisis since the 1930s, a crisis that has precipitated a sharp downturn in the global economy. The epicentre of the present crisis is in the USA. President Obama, in his Georgetown University lecture says that present recession was not caused by a normal downturn in the business cycle, but was caused by a perfect storm of irresponsibility and poor decision-making that stretched from Wall Street to Washington to Main Street (Obama, 2009). As USA's share in world GDP is by more than $1/5^{th}$, its crisis has global effects; so to understand it is important.

This paper runs into six sections. The first explains how the home-owning democracy led to housing bubble; the second deals with the financial deregulation, leading to housing bubble; the third analyses how the bursting of housing bubble led to financial crisis; the fourth accounts for the process of economic crisis over a decade; the fifth examines the bailouts and beneficiaries; and the last one portrays conclusion.

HOME-OWNING DEMOCRACY TO HOUSING BUBBLE IN USA

"By radically increasing the opportunity for Americans to own their own homes, the Roosevelt administration pioneered the idea of a *property-owning democracy*. It proved to be the perfect antidote to *red revolution*", (Ferguson, 2008a; p. 246). The notion, that property ownership enhances citizenship, and that therefore a property-owning democracy is more socially and politically stable than democracy divided into landlords and tenants, was invented just 70 years ago in USA. The federal government encouraged Americans to own their own homes, by borrowing. Mortgage-interest payments were always tax-deductible, from the inception of the federal income tax in 1913 (Ferguson, 2008b).

Before the 1930s, little more than 40.0 percent of American households were owner-occupiers. The few people who did borrow money to buy their own houses in the 1920s found themselves in deep difficulties when the Great Depression struck. Mortgages were short-term (3-5 years), and unamortized. Interest used to be paid first, and principal at the end of the term. This led to repayment problems. In 1932 and 1933 there were over a half million foreclosures and by mid-1933, over a thousand mortgages foreclosed every day (Ferguson, 2008a; pp. 241 and 242).

I. Home Ownership Encouragement: Fannie Mae, Ginnie Mae, and Freddie Mac

During the Depression, the Roosevelt administration created Federal Home Loan Bank Board in 1932 to encourage and oversee local mortgage lenders known as savings-and-loans (S & Ls)—mutual associations that took in deposits and lent to homebuyers.

Under the New Deal, the Federal Housing Administration (FHA) formed in 1934 sought to encourage large (up to 80 percent of the purchase price), long (20-25 years), fully amortized, low-interest loans. The FHA laid the foundation for a national secondary market. This market came to life in 1938, when a new Federal National Mortgage Asociation—*Fannie Mae*—was authorised to issue bonds and use the proceeds to buy mortgages from the Savings and Loans. *Fannie Mae* was restructured into the Government National Mortgage Association (*Ginnie Mae*) in 1968; and the Federal Home Loan Mortgage Corporation (*Freddie Mac*) in 1970. The overall effect was to broaden the secondary market for mortgages, and to lower mortgage rates. Further, the Community Reinvestment Act of 1977 encouraged lending to poorer minority communities. With the underwriting by Fannie, Ginnie and Freddie, housing market flourished and it seemed to realise *the property-owning democracy* (*ibid.*, pp. 248-51).

But, the US Savings and Loan (S&L) crisis of the 1980s and 1990s was caused by lending institutions, as they exploited government's encouragement and incentives (insurance, etc.) for home loans, by lending more money in home loans than was prudent and then getting hit by rising interest rates. Fraud was also a big factor. The government's bail-out cost about $300 bn (2008 dollars) and when the assets were sold, it got back about 80 percent of what it paid (Reuben, 2008).

2. Subprime Mortgages

By mid-1990s, home-equity loan, also known as a second mortgage, permitted homeowners to borrow money by leveraging the equity in their homes. Home-equity loans exploded in popularity in 1996. With a home-equity loan, homeowners can borrow up to $100,000 and still deduct all of the interest when they file their tax returns. Thus, the home loans could increase over a period. It was on the higher scale after subprime loans were allowed.

There is no one definition of a subprime mortgage. The classification "subprime" generally is a lender-given designation for loans extended to borrowers with some sort of credit impairment, say, due to missing instalment payments on debt or the lack of a credit history. Subprime mortgages can have fixed or adjustable interest rates. Interest rates on adjustable rate mortgages (ARMs) are pegged to a benchmark rate, such as the six month Libor rate or the one-year Treasury bill rate. Subprime interest rates were 1.8 to 4.0 percentage points higher compared to the conventional 30-year fixed rate of about 6.2 percent (Federal Reserve Bank of San Francisco, 2007). The combination of declining long-term interest rates and ever more alluring mortgage deals did attract new buyers into the housing market, because of *teaser loans* which are usually offered to low-income home buyers. In fact, these loans are *NINJA* (no income no job and assets) *loans*, or *liar loans* (low-documentation or no-documentation mortgages).

3. Securitisation of Home Loans

This securitisation of mortgages was the dawn of a new era in American finance and it was a necessary prelude to the *age of leverage*. This was the so called financial alchemy or engineering. The mortgage backed securities (MBSs) and collateralised debt obligations (CDOs) are the two important financial instruments. The process of mortgage operation involves the direct players: (1) *mortgage brokers*, (2) *mortgage originators*, (3) *borrowers*, (4) *investment banks*, (5) *structured investment vehicles (SIVs)*, (6) *final investors*, and (7) *servicers*. The indirect players are (8) *underwriters* and (9) *credit rating agencies*.

The process starts with *mortgage brokers* who entice subprime borrowers and attach them to *mortgage originators*. Mortgage originators issue home loans to *borrowers*. Then the originators rather than holding the loans in their own portfolios sell the loans to *investment banks*, which aggregate mortgage loans into large pools to issue bonds known as a mortgage-backed securities (MBSs). In turn, investment banks set-up a new type of off-balance sheet operation known as *SIVs* for buying up mortgage loans (MBSs), that are restructured into CDOs. The SIVs slice CDOs into various 'tranches' and distribute them to *final investors. The servicers* collect instalment EMIs from the borrowers (by charging 0.25 to 0.50 percent) to arrange to credit them into the accounts of final investors. The *underwriters* operate as guarantors for the issue of bonds by SIVs. The *credit rating agencies* charge fees to rate CDOs with good rating, i.e., AAA.

"Tranches" depend on their level of exposure to losses from defaults: (i) *senior* tranches, (ii) *mezzanine* tranches, and (iii) *equity* tranches. The senior and mezzanine tranches get full even in the case of defaults, leaving losses, if any, to the equity tranches as they get from what is left. Hedge funds and other aggressive investors invest in lower tranche (equity) which has high risk and so gets a higher rate of return. Several thousand mortgages may go into a single MBS and as many as 150 MBSs can be packaged into a single CDO (Beitel, 2008; Dodd, 2007; Crotty, 2009).

4. Credit Default Swap (CDSs) as Credit Insurance

Credit Default Swap (CDS), a credit derivative, is an important contributor to the financial crisis of 2007-08. CDS is an insurance against credit risk in case of default. A CDS contract involves the transfer of the credit risk market bonds, mortgage-backed securities, or corporate debt between two parties. It is similar to insurance. The CDS market expanded into structured finance, such as CDOs, that contained pools of mortgages. It also exploded into the secondary market, where speculative investors, hedge funds and others would buy and sell CDS instruments, which have no direct relationship with the underlying investment. They are betting on whether the investments will succeed or fail. It is like betting on a sports event without playing in the game, but people all over the country are betting on the outcome. The market for CDSs is over-the-counter (OTC) and unregulated.

The CDS market exploded over the past decade. The value of credit default swaps hit $62 trillion in December 2007 while the maximum value of debt that might conceivably be insured through these derivatives was only $5 trillion. Thus, it is evident that massive speculation by banks and others, not just hedging, was taking place (Crotty, 2009). This is roughly twice the size of the U.S. stock market (Morrissey, 2008). George Soros said that it was equal to 50 percent of the US household wealth or five times (500 percent) the national debt.

5. Fraudulence of Players in Securitisation

All the players mentioned in securitisation, from mortgage broker to credit rating agencies, get fees and commissions at each stage. SIVs depend on asset backed commercial paper (ABCP), which is a short-term borrowing for 90 days from other financial institutions, i.e., *borrow short and lend long*. The ABCP has a lower interest near to the FED rate, but they lend to the subprime borrowers, above 4-6 percentage points. This much margin is kept to cover the fees and commissions of investment banks. Further, employees get tremendous incentives by pay for performance. The underwriters do not follow scrupulous standards. The rating agencies rate the CDOs, etc., on their whims and fancies. Borrowers are carried away by speculative and Ponzi spirit.

Mainly it is dangerous, when credit rating agencies, like Standard and Poor's, Mody's, certify ratings by collecting money from the firms which are being rated. It is like professors accepting money from their students before grading them. John Moody, in his autobiography in 1934, said very clearly that the rating agency should never, as a rater, accept money (Shiller and Steil, *et al.*, 2009).

6. Subprime Mortgages Leading to Rise in Home Ownership Rates

After the subprime mortgage lending rose, the percentage of homeowners in all US householders increased to 69 percent in 2005 from 64 percent in 1995. Over a decade (1995-05), about half of that increase could be attributed to the subprime-lending boom. President Bush urged lenders to create 5.5 million *new minority homeowners* by the end of the decade, signed the American Dream Downpayment Act in 2003, a measure designed to subsidize first-time house purchases in low-income groups. Between 2000 and 2006, the share of undocumented subprime contracts rose from 17 to 44 percent. Fannie Mae and Freddie Mac also came under pressure from the Department of Housing and Urban Development to support the subprime market (Ferguson, 2008b). The home-ownership rates rose for all age groups, all racial groups, and all income groups. The increases in home-ownership were largest in the West, for those under the age of 35, for those with below-median incomes, and for Hispanics and blacks (Shiller, 2008a, p.5).

FINANCIAL DEREGULATION: THE CAUSE OF FINANCIAL CRISIS

1. Regulation to Deregulation of Financial Sector in USA

In the United States of America (USA), between 1792 and 1933, there were several financial panics and crises every fifteen to twenty years. In fact, the USA did not suffer another major banking crisis for just about 50 years between 1933 and 1982. The fifty years of relative financial calm that followed the Glass-Steagall Act of 1933, the Securities Exchange Act of 1934, and the Banking Act of 1935 strongly suggest that sound public risk management can make a positive difference. This role began to take shape in 1933 with passage of Glass-Steagall, which introduced federal deposit insurance, significantly expanded federal bank supervision, and required the separation of commercial from investment banking (Moss, 2009).

Under the influence of Milton Freidman's free market ideology, Nixon encouraged Chicago boys to disrupt Chile (outside USA), but within USA he claimed, "we are all Keynesians." It was Carter who started the deregulation of trucking and natural gas and broadcasting in the late 1970s (Kutner, 2008). By the time of Reagon and under his tenure, the financial regulation began to get dismantled with the passage of the Depository Institutions Deregulation and Monetary Control Act of 1980 and the Depository Institutions Act (Garn-St. Germain) of 1982, which commenced the drive for financial deregulation.

The repeal of the Glass-Steagall Act was passed by Congress in November 1999, under the influence of Phil Gramm, the Senator, Milton Friedman fanatic. It involved a $300 million lobbying effort by the banking and financial-services industries. The repeal of Glass-Steagall brought investment and commercial banks together, the investment-bank culture of speculation came out on top (Stiglitz, 2009a).

Alan Greenspan, who was a believer in free market philosophy, was appointed as the Federal Reserve Chairman in 1987, by president Reagon. Greenspan, in his long tenure of 19 years (1987-2006), adopted free market policies. In 1997, together with then-Federal Reserve chairman Alan Greenspan, Rubin, the Secretary Treasury, strongly opposed the regulation of derivatives. In 2000, the American parliament amended Securities Exchange Commission (SEC), exempting the derivatives from the purview of the Government's regulation (Bello, 2008b).

2. Global Savings Glut: Debt Dependence and Declining Interest Rates in USA

As dollar is reserve currency of the world, today's "paper

gold", USA imports foreign goods, buys foreign assets and pumps dollars into the world economy without providing any quid pro quo (Hudson, 2002). But, the earners of paper dollars have no other alternative than to invest in USA. In addition, 2/3rds of global reserves are in dollar terms. Thus, there has been *global savings glut,* which flows into USA. This leads supply of credit at cheap rate in USA.

Further, prior to 1997-98 Asian financial crisis, in developing countries when there were surpluses in foreign exchanges they used to spend because of lax monetary policy and fiscal profligacy. But, after 1997-98 crisis, the developing countries began to maintain foreign exchange reserves in their economies. The intention is to protect against rainy day. This is possible by tightened monetary and fiscal policies. When China, India ASEAN countries are maintaining FE reserves and sending them to USA for investment. Thus, the USA is expending beyond its means. By which the saving rate in USA has fallen down to zero (from 11 percent in 1982) and became *World's Consumer of Last Resort.* As the foreign exchange surpluses were being poured into USA, the FED used to maintain low interest rates. The people used to borrow and invest in home market (under subprime mortgage), as the home prices were rising (Stiglitz, 2009b; Sachs, 2009a).

3. Speculative Finance

As the FE reserves were pouring into USA, the FED adopted a very expansionary monetary policy, by keeping interest rates low, starting in the late 1990s. After the East Asian crisis and after the Russian crisis they really worried about the crisis spilling over to the USA and so the FED loosened. Before trying to tighten a little bit, the 9/11 terrorist attack was feared to lead to a major financial crisis. The Fed again loosened considerably. This was the environment that led to monetary expansion, that provided the credit, and the easy access to credit that fueled the booms (Bordo in Steil, *et al.*, 2009; Sachs, 2009b).

By keeping interest rates low, the Federal Reserve made it easy to borrow so as to encourage investment in financial assets, called as FIRE (finance, insurance and real estate) sectors. The common people were also attracted by home mortgages, being subprime loans. As asset prices soared, corporations and households experienced huge increases in their wealth, at least on paper. They were therefore able to borrow on a titanic scale, vastly increase their investment and consumption, and in that way, drive the economy. So, private deficits replaced public ones, i.e., *asset price Keynesianism* replaced *traditional Keynesianism*. Capital accumulation has come literally to depend upon historic waves of speculation, carefully nurtured and rationalised by state policy-makers and regulators, leading to *first the historic stock market bubble of the later 1990s, then the housing and credit market bubbles from the early 2000s* (Brenner, 2009).

James Tobin, Nobel laureate in economics, pointed out in 1984, that capitalism was becoming inefficient by devoting its surplus capital increasingly to speculative, casino-like pursuits, rather than long-term investment in the real economy: "We are throwning more and more of our resources...into financial activities remote from the production of goods and services, into activities that generate high private rewards disproportionate to their social productivity" (Foster, 2007). In 1936, Keynes also said, "the position is serious when enterprise becomes the bubble on a whirlpool of speculation. When the capital development of a country becomes a by-product of the activities of a casino, the job is likely to be ill-done" (Keynes, 1978, p. 159)

4. Greenspan did not Care Warnings

Warren Buffet described credit derivatives like CDSs as *"financial weapons of mass destruction"*, and George Soros portrayed them as *"instruments of destruction."* Soros, the successful Hedge Fund Manager, has been insisting on the government regulation in the international financial markets, basing on his theory of reflexivity (Soros, 2008). It is from this perspective only Bhagawati (2004, p. 8), Krugman (2007) and some other economists support only free trade in goods and services but oppose unbridled liberalization of financial markets. Fukuyama (2008) noted that between 2002 and 2007, Washington *failed to adequately regulate the financial sector* and allowed it to do tremendous harm to the rest of the society. Shiller argued in 2005 that the US economy was in the middle of a dangerous housing bubble (Shiller, 2008b). Edward Gramlich, a member of the Board of Governors from 1997 to 2005, frequently testified before

Congress on problems in home finance and called for action to halt abuses. But *Greenspan was consistently unsympathetic, and the Federal Reserve neither took action on its own nor supported action by other agencies* (Friedman, 2008).

BURSTING OF HOUSING BUBBLE INTO FINANCIAL CRISIS IN USA

I. Bursting of Housing Bubble

The Fed's interest rate downward manipulation (which is inter-bank lending rate) led to the housing bubble. The Fed rate was 6.25 percent in 2000 and came down to 1.00 percent by June 2003. Thereafter, Greenspan increased gradually to 4.5 percent by the time of his retirement (January 31, 2006). Later Ben Bernanke, next FED chairman, also began to rise Fed rate and it reached maximum 5.25 percent by June 29, 2006. *The people suspected that the Fed's tightening monetary policy was to control inflationary trend.* Depending on Fed's rate going up, the home loan interest rate also began to go up. As a result, monthly payments (EMIs) increased on adjustable rate mortgages. Home prices, that rose in real terms almost doubly between 1997 and 2006, are now down over 40 percent (Shiller in in Steil, *et al.*, 2009).

Minsky attributed this behaviour to Ponzi finance and propounded financial instability hypothesis. He says: "It is obvious that Ponzi finance unit's present value depends on interest rates and the expectation of cash flows in the future. Rising interest rates increase the rate of increase of outstanding debts and can transform positive present values into negative present values. Inflation will often lead to financing relations which can be validated only if inflation continues. Acquiring assets because of inflationary expectations bids up the price of favoured assets and the financing bids up interest rates. A decline in inflation expectations will lead to a drop in these asset prices which can lead to the debts exceeding the value of assets" (Minsky, 1982, p. 28)

When the home prices were rising, borrowers began to assume difficult mortgages in the belief they would be able to quickly refinance at more favourable terms. However, once interest rates began to rise and housing prices started to drop moderately in 2006-07 in many parts of the US and refinancing became more difficult. *Defaults* and *foreclosure* activity increased dramatically as easy initial terms expired, home prices failed to go up as anticipated, and ARM *interest* rates reset higher. The resulting defaults among marginal new owners led to a fall in house prices. This led to an ever increasing number of owners owning more on their houses than they were worth, creating more defaults and a further fall in house prices. *Thus the housing bubble burst.*

It was expected that around 15 percent of all borrowers with negative equity could lose their homes by December 2008; as Moody's Economy.com reckoned that around 13.4 million homeowners were underwater, so it was reasonable to project that over 2 million would lose their homes, in addition to the 2 million the banks had already sold (Tully, 2008).

2. Precipitation of Financial Crisis

The ongoing foreclosure epidemic of home loan mortgages began in late 2006 in the US, as the Fed rate began to increase by mid-2006, reaching 5.25 percent, which signaled that Fed rate might go up to control inflationary surge in the home markets. The inter-bank credit, which depends on the Fed rate, became difficult for the short-term purpose particularly on ABCP. Thus, the credit crunch was arrived in. The credit crunch was caused because banks became less willing to lend to each other after they suffered large losses on investments linked to the US housing market, and the subprime sector in particular. To ease credit, again a regime of cuts in Fed rate began. Fed rate was reduced gradually to 3.00 percent by January 30, 2008, thereafter to 1.00 percent by October 29, 2008 and further to 0.25 percent by December 16, 2008.

But, the situation did not turn better in credit flows, because the investment banks began to bring the off-balance sheet accounts into their books. For doing this, they have to reduce lending and raise interest rates, both to other financial institutions and households and non-financial institutions. This process, from *over-leveraging* to *de-leveraging* resulted in the credit squeeze, which in turn led to the fall in home prices and mortgage defaults, causing additional bank losses. Thus, the de-leveraging process froze credit markets. Since modern non-financial business and household sectors run on credit, the shrinking availability and rising cost of borrowing led to financial crisis in USA, that slowed down economic growth (Crotty, 2009).

Thus, the bursting of housing bubble caused big bank failures, undoing the 'too big to fail' concept in banking sector. By March 14, Bear Stearns collapsed and the Federal Reserve funded JP Morgan Chase to take over assets of Bear Sterns. Further the Major Banks, Lehman Brothers and Merryl Linch, collapsed around September 14, 2008. The mortgage lenders and guarantors, Fannie Mae and Freddie Mac (September 7); and American International Group (AIG), the giant insurance company of the world (September 16) were taken over by the government.

RISING FINANCIALISATION AND LACK OF AGGREGATE DEMAND OVER A DECADE: THE CAUSE OF ECONOMIC CRISIS

1. Excessive Financialisation Relative to Real Sector Economy

Financialisation elevates the significance of the financial sector relative to the real sector, transfers income from the real sector to the financial sector and increases income inequality and contributes to wage stagnation (Palley, 2008). The disconnect between the real and the financial is not accidental, that the financial economy expanded precisely to make up for the stagnation of the real economy. Over several decades, these developments inflated the size of financial markets relative to the real economy (Bello, 2008a).

The extent of financialisation in USA is seen from the fact that by 2004-06, financial services represented 20 to 21 percent of gross domestic product, keeping manufacturing just at 12 to 13 percent. And finance enjoyed an even bigger share of corporate profits (Phillips, 2008, p. viii). Further, the value of all financial assets in the US grew from four times GDP in 1980 to 10 times GDP in 2007. In 1981 household debt was 48 percent of GDP, while in 2007 it was 100 percent. Private sector debt was 123 percent of GDP in 1981 and 290 percent by late 2008. The financial sector itself saw the fastest rate of debt accumulation: from 22 percent of GDP in 1981 to 117 percent in late 2008 – or *in a decade, 1997-2007, borrowing by US financial institutions rose from 62 percent to 114 percent of GDP.* The share of corporate profits generated in the financial sector rose from 10 percent in the early 1980s to 40 percent in 2006 (Crotty, 2009).

2. Lack of Aggregate Demand

The financial sector problems are concerned with foreclosure in housing sector. But the problem underlying this financial crisis is *the macroeconomic problem: the insufficiency of aggregate of demand.* It is because of income inequality and the absence of redistribution of income from the rich to the poor., i.e., from those who have low MPC to those who have high MPC (Stiglitz, 2009b). When newly industrialised countries (NICs) began to produce the same goods and services as those of USA, at cheaper prices, USA's exports got affected. USA also got cheap imports from NICs. Thus, oversupply in USA reduced prices and as a concomitant reduced profits, despite cut in real wages. As a result private investment, consumption and government expenditure (social sector) were reduced. *The consequence of all these cutbacks in spending has been a long-term problem of aggregate demand* (Brenner, 2009).

3. Process of Economic Crisis Over a Decade

Though the recent downtrend in the US economic growth is attributed to the subprime debacle, weaknesses in the US economy for over a decade have been well observed. In the USA, during 2001-07, GDP growth was by far the slowest of the postwar epoch. Economic performance was weak, despite the enormous stimulus from the housing bubble and the Bush administration's huge federal deficits. Economic growth was driven entirely by personal consumption and residential investment, made possible by easy credit and rising house prices. Real wages were basically flat. There was no increase in median family income for the first time since WW-II. Housing by itself accounted for almost one-third of the growth of GDP and close to half of the increase in employment in the years 2001-05. When the housing bubble burst, consumption and residential investment fell and the economy plunged (Brenner, 2009). Further, the income inequality went up as the top 1 percent population had 8 percent GDP in 1980, whereas the top 1 percent population in 2007 had 23 percent GDP (Reich, 2009; Zakaria, 2008a, p. 202).

A sharp decline in the share of wages and salaries in GDP has been observed; it was 54 percent in 1971 and 45 percent in 2006 (Foster, 2008). Real wages (i.e., taking *inflation* into account) in the US peaked in 1971, when Richard Nixon was president, and by 2008 had fallen back to 1967 levels, when Lyndon Johnson was president (Foster, 2009).

BAILOUT BENEFICIARIES: BANKS NOT HOMEOWNERS

As the cuts in Fed interest rate did not ease credit markets and revive confidence, and the American economy was on the verge of recession, by the end of 2007; in first week of February 2008, President Bush passed the *economic stimulus package,* as tax rebates of $ 150 billion to tax payers and investing industry.

By September 18, 2008, Treasury Secretary, Paulson, hastily devised plan Troubled Asset Relief Program (TARP) for $ 700 billion. Even after modification, it was rejected by the Congress after 11 days (September 29, 2008). It was passed after four days., i.e., by *October 3, 2008*. Greenspan was called to House of Representatives to explain on October 4, 2008, where he confessed that regulation of financial markets was necessary; though he did not agree that there was regulatory failure in financial markets even after the collapse of Bear Stearns (March 14, 2008).

The bailout of banks was supported by Bernanke, the Fed Chairman, from his logic that in lieu of tax cuts, the government could reverse deflation by printing money to increase spending on current goods and services or even acquire existing real or financial assets, even when *liquidity trap* conditions were there (Fed rate being near zero). This is Milton Friedman's famous *'helicopter drop'* of money (Brown, 2009). In this spirit only, around the late September and early October 2008, *the dollars were printed/created at a rate of a trillion dollars a week* and were flooded into the banking system (American Chinese Medicine Association, 2008). It appears that the Federal Reserve followed John Law, who printed the first large-scale issue of paper money to finance the profligacy of early 18th-century French royalty, to subject US economy to *reflation* (Feguson, 2008a, p. 142).

Under the Troubled Asset Relief Program (TARP), $700

billion Bush's bailout plan was to purchase toxic or dodgy assets from failed banks, as Stiglitz rightly called it Paulson's plan of *'cash for trash'*. In fact, the home owners were not bailed out. Thus, main plank of the government bail-out is to protect institutions burdened with worthless mortgage backed securities rather than help homeowners or those looking for credit to finance homeownership (Chandrasekhar, 2008). On April 14, 2009, Obama spoke implying that it would be better to spend government money on banks (by bail out) instead of families and businesses, because bank dollars when lent to families and businesses, *would have a multiplier effect (8 or 10 times) which ultimately leads to a faster pace of economic growth* (Obama, 2009).

Bail-out money is going to the people who do not need any money, but not to the people who need money. In fact, from the first round funding (October, 2008) of $250 billion, Bush government had pledged $172 billion to a total of 52 banks, $125 billion to nine major banks, and $47 billion to the 43 remaining banks (Goldman, 2008). The cost of all the bailouts to the taxpayer is a whopping $8,750 per household, more than two and half times what it was over 20 years ago during the savings and loan (S & L) crisis. Banks used this bailout dollars for payment of high salaries, bonuses, and holidayings to their employees. Each CEO of the nine banks bailed out by government took home on average, $32.2 million each, nearly triple the average CEO pay at the 500 biggest US companies. This is more than $600,000 a week (Winship, 2008). Further, no penalties for the bankers who generated the crisis; nobody is being sacked and the boards of the banks will remain in place; this is *crony capitalism* (Chakravarthy, 2008).

Of $700 billion bailout package of Bush, the Obama government got nearly $300 billion (Ericson *et al.*, 2009). Obama also has economic stimulus package having four components. The first is bailout for $787 billion. Within this, 38.0 percent ($300 billion) is for tax cuts, another 38.0 percent ($300 billion) for providing aid (unemployment food stamps, medical aid, etc.), and the remaining goes for federal spending (but only $ 27 billion this year). The second component is Public-Private Investment Fund which gets $190 billion left over from that $700 billion TARP fund. The third one is Term Asset-Backed Securities Loan Facility with $1000 billion ($200 billion old). The fourth is Homeowner Affordability and Stability Plan with only $75 billion, *a paltry sum for targeting subsidies to mortgage lenders* (Rasmus, 2009).

President Obama, Treasury Secretary, Geithner, and Treasury are bailing out the same people who were being bailed out by Bush. If AIG is bailed out Goldman Sachs would get $ 20 billion, as Paulson's owned Company, which is a single largest counterparty in AIG. So Geithner bailed out AIG to the benefit of Paulson (Hudson, 2009). Following Bagehot's rules, in bailing out, the lender of last resort in a financial crisis can lend money freely on good collateral, but at a penalty rate. But, it is being lent freely on not-so-good collateral, at a rate that is not exactly a penalty rate (Richard Sylla in Steil, *et al.*, 2009).

CONCLUSION

As an antidote to red revolution, in the depression years, president Roosevelt developed the concept of home/property owning democracy. For achieving this goal, lot of infrastructure in his tenure was developed to avoid foreclosure of homes and bank failures. Main piecc of legislation was Glass-Steagal Act 1933, which separated investment and commercial banking. In later years also, with the underwriting of Fannie Mae, Freddie Mac and Ginnie Mae, housing market flourished and seemed to realise *the property-owning democracy.* The financial deregulation started under Carter and Reagon, reached the highest zenith under Clinton, when Glass-Steagal was repealed in 1999. By that time, due to global savings glut, lot of surplus reserves (dollars) began to flow into the USA, and this led to easy credit by lowering Fed interest rate (1.0 percent in 2003). Alan Greenspan, Fed chairman, used manipulative interest rates to counter the impending recessions after dot.com bubble and 9/11 terrorist attacks (2001). This led to housing bubble, with rise in the home prices and home loans.

New type of securitisation in home market, with new fianancial instruments mortgage backed securities (MBSs), collateralised debt obligations (CDOs) and credit default swaps (CDSs) led to speculative and Ponzi finance. This encouraged subprime mortgages, by extending loans to households who have no good credit histories. As home prices were increasing, the borrowers and investment banks all were in euphoric mood. This mood was affected as soon as the Fed interest rates began to go up from 1.00 percent to 5.25 percent (June 2003 to June 2006). As banks increased interest rates for inter-bank and housing loans, the credit became difficult. Collapse of banks and foreclosures by homeowners became the order of the day. Consequent falling home prices and instalment hikes led to the financial crisis. *Excessive leveraging now turned into de-leveraging for banks and households.* This led to credit crunch and financial crisis. Thus, even as per Bernanke (2009), the cause of the crisis was the housing bubble in the United States and its burst, leading to rise in delinquencies on subprime mortgages, which imposed substantial losses on many financial institutions and shook investor confidence in credit markets.

As the US economy has been dominated by FIRE (finance, insurance and real estate) sectors, the share of real economy is going down. The saving rate has been nil for the past several years. Though the real wages fell, the people were living beyond their means by credit card loans, car loans and home loans. People hoped to get appreciation in home market, to spend by withdrawing home equity. But it fell like a pack of cards. All these led to cut in consumption expenditure in the economy. Government cut social expenditure and private investment fell due to less profitability in commodity (real) sector. The combined effect is deficiency in aggregated demand. This caused economic crisis. The government bailed out only big banks, by purchasing so called toxic or dodgy assets from them, but not the foreclosing home owners.

References

American Chinese Medicine Association (2008), "Printing/Creating Money Is A Hidden Tax, Which Should Be Approved By Taxpayers", ACMA Publication, 2008, Special Report No. 2, October.

Bello, Walden (2008a), "Capitalism in an Apocalyptic Mood", Foreign Policy in Focus, February 20.

_____ (2008b), "Wall Street Collapse: From Where to Where?", Marxist, November 2008, (pp. 12-17) (translated by K. Veeraiah)

Beitel, Karl (2008), "The Subprime Debacle", *Analytical Monthly Review*, Vol. 6, No. 2, May (pp. 25-41).

Bernanke, Ben (2009), The Crisis and the Policy Response, (Transcript), London School of Economics Public Lecture Podcast, January 13.

Bhagawati, Jagdish (2004), In Defense of Globalisation, Oxford University Press, New Delhi.

Brenner, Robert (2009), "A Marxist Explanation for the Current Capitalist Economic Crisis", LINKS, *International Journal of Socialist Renewal*, January 22.

Brown, Ellen (2009), "Reforming Global Finance: In Defense of Bernanke's Helicopters", Ethical Markets, March 28.

Chakravarthy, Manas (2008), "Implications of the US Bailout", *The Wall Street Journal*, September 22.

Chandrasekhar, C.P. (2008), "The Problem as Solution", Review of Shiller's Book, *Economic and Political Weekly*, October, 18.

Crotty, James (2009), "Profound Structural Flaws in the US Financial System that Helped Cause the Financial Crisis", *Economic and Political Weekly*, Vol. XLIV, March 28, (pp. 127-35).

Dodd, Randall (2007), "Subprime: Tentacles of a Crisis", *Finance and Development*, A Quarterly Journal of IMF, Volume 44, Number 4, December.

Ericson, Mathew, *et al.*, (2009), "Tracking the $700 Billion Bailout", *The New York Times*, June 24.

Federal Reserve Bank of San Francisco (2007), The Subprime Mortgage Market: National and Twelfth District Developments, 2007, Annual Report, San Francisco.

Ferguson, Niall (2008a), The Ascent of Money: A Financial History of the World, Allen Lane, Penguin Books Ltd., London.

_____ (2008b), "Wall Street Lays Another Egg", Vanity Fair, November 10.

Foster, John Bellamy (2009b), "Financial Crisis: A Whole Other Struggle is Emerging", *International News*, Green Left Weekly, Issue #786, 11 March (Interview was made on March 6, 2009).

_____ (2008), "Financial Implosion and Stagnation: Back To The Real Economy", *Monthly Review*, December.

_____ (2007), "The Financialization of Capitalism", *Monthly Review*, April.

Friedman, Benjamin M. (2008), "Chairman Greenspan's Legacy: Review of 'The Age of Turbulence: Adventures in a New World", *The New York Review of Books*, Vol. 55, No. 4, March 20.

Fukuyama, Francis (2008), "The Fall of America, Inc.", *Newsweek*, October 04.

Goldman, David (2008), "Where the Bailouts Stand?", CNNMoney.com, November 12.

Hudson, Michael (2002), "Pluto Press Release of November 25, 2002", in Super Imperialism: The Economic Strategy of American Empire, Pluto Press, London, 2003 (2nd edition).

_____ (2009), The Way We Were and What We Are Becoming (audio), Guns and Butter, KPFA Radio, March 2004.

Keynes, John Maynard (1978): The General Theory of Employment, Interest and Money, Macmillan Cambridge University Press (for the Royal Economic Society), London.

Krugman, Paul (2007), Trade and Inequality, London School of Economics, Public Lecture, May 2004.

Kuttner, Robert (2008), The Squandering of America: How the Failure of Our Politics Undermines Our Prosperity, (transcript of discussion with

Joanne J. Myers), the Carnegie Council, November 12.

Minsky, Hyman P. (1982), Inflation, Recession and Economic Policy, Wheatsheaf Books, Brighton, Sussex.

MORRISSEY, Janet (2008), "Credit Default Swaps: the Next Crisis?", *Time*, March 17.

Moss, David (2009), An Ounce of Prevention: The Power of Public Risk Management in Stabilizing the Financial System, Working Paper 09-087, Harward Business Schoo, January 05.

Obama, Barack (2009), A Speech on the Economy: Broad Domestic Agenda—the Path to Recovery , Georgetown University, Washington, April 14.

Palley, Thomas I. (2008), Financialization: What it is and Why it Matters, IMK Working Paper 04/2008, Hans-Böckler-Straße 39D-40476 Düsseldorf, Germany.

Phillips, Kevin (2008), Bad Money: Reckless Finance, Failed Politics, and The Global Crisis of American Capitalism, Viking, Penguin Group (USA) Inc., New York.

Rasmus, Jack (2009), "Barack Obama's Economic Recovery Plan", *Global Research*, March 2008.

Reich, Robert B. (2009), What Lurks around the Financial Corner in 2009, (audio), the Commonwealth Club of California. San Francisco, CA, January 14.

Reuben, Anthony (2008), "Have Bail-outs Worked in the Past?", *BBC News, Business Reporter*, October 13.

Sachs, Jeffrey (2009a), Global Capitalism—New Forms of Capitalism, Dicussion Mathew Bishop, Fora-TV, New York, March 03

______ (2009b), Global Effects of Crisis, Columbia Business School, New York, Fora-TV, New York, April 14 (www.foratv.com)

Shiller, Robert J. (2008a), The Subprime Solution: How Today's Global Financial Crisis Happened, and What to do About It, Princeton University Press, Princeton

______ (2008b), "Challenging the Crowd in Whispers, Not Shouts", *New York Times* (Economic Review), November 2002.

Soros, George (2008), New Paradigm for Financial Markets: The Credit Crisis of 2008 and What It Means, LSE Public Lecture, May 21, 2008.

Steil, *et al.* (2009), Crisis and Capitalism: Does History Suggest Where We're Headed?, (Transcript) , (Michael Bordo, Jerry Muller, Robert Shiller and Richard Sylla), January 12.

Stiglitz, Joseph (2009a), "Capitalist Fools", Vanity Fair, January.

______ (2009b), Lecture at Columbia Business School (Audio), February 19.

Tully, Shawn (2008), "Best Housing Bailout May be no Bailout", November 19.

Winship, Michael (2008), "For Whom Bailout Tolls", *Bill Moyers Journal*, October 24.

Zakaria, Fareed (2008), The Post-American World, Viking, Penguin Books India Pvt. Ltd., New Delhi.

Global Meltdown and India's Response

MITHILESH KUMAR SINHA AND ASHWANI KUMAR SRIVASTABA

PROLOGUE

The year 2008 saw the emergence of a global economic crisis. In Korea, exporters are suddenly struggling. In India, industrial growth has slowed substantially. In Sweden, Volvo is cutting thousands of jobs. In Japan, which thought it was immune to the current market chaos, a credit squeeze seems to be forcing small companies into bankruptcy. Around the world, fears of recession have fed a stock market panic, as worries about toxic assets spread from the financial sector to the credit markets and now to the broader economy. Companies from Germany to Asia are hoarding cash because credit markets are tight. The sheer uncertainty of it all is upending plans for businesses to expand. Consumers have pulled back, just as they received some relief from high oil prices. Even credit-worthy companies cannot get money in Europe. And across Asia, export growth has slowed to a crawl or started declining in real terms. The United States, once the engine of the global economy, is ailing and in no position to inspire confidence, much less point the way around or out recession. Americans are seen as both the root of the problem, and powerless to solve it.

I

Evolution of Meltdown

The crisis began in June 2007 with the advent of sub-prime market crisis hitting the US market. Sub-prime crisis refers to the crisis faced by the mortgage companies that were in loaning business that due to adverse situations ran in trouble. As a result the number of defaulters increased resulting in huge bad debt for the mortgage companies. This type of lending was advanced mostly by the mortgage funding agencies. However, as long as situation in both the markets that is properly market and capital remained tacit the things were okay. With time the house prices initially rising and then falling these agencies started making huge on account of defaulting loans and decreasing prices of mortgaged houses. This led to credit crunch for other sector thus the whole financial market came under this grip. Also recently some of the America's top investment banks like Lehman brothers, Merrill Lynch, Wacchovia also started falling as the assets valuation began to decrease and liabilities rose for those institutions. This is what is known as financial mayhem.

Stages of U.S. Sub-prime

The U.S sub-prime has had three stages:

- The first phase was August 2007 t0 March 2008 an eight month period for markets to adapt a new or world order.
- The second phase was from Bear Stearns to Lehman in September, or a 13-month period from when the story of sub-prime broken down.
- The third period is September 2008 to now and continuing.

NATURE OF RECESSION

The current recession looks more Hayekian than Keynesian with Fisherian consequences. A Keynesian recession represents a sudden fall in demand, and can be remedied within six months by pumping enough purchasing power into the economy. A Hayekian recession, however, is caused by misallocation of resources over a long period, driven by unrealistic interest rates, ending in a bust that requires years of structural adjustment. Such a recession can last a decade (as in Japan in the 1990s) (Aiyar, 2009). Hayek provides the best diagnosis of the cause of the current crisis, neither he nor Keynes provide an adequate explanation of the financial aspects of business cycles, assuming these are endogenous to the flactuations in the real economy. It is Irving Fisher ("The Debt-Deflation Theory of Great Depression", *Economtrica*, 1933) who provides the correct diagnosis of the nature and cures for the current crisis. Fisher saw a 'balance sheet recession' as an essential element in the Great Depression. He argued that, whilst there were many cyclical factors behind trade cycles, for Great Depression the two dominant factors are "over-indebtedness to start with and deflation following soon after" (p. 348). This provides a succinct explanation of the current crisis and pointers to its cure. We have a Hayekian recession with Fisherian consequence (Lal, 2009).

MURDERERS OF FINANCIAL SYSTEM

Murderers of financial system are: The Federal Reserve Board; US Politics; Fannie Mae and Freddie Mac; Financial Innovators; Regulators; Banks and Mortgage Lenders; Investment Banks; Rating Agencies; The Based Rules for Banks; US Consumers; Asian and OPEC Countries. In my view, everybody including States, Institutions and Markets was guilty for meltdown.

What it is a Global Crisis?

We need to recognize that we are grappling with three separate crises that, though interwoven are also quite distinct. The solution to any one of them won't automatically resuscitate the larger economy if the others remain untreated and unchanged. Here are the three:

First: the collapse of consumer spending. American consumers represent 70% of the economy. Traumatised by plunging home values and stock prices—which have shaved at least $7 trillion from personal wealth—they have curbed spending and increased saving. That's led directly to layoffs. In December 2008, vehicle sales were down 36% from year-earlier levels.

Second: the financial crisis. Lower lending deprives the economy of the credit to finance business, homes and costly consumer purchases (cars, appliances). The deepest cuts involve 'securitization'—the sale of bonds. Investors have gone on strike. In 2008, the issuance of bonds backing credit card loans fell 41% and those backing car loans 51%.

Third: a trade crisis. Global spending and saving patterns are badly askew. High-saving Asian countries have relied on export-led growth that, in turn, has required American consumers to spend ever-larger shares of their income. Huge trade imbalances have resulted: US deficits, Asian surpluses. As Americans cut spending, this pattern is no longer sustainable. Asia is tumbling into recession. Overcoming any of these crises alone would be daunting. Together, they're the economic equivalent of a combined Ironman triathlon and Tour de France.

Indeed, if the rest of the world does not buy more from America, any US recovery may be feeble. What are needed are policies that correct the imbalances in spending and saving. As Americans save more of their incomes, Asians should save less and spend more, so that they rely more on producing for themselves rather than exporting to us. The great trade discrepancies would shrink. But this sort of transformation requires basic political changes in Asia. Whether China and other Asian societies can make those changes is unclear. The implications are sobering (Samuelson, 2009). A recent paper by Carmen M. Reinhart of the University of Maryland and Kenneth S. Rogoff of Harvard University examines the depth and duration of the slump that invariably follows severe financial crisis. It looks at all the major post-war banking crises in the developed world (a total of 18) with special emphasis on the ones dubbed "the big five" (Spain, 1977; Norway, 1987; Finland, 1991; Sweden, 1991, and Japan, 1992) as a number of famous emerging market episodes: the 1997-98 Asian crisis (Hong Kong, Indonesia, Korea, Malaysia, the Philippines, and Thailand); Colombia, 1998; and Argentina, 2001.

In a nutshell, it finds financial crisis are protracted affairs. They have deep and lasting effects on asset prices, output and employment. Unemployment rises and housing price declines extend out five and six years, respectively. On the encouraging side, output declines last only two years on average. And hard as it might be to believe at the moment, even recessions sparked by financial crises do eventually end, albeit almost invariably accompanied by massive increases in government debt.

More often than not, the aftermath of severe financial crises share three characteristics. First, asset market collapses are deep and prolonged. Real housing price declines average 35% stretched out over six years, while equity price collapses average 55% over a downturn of about three and a half years.

Second, the aftermath of banking crises is associated with profound declines in output and employment. The unemployment rate rises an average of 7 percentage points over the down phase of the cycle, which lasts on average over four years. Output falls (from peak to trough) an average of over 9%, although the duration of the downturn average roughly two years, is considerably shorter than for unemployment.

Third, the real value of government debt tends to explode, rising an average of 86% in the major post-world war II episodes. Interestingly, it finds the main cause of debt explosions is not the widely cited costs of bailing out and recapitalizing the banking system. rather the big drivers of debt increases are the inevitable collapse in tax revenues that governments suffer in the wake of deep and prolonged output contractions, as well as often ambitious countercyclical fiscal policies aimed at mitigating the downturn (NBER, Working Paper).

Spread of Crisis

Again, later in July and August 2008, the Fannie Mae and Freddie Mac the mortgage giants faltered. Federal Reserves pumped in 200 billion to ease the credit situation. Even before the situation could improve the Lehman Brothers one of the oldest investment banking institution in US filed for bankruptcy. However, the company could not sustain the market pressures. The other two mega giants AIG and Merrill Lynch were also on the brink of falling. However, these were rescued by the Bank of America that bought the Merrill Lynch and Fed lend $85 billion loan to AIG thus averting the crisis for the two companies. In addition Wachhovia group came under pressure.

The initial impact was fall in the total financial assets for the US economy. However, it was not only restricted to fall in total capital asset worth as the share market also tripped shedding more points than ever. The valuation of the company with increasing global integration the shake in the US market also had spill over effects to other markets. The well known historically financial behemoth UK capital market also fell to the whims and fancies of the catastrophe. In aftermath of the crisis, some of the well known institutions in UK and its currencies came under pressure.

II

GLOBAL CRISIS AND WORLD'S GDP GROWTH RATE

Boosted by the strength of India and China, developing nations would grow 1.2 per cent in 2009, but without the two, these economies would shrink 1.6 per cent, according to World Bank. Warning that the world is entering an era of "slower growth", the multilateral lending agency has projected the global economy to shrink 2.9 per cent in 2009. The world Bank in its latest report titled "Global Development Finance 2009: Charting a global recovery" has said that "excluding India and China, the developing economies would shrink 1.6 per cent in 2009. Developing countries are expected to grow by only 1.2 per cent in 2009, after 8.1 per cent growth in 2007 and 5.9 per cent growth in 2008. When China and India are excluded, GDP in the remaining developing countries is projected to fall by 1.6 per cent, causing continued job losses and throwning more people into poverty", the report said. The Bank anticipates the global economy to contract 2.9 per cent in 2009 but to grow in 2010. Earlier, the Bank projected the world GDP to shrink 1.7 per cent. Global growth is also expected to be negative, with an expected 2.9 per cent contraction of global GDP in 2009, the report noted. Presenting an optimistic outlook, the Bank has projected the developing economies to grow at 4.4 per cent and 5.7 per cent in 2010 and 2011, respectively. Global GDP is expected to rebound to two per cent by 2010 and 3.2 per cent by 2011. In developing countries, the growth is expected to be higher, at 4.4 per cent in

2010 and 5.7 per cent in 2011, albeit subdued relative to the robust performance prior to the current crisis.

The crisis is reckoned to have begun in August 2007. We note that though the unfolding of the crisis over nearly 14 months up to October 2008, the growth forecast for 2008 goes down only by about 1 percentage point relative to the forecast in April 2007. The forecast of 3.9% for global economic growth is impressive going by the growth record since the Second World War (Mohan, 2009), (Table 1). Even in January 2009, the forecast for 2008 remains a respectable 3.4%. It is the forecast for 2009 that changes drastically.

TABLE 1

IMF Growth Forecasts for the World Economy

	2008	*2009*
April 2007	4.9	-
September 2007	4.8	-
April 2008	3.7	3.8
October 2008	3.9	3.0
January 2009 (Update)	3.4	0.5

Source: IMF'S World Economic Outlook.

IMF cuts 2009 growth estimate to less than a fourth since November 2008. In November, the estimate for growth in 2009 was 2.2% and it was 3.8% for 2010 (Table 2).

TABLE 2

Growth Estimate

(GDP growth in %)

	2007	*2008*	*2009**	*2010**
World	5.2	3.4	0.5	3.0
Advanced economies	2.7	1.0	-2.0	1.1
United States	2.0	1.1	-1.6	1.6
Euro area	2.6	1.0	-2.0	0.2
Russia	8.1	6.2	-0.7	1.3
Developing Asia	10.6	7.8	5.5	6.9

* Projections

Source: IMF, World Economic Outlook Update.

Growth of the seven biggest economies in the world is set to weaker further, OECD signalled on 8 August 2008, pointing also to a mixed outlook for big emerging economies. The warning fits the picture of sharp slowdown in many advanced countries which has emerged so far 2008 as the repercussions of the credit crisis, and high oil prices, reached ever deeper into activity and lending. A similar signal for the Eurozone from European Central Bank on 7 August 2008, when the bank held its key rate steady, pushed down the euro against the dollar, a movement which continued on 8 August 2008. The OECD said its composite leading indicators for June "indicate a continued weakening outlook for all the major seven economies." It said, "The latest data for non-OECD member economies tentatively point to expansion in China and Brazil and a downturn in India and Russia." The indicator for all 30 countries in the OECD fell by 0.6 points in June 2008, and was a full five points lower than in June 2008, the OECD said. The figure for the US economy fell by 0.2 points and was 5.4 points down over 12 months. The Eurozone indicator fell by 0.8 points in June for a 12-month fall of 5.2 points. The June figure for Japan was unchanged but showed a fall of 4.1 points over 12 months. The OECD explained that its indicator, which had to be used with caution, "is designed to provide early signals of turning points (peaks and troughs) between upswings and down-swings in the growth cycle of economic activity." Other main figures were: Britain down 0.8 in the month and 4.8 points over 12 months, Canada down 1.1 and 3.9 points, France down 0.9 and 5.1 points, Germany down 0.9 and 5.4 points and Italy down 0.7 points and 4.5 points. The indicator for China was steady in June and rose by 0.8 points on a 12-month basis. The figure for India fell by 1.5 points in May 2008 and was 4.4 points down from the May 2007 level (Table 3).

The forecasts for economic growth in 2009 are subdued. Goldman Sachs projects it as low as 1.5 per cent; in Russia Goldman Sachs and Barclays Capital project a big decline in investment and hardly any growth in 2009; in India the World Bank, Goldman Sachs and Citi all expect economic growth in 2009 to be below 6 per cent; Goldman Sachs expects China's growth to slump to 6 per cent (Acharya, 2008) (Table 4).

TABLE 3

Slowdown in Points in some Countries (June 2008)

Countries	*Slowdown in Points*
OECD countries	0.6
US	0.2
UK	0.8
Canada	1.1
France	0.9
Germany	0.9
Italy	0.7
India (May 2008)	1.5*

Source: *The Economic Times* (2008), 9 August.

TABLE 4

Growth Rate of BRICs

	2007	*2008 (E)*	*2009 (F)*		
			WB	*GS*	*Citi*
Brazil	5.4	5.2	2.8	1.5	3.0
Russia	8.1	6.0	3.0	0.5	4.5
India	9.0	6.3	5.8	5.8	5.5
China	11.9	9.4	7.5	6.0	8.2

Notes: E = Estimate; F = Forecast; WB = World Bank; GS = Goldman Sachs. Data for India refer to fiscal year.

Sources: World Bank (Global Economic Prospects), Goldman Sachs Citi (all publications/forecasts are dated December 2008). Data for 2007 and 2008 from World Bank.

ADB REPORT

Asian Development Outlook, 2008 (ADO) shows that favourable policy conditions and impressive productivity growth associated with Asia's economic modernization and structural transformation will continue to keep the region on a strong growth path. A key message of ADO 2008 is that, although problems will spread from the global economy to developing Asia—a process that is already visible in high-frequency trade and financial data—the region's growth in 2008 is much more likely to moderate than to lurch down. There should be no room for complacency. Asia's growth is neither preordained nor guaranteed, and if economic vigor is to last, countries must address a raft of challenges (Table 5).

Important points of Asian Development Outlook 2008 (ADO) are following:

- Asia's economy is expected to expand by 7.6% in 2008, picking up a shade to 7.8% in 2009. These projections suggest a slowdown from 2007's outcome, now estimated at 8.7%, the highest in 19 years.
- Still, growth projections for the next 2 years are only slightly below the recent historical trend and would constitute a solid performance in an unsteady global economy.
- Growth is expected to decelerate in most of the developing Asia's economies in 2008.
- People's Republic of China (PRC) and India are projected to cool.
- In India, where domestic demand accounts for most output growth, a modest slowdown is seen.
- Rising food and fuel prices are stocking headline inflation, but economic speed limits have also been tested, with recent output growth straining capacity. On the demand side, sustained balance-of-payments surpluses have seeped into domestic liquidity and credit expansion.
- A coincident slowdown of output growth in the G3 economies—United States (US).
- European Union (EU), and Japan now looks set for 2008, with only a moderate and highly uncertain pickup forecast in 2009.
- If the global slowdown is concentrated in sectors such as electronics, textiles and garments, and toys, as recent data appear to suggest.
- Developing Asia is now exporting more to other emerging economies—the Middle-East, Russian Federation, and elsewhere.

TABLE 5

Growth Rate of per Capital GDP

(% per year)

	2003	*2004*	*2005*	*2006*	*2007*	*2008*	*2009*	*Per capita GNP. US $. 2006*
East Asia	**6.8**	**7.8**	**7.6**	**8.5**	**8.7**	**7.6**	**7.7**	
China. People's Rep. of	9.4	9.4	9.6	10.4	10.8	9.4	9.2	2.010
Hong Kong, China	3.2	7.6	6.6	6.3	5.2	3.6	4.0	28.460
Korea. Rep. of	2.6	4.3	4.0	4.8	4.6	4.7	4.9	17.690
Mongolia	4.7	11.4	7.0	5.6	8.1	8.3	7.8	880
Taipei. China	3.1	5.8	3.8	4.4	5.2	3.7	5.0	17.230
South Asia	**6.1**	**5.7**	**7.47.4**	**6.8**	**6.3**	**6.8**		
Afghanistan, Islamic Rep.	10.3	5.3	12.1	2.1	10.9	6.2	6.2	
Bangladesh	3.8	4.9	4.6	5.1	5.1	4.3	4.7	480
Bhutan	3.8	5.6	5.6	6.4	15.4	12.8	5.7	1.410
India	6.7	5.8	7.8	8.1	7.2	6.5	6.9	920
Maldives	6.8	8.0	-6.2	16.4	5.1	6.4	-	2,680
Nepal	14.4	2.1	0.6	0.9	0.1	-	-	290
Pakistan	2.6	6.0	6.9	4.7	4.6	-	-	770
Sri Lanka	4.5	4.3	5.1	6.6	-	-	-	1.300
South East Asia	**4.3**	**4.8**	**3.9**	**4.8**	**4.5**	**3.7**	**4.2**	
Cambodia	6.7	8.2	11.2	8.2	7.2	5.8	4.2	480
Indonesia	3.5	3.7	3.4	5.1	4.7	4.4	5.0	1.420
Lao People's Dem. Rep.	2.9	4.0	-1.4	6.0	6.4	5.9	6.0	500
Malaysia	3.6	4.6	2.8	3.9	4.3	3.7	4.2	5,490
Myanmar	11.6	11.4	11.4	10.5	-	-	-	-
Philippines	2.7	4.2	2.8	3.4	5.3	3.9	4.2	1,420
Singapore	4.9	7.6	4.8	4.8	3.3	4.0	4.6	29,320
Thailand	6.2	4.6	4.5	4.8	4.0	1.6	1.8	2,990
Vietnam	5.8	6.3	7.0	6.8	5.6	5.6	6.7	690

Source: Asian Development Outlook, 2008.

III

GLOBAL CRISIS AND INDIA'S RESPONSE

Globalisation has ensured that the Indian economy and financial markets can not stay insulated from the ongoing financial crisis in the developed economies. The global financial and economic crisis, which became full-blown in the second half of 2008 interrupted India's growth momentum through the contraction of export demand and constrained external financing conditions. As a result, India's economy grew by 6.7% in 2008-09 after clocking annual growth of 8.9% on an average over the preceding five years. The growth slowdown was more pronounced in the second half of 2008-09. With the assumption of normal monsoon, the RBI has placed the GDP growth for India at 6.0% for 2009-10 but on the basis of ten indicators* ICRIER has forecasted GDP growth for half (H1) 6.8% without shock and 3.9% with shock in 2009-10.

How Resilient India is to Withstand the Storm with Minimal Damage!

In the light of the fact that the Indian economy is linked to global markets through a full float in capital account (trade and services) and partial float in capital account (debt and equity), we need to analyze the impact based on three capital factors: Availability of global liquidity; demand for India investment and cost thereof and decreased consumer demand affecting Indian exports.The concerted intervention by Central Banks of developed countries in injecting liquidity is expected to reduce the unwinding of India investments held by foreign entities, but fresh investment flows into India are in doubt. The impact of this will be three-fold: The element of GDP growth driven by off-shore flows (along with skills and technology) will be diluted; correction in the asset prices which were hitherto pushed by

* For constructing the leading indicators index, the following ten indicators have been used: (i) production of machinery and equipment, (ii) sales of heavy commercial vehicles, (iii) non-food credit), (iv) railway freight traffic, (v) cement sales, (vi) sales of the corporate sector, (vii) fuel and metal prices, (viii) real rate of interest, (ix) BSE Sensex, and (x) GDP growth rates of the US and Europe.

foreign investors and demand for domestic liquidity putting pressure on interest rates.

Indian companies which had access to cheap foreign currency funds for financing their import and export will be the worst hit. Also, foreign funds (through debt and equity) will be available at huge premium and would be limited to blue-chip companies. The impact of which, again, will be three-fold: Reduced capacity expansion leading to supply side pressure; increased interest expenses to affect corporate profitability and increased demand for domestic liquidity putting pressure on the interest rates. Consumer demand in developed economies is certain to be hurt by the ongoing crisis, thus affecting the Indian exports. The impact of which, once again, will be three fold: export-oriented units will be the worst hit impacting employment; reduced exports, will further widen the trade gap to put pressure on rupee exchange rate and intervention leading to sucking out liquidity and pressure on interest rates.

Impact on Financial Market

The impact on the Financial markets will be the following: Equity market will continue to remain in bearish mood with reduced off-shore flows, limited domestic appetite due to liquidity pressure and pressure on corporate earnings; while the inflation would stay under control, increased demand for domestic liquidity will push interest rates higher and we are likely to witness gradual rupee depreciation and depleted currency reserves. Overall, while RBI would inject liquidity through CRR/SLR cuts, maintaining growth beyond 7% will be a struggle. As far as banking industry is concerned, the first half of 2008-09 offered challenges to banks in the form of rising inflation due to accelerated levels of global commodity prices, sustained monetary tightening and consequent pressures on margins and profitability.

As the beginning of the second half, however, the global crisis created intense uncertainties for funding liquidity. The RBI had to ensure adequate provision of liquidity of the market through banks, with the aim of restoring normal functioning of the market, and thereby facilitating adequate flow of credit to the productive sectors of the economy. The Monetary Policy stance of the Reserve Bank shifted from concerns related to inflation in the first half of 2008-09 to maintaining financial stability and accelerating growth momentum in the second half. The performance indicators of the banking industry during 2008-09 reflected the rising strains on India's real sector. The growth of bank credit to commercial sector decelerated sharply in 2008-09. It increased only by 16.9% in 2008-09 compared to 21.0% a year ago. The lower expansion of credit against the deposit mobilization at 19.8% (y-o-y) resulted in a decline in incremental credit-deposit ratio (y-o-y) of banking industry to 64.4% at end-March 2009 compared to 73.6% at end-March 2008. The RBI data showed that while the deceleration in bank credit was observed across the banking system, it was shaper for the private and foreign banks (Mallya, 2009).

The sectoral deployment data of credit of SCBs during 2008-09 indicated that the incremental credit expansion was primarily channelised to infrastructure, petroleum, coal products and nuclear fuels, iron and steel, engineering, construction and chemical and industries. While the credit flows to small industries and personal borrowers moderated, those to agriculture sector posted an increase. Despite this, Indian banks posted healthy financial results during 2008-09 compared to their global peers. The outlook of the Indian banking industry remains positive in 2009-10 on the backdrop of its stricter prudential regulation by the RBI financial indicators and stable political regime.

Impact on Export Growth

The ongoing global financial crisis is likely to have impact on India's export growth rate. The impact of the global slowdown made itself felt with Indian exports dipping for the first in seven years owning to slackening demand from US and Europe, rupee depreciation and a high base effect. In dollar terms, export in October, 2008 dropped 12.1 per cent to $12.82 billion against a 50.93 per cent jump in the same month in 2007. Exports stood at $14.58 billion in October 2007.

Analysts cite the decline in exports as an early indicator of sharp deceleration in the Indian economy, with most economists predicting less than 7 per cent growth in the second half of 2008. In rupee terms, however, the depreciation of the Indian currency by 24 per cent (October to October) helped exports grow 8.2 per

TABLE 6

Export and Import Growth

	($)				(Rs.)			
	Oct. 07	*Oct. 08*	*April -Oct. 07-08*	*April - Oct. 08-09*	*Oct. 07*	*Oct. 08*	*April - Oct. 07 - 08*	*Apri - Oct. 08-09*
Exports (% growth)	50.93	-12.1	23.33	23.7	29.27	8.2	8.98	32.0
Imports (% growth)	28.18	10.6	28.89	36.2	9.76	36.2	13.45	45.6

Source: Development of Commerce and RBI.

cent to touch Rs. 23,360 crore. Though a fall in the value of local currency makes exports cheaper for consumers, it erodes earnings in dollar terms. Imports grew at a much lower rate of 10.6 per cent in October 2008 to touch $23.36 billion.With exports declining and imports registering modest growth, the trade deficit- the difference between the two—went up 62 per cent to touch $10.53 billion in October 2008 (Table 6).

"India's export performance is expected to be lacklustre for the rest of the year 2008 and also much of 2009 as consumers and businesses around the world have cut back expenditure" said Sherman Chan, economist with Moody's economy.com. "Slowing external orders will also hurt local manufacturers, which will in turn, curb job creation," she added. Meanwhile, non-oil imports in the October 2008 expanded just 5.5 per cent to $15.4 billion against $14.6 billion in October 2008. Trade experts said non-oil exports were increasing by about 35 per cent for the period between July and September 2008. "This is a cause for concern as well. Though desegregated data is not available in the moment, the decrease in growth of non-oil imports could be because of lower machinery and capital goods imports," said Shubhada Rao, chief economist with Yes bank.

Oil imports in October 2008 grew 22 per cent and stood at about $8 billion against $6.52 billion in the corresponding month of 2007.Exporters have already started demanding fiscal sops from the government citing the global financial crisis. They claim difficulty in accessing bank credit and slowing demand from customers in US and Europe. Curiously enough, the most important demand-reducing factor operating in the pre-crisis period was the sharp slowdown in exports. According to Central

Statistical Organization (CSO) data, 2007-08[1] saw export growth plummeting to 7.5% from 18.9% registered in the earlier year (Table 7). Even this constitutes an underestimation of the decline in external stimulus to the domestic economy. The CSO estimates of export growth are obtained by deflation nominal export earnings by the export price index. This yields the per4centage change in the volume of export. However, for estimation of the demand generation impact of exports (a la the foreign trade multiplier analysis) what is relevant is the command of export earnings over domestic consumption and investment. Hence, the need for using the GDP deflator rather than the export price index.[2] Again, to the extent some exports directly involve use of imported items (for example uncut diamonds or gold in the export of gems and jewellery), it is export earnings less the value of the items that denote the autonomous component of domestic demand arising from trade.[3]

In the context of these observations it is easy to see how important export slowdown was in causing the decline in GDP growth in general and industrial growth in particular during 2007-08. Exports (of goods and services) less export-related imports (ELEM) were a little over 20% of GDP in 2006-07, but their share in total autonomous expenditure was nearly 30%. This together with the fact that between 2006-07 and 2007-08 there was a 15.8 percentage fall in ELEM attests to the enormous significance of exports in engineering the GDP deceleration. The decelerating trends of industrial and GDP growth started, let us remember, from April 2007 and the first quarter of 2007-08, respectively. Though quarterly data for ELEM are not available, our estimates of export growth (gross of export-related imports) indicate how closely this turning point corresponds to the behaviour of export earnings. Export growth started decelerating from the third quarter of 2006-07, plummeted from 13.2% to 0.6% in the first quarter of 2007-08, and declined further to minus 3.1% in the second quarter of 2007-08.[4] It is thus clear that the two most important factors behind the deceleration of GDP in general and industrial production in particular[5] were in operation well before the onset of the global crisis (Rakshit, 2009).

TABLE 7

Export and Import Growth Rate

(in %)

	2006-07				2007-08 (QE)				2008-09 (AE)		
	Q1	*Q2*	*Q3*	*Q4*	*Q1*	*Q2*	*Q3*	*Q4*	*Q1*	*Q2*	*Q3*
Exports of goods and services $	24.6	28.1	14.9	11.4	14.5	-2.0	15.8	12.1	21.4	14.4	6.2
Export of good and services#	28.5	32.0	17.4	13.2	0.6	-3.1	14.7	9.6	22.2	18.6	6.0
ELEM#	25.6				5.1						
Export of goods	22.8	28.8	13.3	9.2	3.1	-0.2	16.2	3.4	14.9	24.6	
ELEM of goods only#	24.4				8.6						
Export of services#	38.4	36.4	23.1	18.3	0.1	-5.7	4.8	-5.6	9.7	36.6	18.4
Import of goods and services $	25.6	35.2	20.4	18.5	6.4	2.6	10.7	7.9	21.7	20.5	21.7
Import of good and services#	23.1	32.2	16.9	14.4	3.0	2.0	10.3	6.1	25.7	24.6	
ILEM#	24.4				8.2						
Import of goods#	22.2	27.9	16.0	7.2	3.4	1.0	20.7	18.2	25.3	46.0	
Import of services#	13.9	40.1	10.0	34.9	1.7	-4.8	-5.8	-4.0	7.1	18.1	

Note: AE: Advance Estimate; QE: Quick Estimate. ELEM: Export (of goods and services) less export-related imports; ILEM: Import (of goods and services) less export-related imports. $ Based on CSO figures of real exports of goods and services, estimated by using export price indices as the deflator. # Growth based on real exports and imports of goods and services and remittances estimated using GDP deflator.

Source: Central Statistical Organisation, GoI, National Accounts Statistics, 2008 and various press releases; RBI's web site.

Impact on Gross Domestic Product Growth Rate

The world-meltdown has affected the gross domestic growth badly. After seeing a growth rate of 9 per cent or more during the last three years, i.e., 2005-06, 2006-07 and 2007-08 (Table 8) it declined to 6.7 per cent in 2008-09. The median view of 20 forecasters who participated in the policy survey of the central bank is that the economy would grow by 8 per cent in the 2009-10. The median view is industrial sector would improve to 7.7 per cent and services would grow at a slightly slower 9.4 per cent. On the monetary policy front, the forecasters expected the repo rate to ease to 8.4 per cent and CRR to 8.5 per cent by the end of 2009-10. When it comes to fiscal consolidation the optimism petters out. The median view is that Centre's fiscal deficit for the current year may rise to 3.9 per cent, against 2.5 per cent estimated in the budget 2008-09, and then fall to 3.4 per cent in 2009-10 (Table 9).

TABLE 8

GDP Growth Rate during the Last Six Years

Financial Year	*GDP (in %)*
200203	3.8
200304	8.5
200405	7.5
200506	9.4
200607	9.6
200708	9.0

TABLE 9

Growth Forecast

	2007-08	*2008-09*	*2009-10*		
			Maximum	*Minimum*	*Median*
Real GDP Growth	9.0	6.7	8.8	6.2	8.0
Agriculture and Allied Activities	4.9	1.6	5.0	2.5	3.3
Industry	8.2	2.4	9.0	5.5	7.7
Services	10.7	9.0**	10.8	7.0	9.4
Pvt.Final Consumption Expenditure	8.3	7.1^	8.5	6.0	7.1
Gross Domestic Savings	37.9	-	37.0	30.0	35.0
Gross Domestic Capital Formation*			43.9	32.9	37.0
Gross Fixed Capital Formation*			37.6	30.9	34.0
Combined Gross Fiscal Deficit*			9.0	4.8	6.5
Central Govt Fiscal Deficit			6.5	2.5	3.4
Repo (end period)	7.7	8.9^	9.0	6.0	8.4
Reverse Repo (end period)	6.0	9.1^	7.0	5.0	6.3
CRR (end period)	7.5	9.1^	9.3	5.0	8.5

Note: *Median view of 20 forecasters *as a % of GDP at current market price **Trade, hotels and restaurants, transport and communication (together).

Source: RBI and Economic Survey 2008-09.

Citing OECD data, Surjit Bhalla says India actually had negative growth (-3.6%) in Q4 of 2008, not the 5.3% claimed by the government. Moreover compared with 8.2% growth in Q4 of 2007 (again using OECD calculations), Bhalla says the total growth swing between the fourth quarters of 2007 and 2008 is a massive -11.8. On this swing criterion, Indian growth is far worse

TABLE 10

GDP Growth Estimated as Q-o-Q Gtowth Seasonally Adjusted and Annualised

	Non - Agri.Growth (%)	Total Growth (%)		Non -Agri. Growth	Total Growth
2001 Q1	2.7	2.8	2005 Q1	8.0	9.6
2001 Q2	7.5	12.0	2005 Q2	13.3	12.0
2001 Q3	4.5	4.4	2005 Q3	8.3	7.6
2001 Q4	9.9	8.0	2005 Q4	10.1	9.2
2002 Q1	3.0	2.4	2006 Q1	11.6	10.4
2002 Q2	10.6	5.6	2006 Q2	13.2	10.0
2002 Q3	6.1	2.0	2006 Q3	9.2	9.2
2002 Q4	7.2	-2.0	2006 Q4	9.0	7.6
2003 Q1	5.7	10.0	2007 Q1	9.8	10.4
2003 Q2	8.2	11.6	2007 Q2	11.3	8.4
2003 Q3	13.7	13.6	2007 Q3	8.4	8.8
2003 Q4	6.4	9.6	2007 Q4	7.6	7.2
2004 Q1	1.9	-2.8	2008 Q1	11.6	9.6
2004 Q2	14.9	12.0	2008 Q2	7.5	5.6
2004 Q3	10.3	8.4	2008 Q3	6.0	7.2
2004 Q4	8.0	4.8	2008 Q4	3.5	-1.6

Source: *The Economic Times,* March 25, 2009, Cited by Swaminathan S. Anklesaria Aiyar.

than in the US (-6.2%), UK (-8.4%) or European Union (-8.2%), though better than in Japan (17.8%) or Korea (-28.8%) (Table 11).

Why are Bhalla's figures so dramatically different from Indian official figures? Our Central Statistical Organization (CSO) calculated GDP growth comparing GDP in Q4 of 2008 with Q4 of 2007. But the world over, says Bhalla, countries calculated GDP growth quarter on quarter (Q4 against Q3 in this case), seasonally adjusting and annualizing the estimate (multiplying QoQ growth by 4). India does not use this standard global methodology, arguing that its agricultural data are notoriously volatile and rain-dependent. Aiyar have done his own calculations of QoQ growth seasonally adjusted and annualized, using data available in Washington DC and standard X-12 methodology for seasonal adjustment. Since agriculture is highly volatile, he has also listed non-agricultural annualized GDP growth (Table 10). According to him overall annualized GDP growth in Q4 of 2008 was negative (-1.6%). This is not bad as Bhalla's cited estimate (-3.6%). But it is much worse than the 5.3% claimed by the government using the CSO methodology. Even overall growth (including agriculture) in Q4 of 2008 (-1.6%) was not the worst in recent years. It was worse in Q1 of 2004 (-2.8%) and in Q4 of 2002 (-2.0%). There was no global meltdown in those quarters, yet growth was lower. In those cases a sharp downward shift in estimated farm output pushed down overall growth. This warns us to look instead to non-agricultural growth as a more reliable indicator. Non-Agricultural GDP growth in Q4 of 2008 (3.5%) was low, but by no means the lowest in recent years. It was lower in Q1 of 2001 (2.78%), Q1 of 2002 (3.0) and Q1 of 2004 (1.9%). So, while India is in trouble right now, non-agricultural data show it was worse in earlier periods that did not have a meltdown. So let's not view the current situation too darkly. Finally, even including agriculture and looking at the overall swing between the same quarter in successive years, the swing ending in Q4 of 2008 was less (-8.8%) than in Q4 of 2002 (-10%) or Q1 of 2004 (-12.8%). So while India has certainly slow down, the situation looks more comforting when we see how much worse such swings have been in the past.

TABLE 11

GDP Growth Rate Difference of Selected Countries

Country	*GDP Growth 2007 Q4 (in %)*	*GDP Growth 2008 Q4 (in %)*	*Difference*	*Country*	*GDP Growth 2007 Q4 (in %)*	*GDP Growth 2008 Q4 (in %)*	*Difference*
Australia	3.8	-2.1	-5.9	Hungary	2	-4	-6
Austria	2.8	-0.8	-3.6	India	8.2	-3.6	-11.8
Belgium	1.6	-5.2	-6.8	Iceland	-3.8	-3.7	0.1
Canada	0.8	-3.4	-4.2	Israel	6.6	-0.5	-7
Switzerland	4.4	-1.2	-5.6	Italy	-1.1	-7.2	-6.1
Germany	1.4	-8.4	-9.8	Japan	4.4	-13.4	-17.8
Denmark	0.5	-8	-8.6	Korea	6.2	-22.6	-28.8
EMU	1.6	-5.9	-7.5	Mexico	2.5	-10.8	-13.3
Spain	2.5	-3.9	-6.4	Netherlands	6.2	-3.4	-9.6
European Union	2.2	-5.9	-8.2	Norway	5.7	5.4	-0.3
Finland	6	-5.1	-11.1	Poland	8.3	1.4	-6.9
France	1.6	-4.7	-6.4	Portugal	2.3	-8	-10.3
G7	1	-7.4	-8.4	Slovak Republic	27.9	8.5	-19.4
United Kingdom	2.2	-6.1	-8.3	Sweden	5.9	-9.7	-15.6
Greece	2.5	1.2	-1.3	USA	-0.2	-6.4	-6.2

Notes: The GDP growth figures are for the quarter indicated over the preceding quarter; all figures have been seasonally adjusted and annualized by OECD.

Source: OECD, www.oecd.org

All the evidence suggests that India's policy response to the financial crisis is some considerable distance towards ugly. Indian policy-maker expectation would be that the decline in GDP growth rate in India should be one of the lowest in the world. This is wrong. The Indian economy is among the worst (sixth from the bottom among 27 countries) with a value of minus 11.8 per cent. This number is obtained as follows: Growth in 2007, fourth calendar quarter, and 8.2 per cent. Growth in 2008, fourth calendar quarter, is -3.6 per cent. Decline in growth rate, is -11.8 per cent (Table 11)

Employment Dimension

As the financial meltdown played out on Wall Street, the winds that blew away the jobs at Lehman and Merrill Lynch hit India too, in a big way and the hot shot MBAs started to lose the spring in their step. Job-cuts and lay-offs are the harsh realities that existing and prospective numbers of the Indian job market cannot rurn their back on. The findings of a recent study conducted across 21 companies show that over 65,000 people in India have been handed over the pink slip between August and October 2008, due to the economic slowdown. And this is only the beginning of the change that is expected in the job market in the next one year (Thomson, 2008). Rising unemployment is likely to trouble US. US unemployment rates are around 6.7 per cent in 2008 and are forecast to rise to around 8.2 per cent in June 2009. According to Okun's law, cited in one of the latest research notes put out by JP Morgan Chase Bank a real GDP growth of 1 per cent leads to reduction in unemployment by around 0.4 per cent. So, if the unemployment rate is around 8 per cent, it will take 12 quarters of 4.2 per cent growth to get the unemployment rate back to 6 per cent for unemployment levels to reach that level in 8 quarters, a GDP growth of 5 per cent is required (Jain, 2009) (Tables 12a and b).

GDP-Unemployment Tradeoff

There is certainly a deep recession as far as jobs for the highly educated are concerned. Ironically, this may be the first time in India's history when it is more difficult for the professional graduates to find employment or appropriate employment, compared to the less educated millions. Those who

TABLE 12(a)

GDP Growth Required to Lower Unemployment Rate Back to 6 per cent

(GDP growth in %)

	If peak unemployment rate is:		
Time required	7%	8%	9%
4 quarters	5.0	7.5	10.0
8 quarters	3.8	5.0	6.3
12 quarters	3.3	4.2	5.0

TABLE 12(b)

Sector-wise Job Lost in U.S.A. in the month of February, 2009

Sector	*Job Lost*
Construction	104,000
Factories	168,000
Retailers	40,000
Professional and Business Services	180,000
Temporary Help Agencies	78,000
Finance COS	44,000
Leisure, Hospitality	33,000

Note: In December 2008, The U.S.A. Economy lost 681,000 jobs and another 655,000 in January, 2009.

are currently struggling to find a decent job include engineers, management graduates, IT sector-trained professionals, fashion designers, pilot and other retail sector professionals, pilots and other aviation industry staff, and other professionals. The problem is even more acute for those in the middle and senior management functions who have lost their jobs in the last few months.

To compound the misery further for those job seekers, even if the over-all business sentiment improves in India during 2009 sometime, it is very unlikely that prospective employers will back to aggressive hiring of professional staff anytime during the next 12-18 months. During most of the 1990s and early 2000s, developed countries such as the US and EU shed hundreds of thousands of middle-management jobs. Even in the boom times of the last five years, many of those jobs were never really filled up. The job creation actually happened in different sectors, e.g. real estate and housing, financial services, travel and hospitality, retail and healthcare, to list just a few. These job-seekers will also be facing the adverse fallout of the otherwise much heralded demographic dividend of India. In the next 12 months, (i.e., 2009) India will add more than three million graduates to the employable pool. Of these, there will be more than 10,000 engineers from just the top 25 colleges alone (including the IITs), more than 5,000 MBAs from the top 25 business schools, more than 500 textile, apparel and accessories designers from the top 10 fashion institutes, more than 2000 retail sector professionals (corporate staff level) from the miscellaneous substreams of specialization, and more than 2500

TABLE 13(a)

Trends in Average Employment, India

(million)

Period	*Average Employment*	*Percentage Change*
September 2008	16.2	
October 2008	16.0	-1.21
November 2008	15.9	-0.74
December 2008	15.7	-1.12
Average monthly change	-1.01	

TABLE 13(b)

Percentage Change in Employment of Exporting and Non-exporting units

Period	*Exporting Units*	*Non-exporting Units*	*Overall*
October 2008	-1.3	-1.05	-1.21
November 2008	-0.45	-1.24	-0.74
December 2008	-1.66	-0.15	-1.12
Average monthly change	-1.13	-0.81	-1.01

aviation sector professionals (cockpit and cabin staff level), etc. And finally, a trickle has already begun of professionals of Indian origin returning to India as job opportunities dry up in the US and other developed economies (Singhal, 2009).

Unemployment in India's industrial and services sectors is on the rise. If earlier growth was being describe as "jobless", the problem now is that is lower comes with job losses. On the basis of one study, the total employment in all the sectors covered by the survey is estimated to have declined from 16.2 million during September 2008 to 15.7 million during December 2008, implying a job loss of about half a million (Table 13a). However, the survey does suggest that employment fell in every month in the period studied. After September 2008, employment in all industries declined at an average rate of 1.01 per cent a month. A comparison of employment in export and non-export units indicates that employment declined at an average monthly rate of 1.13 per cent in the former, as opposed to 0.81 per cent in the latter (Table 13b).

IV

MITIGATING GLOBAL FINANCIAL CRISIS

It is now clear that the global financial and economic crisis, even though originating in the western world has affected the developing countries very badly. It is threatening to set back the gains made over the past decades in terms of poverty alleviation and achievement of the millennium development goals by developing countries. Millions of people have lost their jobs and have been pushed back into poverty. The impact is particularly severe in developing countries because of very large concentration of poor, unorganized and vulnerable people combined with a general lack of social security system and limited capabilities of the governments to take care of the affected sections. While the so-called 'green shoots' of recovery are beginning to be spotted, the western economies are unlikely to regain their status of being the engines of growth for the world economy in the near future.

A global crisis of such proportions obviously needed a global response even though the national governments across the world have been adopting fiscal stimulus packages to revive demand depending upon their capacities. To be fair, the international community has responded to it in a spirit of cooperation and to contain further deepening of the crisis. In October 2008 itself the president of the UN General Assembly appointed a Commission on Reforms of International Monetary and Financial System chaired by Nobel Laureate Professor Joseph Stiglitz and with senior experts from different regions including Dr. Y.V. Reddy, the former governor of the RBI. The G-20 leaders met in Washington DC in November 2008 and in London in April 2009 to chart out a global plan for recovery and reform. The UN Conference on the World Financial and Economic Creisis and its Impact on Development was held on 24-26 June 2009 with leaders and ministers of many countries and adopted an outcome document containing some proposals for addressing the concerns of developing countries, specially the poorer and smaller ones not reprented in G-20.

The two initiatives need to be seen in a complementary manner. The G-20 process addressed the most immediate task of restoring confidence and assisting recovery by providing a package of $1,100 billion at the disposal of international financial institutions and multilateral development banks to restore lending. The UN Conference being able to bring together nearly all of the humanity came up with a more inclusive in the medium and longer-term. It was able to highlight the challenges faced by developing, especially the poorer, countries underlining, for instance, the plight of developing countries with the sudden reversal of private capital flows, large and volatile movements in exchange rates, falling revenues and reduced fiscal space for taking corrective measures. It called for a coordinated and comprehensive global response focusing on restoration of the flow of development finance without unwarranted conditionalities and debt relief to developing countries for 'fostering an inclusive, green and sustainable recovery', among many other measures. It also emphasized on the importance of South-South cooperation and triangular cooperation for assisting the developing countries in recovery. More importantly, it emphasized the importance of the long pending reform of international financial architecture to enhance the voice and participation of emerging markets and developing countries and acknowledged the importance of examining the calls for reform of current global reserve currency system. It recognized the importance of regional financial cooperation and its potential to complement global initiatives (Kumar, 2009).

Indian Way to Handling Crisis

India have taken a number of steps to address the problem of liquidity crunch. Between October 6, 2008 and October 15, 2008, the RBI cut the CRR by a total of 250 basis points. The SLR requirements were relaxed initially by one percentage point and subsequently an additional window of 0.5 percentage points was introduced specifically to enable banks to draw funds to provide liquidity to mutual funds. The call money rate today is around 6.8 per cent.Government also arranged to provide, in advance, a sum of Rs. 25,000 crore (Rs. 250 billion) to the banking system under the Debt Waiver and Debt Relief Scheme. The limit of the investment by Foreign Institutional Investors in corporate bonds was increased from $3 billion to $6 billion. Both RBI and government are carefully monitoring the flow of credit and will ensure that the additional liquidity infused into the system translates into actual credit. They will not hesitate to do more if needed. Three stimulus packets have been given so far to recover the crisis.

CONCLUSION

To conclude, therefore, time has come to take the proposals of international and regional cooperation in the era of finance to the next level. As the emerging centre of gravity of the world economy, Asia should take the lead in exploiting the potential of regional financial cooperation for generating additional demand for expediting the recovery of the world economy from the worst crisis since the Great Depression while pursuing an agenda for inclusive and sustainable growth.

NOTES AND REFERENCES

1. Note that though the global financial turmoil started in the third quarter of 2007-08, world GDP growth did not fall significantly during the financial year. In fact, in calendar year it increased by 10 basis points to 5.2% (IMF, 2008, 2009).

2. To illustrate, suppose prices of country's export go up, but the amount exported remains the same. If the increase in domestic prices of consumption and investment goods is less than that in export prices, there would be an increase in the country's GDP both directly and through additional consumption demand arising therefrom.
3. The reason, the perceptive reader must have realized, is that in the case of such exports the leakage due to their related imports occurs in the very first round of the additional income generated (through exports). Hence the foreign trade multiplier operates on exports less export-related imports.
4. Curiously enough, the growth jumped to 14.7% in the third quarter of 2007-08., just when the global financial crisis had broken out.
5. Note that investment and export constitute major sources of demand for industrial goods.

References

Aiyar, Swaminathan, S. Anklesaria: *The Economic Times* 25 March 2009, GDP Growth: Closer to 3.5% than 5.3%.

Acharya, Shankar (2008): "Tottering BRICs?", *Business Standard*, Vol. XXXIV, No. 270, December 25.

Aiyar, S. Anklesaria (2009): "Beware: Recession may be Hayekian" , *The Economic Times*, January 28.

Jain, Sunil (2009): "Barack's Burden", *The Business Standard*, Vol. XXXIV, No. 304, January 29, 2009.

Kumar, Nagesh: "Mitigating Global Financial Crisis", *The Economic Times*, July 3, 2009.

Lal, Deepak (2009): "A Hayekian Recession with Fisherian Consequences."

Mallya, M.D. (2009): Statement at the 13th Annual General Meeting of Shareholders at Vadodara, 2nd July, 2009.

Mohan, T.T. Ram (2009): "The Impact of the Crisis on the Indian Economy" , *Economic and Political Weekly*, Vol. XLIV, No. 13, March 28, 2009.

Rakshit, Mihir (2009): "India Amidst the Global Crisis", *Economic and Political Weekly*, Vol. XLIV, No. 13, March 28, 2009, pp. 99-100.

Samuelson, Robert J.: Washington Post-Writers Group, 2009, *The Economic Times*, 30 January, 2009.

Singhal, Arvind (2009): "The Job Recession", *The Business Standard*, Vol. XXXIV, No. 304, January 29, 2009.

The Business Standard, March 31, Kolkata.

The Aftermath of Financial Crisis, NBER, Working Paper No. 14656.

Thomson, Lisa Mary (2008): "The Line of Fire", *The Economic Times*, December 7, 2008.

Recent Global Economic Crisis: Outsourcing and India

Abhay Narayan Rai, Rakesh Kumar Singh and Manmohan Krishna

Most countries of the globe are facing recessionary tendencies at present. Although the present slow down is not comparable to the great depression of 1930's in magnitude and geographical penetration, yet all indicators suggest that recession is deep and widespread. Indian economy is also facing severe impact in terms of slowing down of GDP growth, reduction in employment and more importantly negative export growth especially in the sector of IT enabled services. The present paper tries to analyze the causes and impact of present recession in Indian reference and based on these finding makes suggestions to the policy-makers as to how the adverse effects of global recession could be minimized? The paper is divided into four parts. In Part-I, detailed analysis of present crisis and its causes are presented. In Part-II, causes of outsourcing and its impact for developed and developing countries with reference to India are presented in Part-III. Impact of global recession and its impact on outsourcing on Indian IT enabled services is studied. In Part-IV, based on the findings of Part-III certain conclusions are drawn and policy recommendations are made.

ECONOMIC CRISIS—HISTORY, CAUSES AND SIGNIFICANCE

The financial crisis, which is now a full-fledged global recession cannot be attributed to only one cause. In fact every economic crisis or problem is such that its causes can not be isolated. The present crisis is also due to various factors related not only to financial sector but also to macroeconomic management of some important countries. The famous economist J.M. Keynes in dealing the depression of 1930's quoted 'Lack of effective demand' as the major cause of it and suggested ways and means mostly related with financial expansion which in turn would create money illusion, that would enhance aggregate demand and effective demand which in turn would lead to higher monetary investment and because of large scale unemployment monetary investment world automatically turn into real investment, higher employment, higher income and a near full employment equilibrium. This short-term, specific circumstance model has been used by different countries in deferent circumstances and each time it has resulted in severe economic crisis. Increasing effective demand may prove useful in short-run in generating aggregate demand which may lead to recovery in a country but large financial expansion or huge fiscal deficits if practiced for long periods create a bubble, which must burst and generally results in recession. Moreover, the present financial system is much different from Keynesian times. Financial institutions and instruments have been completely revolutionized in 21st century. Now Government do not have the same level of control and domination in financial sector as was available in Keynesian era. Thus, it can easily be concluded that Keynesian policy prescriptions need to be revised from time to time with additional information, which one receives after every recessionary period. The present crisis also has its genesis in Keynesian theory where large fiscal deficits and financial expansion was done to generate effective demand and earn huge profits. Several causes may be attributed to present crisis. Some of the important causes are given below.

Planners and entrepreneurs in search of ever growing (mirage) economy opted for huge expansion in economic activities, which was not consistent with actual growth in output of goods and services. This lead to large current account deficits, especially in U.S*, U.K. and Australia. (Table 1).

TABLE 1

Balance of Current A/C of Few Major Countries of the World

Country	*Years*		
	1990	*2002*	*2007*
United States	-78,960	-480,859	-738,641
United Kingdom	-38,811	-14,414	-115,243
Australia	-15,950	-17,264	-56,783
China	11,997	35,422	249,866
Germany	44,674	46,586	150,746
Japan	44,078	112,447	210,490
India	-7,036	4,656	-9,415

Source: World Development Reports (World Bank)—2004, 2008.

Central banks of different countries also did not focus their attention at appropriate policies because most of world was being managed by market friendly policies, i.e. the policy of least interference in economic activities.(3) At certain places central banks were too much obsessed by the objective of price stability and adequate liquidity that it did not oversee the risk involved with it. There were too many financial instruments having different characteristics. Banks (commercial and central) either intentionally or due to lack of skill could not simply understand the complexity of these instruments. Managers of financial system and even regulators were quite puzzled by the behaviour of the market and actually did not respond to whatever weaknesses the system had. Some economies especially the Chinese, German and Japanese had surplus in saving and BOP (domestic savings could not be invested domestically and exports were greater than imports for quite long period) which in turn resulted in huge foreign exchange reserves (as shown in the Table 1). This lead to imbalances in saving and investment as well as exports and imports at global level. There was only one currency in which most global reserves were held, i.e. US $ and similarly US was considered to be most important economy which is looked at for generating effective demand. So much dependence on one economy for both creation of aggregate demand and for global liquidity has more adversities than positives. It can be concluded that there cannot be a single reason attributed to the crisis.

As per the immediate causes of bursting the bubble is concerned, the credit goes to US economy as was to case of the great depression of 1930s. But unlike the depression of 1930's whose impact fell more on Europe than other economies, the impact of this recession was more on U.S. than other economies of Europe or Asia. The crisis began when the U.S. financial companies led by business professionals started thinking big. In search of excessive profits first the loans will be given to one and all for generating greater demand in various sectors. When there were payment failures these loans were sold to other financial companies through other derivatives and this phenomenon had cascading effect. These financial planners taking political and media support created funds and bonds which were not matched or balanced by growth of real output. Based on information asymmetry the government and the public believed that US economy had entered a phase of boom. There were many warning signals but were ignored not in US alone but by the investors of funds from foreign countries as well. Thus the model developed by financial manager which distributed credit risk to all those who participated in it due to excessive greed resulted in building of a bubble that had to burst. Had this not been sub-prime lending business it could have been some others sector or business. Like every other recession this was also caused by both Market failure as well as government failure. Market failed because in the expectation of too high profits too much speculative activities took place and the government failed to regulate probably because of complex behaviour of financial sector which was neither well understood nor anticipated. Financial crisis of US became economic crisis of the world simply because of too much dependence on US economy and the policy of globalization being followed by almost every nation where every economy is deeply integrated with the global economy. The impact of present recession on global economy has been clearly shown in Table 2 and Table 3 which have estimated by IMF and World Bank respectively.

TABLE 2

World Economic Outlook

	Year-wise Status		
Country	*2007*	*2008*	*2009*
World Output	5.0	3.9	3.0
Advance Economies	2.6	1.5	0.5
Euro Area	2.6	1.3	0.2
Emerging and Developing Economies	8.0	6.9	6.1

Source: World Economic Outlook 2008 (IMF).

OUTSOURCING: RATIONALE AND SIGNIFICANCE

A rational consumer would always like to purchase the good quality commodity at cheapest rates. He does not care whether it is produced by domestic industry or has been imported. Similarly, a producer would like to produce goods at lowest cost he does not care that resources are domestic or foreign. Similarly, a factor would settle in an occupation where the rewards are maximum. Thus, economic theory and practice believes in the freedom of consumption, production and employment. However, nation states factors among the countries. However, individuals and institutions in quest of better quality, lower price and high profits move across nations. International trade is the first option. "International Trade is an alternative to movement of factors of production," wrote Bertil

TABLE 3

Outsourcing: Rationale and Significance

Country	*2006*	*2007*	*2008*	*2009*	*2010*
Euro Countries	2.9	2.6	1.1	-0.6	1.6
USA	2.8	2.0	1.4	-0.5	2.0
Japan	2.4	2.1	0.5	-0.1	1.5
Brazil	3.8	5.4	5.2	2.8	4.6
Russia	7.4	8.1	6.0	3.0	5.0
India	9.7	9.0	6.3	5.8	7.2
China	11.6	11.9	9.4	7.5	8.5

Source: World Bank.

Ohlin in 1930s. If factors are not allowed to move out of the country, then free movement of the goods and services will lead to factor prices being equated all over the world because each country would produce and export the good in which it has abundant resources and import in which its resources are scarce. But this could happen only when the movement of goods and services is free. Unfortunately, that is not, so other methods of trade are adopted. Movement of capital and technology via aid, loan and investment, labour migration and Outsourcing are examples of such indirect trade. A country having large capital if does not find enough profitable avenues to invest, they capitalists in search of more profits move beyond the country frontiers and invest or lend to capital scarce people and country. Various kinds of loans and investments are being made by capital rich developed countries. But the movement of labour is restricted by toughening the migration laws. But this did force labour abundant countries search other systems because trade is a bilateral affair. Every country has to export if it wants to import. China was the first developing country which using appropriate (labour intensive yet efficient) technology started competing with machine made goods of developed countries. By the last decade of 20th century China out competed the U.S and the E.U. in most manufactured goods. When the European and US Companies could not compete with China and some other Asian countries they opted for a new process, which in general term, is addressed as **"Outsourcing"**.

The term outsourcing is very wide in use and scope but it generally refers to a situation where any industry or corporation gets semi manufactured, intermediate goods or certain processes being performed at a place which is out side its main premises. The outsourcing can be 'inshore and offshore' depending upon the location of main producer and its subsidiaries. In fact, Outsourcing is not a new process but its scale and diversity in various fields is new. Outsourcing earlier was done to take advantage of skills and minerals of poor nations. The larger MNC's used to open their workshop, or hire local people to take advantage of low cost minerals or skills of developing nations in as early as 18th century. Most of the petrol refineries of Arab nation were owned by British or other people of developed world. New outsourcing process is used to take advantages of low wages of poor nations. The method and scope has changed only because of development in science and technology. There are two major ways of outsourcing utilized by big companies at present, first is to open an industry or workshop in a poor country employing local people (which may be semi skilled or highly skilled) to produce intermediate goods. second is when a whole process or semi finished products are outsourced, i.e. the production house of the developing countries own and produce goods to the final requirements of large industries. So the companies of developed nations use latest capital intensive technology and add it with cheap labour to reduce the cost of production for the race to bottoms. In this case labour remains where it is (no migration is required) and its produce is exported. This method may not look like 'International trade' in a 'Text book fashion' but actually is export of labour without migration. It leads to a win-win situation for all. Producers reduce their cost by increased efficiency and productivity (producers equilibrium is attained) consumers get commodity at lower price (consumers equilibrium is attained) and enough jobs are created in poor countries at no extra Government Burden (Social welfare is attained). So the system is Pareto Optimal at global level.

However, certain countries have started opposing this method. They have opposed the strategy of outsourcing by big industries/companies. The arguments they provide are narrow, shallow and weak as most of the arguments are in favour of protection. For example: *Argument (1):* Domestic employment is reduced. In principles of economics if a low cost input replaces a high cost input it leads to lowering of cost, increased productivity, production, consumption and social welfare. This is trade creation *Argument (2):* Gains are unevenly distributed, i.e. labour abundant countries would gain. This is a myth because by employing cheap labour these industries remain competitive and expand their business. They only outsource low end labour intensive services thus there is no significant loss of employment. Many surveys have proved this. Moreover these nations are happy when capital moves from them and earns profit, dividend and interest. Is this distribution not uneven? *Argument (3):* In trade goods and services move from one country to another while in outsourcing it does not. What happens trade of such services where no factor moves and yet revenues take place as in case of cross border consumption. *Argument (4):* This trade is not based on comparative advantage. Why not? Labour is relatively cheap in comparison to capital in poor countries. People with same level of skill are available at much lower wages in poor counties which is exported by developing countries and capital goods are imported by developing countries which are comparatively costlier. All other arguments are similarly farcical to say the least. In fact every argument in favour of protection is practiced only in cases where domestic resources are inferior and inefficient. Every country preaches fair trade if domestic resources are superior.

RECESSION AND THE INDIAN ECONOMY

The present recession had adverse impacts on Indian economy despite Indian macroeconomic policies and structure being very sound. The regulatory policies adopted by India are very sound* but once a country opts for globalization it is bound to be affected by economic events held outside its geographical area. What can be done is that these effects could be minimized. The impact on Indian economy was mainly from two fronts: (1) Financial sector where many Indian banks and financial institution held stakes with International financial institutions. In globalization, the financial sector can not be insulated, against such happening. (2) The export sector where the reduced demand of Indian goods effected its growth adversely. (The effect of present global economic crisis on various sectors of Indian economy has been shown in Table 4).

In this sector major effect was felt in IT enabled services. IT sector in fact was the fastest growing sector of Indian economy. According to Nasscom-Delloitte study the contribution of IT sector in India's G.D.P. was 0.04% in 1988. It rose to 1.2% in 1998 and by 2006 it rose to 5.0%. In field of employment the growth was not spectacular, yet from .4 million in 1980 it rose to 1.64 million by 2006. In respect to imports this sector registered fastest growth rate since 21st century began. The IT enabled services were well diversified at the down of 21st century in terms of both geographical penetration and portfolio. In the beginning India was a supplier of labour intensive low

TABLE 4

	2003-04	2004-05	2005-06	2006-07	2007-08	2008-09
Agriculture, forestry & fishing	10.0	0.0	5.8	4.0	4.9	1.6
Mining & quarrying	3.1	8.2	4.9	8.8	3.3	3.6
Manufacturing	6.6	8.7	9.1	11.8	8.2	2.4
Electricity, gas & supply	4.8	7.9	5.1	5.3	5.3	3.4
Construction	12.0	16.1	16.2	11.8	10.1	7.2
Trade, hotels & restaurants	10.1	7.7	10.3	10.4	10.1	*
Transport, storage & communication	15.3	15.6	14.9	16.3	15.5	*
Financing, insurance, real estate & business services	5.6	8.7	11.4	13.8	11.7	7.8
Community, social & personal services	5.4	6.8	7.1	5.7	6.8	13.1
Total GDP at factor cost	8.5	7.5	9.5	9.7	9.0	6.7

Source: Economic Survey, 2008-09.

end services such as data entry, payroll making, call centers but since 2004 India has become a reliable supplier of high end services such as Customs Application, Development and Maintenance (C.A.D.M.), System Integration, Infrastructure Management and Consultancy, etc. India is all set to enter more mature areas of K.P.O., T.P.O. and legal processing on both 'On site' as well as 'Off site' services. The present recession has acted as a big hindrance in the progress of IT sector. In fact now-a-days business activity is less affected by performance or efficiency and more by future expectation. As the news of global slowdown started appearing various agencies started projecting growth slowdown in ITes. Nasscom Dioltte survey announced that global IT sector would grow at 3.7% in 2008 and 2.9% in 2009 while it was growing at above 5% between 2002 to 2007. This along with some IT-based industries and companies of U.S. (where India export 61% of total IT services) forced Indian companies to relook into their future strategy. During the period Feb. 2007-08 the value of Indian rupee also appreciated *vis-à-vis* US $ which naturally reduced the level of profit of large Indian IT exporters such as TCS, Infosys, Satyam, HCL, Wipro. So the financial planners of these companies started taking steps to meet the slowdown. The first step was wage freeze along with freeze in new appointments. Some companies started sacking their employees and those who had been selected by companies were asked to wait. If one looks at the profits earned in Q1, Q2, Q3 of 2008 of Infosys, TCS or any other company except Satyam, they have increased regularly. Their business has also expanded during this period. Infact there are large domestic projects in queue for these companies such as ERP Railway project, BSNL system integration project, private telecom industry project, banks and other financial institutional project. The estimated cost of these projects is more than 100 US billion $ which is almost twice the amount of their present turnover. But as said earlier the forecasts by any Tom, Dick and Harry are more important these days than actual performance. The media hypes can generate 300% price rise in any commodity these days. Infact the information asymmetry leads to high speculative activities and financial adverse make profit while the consumer and society suffers. Thus the present recession forced various IT companies to shelve various infrastructures, research programmes which could have put India much ahead of its competitors in the field of IT exports and because of an estimate job loss around 1.71 lakh in IT area. The backward linkage industry also suffered and propelled the recessionary trends in the whole economy.

FINDINGS AND CONCLUSIONS

It is certain that whenever a country integrates with the rest of the world events and incidents outside its main land will have effect on it. Indian economy is also effected by financial/ economic crisis but Indian economy did not plunge into economic recession as most of the European economies, U.S. and Japan have. In India export growth has been negative, employment of opportunities have also declined but the major indicators of recession are absent, yield curve is not inverse although it has been flat for some time. Net employment has grown, i.e. in some sectors people have lost job but overall employment has grown during this period. GDP never saw a negative growth rate in any quarter. Annual GDP growth has been maintained well above 5% although the growth rate has declined from a high 8 to 9% to moderate 5% to 6%. . The rate of capital formation and investment has not been effected. There have been losses in valuation in both real estate sector and sensex but they are more dependent on hopes and expectation (Infact India and China are the two countries because of whom the world GDP has not been negative). Otherwise, the growth in manufacturing, construction and even in services has been maintained. The reason for such resilience is 'balance'. Infact all economic theories are based on the concept of Balance. Balance between aggregate demand and aggregate supply, imports and exports, government revenue and expenditure. Even the environmental balance is necessary for global health. Minor variations in different circumstances can be corrected but huge imbalances are bound to create crisis.

But maintaining balance at domestic level does not insulate any economy from foreign pressures and happenings, e.g. if a country has balance of trade (Exports match Imports) and recession takes place in those economies where domestic exports are directed, then exports decline. This incident will affect the whole of the economy because through decline in exports the employment, income and Aggregate demand would be reduced. Balance of Trade would become adverse and so protective measures would be adopted and thus a whole chain of reactions will set in place. This is what actually happened to India. Its Software exports were hurt because they were largely counteracted to U.S. and then it effected the whole set of economic activities. The only saving grace for Indian economy was its vibrant domestic sector which created enough demand and restrained the pace of recession.

Globalization is a reality and no country can live without it at present. So what one has to plan is reap maximum benefit when going is good and minimize loses in adverse whether. For this long-run foreign trade and foreign capital policies have to be made because these are the two sectors in which a country is directly and significantly related with the rest of the world. In trade a strategic planning required. There shall be no doubt in any ones mind that in 20th century trade is not based on Natural comparative advantage but on attained comparative advantage. Japan Automobile and electronic Industry are famous examples in which Japan strategically invested and out competed the world leader U.S.A. Similarly China has become the largest manufacturing exporters of a large no. of commodities. Porter in his diamond edge model competitive advantage theory demonstrates as to how trade is based on competitive adventives and not on comparative advantage. Gone are the days when a country could depend on 'Vent for Surplus'. Indian Software Industry is also one of the examples of attained comparative advantage but research and investment in the Industry must continue to maintain the competitive advantage. But no country should put all eggs in one basket so many areas especially of traditional art and skills in which India should devoted. Diversification is the key word both in terms of Geographical penetration and export structure. As the funds are not abundant, areas should be selected on the priority basis and then leading sectors could be created who will pull back the others. The more diversified is the portfolio the grater is the chance of fighting a recession.

Foreign capital is an important source of investment and modern technology but too much dependence on it creates more problems then it solves. At present, Indian economy need not worry about this as foreign Capital accounts for 8% of total Capital investment in India and out of it only 10% is of short-term nature. Indian policy-makers must keep the examples of East Asia and Mexico before rushing into any nasty decision of opting full Capital Account convertibility especially in the case of large balance of trade deficits.

References

Global Economic Prospect, 2009, World Bank.

B. Ohlin, Inter-regional And International Trade, Cambridge, Mass.

C.L. Mann, Perspectives on the US Current Account Deficit and Sustainability, *Journal Of Economic Perspectives*, Summer 2002.

D. Salvatore, International Economics, 8th ed., John Wiley & Sons (Asia) Pvt. Ltd., 2004.

D.A. Irvin, Free Trade Under Fire, Princeton University Press, 2001.

G.M.B. Tootel, Globalization And US Inflation, Federal Reserve Bank of Boston, *New England Economic Review*, July-Aug 1998.

Harvard University Press, 1983.

J.N. Bhagwati, Free Trade Today, Princeton University Press, 2002.

J.N. Bhagwati, Dependence and Interdependence, Cambridge Mass: MIT Press, 1985.

J.M. Keynes, The General Theory of Employment, Interest and Money, London: Macmillan, 1936.

J.N. Bhagwati, Protectionism, Cambridge Mass: MIT Press, 1988.

K.A. Elliot, Can Labour Standards Improve Globalization?, Washington, DC, International Economic Institute, 2001.

K.G. Klettzer, Jobloss from Imports: Measuring the Costs, Washinton, DC, International Economic Institute, 2001.

P. Krugman, Has the Adjustment Process Worked?, Washinton, DC, International Economic Institute, 1991.

P.R. Krugman, Is Free Trade Passe?, *Journal of Economic Perspectives*, 1987.

Rahees Singh, World Under Economic Crisis, *Yojana* (Hindi), Jan. 2009.

Rahees Singh, Worrying on slowdown of World Economy, *Yojana* (Hindi), Aug. 2009.

Global Financial Crisis: Response to RBI as a National Regulator

BHAVIK M. PANCHASARA AND HEENA S. BHARADIYA

INTRODUCTION

The global financial crisis has called into question several fundamental assumptions and beliefs governing economic resilience and financial stability. What started off as turmoil in the financial sector of the advanced economies has snowballed into the deepest and most widespread financial and economic crisis of the last 60 years? With all the advanced economies in a synchronized recession, global GDP is projected to contract for the first time since the World War II, anywhere between 0.5 and 1.0 per cent, according to the March 2009 forecast of the International Monetary Fund (IMF). The emerging market economies are faced with decelerating growth rates. The World Trade Organization (WTO) has forecast that global trade volume will contract by 9.0% in 2009. Governments and central banks around the world have responded to the crisis through both conventional and unconventional fiscal and monetary measures. Indian authorities have also responded with fiscal and monetary policy measures.

IMPACT OF GLOBAL CRISIS ON INDIA

The direct effect of the global financial crisis on the Indian banking and financial system was almost negligible, thanks to the limited exposure to riskier assets and derivatives. The relatively low presence of foreign banks also minimized the impact on the domestic economy. However, the crisis did have knock on effects on the country, broadly, in three ways. First, the reduction in foreign equity flows—especially FII flows - impacted the capital and forex markets and the availability of funds from these markets to domestic businesses; second, the shrinking of credit markets overseas had the impact of tightening access to overseas lines of credit including trade credit for banks and corporate. Both these factors led to pressure on credit and liquidity in the domestic markets with the knock on effects, and third, the fall in global trade and output had impact on consumption and investment demand. The cumulative impact of all this was a slowing down of output and employment. Despite the slowing down, India is still the second fastest growing economy in the world.

MODERATION IN GROWTH RATE

After clocking an average of 9.4% during three successive years from 2005-06 to 2007-08, the growth rate of real GDP slowed down to 6.7% (revised estimates) in 2008-09. Industrial production grew by 2.6% as compared with 7.4% in the previous year. In the half year ended March 2009, imports fell by 12.2% and exports fell by 20.0%.

The trade deficit widened from $88.5 billion in 2007-08 to $119.1 billion in 2008-09. Current account deficit increased from $17.0 billion in 2007-08 to $29.8 billion in 2008-09. Net capital inflows at US $ 9.1 billion (0.8% of GDP) were much lower in 2008-09 as compared with US $108.0 billion (9.2% of GDP) during the previous year, mainly due to net outflows under portfolio investment, banking capital and short-term trade credit. As per the estimate made by the RBI in its Annual Policy announced on April 21, 2009, GDP is expected to grow by 6% in 2009-10.

MULTIDIMENSIONAL ROLES OF THE RBI

The RBI is entrusted with several functions, one of the most important one being the monetary authority of the country. As monetary authority, the RBI has as its objectives price stability, growth and financial stability. The weight and emphasis accorded to each of these objectives would vary depending on the overall macroeconomic conditions. In addition to its role as monetary authority, the RBI has responsibilities for forex management and Government domestic debt management—both national and sub-national. It is also the banking regulator—it regulates commercial banks, cooperative banks (both rural and urban), financial institutions and non-banking financial companies. It has a developmental role to ensure inclusive growth—thus, policies on rural credit, SME and financial inclusion are an integral part of its functions.

RBI'S RESPONSE AS MONETARY AUTHORITY

Till August 2008, the RBI followed a tight monetary stance in view of the inflationary pressures arising from crude, commodity and food prices. In mid-September 2008, severe disruptions of international money markets, sharp declines in stock markets across the globe and extreme investor aversion brought pressures on the domestic money and forex markets. The RBI responded by selling dollars consistent with its policy objective of maintaining orderly conditions in the foreign exchange market.

Simultaneously, it started addressing the liquidity pressures through a variety of measures. A second repo auction in the day under the Liquidity Adjustment Facility (LAF) was also re-introduced in September 2008. The repo rate was cut in stages from 9% in October 2008 to the current rate of 4.75%. The reverse repo rate was brought down from 6 per cent to 3.25%. The cash reserve ratio which was 9% in October 2008 has been brought down to 5%. To overcome the problem of availability of collateral of Government securities for availing of LAF, a special refinance facility was introduced in October 2008 to enable banks to get refinance from the RBI against a declaration of having extended *bonafide* commercial loans, under a pre-existing provision of the Reserve Bank Act for a maximum period of 90 days. The statutory liquidity ratio requiring banks to keep 25% of their liabilities in government securities was reduced to 24%. These actions of the RBI since mid-September 2008 resulted in augmentation of actual/potential liquidity of nearly $50 billion. (Table 1)

TABLE I

Actual/Potential Release of Primary Liquidity—since Mid-September 2008

(Rs. Crore)

	Measure Facility	*Amount*
1.	CRR Reduction	1,60,000
2.	Unwinding/Buyback/De -sequester ing of MSS Securities	97,781
3.	Term Repo Facility	60,000
4.	Increase in Export Credit Refinance	25,512
5.	Special Refinance Facility for SCBs (Non -RRBs)	38,500
6.	Refinance Facility for SIDBI/NHB/EXIM Bank	16,000
7.	Liquidity Facility for NBFCs through SPV	25,000*
Total (1 to 7)		**4,22,793**
Memo: Statutory Liquidity Ratio (SLR) Reduction		40,000

* Includes an option of Rs. 5,000 crore.

FINANCIAL STABILITY OBJECTIVE—RBI's RESPONSE

The immediate result of tightening of the money and credit markets in October 2008 created demands on banks that were already expanding credit well beyond the resources raised from the public by way of deposits. Companies which were substituting overseas credit and capital market sources with bank funds started withdrawing funds parked with mutual funds and utilizing their undrawn limits with banks. Some of the companies that had issued commercial paper in the market—especially the real estate companies and the non-banking companies—found it difficult to roll over the maturing paper. The Commercial Paper and Certificates of Deposit markets became illiquid and mutual funds started facing severe redemption pressures. Hence, in the interest of maintaining financial stability, the RBI instituted a 14-day special repo facility for a notified amount of about $4 billion to alleviate liquidity stress faced by mutual funds, and banks were allowed temporary use of Statutory Liquidity Ratio (SLR) securities for collateral purposes for an additional 0.5 per cent of Net Demand and Time Liabilities exclusively for this. Subsequently, this facility was extended for non-banking finance companies (NBFCs) and later to housing finance companies (HFCs) as well. The relaxation in the maintenance of the SLR was enhanced to the extent of up to 1.5 per cent of their NDTL. (Table 2)

TABLE 2

Interest Rates—Monthly Average

(Per cent)

Segment Instrument	*March 2008*	*October 2008*	*January 2009*	*March 2009*	*June 2009*
Call Money	7.37	9.90	4.18	4.17	3.25
Commercial Paper	10.38	14.17	9.48	9.79	6.06*
Certificates of Deposit	10.00	10.00	7.33	8.61	3.70
91-day Treasury Bills	7.33	7.44	4.69	4.77	3.22
10-year Government Security	7.69	7.80	5.82	6.57	6.83

*Relates to May 2009.

In order to curtail leveraging, commercial banks, all-India term lending and refinancing institutions were not allowed to lend against or buy back CDs held by mutual funds. This restriction was relaxed in the context of the drying up of liquidity for CDs and CPs. Considering the systemic importance of the NBFC sector, the Government in consultation with the RBI announced setting up of a special purpose vehicle (SPV) that could raise funds from the RBI against Government guaranteed bonds to meet the temporary liquidity constraints of systemically important non-deposit taking non-banking financial companies (NBFCs-ND-SI).

RBI's RESPONSE AS FOREX MANAGER

The RBI assured the markets that it would continue to sell foreign exchange (US $) through agent banks to augment supply in the domestic foreign exchange market or intervene directly to meet any demand-supply gaps, and did so, especially in October 2008. It also provided forex swap facility with a three month tenor, to Indian public and private sector banks having overseas branches or subsidiaries—this acted as a strong comfort to such banks in the context of the drying up of the overseas money markets. Further, for funding the swap facility, banks were allowed to borrow under the LAF for the corresponding tenor at the prevailing repo rate. The forex swap facility of tenor up to three months was extended up to March 31, 2010. The prudential limit on overseas borrowing by banks has been doubled. Taking into account the difficulties faced by exporters, as orders got cancelled and receivables mounted, the RBI extended the period of concessional pre-shipment and post-shipment export credit.

The export credit refinance available to banks from the RBI was also increased. Interest rates on dollar and rupee deposits kept in Indian banks by NRIs are capped by the RBI in order to prevent hot money flows. In order to address the impact of slow down in capital flows, the ceiling rates on these deposits were raised. The ceiling on the interest rates at which companies could raise funds from abroad were increased and the end use restrictions that were placed on the deployment of such funds, to deal with the huge inflows in 2007-08, were restored to the *status quo* position. Systemically important NBFCs that were not otherwise permitted to resort to overseas borrowing were allowed to raise short-term foreign borrowings; housing finance companies were also allowed to access External Commercial Borrowings (ECBs) subject to Reserve Bank approval. Taking advantage of the discount on Foreign Currency Convertible Bonds (FCCBs) issued by Indian companies in overseas markets, they were allowed to prematurely buy back their FCCBs at prevailing discounted rates.

REGULATOR OF BANKS AND NBFCs—RBI's RESPONSE

As indicated earlier, the Indian banking system was not affected by the global crisis and all financial parameters have remained strong with capital adequacy ratio for the system at 13.65% (tier I ratio at 8.95%), return on assets over 1%, non-performing loans around 2% as of March 2009. All commercial banks meet the minimum capital adequacy norm of 9% and throughout the crisis period, inter-bank markets for money, forex and debt have been functioning smoothly.

The impact of the crisis in India, as in many Emerging Market Economies (EMEs), spilled over from the real sector to the financial sector. Industry and businesses, especially the Small and Medium Enterprises (SME) sector had to grapple with a host of problems such as delay in payments of bills from overseas buyers as also domestic buyers affected by the global slowdown; increase in stocks of finished goods; fall in value of inventories, especially raw material, which in many cases were acquired at higher prices such as metal and crude oil-based products; slowing down of capacity expansion due to fall in investment demand; demand compression for employment intensive industries, such as, gems and jewellery, construction and allied activities, textiles, auto and auto components and other export-oriented industries. Hotels and airlines apart from IT also saw fall in demand due to global downturn.

Recognizing that the unexpected and swift turn of events could lead to problems of a spiraling downturn, the RBI took a series of regulatory measures in addition to providing liquidity and special refinance. During the years from 2005-06 onwards, in the context of high growth in bank credit to certain sectors, the RBI had raised the risk weights for these sectors in stages and had also increased the provisioning requirements for standard assets. In November 2008, as a countercyclical measure, the additional risk weights and provisions were withdrawn and restored to previous levels.

The prudential regulations for restructured accounts were modified, as a one-time measure and for a limited period of time in view of the extraordinary external factors, for preserving the economic and productive value of assets which were otherwise viable. The modified regulations were in operation for applications for restructuring received up to March 31, 2009 and restructured packages implemented within 120 days of receipt of application or by June 30, 2009, whichever was earlier.

Banks were, therefore, required to take swift action for detecting weaknesses and putting in place the re-structured packages in order to avail of the benefits in assets classification under the modified prudential regulations. The modifications permitted the restructured accounts to be treated as standard assets provided they were standard on the eve of the crisis, viz., September 1, 2008, even if they had turned non-performing when restructuring had been taken up. This special regulatory treatment for restructured accounts was extended to most cases of second restructuring and for first restructuring of exposures to commercial real estate in view of the sudden downturn. To take care of the problem of restructured accounts that had become unsecured due to loss in the value of inventories, special regulatory treatment for asset classification was permitted if additional provisions were made as prescribed for the unsecured portion. In the case of NBFCs, having regard to their need to raise capital, they were allowed to issue perpetual debt instruments qualifying for capital. They were also allowed further time of one more year to comply with the increased Capital to Risk- Weighted Asset Ratio (CRAR) stipulation of 15% as against the existing requirement of 12%. Risk weight on banks' exposures to NBFCs which had been increased earlier was brought down. The impact of liquidity easing and prudential measures is reflected in the credit growth in the year ended June 2009 at 15.8% against 26.3% in the previous year. Though there was slowing down in the period after October 2008, the credit growth in the period October 2008 to June 2009 clocked annualized rate of 8.9%. The credit growth during November 2008 - May 2009 was higher than average for sectors such as infrastructure, real estate, NBFCs, SMEs, agriculture and certain industries like iron and steel.

EMPLOYMENT INTENSIVE SECTORS—RBI's RESPONSE

Following the announcement in the Union Budget 2008 in February 2008, the commercial banks, cooperative banks and regional rural banks implemented in the period till June 2008, the debt waiver (100% waiver) program for small and marginal farmers and debt relief (25% relief) program for other farmers, covering an estimated 40 million farmers to the extent of nearly Rs. 71,000 crore or $14.5 billion. The RBI took sector-specific measures to alleviate the stress faced by employment intensive sectors such as SMEs, exports and housing. In order to address the problems faced by the MSEs, meetings of the State Level Bankers' Committee were convened almost on a monthly basis in the first half of this year. During these meetings State Governments and banks were sensitized about the need to respond promptly to the credit needs of the sector to ensure that units do not get into distress. The RBI guidelines on restructuring were disseminated at such meetings. The RBI extended special refinance of $1.4 billion to Small Industries Development Bank of India (SIDBI) to enable it to on-lend to banks and financial institutions towards incremental SME loans. Banks were advised to carve out and monitor separate sub-limits of large companies to meet payment obligations to micro and small enterprises. MSME (Refinance) Fund of Rs. 2000 crore ($400 million) was instituted and banks were asked to contribute towards this fund against their shortfall in their lending to the weaker sections as low interest deposits with SIDBI to be used by the latter for providing assistance to the MSME sector.

Considering the knock on effects on the housing sector, and the role of HFCs in providing housing loans, the National Housing Bank (NHB) was made available a refinance limit of $800 million to assist the sector. As in the case of SIDBI, banks were asked to deposit specified amount against the shortfall in their lending to the weaker sections with NHB. Loans to HFCs were made eligible for the special repo window opened for bank lending to mutual funds. HFCs were also allowed to borrow abroad from bilateral and multilateral agencies with prior approval from the RBI. The period of concessional export credit was extended and the entitlement of banks under the export refinance facility from the RBI was enhanced. Export-Import Bank of India (EXIM Bank) was given a special refinance limit of $1 billion as also extended a special forex swap facility as in case of banks with overseas branches.

RBI's RESPONSE AS DEBT MANAGER

To contain the knock on effects of the global slowdown, the Government of India announced three fiscal stimulus packages during December 2008-February 2009. These stimulus packages were in addition to the already announced post-budget expenditure towards farm loan waiver, rural employment guarantee and other social security programs, enhanced pay structure arising from the Sixth Pay Commission, etc. As a result, the net borrowing requirement for 2008-09 increased by nearly 2.5 times the original projection in 2008-09 from 2.08% of GDP to

5.89% of GDP. The Reserve Bank of India's managed the additional borrowings in a non disruptive manner through a combination of measures including unwinding under the market stabilization scheme (MSS), open market operations (OMOs) and easing of monetary conditions. The MSS was introduced in 2004 to help the Reserve Bank sterilise the impact of capital flows when huge accretion to reserves added primary liquidity to the system. Under an agreement entered into between the Government of India (GoI) and the RBI, GoI agreed to issue bills and bonds, the proceeds of which were immobilized with the RBI and thereby the liquidity impact of forex purchase by the RBI realized. The MSS operates symmetrically, and acts as a store of liquidity and hence has the flexibility to smoothen liquidity in the banking system both during episodes of capital inflows and outflows. When capital outflows were experienced in 2008, and the borrowing requirement of Government increased, it was decided to buy back MSS securities while simultaneously issuing new securities under the borrowing program. The agreement between the Reserve Bank and GoI alluded to earlier was amended in February 2009 to allow the funds immobilized under the MSS to be de-sequestered instead of going in for fresh borrowing. So far between March and May this year, cash balances of nearly $8 billion have been de-sequestered. Keeping in view the government market borrowing in 2009-10 as provided in the interim budget, coming on top of a substantial expansion in market borrowing in 2008-09, it was important for the RBI to provide comfort to the market so that the borrowing programme is conducted in a non-disruptive manner. Accordingly, the RBI simultaneously indicated its intention to purchase government securities under OMOs for an indicative amount of Rs. 80,000 crore ($16 billion) during the first half of 2009-10. The distribution method for the primary issuances was also shifted to uniform price auction in view of the uncertain market conditions. Offers of shorter term bonds and benchmark securities have also helped meet investor preference and stabilize yields. The general easing of monetary conditions, in addition to the above measures have also ensured that the additional borrowing needs of the Government do not result in crowding out of credit to the private sector and helped in maintaining stable conditions in the government securities markets.

FACTORS THAT HELPED IN RESPONDING SWIFTLY AND EFFECTIVELY

There are certain factors that enabled the RBI to respond swiftly and effectively to the unfolding crisis. The single most important concern that needed to be addressed in the global crisis was the liquidity issue. The RBI had in its arsenal a variety of instruments to manage liquidity, viz., CRR, SLR, LAF, Refinance, OMO and MSS. Through a judicious combination of all these instruments, the RBI was able to ensure more than adequate liquidity in the system. At the same time it was ensured that the growth in primary liquidity was not excessive. The inherent synergies in its multiple roles enabled the RBI to ensure orderly functioning of money, forex and government securities markets while dealing with capital flows, managing additional government market borrowing and ensuring adequate credit to restore growth momentum.

As regulator and forex manager, the RBI was able to build reserves, calibrate capital controls and take prudential countercyclical measures which could be reversed when the need arose. Both, macro-prudential and micro-prudential policies adopted by the RBI have ensured financial stability and resilience of the banking system The timely prudential measures instituted during the high growth period especially in regard to securitization, additional risk weights and provisioning for specific sectors, measures to curb dependence on borrowed funds, and leveraging by systemically important NBFCs have stood us in good stead. The reserve requirements—both cash and liquidity—acted as natural buffers preventing excessive leverage. While credit expansion by private sector and foreign banks was significantly lower during 2008-09, especially to retail and SME borrowers, public sector banks (covering nearly 70% of banking assets) maintained their credit growth to employment impacting sectors such as SMEs, agriculture, real estate and infrastructure, even as regulatory policies have ensured that prudential norms and financial soundness were not compromised.

CONCLUSION

Going forward, the RBIs policy stance will continue to be to maintain comfortable rupee and forex liquidity positions. The Annual Policy Statement, 2009-10 announced on April 21, 2009 stated the following policy stance:

- Ensure a policy regime that will enable credit expansion at viable rates while preserving credit quality so as to support the return of the economy to a high growth path.
- Continuously monitor the global and domestic conditions and respond swiftly and effectively through policy adjustments as warranted so as to minimize the impact of adverse developments and reinforce the impact of positive developments.
- Maintain a monetary and interest rate regime supportive of price stability and financial stability taking *into account the emerging lessons of the global financial crisis.*

The RBI has been actively engaged in policy action to minimize the impact of the global crisis on India. The policy response of the RBI has helped in keeping India's financial markets functioning in a normal manner and in arresting the growth moderation. The RBI will continue to maintain vigil, monitor domestic and global developments, and take swift and effective action to minimize the impact of the crisis and restore the economy to a high growth path consistent with price and financial stability. Finally, the close coordination and interaction between the Government and the RBI ensured that appropriate package of measures were put in place promptly to deal with the crisis and restore the growth momentum.

References

Economic and Political Weekly.
economictimes.indiatimes.com
Reserve Bank of India.
The Economic Times.

The Impact of the Current Global Financial Crisis on South Asian Countries

CH. PARAMAIAH

The current financial and economic crisis, which is the most severe crisis since World War II, is expected to have a major impact on South Asia by influencing the real and financial sectors. The crisis impacted those countries of region which are commodity exporters. They have been hit hard by the sharp decline in the demand for their commodities and their prices. Compared to any other previous business cycles, the present situation was unavoidable while many reasons led to the collapse on the global level. The crisis started in the advanced economies but the consequences have been felt all over the globe, including in the developing countries. Impact of the crisis can be assessed on different levels and in the different areas.

The objective of this paper is to assess the impact of current global financial crisis on South Asian economies by examining the trends in global and regional output growth rates, key macroeconomic indicators, remittances (coming from migrant workers), foreign direct investments (FDI) and net capital flows. The global output growth is expected to decline in 2009 by 1.3 percent for the first such contraction since the World War II. However, the South Asia economies are set to grow 6.3 percent in 2009 as again 8.4 per cent in 2007 and 6.3 percent in 2008. The slowdown will be particularly notable for India and Pakistan. On a net basis, the total private and official capital flows to the region declined from a record-high $116.5 billion in 2007 to $77 billion in 2008. The contraction was led by a halving of portfolio equity inflows plunging private creditor bond issuance and syndicated bank loans, which contracted by 84 percent and 67 percent, respectively. The huge loss of income from the terms of trade was partially compensated by rising remittances prior to the crisis, but the same did not happened in the crisis period.

INTRODUCTION

The genesis of the current global financial crisis is complex interaction of a number of interrelated forces. Some of these created by the phenomena of market forces, product of market failures and some were the result of incentives created by policy-makers; together they produced a substantial financial peak stage on a global scale. Real short-term interest rates were reduced around the world, following a nearly decade long secular decline in inflation rates, a slowdown in growth at the turn of this decade and subsequent deflation. The current financial crisis can be traced back to the global capitalist crisis that erupted in the late 1970s. It was during this period that the post-war boom started to come to an end and the global economy began to stagnate.

The deregulation process, banks, pension fund companies and mutual funds from across the world were also allowed to begin speculating on currencies, bonds and shares. With this massive expansion of the financial markets, the value of a company's stock became far more important than in the past. Companies wanted their shares to be valued higher to attract investors, like banks and pension funds. To boost share values, most of the biggest companies also borrowed massive amounts of money to buy back their own shares and thereby inflate the prices. Even companies that were traditionally manufacturers restructured their operations to become partial investment vehicles and often borrowed colossal amounts of capital to speculate on financial markets and in real estate.

Impacts of the crisis can be assessed on different levels and in the different areas. The main objective of this paper is to assess the impact of current global financial crisis on South Asians economies by examining the trends in global and regional output growth rates, key macroeconomic indicators, remittances (coming from migrant workers), foreign direct investments (FDI) and net capital flows.

SOURCES OF THE CURRENT FINANCIAL CRISIS

(i) Real Estate Speculation

U.S. real estate markets have experienced dizzying price increases between 1998 and 2005, including Florida, Nevada, New York, Arizona and California. Manufacturers have increased housing starts until there was a surplus of inventory. It led to a downward spiral on prices, higher interest rates and defaulting owners tied to variable mortgages. When we talk about real estate speculation, we believe, among others, about Flipping. Nearly 40% of residential transactions in the United States did not acquire a main property (residence).

(ii) Sub-prime Mortgages

One of the important sources of the current financial crisis is sub-prime mortgage system. How? It is suggested that the products to customers were in some cases depending on the premium payment received by the broker. The sub-prime mortgages are at the heart of the crash of the U.S. financial sector. From 1994 to 2006, the share of these "tools" increased from 5% to 20%. One of the sub-prime instruments was the most popular ARM (interest-only adjustable rate mortgage). According to estimates made in 2004 by a former Fed Governor of the U.S., over 50% of sub-prime loans were made without any guidance from the federal government.

(iii) A Complex Structure of Financial Instruments

The structure of financial instruments has become very complex in US. The leaders of institutions and boards are currently suspected of incompetence, by their ignorance of the risk factors involved in their investment process. The structure of the remuneration of such leaders would also be a source of the current crisis. These instruments allowed investors to buy insurance or protection against a broader range of individual credit risks, such as the default by a home owner or a company. Issuance of asset-backed securities (ABS), collateralized debt obligations (CDOs) and collateralized loan obligations (CLOs), as well as credit default swaps (CDS), expanded on a dramatic scale, particularly from 2005 through to mid-2007. And over this same period, the composition of the assets in ABS, as well as in CDOs and CLOs, shifted to higher credit risk mortgages and loans issued by non-investment grade companies.

(iv) Monetary Policy and Government Policy

Nobel laureate Milton Friedman: "A Monetary History of the United States." It revolutionized thinking on the causes of the Great Depression when published in 1965. The book blamed the Fed for causing the slump. The bank failed to use its full bag of tricks to stop the implosion of the money stock, and turned a bust into calamity by raising rates. Both policies are identified: the monetary policy of Alan Greenspan and the policy of Housing and Urban Development Department (HUD). Schwartz warns against facile comparisons between today's world and the gold standard era. "This is nothing like the Depression. I don't really believe the economy as a whole is going to fall apart. Northern Rock has been the only episode of a bank failure so far," she says.

(v) Consumer Behaviour

The U.S. consumer is also a source of current financial crisis, because of its lack of vision, responsibility and the use of credit feverish. In 2004, the U.S. Fed estimated the total debt of U.S. consumers more than 2 trillion (2000 billion) dollars, **excluding mortgages**. Simply by debts of credit cards, the average American was (before the crisis!) an estimated $9,000 and $13,000 in debt.

(vi) The Absence of Financial Regulations

The rational actions taken by even the strongest financial

institutions to reduce exposure to future losses have caused significant collateral damage to market functioning. The most common failures were in how firms dealt with uncertainty about the scale of losses they would face in a less benign economic and financial environment; the scale of the cushion they built up against that uncertainty; how well they managed the internal tension between risk and reward; and how quickly they moved to mitigate risk as conditions deteriorated.

IMPACT OF THE CRISIS ON SOUTH ASIAN COUNTRIES

The global economy is expected to decline in 2009 by 1.3 percent for the first such contraction since the World War II (Table 1). However, the data reveals significant differences

TABLE I

World and Regional Output Growth Rates (Real GDP)

(Annual percent change)

	Average 1991-2000	*2001*	*2002*	*2003*	*2004*	*2005*	*2006*	*2007*	*2008*	*2009f*	*2010f*	*2014f*
World	3.1	2.2	2.8	3.6	4.9	4.5	5.1	5.2	3.2	-1.3	1.9	4.8
Advanced economies	2.8	1.2	1.6	1.9	3.2	2.6	3.0	2.7	0.9	-3.8	0.0	2.6
Developing economics	3.6	3.8	4.8	6.3	7.5	7.1	8.0	8.3	6.1	1.6	4.0	6.8
Africa	2.4	4.9	6.5	5.5	6.7	5.8	6.1	6.2	5.2	2.0	3.9	5.4
Central and Eastern Europe	2.4	0.0	4.4	4.9	7.3	6.0	6.6	5.4	2.9	-3.7	0.8	4.0
Developing Asia	7.4	5.8	6.9	8.2	8.6	9.0	9.8	10.6	7.7	4.8	6.1	8.8
Middle East	4.0	2.6	3.8	7.0	6.0	5.8	5.7	6.3	5.9	2.5	3.5	4.5
Western Hemisphere	3.3	0.7	0.6	2.2	6.0	4.7	5.7	5.7	4.2	-1.5	1.6	4.3
European Union	2.2	2.1	1.4	1.5	2.6	2.2	3.4	3.1	1.1	-4.0	-0.3	2.6
SOUTH ASIA												
Afghanistan	...	...	...	15.1	8.8	16.1	8.2	12.1	3.4	9.0	7.0	9.2
Bangladesh	4.9	4.8	4.8	5.8	6.1	6.3	6.5	6.3	5.6	5.0	5.4	7.0
Bhutan	5.0	6.8	10.9	7.2	6.8	7.0	8.8	17.9	6.6	5.7	6.6	6.7
India	5.6	3.9	4.6	6.9	7.9	9.2	9.8	9.3	7.3	4.5	5.6	8.0
Maldives	7.5	3.5	6.5	8.5	9.5	-4.5	18.0	7.2	5.7	-1.3	2.9	5.5
Nepal	5.0	5.6	0.1	3.9	4.7	3.1	3.7	3.2	4.7	3.6	3.3	5.5
Pakistan	3.9	2.0	3.2	4.8	7.4	7.7	6.2	6.0	6.0	2.5	3.5	7.0
Sri Lanka	5.2	-1.5	4.0	5.9	5.4	6.2	7.7	6.8	6.0	2.2	3.6	5.5

Note: f – forecasted.

Source: IMF, World Economic Outlook April, 2009.

among countries and different regions. The severely affected regions of the crisis includes emerging Europe, the CIS countries and the newly industrialized Asian economies, each of which is expected to see contractions in GDP in 2009 near or even above five percent.

Some of the regions are expected to do much better, including the emerging market countries of South Asia, Africa and the Middle-East. But there is a wide range of projections even within regions. Most notably, while emerging Asia as a whole is projected to grow by 2.5 percent this year, the developing countries within the region are set to grow at 4.8 percent (Table 1).

The strong performance was led by the economies of South Asia (Figure 1), dominated by India at 9 percent. After a decade of sustained growth India's gross national income (GNI) per capita (using the World Bank Atlas method) now places it with China among the lower middle-income economies. Bangladesh, Pakistan, Sri Lanka in South Asia grew faster than 6 percent before 2007, as did all South Asian economies including Afghanistan, Bhutan, Maldives and Nepal are severely hit by the current financial crisis.

FIGURE 1

Output Growth Rates (Real GDP)

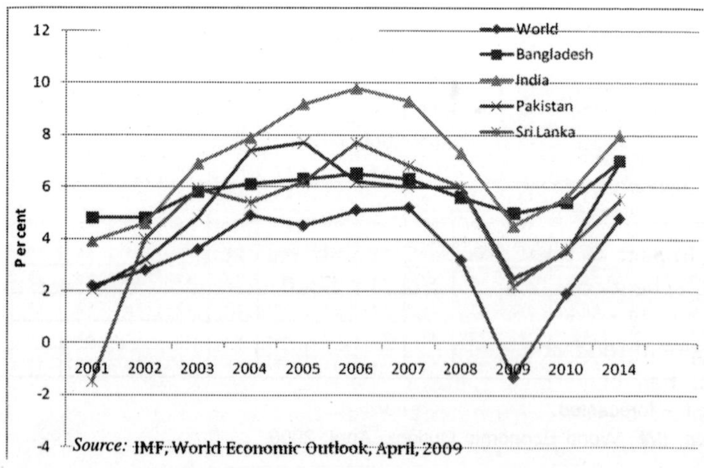

Source: IMF, World Economic Outlook, April, 2009

Although the global crisis did not originate in Asia, and indeed, the direct damage to financial sector in Asia has been much less than in Europe and the US. As a result, GDP growth has dropped sharply across the South Asia region (figure 2).

The global crisis in 2008, GDP growth in South Asia registered a relatively resilient 6.5 percent in 2008, down significantly from the robust 8.4 percent outturn of 2007, on a calendar-year basis a 1.9 percentage point falloff in South Asia's growth (Figure 2). All major economies in the region showed decline in year-on-year growth. Since 1980, South Asia has been on a rising growth path, reaching a peak of 9 percent in 2006. Growth has been on a declining trend since then. The onset of the global financial crisis predicts a significant slowdown in South Asia's growth prospects for 2009-10 (Figure 2). The slowdown will be particularly notable for India and Pakistan.

FIGURE 2

GDP Growth Rates in South Asia

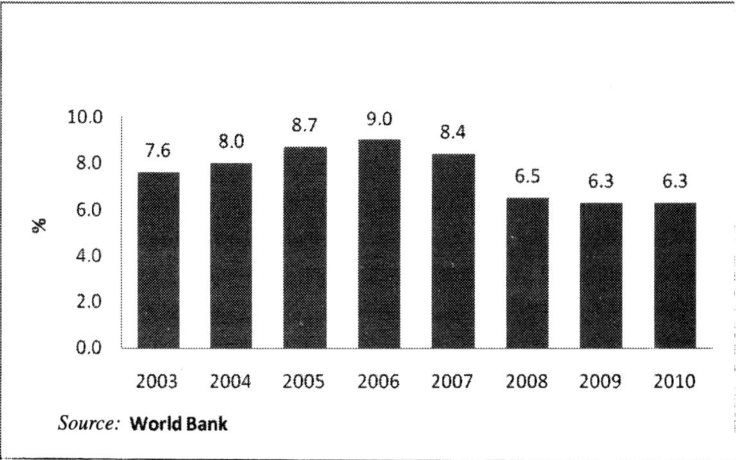

Source: World Bank

The Impact of the Crisis on Economic Indicators

The global financial crisis hit South Asia at a time when it had barely recovered from severe terms of trade shock resulting the global food and fuel price crisis. India, big brother in South Asia, has been facing major challenges owing to the global financial crisis. The immediate effects are stock prices, a net inflow of foreign direct investment, merchandise exports and imports, large reduction of foreign reverses and inflation. As a result, manufacturing production has taken a hit and activities in the organized services sector (housing, construction, IT) are declined very sharply.

TABLE 2

South Asian Countries and Key Macroeconomic Economic Indicators

	2004	2005	2006	2007	2008 e	2009 p	2010 p
Growth rate of merchandise exports (% per year)							
Afghanis tan	-13.2	9.2	0.9	1.3	17.5	-6.1	11.2
Bangladesh	15.9	14.0	21.5	15.8	15.7	14.0	13.0
Bhutan	39.7	34.5	47.2	64.5	-8.5	-12.2	6.7
India	28.5	23.4	22.6	28.9	11.9	-9.1	8.9
Maldives	19.1	-10.7	39.7	1.2	52.6	-	-
Nepal	14.8	11.4	2.6	1.9	12.8	-	-
Pakistan	13.8	16.2	14.9	4.4	16.5	-6.0	2.0
Sri Lanka	12.2	10.2	8.5	11.0	6.5	-22.0	4.6
Growth rate of merchandise imports (% per year)							
Afghanistan	16.1	20.5	10.0	16.2	12.3	-1.2	0.3
Bangladesh	13.0	20.6	12.1	16.6	25.6	18.0	17.0
Bhutan	27.3	75.5	-5.6	15.1	9.1	-17.9	-5.0
India	48.6	32.1	21.4	35.2	15.6	-10.9	11.5
Maldives	36.3	16.1	24.4	18.3	32.3	-	-
Nepal	15.9	12.5	17.8	13.1	26.3	-	-
Pakistan	20.0	37.8	33.3	8.0	31.2	-14.5	-5.0
Sri Lanka	19.9	10.8	15.7	10.2	24.0	-10.8	4.0
Growth rate of value added in serices (% per year)							
Afghanistan	36.6	-	-	-	-		
Bangladesh	5.7	6.4	6.4	6.9	6.7		
Bhutan	10.3	13.3	11.4	7.3	8.7		
India	9.1	10.6	11.2	10.9	9.6		
Maldives	9.7	-8.2	21.3	9.1	6.0		
Nepal	6.8	3.3	5.6	4.5	7.0		
Pakistan	5.8	8.5	6.5	7.6	8.2		
Sri Lanka	6.7	6.4	7.7	7.1	5.6		
Growth rate of value added in industry (% per year)							
Afghanistan	32.4						
Bangladesh	7.6	8.3	9.7	8.4	6.9		
Bhutan	5.8	3.5	5.5	30.6	19.2		
India	10.3	10.2	11.0	8.1	4.8		
Maldives	12.9	2.9	15.8	10.0	6.9		
Nepal	1.4	3.0	4.5	3.9	4.6		
Pakistan	16.3	12.1	4.1	8.0	4.6		
Sri Lanka	5.4	8.0	8.1	7.6	5.9		
Foreign Direct Investment (US $ million)							
Afghanistan	187	271	238	243	300		
Bangladesh	385	800	743	793	650		
Bhutan	3	9	6	73	30		
India	5,987	8,901	21,991	32,327	20,700		
Maldives	15	10	14	15	16		
Nepal	0	2	-6	5	5		
Pakistan	906	1,459	3,450	5,026	5,078		
Sri Lanka	217	234	451	548	313		

Note: e-estimated and p-projected.

Source: Asian Development Outlook, 2009.

The largest economy in region, India's merchandise exports is estimated 11.9 per cent in the year 2008 and it was forecasted -9.1 percent in the year 2009. The weak performance of exports declining year on year since October 2008 becomes a big challenge to maintain macroeconomic management to the government. The items like textile, garments, gems and jewelry, readymade garments, and petroleum products all saw declines. Worsening global crisis in advanced and industrial economies is affecting India's exports of information technology and business services. Asian development outlook reports that India's merchandise export forecasted positively, i.e. 8.9 percent per year for the year 2010. The similar trend can be seen from the Table 2 for all South Asian economies in terms of growth rate of merchandise exports and imports.

Growth rate of value added in services (% per year) are shown in the Table 2 which gives the growth rates of value added in services. In India growth rate of value added in services as % per year was registered 10.9 in 2007 which is sector's share of 55.7 in the same year but it was declined to 9.6 per year in the year 2008. It is also evident from the Table 2 the growth rate of value added in industry (% per year). Table 2 provides the growth rates of value-added in industry and its corresponding share in 2006. This sector comprises manufacturing, mining and quarrying, construction, and utilities.

Gross capital inflows international syndicated bank lending, equity placements, and bond issuance to South Asia had surged in recent years, but collapsed in the aftermath of the crisis. Flows to South Asia fell by 29 percent in 2008, among the sharpest declines posted among developing regions. In the first quarter of 2009, inflows to Bangladesh, Pakistan, and Sri Lanka fell to zero, while in India they were extremely subdued, down 64 percent relative to inflows recorded during the first quarter of 2008. In India, gross inflows were primarily composed of bank loans, with a trickling of equity inflows for the first quarter of 2009. FDI inflows had become a significant source of finance for the rapid rise in regional investment (particularly for corporate capital expenditures in India) and a key driver of regional GDP growth over recent years (see Table 2 above). As a consequence, their reversal has contributed to a sharp falloff in regional investment growth. For example, in India, FDI contributes US $ million 32,327 in the year 2007 it was projected to decline by US $ million 20,700 in 2008. The second largest economy, Pakistan, is much more fragile and facing the most vulnerability in South Asia, the contribution of net exports to growth turned negative aroused by the prices and continued slowdown in textile exports from the country. Growth in services and industry was much less than the targets for year 2008 and industrial growth remained subdued.

TRENDS IN NET CAPITAL FLOWS IN SOUTH ASIA

Net private and official flows to the region were declined from US $ billions 116.5 in the year 2007 to US $ billions 77 in the year 2008. The large loss of income from the terms of trade shock was partially compensated by rising remittances. There has been a tremendous negative impact on the current account balances in South Asia. The rapid deterioration in the current account balance, which from a surplus of US $ billions 12.5 in 2003 to a deficit of $ -20.5 billions in 2007 and it is projected to decline $ -59.1 billions in 2008.

These effects reflect a number factors including: relative magnitude of terms of trade, the differences in compensating growth of remittances, and policy responses. As a result, the reversal has contributed to a sharp falloff in regional investment growth. In India, Foreign Direct Investment inflows fell from 4.6 percent of gross domestic investment in the third quarter of 2008 to only 0.7 percent during the fourth quarter of the same year. In contrast, in Bangladesh, FDI has been relatively resilient. On a net basis, total private and official capital flows to the region contracted by one-third in 2008 from a record-high $116.5 billion in 2007 to $77 billion (Table 3). The contraction was led by a halving of portfolio equity inflows plunging private creditor bond issuance and syndicated bank loans, which contracted 84 percent and 67 percent, respectively. The marked deterioration in investor confidence, collapse in capital flows and plummeting external demand and trade are translating into a significant falloff in industrial production. High frequency data for South Asia (where available) show a decidedly sharp slowdown—if not outright contraction—in economic activity in recent months (World Economic Outlook, April 2009).

Net Capital Flows to South Asia from 2003 to 2008

(US $ billions)

	2003	2004	2005	2006	2007	2008p
Financial Flows						
Current Account Balances	12.5	-1	-12.4	-16.6	-20.5	-59.1
as % of GDP	1.6	-0.1	-1.2	-1.5	-1.5	-3.9
Net private and official flows	13.8	25.4	28.6	76.6	116.5	77
Net private flows (debt + equity)	15.5	24.3	25.4	71.9	112.5	66.5
Net equity flows	13.4	16.8	22.7	33.6	66	65.5
Net FDI inflows	5.4	7.8	10.3	23.2	29.9	47.5
Net portfolio equity inflows	8	9	12.4	10.4	36.1	18
Net debt flows	0.4	8.6	5.9	43	50.5	11.5
Official creditors	-1.7	1.1	3.2	4.7	4	10.5
World Bank	-0.1	2.1	2.3	1.9	1.9	1.4
IMF	-0.1	-0.3	0	-0.1	-0.1	3.2
Other officials	-1.5	-0.7	0.9	2.9	2.2	5.9
Private creditors	2.1	7.5	2.7	38.3	46.5	1
Net medium- and long-term debt flows	1.4	4.9	1.1	20.3	27.2	1.8
Bonds	-3.1	4.1	-2.9	4.3	9.5	1.5
Banks	4.5	1.1	4.1	16	17.7	5.9
Other private	0	-0.3	-0.1	0	0	-5.6
Net short-term debt flows	0.7	2.6	1.6	18	19.3	-0.8
Balancing item a	9.6	3	-10.4	-19.8	5	-44.8
Change in reserves (- = increase)	-35.9	-27.3	-5.8	-40.2	-101	27

Note: p = projection.

Sources: World Bank. All forecasts and databases for the Global Development Finance 2009 Report.

IMPACT ON WORKERS' REMITTANCES

One of the important sources of income and foreign exchange in South Asian economies is remittances. Total remittances to South Asian countries were over US $55,490 million in 2007 and are estimated to have reached more than $73,676 million in 2008 (Table 3).

However, this was apparently temporary phenomenon, because migrant workers who have lost foreign jobs are reported to the returning to their home countries with accumulated saving. Recently, remittance inflow to India has drastically slowdown, it was estimated to declined from $51 billion in 2008 to $51 billion in 2009 (Table 3). The outflow of migrant workers and the inflow of overseas remittances have had a profound impact on the economies of South Asia.

TABLE 3

Workers' Remittances Inflows in South Asian Countries

(US $ million)

	2001	2002	2003	2004	2005	2006	2007	2008[e]	2009[f]	2010[f]
World	146,793	169,546	207,280	236,351	270,504	309,137	380,050	433,086	-	-
South Asia	19,173	24,137	30,366	28,694	33,092	39,615	55,490	73,676	46,000	57,000
Afghanistan		-	-	-	-	-	-	-		
Bangladesh	2,105	2,858	3,192	3,584	4,314	5,428	6,562	8,985	6,700	7,800
Bhutan	-	-	-	-	-	-	-	-		
India	14,273	15,736	20,999	18,750	21,293	25,426	38,666	51,974	30,000	40,000
Maldives	2	2	2	3	2	3	3	3		
Nepal	147	678	771	823	1,212	1,453	1,734	2,735		
Pakistan	1,461	3,554	3,964	3,945	4,280	5,121	5,998	7,032	6,800	6,900
Sri Lanka	1,185	1,309	1,438	1,590	1,991	2,185	2,527	2,947		

Note: e – estimated, f – forecasted.

Source: World Bank staff estimates based on the International Monetary Fund's Balance of Payments Statistics Yearbook 2008.

FIGURE 3

Workers' Remittance Inflow

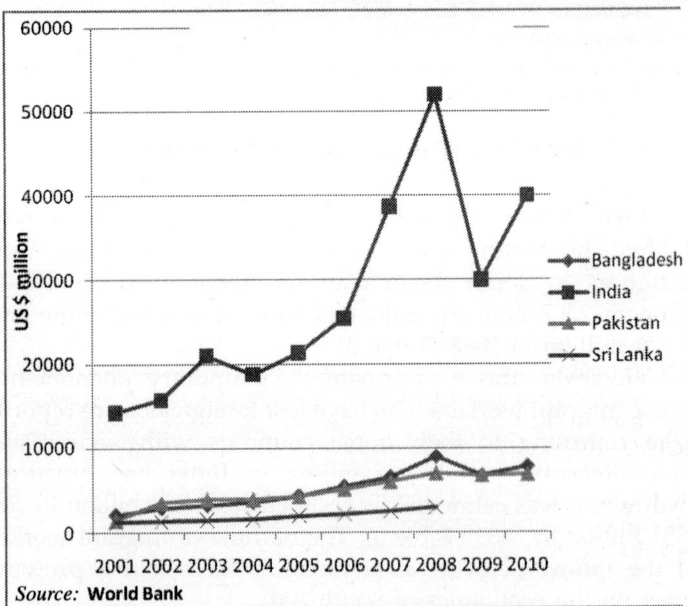

CONCLUSION

During the time of 1930's Great Depression, then US President Roosevelt launched a series of wide ranging programs to prevent the situation at that time to provide employment, reform tax policies and business incentives and stimulate the US economy. Those programmes including building homes, roads, schools, dams and electrical goods, to put the million of the people back to work which helped the country to sophisticate its technology and infrastructure to bring competitiveness in the world. It is time for South Asia to reclaim the debate on its development and take responsibility for it. Today's financial crisis needs the same kind of the determination, leadership and non-conventional measure from South Asia.

References

Asian Development Bank (2009), Asian Development Outlook, Mandaluyong City, Philippines.

IMF (2008), World economic outlook update, rapidly weakening prospects for new policy stimulus. November 6. Washington, DC.

IMF, 2009a, "Lessons of the Financial Crisis for Future Regulation of Financial Institutions and Markets and for Liquidity Management", (Washington: International Monetary Fund.

International Monetary Fund (2009), *World Economic Outlook*, October, Washington, D.C.

Milton Friedman and Anna Jacobson Schwartz (1965), "A Monetary History of the United States, 1867-1960", Princeton University Press, Princeton.

Stiglitz JE (2008), Towards new global economy compact: principle for addressing the current global financial crisis. A communication to the United Nations General Assembly,. New York, United Nations.

UNCTAD (2008), World Investment Report, 2008, Transnational Corporations and the Infrastructure Challenge (New York and Geneva: United Nations), p. 105.

UNCTAD (2008a), World Investment Prospects Survey 2008–2010. New York and Geneva. United Nations Publication.

UNCTAD (2008b), World Investment Report, 2008: Transnational Corporations and the Infrastructure Challenge. New York and Geneva, United Nations Publication.

UNCTAD (2008c), The crisis of a century, UNCTAD Policy Briefs, No. 3, October.

United Nations (2009), Word Economic Situation and Prospects, 2009, New York and Geneva, United Nations Publication, January.

World Bank (2009), Global Economic Prospects, 2009, Commodities at the Cross Road. Washington, DC, January.

10

Impact of Global Meltdown on India's Real Estate

TAPAN KUMAR SHANDILYA AND SURAJ KUMAR

The US financial crisis has caused disturbing impact on the Indian real estate market, which is facing a plunge in real estate demand. The industry is facing crunch of skilled manpower and it remains unorganised, characterised by small players.

Recessions are the result of reduction in the demand of products in the global market. Recession can also be associated with falling prices known as deflation due to lack of demand of products. Again, it could be the result of inflation or a combination of increasing prices and stagnant economic growth in the west.

Recession in the West, specially the United States, is a very bad news for our country. Our companies in India have most outsourcing deals from the US. Even our exports to US have increased over the years. Exports for January have declined by 22 per cent. There is a decline in the employment market due to the recession in the West. There has been a significant drop in the new hiring which is a cause of great concern for us. Some companies have laid-off their employees and there have been cut in promotions, compensation and perks of the employees. Companies in the private sector and government sector are hesitant to take up new projects and they are working on existing projects only. Projections indicate that up to one crore persons could lose their jobs in the correct fiscal ending March. The one crore figure has been compiled by Federation of Indian Export Organisations (FIEO), which says that it has carried out an intensive survey. The textile, garment and handicraft industry are worse effected. Together, they are going to lose four million jobs by April 2009, according to the FIEO survey. There has also been a decline in the tourist inflow lately. The real estate has also a problem of tight liquidity situations, where the developers are finding it hard to raise finances.

IT industries, financial sectors, real estate owners, car industry, investment banking and other industries as well are confronting heavy loss due to the fall down of global economy. Federation of Indian chambers of Commerce and Industry (FICCI) found that faced with the global recession, inventories industries like garment, gems, textiles, chemicals and jewellery had cut production by 10 per cent to 50 per cent.

The development of real estate in India is attributed to the off-shoring and outsourcing businesses, such as high-end technology consultation, call centres and programming houses. The demand from the information technology sector has changed the urban landscape. Several multinational companies (MNCs) continue to move their organisational operations to India to take advantage of lower manpower and other costs. Providing human resources and home at their workplace assumes great significance and therefore, the requirement to create space for people to live and work that in turn, causes the development of other related infrastructure. It has been a predominant trend to set-up the world's best business centres, often campus-style establishments bearing a distinguishing corporate stamp. Some of these locations are so distinctive that they are termed as the 'temples of new India'. It is just an indication of the extent to which the development of real estate has been taking place.

The real estate market in India remains unorganised, fairly fragmented, mostly characterised by small players with a local presence. Traditionally, real estate developers were viewed with an element of skepticism. They were often identified dealing with large amounts of unaccounted money, lacking transparency and would use unscrupulous mean to acquire a variety of regulatory approvals.

The tremendous growth of the real estate sector is attributed to various fundamental factors such as growing economy, growing business needs, etc. However, this boom is restricted to areas such as commercial office space, retail and housing sectors. The impending concerns of this sector namely skill shortage, non-availability of statistics, lack of low cost-affordable housing, lack of sustainability and to meet a future that might have downturn due to oversupply.

The industry is presently facing a major resource crunch—an obvious lack of qualified and skilled people from construction firms, etc. Coupled with this manpower shortage is the shortage of availability of relevant statistics, which has created an ambiguity as to how much construction activity is actually taking place and one can't gauge the demand and supply trends accurately.

The opportunities and issues of affordable, low cost housing in India are mainly related with tremendous shortfall of middle class housing as majority of the developers are involved in developing high class housing. So, there is a dearth of low cost affordable units. The negative version of Indian real estate industry is they have complete disrespect for sustainability' and that the concept of green buildings, proper waste disposal methods and the longevity of the product are often dismissed.

Presently, the impact of recession in US economy has caused mammoth impact on Indian real estate market as well, as it is witnessing the recession. Till now, the real estate industry was a booming industry, which were in pace with information technology (IT) industry. Accordingly, the demand for IT space and commercial spaces has been grown. Also, the high net worth of individual investors has created a very fast pace of demand in Indian real estate sector, which has a very high impact image of investing in India.

As the money was coming in terms on investment in from non-resident Indians as well as private equity funds, the well-known developers and real estate players have grown their portfolio as well many small sized players have also created in

Indian market. It has provided a very high supply of real estate segments either in residential or in commercial or in office space. Special economic zone (SEZ) has also creates a very good opportunities for investors as well as corporate to invest and get benefited from Indian real estate market. So, the booming market has created a niche as modern living and created a very mass employment in Indian segment.

The recent changes, which happened in American market such as bankruptcy of Lehman Brother (one of the oldest financial firms of American market) and sell process of PE firm Merry Lynch by the largest US bank, Bank of America, has created a very fast drops/recession in financial industry and created a crisis in all over US economy. Both of these firms were invested their more part of funds into real estate sector without having the proper analyzing or effect. They also have given the funds for mortgage industry of US, which is currently facing the hurdle of sub-prime lending and have affected many players to bankruptcy.

INVESTMENT VALUE OF REAL ESTATE

Present state of uncertainty and volatility encouraged us to assess the investment performance of various assets in India. The investment performance of an asset is judged by comparing the risk and return associated with it. The greater the amount of risk an investor is willing to take on, the higher the expected return. The reason for this is that investor needs to be compensated for taking on additional risk. With a view to analyse the relative performance of real estate in a group of assets like equity and bond.

CALCULATION OF RISK AND RETURN

'Risk' refers to the chance that the actual return of an investment will be different than what was expected. This includes the possibility of losing some or all of the original investment. Risk is usually measured by calculating the standard deviation of the historical returns of a specific investment. The Sensitive Index (Sensex) of the Mumbai stock exchange has been taken as the broad indicator of the Indian equity market. We have derived the average annual return of the Sensex by annualising the average percentage change of the quarterly price series. Similarly, the average annual risk of the Sensex is calculated as the standard deviation of the annualised percentage change of the quarterly price series. Ten-year government bonds have been taken as the indicator of the bond market in India. Government bonds are also known as gilt-edged securities (risk-free assets) as the government does not go default except under extreme circumstances. The only risk associated with these bonds is the expected changes in future interest rate. Bond price and interest rate are inversely related, while bond yield and interest rate are directly related. If the future interest rate is expected to increase, the current bond price declines and bond yield increases. On the contrary, if the future interest rate is expected to decrease, the current bond price increases resulting in a decline in the return. In this paper, the annual bond return has been derived from the annualised quarterly yield to maturity (YTM) of ten-year government bonds. The annual risk associated with the bond is calculated as the standard deviation of the same annualized quarterly yield series. In this paper, 'real estate' means the physical real estate and not any property share or index traded in stock exchange. We have considered seven cities and three sectors to analyse the risk and return in Indian real estate. The cities are Mumbai, Delhi, Bangalore, Chennai, Kolkata, Hyderabad and Pune, while the sectors are commercial, retail and residential. Instead of combining these three sectors into one as real estate, we have considered them separately to gauge their relative performance vis-à-vis equity and bonds. We have defined 'total quarterly returns' of real estate as the sum of the capitalisation rate (initial yields) and capital appreciation from the quarterly data series2. We have first derived the weighted average total quarterly return for the seven cities mentioned earlier and then derived the annual average return by annualising that data series. Risk for investment in real estate is measured as the standard deviation of the annualized average return weighted for the seven cities.

SHARPE RATIO

The Sharpe ratio is the ratio of excess return (actual

return—risk-free return) with standard deviation of the asset's return3. We have used the average annual YTM of the ten-year government bond as 'risk-free return' and derived excess return as the difference of that with average annual return for a different asset class. The asset with the higher Sharpe ratio gives more return for the same risk. It is evident that for most of the years during 2001-08, investment in all the asset classes in real estate was more efficient than investment in the equity market (Figure 1). Among real estate, the residential asset class provided the best efficiency from 2003 to 2008. Moreover, during 2008, efficiency for investment in equity deteriorated much faster than that for real estate investment. Moreover, the Sharpe ratio for equity and retail in 2008 is much lower than that in 2001-the last slowdown that we had witnessed after the 9/11 attack on the World Trade Center in the US.

FIGURE I

The Sharpe Ratio of Various Assets

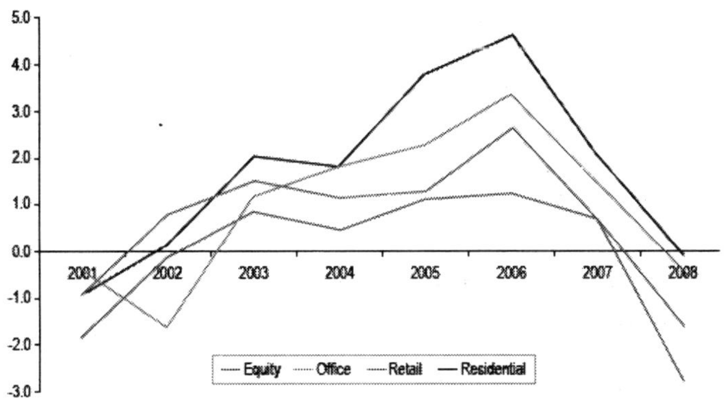

Source: Mumbai Stock Exchange. Real Estate Intelligence Services, Jones Lang LaSalle Mehraj Research.

EFFICIENCY RATIO

While the Sharpe ratio is the ratio of excess return (actual return—risk-free return) with standard deviation of the asset's return, the efficiency ratio is the ratio of the actual return of the asset with its standard deviation. The efficiency ratio or return/

risk ratio tells how much return ('bang') the investor gets per unit of risk ('buck'). The higher the ratio, the more efficiently the investor is 'spending' the risk. If the ratio is less than 1, the investor has expended considerable risk to achieve each point of returns. Investors that seek maximum returns with minimum risk should concentrate on finding assets/portfolios with higher return/risk ratios. We have used this efficiency ratio in our portfolio analysis in the next section. During 2001-04, retail provided an annual average return of 15.8% against 21.3% for equity (Figure 2). However, the efficiency ratio for retail for this period was 2.24 against 0.32 for equity. Clearly, except for bonds,

FIGURE 2

Average Annual Return and Efficiency Ratio: 2001-04

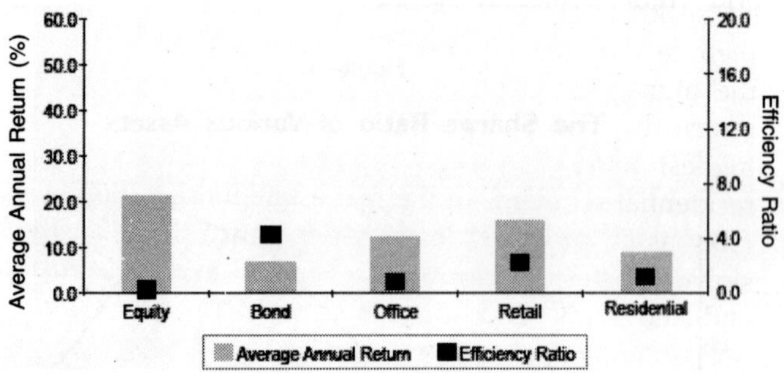

Source: Mumbai Stock Exchange, Reserve Bank of India and Real Estate Intelligence Services.

FIGURE 3

Average Annual Return and Efficiency Ratio: 2005-07

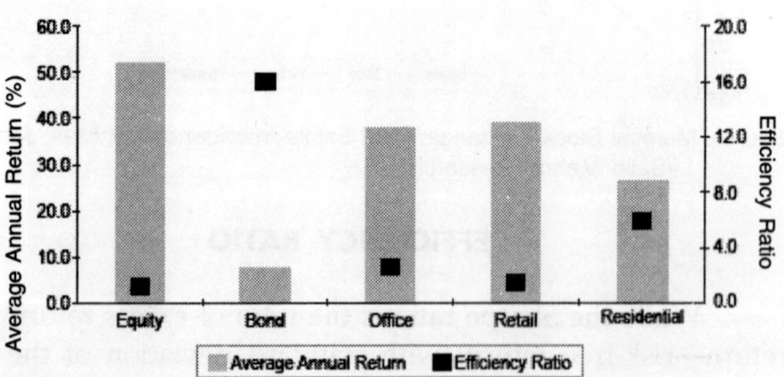

Source: Mumbai Stock Exchange, Reserve Bank of India and Real Estate Intelligence Services.

which provided an average annual return of 7% and efficiency of 4.31, retail had the best efficiency ratio in assets that provided comparable yields in all the remaining four assets. However, retail's efficiency ratio declined significantly to 0.67 during 2005–07 (Figure 3). In contrast, the efficiency ratio for office and residential improved during 2006-07. Moreover, office and retail provided almost equal average annual returns.

HYPOTHETICAL PORTFOLIOS OF EQUITY, BOND AND REAL ESTATE

On the basis of the standard deviation and the Sharpe ratio analysis, equity has been found as the most volatile asset followed by the retail, office and residential segments in the asset class. Bonds are seen as the least volatile, although we consider them as risk free. Following the proposition: 'the higher the risk, the higher the return', equity saw the highest annual average return throughout the 2001-08 period. Retail witnessed the next highest annual average return, followed by the office and residential segments of the real estate market. Bonds, as the least risky asset, provided lesser y-o-y return. In 2008, the economic slowdown resulted in negative annual average return for equity and the retail and office segments of real estate We have

Risk Profile	Composition	Portfolio Name	Equity	Bond	Real Estate (RE)		
					Office	Retail	Residential
Very High Risk	Equity - 100	E	100	0	0	0	0
	Office- 100	O	0	0	100	0	0
	Retail - 100	Rt	0	0	0	100	0
	Residential - 100	Rs	0	0	0	0	100
	RE - 100	S1RE	0	0	33.3	33.3	33.3
High Risk	Equity - 60	S2O	60	10	30	0	0
	Bond - 10	S2Rt	60	10	0	30	0
	RE - 30	S2Rs	60	10	0	0	30
	Equity - 30	S3O	30	10	60	0	0
	Bond - 10	S3Rt	30	10	0	60	0
	RE - 60	S3Rs	30	10	0	0	60
Moderate Risk	Equity - 33.3	S4O	33.3	33.3	33.3	0	0
	Bond - 33.3	S4Rt	33.3	33.3	0	33.3	0
	RE - 33.3	S4Rs	33.3	33.3	0	0	33.3
	Equity - 10	S5O	10	60	30	0	0
	Bond - 60	S5Rt	10	60	0	30	0
	RE - 30	S5Rs	10	60	0	0	30
Low Risk	Equity - 10	S6O	10	80	10	0	0
	Bond - 80	S6Rt	10	80	0	10	0
	RE - 10	S6Rs	10	80	0	0	10
Risk free	Bond - 100	B	0	100	0	0	0

Note: All the numbers are in percentage (%). S1, S2...S6 represents various scenarios from 1 to 6. E=equity; O=office; Rt = retail; Rs=residential; RE=real estate covering all the segments of office, retail and residential.
Source: Jones Lang LaSalle Meghraj Research

constructed 21 alternative hypothetical portfolios to evaluate the risk and return associated with each combination (Table 1). The portfolio return is calculated as the weighted average of the constituent assets' returns whereas the portfolio risk is derived from the standard deviation and correlation of the component assets (Figure 4).

FIGURE 4

Flow of Risk and Return in Alternative Portfolos

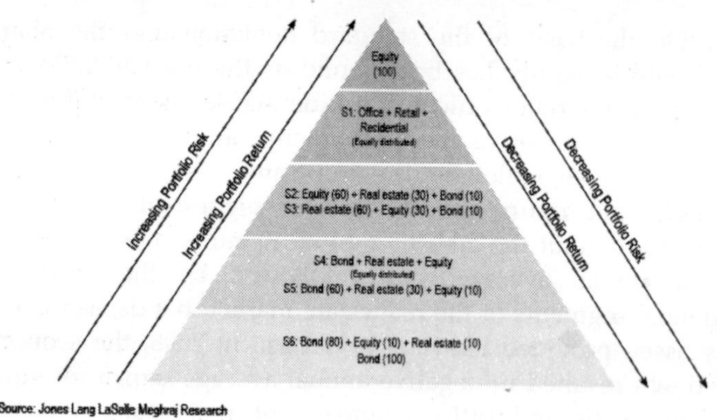

Source: Jones Lang LaSalle Meghraj Research

CHANGES OF AVERAGE ANNUAL RETURNS FOR VARIOUS ASSETS

For the entire 2006-07 period, the BSE Sensex, the realty index and the real estate market provided impressive annual returns, excluding the realty index during 1Q07. From 1Q08, circumstances started to deteriorate due to the negative sentiments fuelled by the crisis that emerged in the US housing market. It further worsened during the remaining part of 2008 due to the financial downturn that the global economy witnessed—starting from Bearn Stearns' collapse and Lehman Brothers' bankruptcy. This is clearly reflected by the negative average annual return for both realty index as well as Sensex for full-year 2008. However, the equity market was fast to react to the crisis that loomed on the global financial market. On the contrary, the real estate market showed some resistance during

1H08, especially the office and residential sectors. Real estate corrected more than the equity market in 1Q09. We may infer that this might be due to the lead time that exists in adjustments in the real estate market. Moreover, this reflects the poor transparency and lower efficiency of the real estate market in realising and adapting to real-time business dynamics. The equity market has witnessed impressive 'bear market rally' towards end-1Q09 reflecting its ability to fast and furious swings in a brief span of time. On the other hand, the real estate market does not have this ability; its movements are slow paced and run with a lag to economy. As such, the amount of 'pain' that the real estate market is expected to witness is not yet complete. Due to the initial lag in the process of correction, real estate is expected to correct more in the next three-four quarters before showing any signs of stabilization.

FIGURE 4

Quarterly Changes of Average Annual Returns for Various Assets

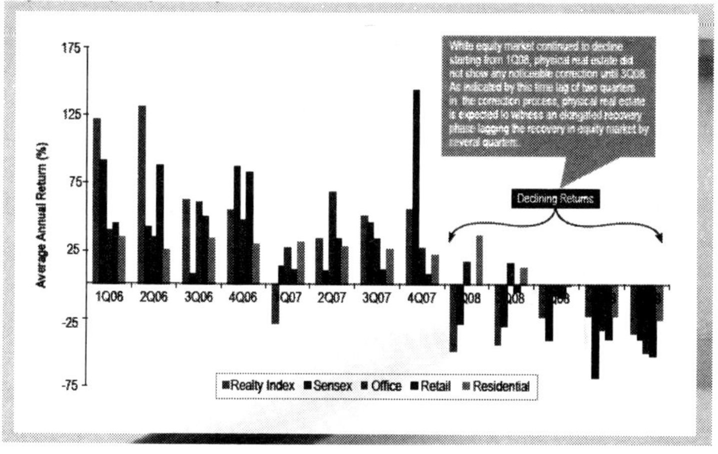

As discussed earlier, real estate provided impressive returns with moderate risk, and a significantly higher efficiency ratio. Real estate in India is currently in the 'pioneer' stage with unlimited growth potential. Although it is unorganized unlike its counterparts in developed countries, this sector is luring foreign investors in a big way.

Due to lesser transparency and lower operational efficiency, risk associated with India's real estate is higher than within the developed economies. However, returns and hence the risk premium in India are significantly higher than in the latter, compensating the investors more than proportionately for the additional risk borne.

However, direct ownership of assets in real estate is not feasible for everyone, especially for small retail investors. This used to be a severe restriction for small retail investors that wanted to reap the benefits of the risk–return profile of real estate investment. This brings us to the emerging opportunities for real estate investment through REMFs and REITs. The essential difference between a REIT and a REMF is that investment made in REITs is only permitted in physical income generating real estate assets whereas REMFs can gain exposure in real estate securities as well. While REMFs are likely to be an active investment tool in the near term, REITs in India are a distant future. The introduction of these investment vehicles in the country are expected to bring in more liquidity, transparency and heighten the organisation level of the emerging real estate market in India.

The recent financial debacle in the US has sent shock waves across the globe and is also projected to impact the Indian real estate sector directly or indirectly, sooner or later. Adequate and timely funding would be a major concern for developers. Already, there are indications of investors—individuals or institutions—withdrawing their funding. While big players consider this shake-up as a temporary phase, most global property consultants anticipate correction in property prices. Buyers are adopting a 'wait and watch' policy and the cascading impact of the US financial tsunami might be felt on real estate too in terms of movement in projects, property prices and stocks of real estate companies. Let us examine the mixed views on the collapse of major US financial institutions on the Indian realty.

Indian realty has two main levels of funding—local and foreign. The US channels funds to Indian realty in three ways—investments by non-resident Indians (NRIs), foreign institutional investors (FIIs) and partnerships with or exposure to finance majors such as Lehman and Merrill Lynch. Though the exact figures of investment by NRIs based in the US is not available due to the non-organised nature of the real estate sector in India, experts estimate it to be to the tune of several billion dollars across the country, mainly in tier-I and tier-II cities.

FIIs hold around 15 per cent of the top 500 shares in the Indian stock market, which includes several real estate companies. Records maintained by the Securities and Exchange Board of India (Sebi) show that net investment by FIIs in Indian equities was around Rs. 2,50,000 crore as on 17th September 2008. In India, many companies such as HDFC Corp, HDFC Bank, ICICI bank, IDFC, India bulls Real Estate, etc. have huge FII exposure. Over the past couple of years, about $4 billion were invested by the US through venture capital funds and FIIs in various real estate projects in India. An additional $14 billion to $16 billion were on their way this year but not any more.

All of these changes in the US economy have affected Indian economy as well as real estate segment as most of the Indian players have their liquidity funded by both of these firms. The IT segment, which was mainly funded by the PE firms or have their export to US markets have noticed very sharp drop of net worth of their firms. This recession also affected the Sensex, which is bullish and brings down the net worth of the leader of Indian real estate player very low. The impact can be shown in share price of DLF, Unitech, GMR group, Reliance Group, Wipro, Satyam, etc. groups. All of these sudden changes in Indian and US market created a point of thinking to investors and individuals that where it will go and what will be the best option in real estate investment. The market rates in India are also dropped by 10 to 30 per cent in most of prominent as well as upcoming cities and the trend appears to be still continuing, till it recovers from the ill-effects of financial crisis.

GLOBAL MELTDOWN AND INDIAN ECONOMY

The inevitable has finally happened. The housing bubble in the US has burst. And the sub-prime crisis that resulted from the real estate bust in the US destroyed investor wealth worth trillions of dollars across the world.

SLOWDOWN IN JOBS

Companies like Lehman Brothers, Merrill Lynch, AIG and Morgan Stanley, to name a few, have their captive research units, brokerage arms, investment banking arms in India employing several hundred thousand people in what is popularly known as BPOs (Business Process Outsourcing) and KPOs (Knowledge Process Outsourcing).

Lehman Brothers' Powai unit itself employed about 2,200 people most of whom will be rendered unemployed unless some other company buys out Lehman's India operations and keeps the wheels running.

Now that the above-mentioned companies are finding it difficult to run their businesses in the US they have either sold out to other companies (Bank of America taking over Merrill Lynch) or to the US government (AIG buyout by the US government).

Obviously, to maintain profits or to just cut even in the current scenario they will start downsizing their workforce wherever they can.

Also, most of these American banking companies have outsourced their technology-related jobs to Indian companies like Satyam, Computers, TCS, Infosys, etc. which might be affected in the near future. The Indian companies, however, maintain that it is an opportunity for them to expand as, in a bid to reduce costs, many US banks will outsource more work to India.

Sectors like real estate, aviation, information technology have already started downsizing their employee strength. There are newspaper reports about DLF (because of the cash crunch) and Kingfisher (rise in aviation oil price and lesser number of flyers taking to the skies) reducing their staff strength by 300.

Technology companies like TCS and IBM had removed more than 500 people each citing poor performance long before the Lehman Brother winds swept across India.

INCREASE IN LOAN RATES

First it was the inflation rate that spoiled the party for Indian borrowers of home loans, personal loans and credit card purchases. Now taking a cue from the US banks—which today are so wary that they are not even lending to each other for the fear that they may not get their money back—Indian banks too have decided to thoroughly scrutinise the repayment capacity of Indian borrowers lest they too go the Lehman Brothers way.

As their cost of money goes up banks will pass on this increase to their customers, ie, borrowers like you and me, at a higher rate of interest. If banks feel that borrowers may not return their money they are going to price it higher to cover the risk of a few defaulting on their payments.

The confidence that borrowers will repay the banks' money with interest every month—at least in the US—is shattered and Indian borrowers will have to bear the brunt of this lack of confidence in the days to come.

CORRECTION IN REAL ESTATE PRICES

There is some good news, though. If experts are to be believed real estate prices in Indian towns and cities are likely to come down by 10-15 per cent in the next few months.

The reason given is most US companies that had bought stakes in Indian real estate companies are facing a cash crunch. Others who had promised to invest in Indian real estate will not do so for the simple reason that the US is no more the place where you can get dollars easily and at a cheaper rate. Most real estate developers who depend on this flow of money may find it difficult to complete their projects. Also, buyers too have dried up because of unaffordably high real estate and interest rates. The outcome could be real estate developers lowering rates to lure buyers.

INCREASE IN GOLD PRICES

Because of the financial problems in the US global investors are losing their faith in the supremacy of the US dollar as a store of value. As a result they are selling dollars to buy some other currency, say the euro or the Japanese yen. Whenever such an event happens investors flock to that ultimate store of value called gold or the noble metal. As the festival season starts with Navratri in India more and more people will demand gold thereby increasing its price further.

However, an increase beyond a particular point is likely to tell on the demand for gold. Just like it is happening with the real estate scene in India.

MORE INFLATION

Increase in oil prices—it jumped a whopping $30 a barrel in intra-day trade today before settling at $108-109 to a barrel — and weakening of the Indian rupee against the dollar will act as a double whammy for Indians.

Crude prices have a multiplier effect. As most goods transported in India use some or the other form of energy it increases the cost of transportation and hence an increase in the price of vegetables, pulses, etc. As the Indian rupee weakens against the dollar—more foreign companies are selling rupees to buy US dollars to take them back to their country—it increases our import bills. For every dollar for which we paid Rs. 39 only a few months back, we will have to pay a good Rs. 45. In this scenario it is small consolation that oil prices have come down from their $140 plus to a barrel at near about $100 to a barrel. Also, if inflation rises further, expect the Reserve Bank of India to further increase your borrowing costs.

SPEED BREAKER AHEAD

Future Group Chairman Kishore Biyani had, way back in 2007, said that 2009 will be a crucial year for the world economy as a whole and particularly India. How very prophetic his words sound today.

With the US economy firmly in the grip of a slowdown owing to the housing price collapse and the subsequent sub-prime drama, this slowdown is fast snowballing across global boundaries and more so India as we depend a lot on the US for the money they bring in. As the US funds tap is expected to run dry in the next 6-12 months Indian companies will be starved of the much-needed cash to expand their businesses. An impact is already visible in the real estate sector as developers scour the world in search of cheap money. If this slowdown impacts the investment climate in India then we can no more dream of the 7.5-8 per cent growth rate that was once upon a time considered a given. A slowdown will force more companies to enter the cost-cutting arena leading to a sizeable dip in job creation.

ROLLERCOASTER RIDE

Be prepared to ride the ups and downs of the global financial markets as India is no more an isolated island. India is likely to follow whatever happens in the US, European or Asian stock markets.

A case in point is how the Sensex closely traced the ups and downs of the Dow Jones and Nasdaq in the previous week. The same is true of the prices of oil, gold, aluminium, copper, steel and any other commodity. Gone are the days when markets defied Newton and gravity. Nobody can expect the markets to move only in one direction.

CONCLUDING REMARKS

The impact of the US financial crisis would be visible after some time. It will reflect mainly on projects, property prices and stocks of real estate companies listed in India and abroad. Real estate and infrastructure companies will be hit the most as this is a capital-intensive sector. FIIs have always been interested in real estate and development projects in India as this segment has been booming for the last four years. So the sharp and immediate fall in share prices of most real estate and infrastructure companies after the US crisis was not a big surprise for experts. Big players, especially those who had huge exposure to Lehman Brothers *et al.*, lost about 7-15 per cent within a couple of hours of the news of the meltdown hitting the market. Though Sensex has recovered slightly, it is still a far cry from the bull ride witnessed over the past few years. Experts see more FIIs selling their stakes in the future in order to shift to safer assets. According to Manish Zaveri, a stock market expert, it is wise to stay away from the stocks of real estate sector as another correction is expected in a few months for various reasons.

Most of the big firms claim that projects will continue unaffected despite the US crisis as they have already received the funds. Market leaders argue that only a handful of big firms are dependent on the foreign entities. NRIs are in for a long-term plan and have invested only their surpluses, so they would wait as the yield here is still higher than in other countries. Many are confident of getting funds from domestic financial institutions. Some are confident that the sector will bounce back in few quarters. This lot does not foresee houses becoming cheaper, at least in big cities.

Another good thing that could happen is greater opportunities in the US for investment in their real estate as the prices are already at ground level. The Indian investor can make big bucks with surplus funds and some patience. Now, FIIs and others will only invest in projects which promise good returns. The level of scrutiny will increase in the pre-investment phase, which in turn will become sensible, responsible financing. As Anuj Puri says, "Sebi and the RBI will also take adequate precautions before going forward."

References

Mumbai Stock Exchange; Real Estate Intelligence Services, Jones Lang LaSalle Meghraj Research 3 Sharpe, W. F. (1994), 'The Sharpe Ratio'. *Journal of Portfolio Management*, 21(1): 49-58.

Mumbai Stock Exchange; Reserve Bank of India and Real Estate Intelligence Services, Jones Lang LaSalle Meghraj Research.

Markowitz, Harry M., (1952), 'Modern Portfolio Theory'.

Toppo Pankaj Anup, Wait Real Estate Meltdown Ahead. topo@outlookindia.com

Recession and real estate in India, 13 Feb. 2009, 0302, hrs 1st, Manoj Pant, ET Bureau.

Recession's positive effects on Indian reality sector, 7 Aug., 2009 0737 hrs 1st, Namrata Kohli, ET Bureau.

Bhola, Subhash Chandra, Kumar, Kiran and Gupta, Abhishek Kiran, The Investment Value of Real Estate). Jones Lang Lasalle Meghraj, Kolkata.

Impact of the Global Economic Crisis on Indian Real Estate Sector

HARVINDER KAUR

INTRODUCTION

Real estate sector in India has grown rapidly after Independence. In 2005, when Government of India allowed 100 per cent Foreign Direct Investment (FDI) in construction business, real estate sector started booming. But, this sector has been witnessing signs of downswing and recently upswing *since first world economic recession of twenty-first century*. Economic recession has hit the countries hard and US remains at the epicenter of the crisis. The sub-prime mortgage crisis in US became a full fledged financial crisis. Many people with no income, no job, no assets were given home loans. It resulted in sub-prime mortgage crisis in US and bankruptcy of Lehman Brothers and the selling process of PE firm Merryl Lynch created a crisis in the entire US economy.

All of these changes in US economy have impacted upon Indian economy as well as Real estate segments as many Indian players have their liquidity funded by both of these firms. However, Global Consumer Recession Index put India in the category of low impact or least affected countries. Whereas Ireland, U.K, Taiwan, Canada, Korea and France have been categorized as the most affected countries (www.globalgiants.com, June 2, 2009).

Similarly, India stood at third place (Australia and China were ranked 1st and 2nd respectively) among the countries perceived to be surviving the economic crisis the best as voted by International Business People (www.labnol.org). No doubt, India is fortunate in having relatively less negative impact, but the signs of slow down in terms of reduced industrial output, reduced liquidity, reduced job opportunities, increased inflation, decline in GDP growth, and decline in growth of IT sector from 23% to 17% are quite glaring. Stock market virtually collapsed for some time. All these factors have led to slow down of real estate sector's growth in India. The impact has been seen in terms of continuously falling share prices of important real estate companies like Unitech, DLF, Orbit Corporation, Parsavnath Developers, HDIL and Puravankra from December 2007 to February 2009. Property prices in India fell 30 by per cent to 45 per cent since the peak of 2007 recession June 30, 2009. Increased prices of construction material due to double digit inflation during June 2008 on the one hand and severe liquidity crunch (a fall out from the US sub-prime crisis) on the other led to reduced demand of realty sector. The projects have been halted. But now some signs of revival, in real estate market in India, especially in the category of affordable residential housing can be seen. In the present paper, an effort is being made to throw light on the following aspects related to real estate in India:

I. Role of Real Estate Sector in Indian Economy,
II. Impact of World Economic Crisis on Indian Real Estate Sector, and
III. Revival of this sector.

ROLE OF REAL ESTATE SECTOR IN INDIAN ECONOMY

Real estate sector plays a significant role in Indian economy. It is second only to agriculture in terms of employment generation and it contributes heavily towards the gross domestic product (GDP). The share of this sector in GDP has reached from less than ten percent in 1999-2000 to 14-15 per cent during 2007-08. The capital appreciation in this sector has remained close to 20-35 per cent per annum. Moreover, the real estate sector is also responsible for the development of many ancillary industries (more than two hundred) and other such related fields of construction. The ups and downs of the real estate market have serious implications on these related fields.

Activities in the real estate sector may broadly be classified into residential, commercial, office premises, the retail segment and hotels. No doubt, real estate development has taken place in all the categories, but almost 80 percent of real estate development in India has taken place in residential space or housing sector. The housing sector has grown at an average of 34 per cent annually in India. The significance of housing sector can be well imagined by the fact that five per cent of the country's GDP is contributed by the housing sector only. Indian Brand Equity Foundation (IBEF) projected in October 2008 that in the next five years, this contribution to the GDP is expected to rise to 6 per cent (*IBEF*, October-December 2008).

The expansion of agriculture economy and rise of new religious centers seemed to be associated with the rise in land prices during 1795 and 1850 (Cohn, 1895). After independence the development of railways, industrialization, urbanization, nuclear families, rapid growth of population, the rise of modern shopping centers, rising slums in cities (Toor and Sidhu, 2005), affordable home loans, increasing disposable incomes, contemporary attitude to home ownership (PR Log, February 19, 2007), revolution in information technology sector, are the several factors which have directly impacted demand, prices and growth of real estate sector in India. Real Estate developers/ firms have also been contributing significantly to the growth of this sector. Some of major national realty firms in India are Unitech, DLF, Orbit Corporation, Parsavnath Developers, HDIL and Purvankra, Anantraj industries, Sobha Developers, Godrej Properties, Ansals, OMAXE, Tata Realty, Akruti Nirman and Orbit Corp.

Real estate sector contains a better money growth than other sectors and on the other hand, risk factor is minimum here. Real estate in India due to these reasons is one of the biggest growing sectors.

IMPACT OF WORLD ECONOMIC CRISIS ON INDIAN REAL ESTATE

World economic recession, especially the recession in US market due to sub-prime crisis has put an adverse impact on Indian real estate sector. The share prices of all the major real estate companies were rising till December 2007. But, real estate stock market had to face bearish trend during 2008 and in early months of 2009. The property prices in India have also declined. A deep reduction in demand for property and decline in investment have halted the construction projects. Foreign players have backed out of their deals which they entered with Indian real estate players during booming conditions of realty sector. Recession in the west has also affected most of the Indian Banks which have branches in the west and they have compelled them to restrict their operations. Since the start of the downturn most realty players have suffered losses as either they have sold their investments at dirt cheap prices or their projects have been stopped or if these have been completed then there are no buyers.

The economic slowdown was aided by fall in stock market during 2008 in India as wealth creation did not happen and there was lack of capital among investors to invest in real estate projects. Also to adjust their share market losses, many investors were forced to sell-off the real estate properties. The impact can be studied with the help of changes in share prices of important real estate companies. Table 1 provides information regarding month-wise share prices of major real estate companies like Unitech, DLF, Orbit Corporation, Parsavnath Developers, HDIL, Puravankara for the period of August 2007 to May 2009. It reveals that the share prices of all these real estate companies were rising till December 2007. Thereafter the share prices of all these companies have continuously declined till Feb.-March 2009. But Unitech suffered the most due to meltdown and has been forced to go in for distress sale of its assets to keep its finances under check (*The Tribune*, May 30, 2009).

The table further reveals that Unitech's share prices plunged to a low of Rs. 28.2 from a high of Rs. 232.5 in May 2008 and Rs. 488 in December 2007, while the share prices of DLF, Orbit Corporation, Parsavnath Developers, HDIL, Puravankara

TABLE I

Important Real Estate Companies and their Share Prices

	Mahindra Lifespace	*Unitech*	*DLF*	*Orbit Corporation*	*Parsavnath Developers*	*HDIL*	*Puravankara*
Aug. 07	575	241.05	592.25	469	302.4	402.22	375.8
Sep. 07	517	307.4	762.95	519	339	469.71	444.55
Oct. 07	639.9	383.65	948	592	338	504.49	454.45
Nov. 07	564.85	382.6	943	760	354.2	615.94	402.9
Dec. 07	688.35	488.25	1073	943	451.1	805.46	456.3
Jan. 08	833.3	378.65	812.55	725	272.35	665.06	325.05
Feb. 08	612.85	359.25	780	635	268.7	642.26	310.95
Mar. 08	536.7	276.15	646	525	209.75	494.03	240.8
Apr. 08	406.5	310.4	705	492	232	579	304.9
May. 08	549.2	232.5	587	466	196	543.34	230.85
June 08	593.4	170.65	396	304	121.8	290.33	175.65
July 08	405.15	163.55	509	247	111.75	337.76	208.5
Aug. 08	459.85	159	493	257.9	115.7	288.35	203.55
Sep. 08	471.8	116.5	352	175.25	90.9	170.2	162.75
Oct. 08	319.95	48.05	220	53.1	40.55	144.25	47.65
Nov. 08	187.95	23.1	198	44.5	35.3	76.85	30.8
Dec. 08	159.3	40.6	281	62.3	47.25	129.95	49.05
Jan. 09	180.3	32.15	177.2	44.4	38.75	96.55	41.35
Feb. 09	127.6	28.2	151	41	34.75	73.4	38.4
Mar. 09	92.6	34.95	167	52.35	36.25	81.9	40.5
Apr. 09	134.4	44.1	230	71.95	48.3	146.8	70.1
May 09	182.55	79.75	403	168.5	96.8	284	107.65
Dec. 07 to Feb. 09% Decline		94%	85.9%	95%	92.4%	90.4%	91.6%
Feb 07 to May 09% Decline		64.6%	62.5%	75.66%	64.10%	74.1%	64%

Source: Capitalmarket.com/stocklogin.asp

came down from a high of Rs. 1073, Rs. 943, Rs. 451, Rs. 805 and Rs. 456 respectively during December 2007 to a low of Rs. 151, Rs. 41, Rs. 34, Rs. 74 and Rs. 38 respectively during February 2009. From December 2007 to February 2009, the property firms Orbit. Corporation and Unitech lost 95 per cent and 94 per cent respectively of their stock value, Parsavnath Developers, Puravankara, HDIL and DLF lost 92.4 per cent, 91.6 per cent, 90.4 per cent, 85.9 per cent, respectively. So the BSE Realty Index became the year 2008's worst performer (June 23, 2009). The biggest loser in all this was the consumer and those people who had invested their hard earned money in the realty sector.

Real estate market in India virtually crashed in October 2008. As a result, property prices, all over India have declined. An average of 30 per cent across India in the second half of 2008 reduction in land prices was observed.

The impact of recession has been quite visible in almost all the regions. For example, prices in Zirakpur have gone down by 20 per cent as compared to prices prevailing in 2007 and 2008 (Khurana, 2009). The property prices and rentals for commercial space in Ludhiana have dropped drastically between 35 to 45 per cent in the first quarter of 2009. Shopping Malls where one could earlier buy property at the rate of Rs. 20-22000 per sq. ft., about eight months back, the same is now available for Rs. 12-15000 per sq. ft. (*The Tribune*, May 2, 2009).

The property market has been attracting only genuine buyers as the demand for affordable homes is rising, but there are no investors. Commercial and retail segments are facing the heat of oversupply, combined with declining rental rates. As a result developers have deferred a majority of the ongoing commercial and retail projects. The country's largest developer (DLF) has stopped construction work on nearly 16 million sq. ft. of office and retail mall space out of 62 million sq. ft. of planned construction. Unitech has also halted work on 8.3 million sq. ft. of commercial projects, out of its projected 21.4 million sq. ft. of projected space. Parsavnath Developers has also put on hold construction work at 11 out of its 17 planned SEZs. Real estate developers are forced to reduce the supply of retail space that was supposed to come up by 2010 by as much as 87 per cent. This happened because of non-availability of Real Estate Investment Trust (REITs), which could not take-off because of complex legal hurdles and the sudden crash in the stock market in 2008 (Thakur, 2009). The real estate businessmen declare this period as 'real estate holiday' (*The Tribune*, April 25, 2009).

Owing to tighter credit and a steep decline in demand, the investments in real estate sector plummeted by 82 per cent between the first and the third quarter of fiscal year 2008-09. According to an Assocham Investment Meter study, the real estate sector investment plans slumped drastically from INR 1,15,326 crore in Q_1, of FY 2008-09 to meek INR 22,482 crore in

Q_3 of the same fiscal year (Real estate investment plunges by 82%, 19 January 2009).

The slowdown of real estate business as a result of world economic recession thus can be held to a large extent responsible for a lower economic growth rate (6.7 per cent) of Indian economy during 2008-09. The states are also not untouched from the heat of recession. The reduction in demand of property and fall in prices has led to decline in revenue of state governments from stamp duty and registry fee. For example, there has been a dip of 27-30 per cent in the revenue of stamp duty and registeries during the past two years in Dehradun. Revenue figures from this source stood at Rs. 342 crore during 2006-07 but plummeted to Rs. 231 crore during 2007-08 (*The Tribune*, June 13, 2009).

SIGNS OF REVIVAL OF REAL ESTATE IN INDIA

Real estate sector in India seems to be getting back on track. Real estate stock market has started coming up. Affordable property is attracting buyers. The BSE real estate index has trebled from its low in March, compared with an 82 per cent slump in 2008. In comparison, the main stock index is up by 91 per cent from its March low (Mehra, 2009). The share prices of important real estate companies like Mahindra Space, Unitech, Parsavnath and Purvankara have also increased by more than 60 per cent and of Orbit corporation and HDIL have increased by nearly 75 per cent from Februrary 2009 to May 2009 (Table 1).

After a considerable drop in property prices and the home loan rates (Behl, 2009) and Lok Sabha elections (Khurana, 2009) a revival of positive sentiment in the reality sector has been noticed. However, the revival is seen mainly in the residential sector. The current mantra seems to be affordable housing and it is this segment where maximum sales are happening (Kamnath and Thakur, 2009). However to attract buyers, the developers have reduced the floor areas by 20-30 per cent at many places. The country's big developers are now concentrating on affordable property rather than the luxury end of the market. In the words of Unitech's managing director, "we made a mistake of only focusing on top two-three per cent of India's population. Now we want to reach the masses ... enter into budget and affordable houses ..." ('Unitech Plans affordable houses', *The*

Tribune, May 30, 2009). Developers have realized that there are seriously under-supplied affordable houses in India. As a state government lottery for about 4000 low cost apartments in Mumbai drew more than 4,30,000 applications, similarly a lottery in Delhi for 5000 flats got 5,00,000 applications ('Affordable homes: Talks of the town', *The Tribune*, May 2, 2009). Realtors are also looking at marginally increasing the prices of affordable homes (Kamnath and Thakur, 2009). Besides it, Indian economy is likely to grow between 6 to 7 percent in 2009-10, slower than earlier years but still among the fastest countries, which could help revive demand for office and retail space (Mehra, 2009).

So, real estate sector in India has started reviving rapidly. Government of India has taken several steps to revive this sector:

- No additional burden of taxes and duties in the Union budget of 2009-10 has been put on the real estate sector so the input costs will remain the same.
- Some of the schemes like Jawaharlal Nehru National Urban Renewal Mission, Golden Jubilee Rural Housing Finance Scheme in India, Approved Rural Building Centres and Indira Awas Yojna are also contributing a lot to the real estate sector's development. Rajiv Awas Yojna on the lines of Indira Awas Yojna is being formulated to promote a slum free India in five years (*The India News*, 2009).
- The Central government has also come out with the 'Interest Subsidy Scheme for Housing the Urban Poor' under its flagship 'affordable housing for all' programme. Households having an average monthly income upto Rs. 3300 (EWS) and between Rs. 3301 to Rs. 7300 (LIG) would be covered under the scheme. The subsidy will be 5 per cent per annum on interest charged on the admissible loan amount over the full period of the loan for construction or for acquisition of a new house (*The Tribune*, May 30, 2009).
- In the budget for 2009-10, The Indian Infrastructure Finance Company (IFC) has been authorized to raise Rs. 1 lakh crore for development of the infrastructure sector. It is an indirect boon to the real estate sector.

- Home loan rates which went up to 12 per cent and higher during 2008 have been reduced. To boost the activities in real estate sector, the interest rates for home loans should be lowered further.
- After realising that demand supply mismatch had proved to be the bane for the real estate, National Housing Bank's move to set-up a Residex (an indicator of property prices) and the RBI's plan to come up with the Housing Start Up Index (a barometer of future housing demand) are other efforts to revive the real estate market (Behl, 2009).

CONCLUDING REMARKS

In the end, it may thus be concluded that real estate sector generates huge employment, has significant linkages with other sectors and investment in this sector has a large multiplier effect on national income. This sector grew rapidly after independence and has witnessed boom after 2005 when Government of India allowed 100 per cent FDI in this sector. But the defaults on sub-prime mortgages (home loan defaults) resulted in a major crisis in the US (during 2006) which further led to Global economic recession. This has negatively impacted Indian real estate market. Indian stock market fell down badly during 2008. From December 2007 to February 2009, the major property firms lost 85 percent to 95 percent of their stock value. The property prices fell down in almost all the regions of India. Inspite of reduced prices, there was steep decline in demand and there were no investors. The period has been declared as 'real estate holiday'.

But now after February 2009, the real estate market has started showing signs of recovery. Real estate share market has been gaining momentum. The share prices of major Real estate companies have increased by 60 to 75 per cent from February 2009 to May 2009. From among the residential, office, commercial and retail segments of real estate business, the residential segment has started witnessing signs of positive sentiment. The Central government has announced some schemes for the revival of real estate sector. No new taxes have been levied on construction sector in the budget for 2009-10. Home loan interest rates have been reduced.

No doubt, all these efforts have had a positive impact on revival of real estate in India. But to further boost this sector, government can initiate public private partnership in low income housing by providing land available with the government to the developers. The increase in the bracket for priority lending for houses can also be helpful. The increase in tax concessions on housing loans can also attract new buyers. The government should focus on evolving a rational structure of stamp duties to be paid on the purchase of land and housing properties. Stamp duty on property is different in all the states of India. It ranges between 4 to 12 per cent. There is a need to fix maximum limit of stamp duty and all states in India should have uniform stamp duty rate. Home loan interest rates need to be further lowered down in order to bring rapidity in real estate sector.

References

Behl, Vinod (2009), 'Hope floats for realty', *The Tribune*, April 25, Syndicate Books, New York.

Cohn S. Bernard (1795), 'Land Control and Social structure in Indian history', Structural Changes in Indian Rural Society.

Kamnath, Raghavendra and Neeraj Thakur (2009), "Realtors believe home market can take price hike", *Business Standard*, 22 June.

Khurana, Sanjay (2009) 'Reviving Reality Sector', *The Tribune*, May 30.

Mehra Prashant (2009), "Reality to pick up on prices activitiy", *The Tribune*, August 1.

PRLog, 'Indian Real Estate Market: An Insight', February 19, 2007.

Thakur, Neeraj (2009), "Realtors homing in on residential projects", Companies, 5 June, *The Tribune*, June 13, 2009.

Toor, M.S. and M.S. Sidhu, (2005), 'Challenge to sustainability of Urban Settlement', *Political Economy Journal of India*, Vol. 14, 28th Issue, July 2005.

Triggers of the Global Financial Crisis and its Impact on the Indian Service Sector

PRADHYUMNA TRIPATHY, ARINDAM DAS AND MOHUA MAZUMDER

INTRODUCTION

The global financial crisis, considered today as the worst since the Great Depression of the 1930's has created havoc across the world. It has shattered the foundations of some of the strongest economics in the world. The unprecedented crisis has had a domino effect in every country across continents, with large-scale job cuts and cost cutting being the most glaring repercussions. Nearly 40 million jobs have been lost. Cumulative losses from bankruptcy of some of the largest investment banks, closures of financial institutions and failed businesses are pegged at trillions of dollars. India inc. has followed a similar path although overall has shown remarkable resilience to the shock. India has experienced a relatively sustainable high growth rate as compared to most of the economies in the world including the developed ones'.

To put it in a simple form, financial crisis refers to a

situation in which the supply of money is outpaced by the demand for money. This means that liquidity is quickly evaporated because available money is withdrawn from banks and banks are forced either to sell other investment to make up for the short fall or to collapse. In this paper an attempt has been made by the authors to identify the factors leading to the financial crisis and impact of the crisis on Indian service sector

The paper is spread over four sections. The first section deals with the concept, objectives of the paper and the plan of the study. The second section is about the contributing factors (triggers) of global financial crisis. The impact of the crisis on Indian service sector is discussed in the third section and the fourth and final section is the epilogue of the study.

CONTRIBUTING FACTORS OF THE GLOBAL FINANCIAL CRISIS

Global Financial Crisis became prominently visible in September, 2008 with the failure of several financial institutions in the United States and a number of European banks and also with decline in the various stock indices worldwide. Though this crisis started in the United States, it spread to other countries of the world. As a result, governments in even the wealthiest nations had to come up with rescue packages to save their financial systems. In this section, the main factors behind this crisis are explored.

Relaxed Monetary Policy

The seeds of crisis were sown during the era of Alan Greenspan, the former chairman of the US Federal Reserve and this period was characterized by a relaxed monetary policy and a free macroeconomic environment in USA. During the Greenspan era, the monetary policy of low interest rates was initiated in response to the collapse of the new economy 'bubble' and the then post-9/11 recession of 2001. As the short-term interest rates reduced to 1% (their lowest level in 50 years) and during this time, an enormous amount of liquidity was pumped into the global monetary system. Accordingly, low interest rates lead to carry trade whereby money went into bonds, stocks, real estate, emerging markets and commodities—anywhere that it might earn a higher return than the very low rates that were on offer in the US and Japan. This low interest rates also made excessive risk taking possible, leading to the sub-prime crisis (Babu, 2008). So, the lax regulation and supervision of Federal Reserve (Fed) and maintaining an artificially low interest rates are the primary factors leading to the crisis.

Reckless Sub-Prime Lending

In the USA, there is a system of giving loans to sub-prime borrowers. By definition, sub-prime borrowers are not prime borrowers and whose credit rating is not high and who do not possess any satisfactory credit history. As there is greater risk associated with sub-prime lending, the rate of interest charged on such loans is also high. While giving loans banks always prefer prime borrowers. But they are not very large in number in reality and all banks try to expand loans to them. Since there is excess supply in the credit market, prime borrowers bargain for lower interest rates. Consequently, as the banks have huge funds and they can also get funds from the Fed at a very low rate of interest, they turned to the sub-prime borrowers who mostly belonged to the lower middle class. Most of these loans in the US credit market were housing loans. Apart from them there were also car loans, credit cards, loans for households consumer durables, etc. If the sub-prime borrowers repay their loans regularly, the banks do not face any problems and certain banks have earned huge profit in this process. In order to earn this type of profits, other lending institutions and bank began to give more and more housing loans to the sub-prime borrowers. When housing loan is granted by a bank, the house purchased is kept as mortgage with the bank. If the borrowers default to pay back the loan the bank will sell the house to get back money (Sarkhel, 2009).

The US government (under both Bill Clinton and George Bush) also encouraged housing loans due to National Homeownership Strategy (1994-2001) and strong US economy as late as 2007. With incentive for aggressive loan disbursement, bank lent billions of dollars of loans into poor households often with incomplete documentation. The share of mortgage sub-prime lending increased from 5% in 2001 to more than 20% in 2006. Between 2001 and 2005, US homeowners enjoyed an average increase of more than 54% in the value of their houses, as measured by the Federal Housing Enterprise Oversight. Housing price continued to increase up to the middle of 2006 and there was a bubble in the housing market and as long as house prices were rising Bush Administration took immense credit for the Goldilocks economy (Babu, 2008).

Unfortunately, a substantial amount of loans given to the sub-prime borrowers became bad debts. Besides, the purchasing power of the borrowers decreased due to hike in oil prices, food prices as well as high rate of inflation. As a consequence, they were unable to repay the housing loans that they availed. So banks started taking possession of mortgaged houses and tried to sell them with a view to recover the loan amount. But during this time as house prices started falling sharply (because of low demand in housing sector), bank failed to recover the same. Banks suffered a serious liquidity crunch that is widely known as the sub-prime crisis (Sarkhel, 2009). This sub-prime mortgage crisis triggered global financial crisis. Basically, the sins the sub-prime crisis got translated into a global misfortune through the presence of certain interlink factors, namely the securitization process, credit derivatives, excessive leverage of the different US financial institution, adaptation of fair value accounting and the role of credit rating agencies.

Securitization

Securitization is a process of converting illiquid assets like mortgage loans, automobile loans, etc. into negotiable securities which may be traded later in the open market. It is a structured process whereby the bank or financial institution or financial company transfers or sells loans of a particular portfolio to a specially created trust which breaks the loan into convenient amounts and raises money from the investors by selling the instruments which represent the loan amounts. Basically, the illiquid assets of the originator are packed, underwritten and sold in the form of securities to investors as other financial institutions through a carefully structured process (Kishore, pp. 886-87). In the USA, government owned corporation (known as Ginnie Mac) and the government sponsored enterprises (GSEs) namely Fannie Mae and Freddie Mac tend to enhance the availability of credit and reduce the cost of credit to the three targeted borrowing sectors, viz., agriculture, home finance and education. However, they largely operate in the residential mortgage-borrowing sector. These GSEs and other investment banks such as Lehman Brothers, Merrill Lynch, Morgan Stanley, etc. encourage mortgage banks countrywide to make home loans and then purchase these mortgage-loans, bundle and package them into large securities called mortgage bank securities. Then, they can either sell those securities to other investors or retain the securities for themselves. On the basis of initial mortgage bank securities, second lien loans are created or third lien loans are formed and so on. Besides, in this situation, the GSEs also enjoyed a special privilege of 'implicit guarantee' as investors tend to believe that if these GSEs failed, the federal government will came to rescue. According to Krugman (2008), "this implicit guarantee means that profits are privatized but losses are socialized. If Fannie and Freddie do well, their stockholders reap the benefits, but if things go badly, Washington picks up the tab. Heads they win, tail taxpayers lose". Since GSEs and other investment banks bear the default risk of the mortgage, this risk arising out of securitization process may be responsible as the source of the financial crisis [Babu (2008) and Chitale (2008)].

Credit Derivatives

The securitization process actually gives birth to different complex credit derivatives products. During the good times in the US mortgage market (i.e., 1990s), GSEs and investment banks grew very large and paid huge salaries to recruit the best and brightest students from top business school, who, in turn helped them to create complex credit derivative instruments from the initial mortgage backed securities. But the risks were not understood by either investors or the top managements of investment bank or GSEs (Duggal, 2008). These credit derivatives are bilateral over the counter financial contracts. "Credit derivatives are defined as off-balance sheet financial instruments that permits one party (beneficiary) to transfer credit risk of a reference asset, which it owns, to another party (guarantor) without actually selling the asset. It, therefore, 'unbundled' credit risk from the credit instrument and trades it separately" (Bhaskar, *et al.*, 2008). Since each of the processes of bundling loans into mortgage backed securities and turning them into derivatives instruments is highly leveraged, at each stage the value goes higher so that finally the total value of the structured products becomes a multiple of the value of the original home for which the initial loan was disbursed to begin with. This is the basis of the 'origination and distribution model' (O & D model) (Babu, 2008). Credit derivatives include the different credit derivative products such as the credit default swap, total returns swap, credit default swaption, etc. There was an excessive growth in credit derivatives products in USA during this time. According to the International swap Dealers Association (ISDA), the notional amount outstanding of credit default swap increased from $ 0.92 trillion (in 2001) to $ 62.2 trillion (in 2007) depicting a compound annual growth rate of 102 per cent. This rapid growth of credit derivatives formed the backbone of the O & D model that proliferated in tandem during the period. In spite of its growth, the market for credit derivatives was highly deregulated and there were no public records showing whether sellers have the assets to pay out if a reference obligation defaults (Chitale, 2008). Accordingly, these derivatives products became toxic due to their illiquid nature, inherently high- leverage, the lack of paper work and absence of transparency. Billions of dollars have been invested by investment banks and financial institutions from all over the world in these toxic products. The life-blood of these products lies in the loan repayment of the housing loans. When these borrowers defaulted, the banks giving loans were in trouble. So the positions of investment banks dealing with derivatives based on home loans were badly affected (Sarkhel, 2009).

Higher Leverage

The good times in the US economy also encouraged banks to take higher leverage in order to earn excess profit. Leverage means borrowing to finance investments and it frequently cited as a contributor to financial crisis (Wikipedia). If the leverage is moderately and widely used, it will increase the potential returns from investment. The banking regulations usually limit the leverage ratio of banks through a minimum capital to risk-weighted assets ratio (CRAR) on an ongoing basis. The Basel II framework evolved by the bank for International Settlement (BIS) in 2006 sets a CRAR of 9 per cent for adoption by banking regulators globally. At the end of 2007, Finnie Mac and Freddie Mae had an effective leverage of 65% and 79% respectively. The leverage ratio for the big five investment banks at the end of 2007 was 27.8% for Merrill Lynch, 30.7% for Lehman Brothers, 32.8% for Bear Stearns, 32.6% for Morgan Stanley and 26.2% for Goldman Sachs (Chitale, 2008). But they did not have sufficient capital to support the risks on their balance sheet. Besides, excessive leverage can also have a damaging impact, because it creates a risk of bankruptcy that means that a firm fails to honour all its promised payments to other firms. It also results in contagion effect thereby spreading from one institution to another (Wikipedia).

Fair Value Accounting (FVA)

The introduction of Financial Accounting Standard No. 157, Fair Value Measurements, has further stimulated the credit crisis. The complex illiquid derivative products are also affected by the introduction of FVA due to following reasons: (a) it brings enormous subjectivity in marking-to-model illiquid credit derivatives with distant settlement dates, (b) in times of crisis, it adversely affects their valuation due to malfunctioning of the orderly sales assumption underlying the accounting framework of fair value and (c) mistaking as realized losses, the extreme marked to market (MTM) losses determined in times of crisis, the financial markets rapidly precipitate a system-wide solvency crisis (Chitale, 2008). The problems in valuing various derivative instruments during the financial market turmoil led to the allegations that FVA exacerbated the meltdown in the US banking system and forced investment and commercial banks to write down well over $100 billion in assets. However, investment banks criticized FVA on the ground that (a) the reported losses are misleading because they are temporary and will reverse as markets return to normal, (b) as fair values are difficult to estimate, there are issues relating to their reliability, and (c) reported losses have adversely affected market prices yielding further losses and increasing the overall risk of the financial system. According to Mott, "Blaming FVA for credit crisis is something like going to a doctor for a diagnosis and then blaming him for telling you that you are sick." Thus, FVA at best remains a side-character in the crisis (Babu, 2008).

Role of Credit Rating Agencies

The role of credit rating agencies for the financial crisis cannot be denied. As many of the structured products like mortgage-backed securities, etc. do not have a market intrinsically, their valuation depends heavily on the rating agencies. Accordingly, in July 2008, Standard and Poor's had downgraded different US structured products that had been originally rated triple-A. The rating agencies did not always disclose the significant aspects of the rating process and they did not always document significant participants in the rating process. Besides, there were issues relating to conflicts of interest and internal auditing process of the rating agencies (Babu, 2008). Thus, the rating agencies cannot avoid their responsibilities for the current financial crisis.

IMPACT OF GLOBAL FINANCIAL CRISIS ON SERVICES SECTOR IN INDIA

According to the World Development Indicators, 2007, World Bank, the contribution of the services sector to GDP is 53 per cent in India. IT services have made India a super power for computer software, Business Process Outsourcing (BPO) and Knowledge Process Outsourcing (KPO). The standard break-up of services in CSO accounts has four major categories: trade and hotels; transport and communications; finance, real estate and housing; and community services (including all government services). As per the Economic Survey, during the Tenth Plan period (2002-07), the average annual growth for trade and hotels was 8.5%, while it was 15.3% for transport and communications. The finance and the real estate category grew by 9.5% and the figure stood at 6.1% for community services.

Now coming to the impact of the global financial crisis on the sunrise sector, it has definitely been adverse. But the fact remains that all the categories under services sector have not been equally hit. While for some categories like trade, exports, etc., it has been really bad, other categories like telecommunications have shown resilience. Exports have declined, as the epicenter of the financial meltdown has been the United States that is coincidentally the destination of most of the exports from India. The slowdown has affected the imports too.

Industrial production has decelerated, affecting domestic trade, although the situation has stared improving in the last quarter (April-June 2009). The occupancy rate of hotels has gone down and so also the tourism industry as a whole. The aviation sector has also been badly affected. The reason can be attributed to the fact that in the face of large-scale job cuts and cost-cutting exercises by almost all organizations across the globe, people are left with little or no disposal income to travel and visit places. Transport has slowed down, but the good news is that telecommunication continues to surge ahead and remain unscathed by the crisis. The percentage share of this industry in total foreign direct investment (FDI) was an impressive 8.3 in 2008. The additional of monthly telecom connections now exceed 10 million. This sector has been resilient during the meltdown and continues to be a boon to the GDP growth of India. Finance and real estate present a mixed picture. Bank lending has started to grow, while real estate is yet to pick up. A combination of lower home loan rates and a significant drop in prices of homes can energize the real estate market on a long-term sustainable basis. This can also fulfil the dreams of millions of Indians to own their own home. Community services on the other hand have been boosted by the implementation of the Sixth Pay Commission recommendation. The pay of government servants has gone up manifold and that is counted as value added. In sum, the result (impact) has been mixed bag. While some categories put up a brave front, others were badly affected. But as every cloud has a silver lining, the service sector that was a restricted domain for foreign capital investment in the past, has become the most sought after area of late. Government policy restriction in the past did not allow foreign investors to invest in service sector as they wished. But as the restrictions have been eased out, FDI has started to flow into this sector generously. It accounted for a substantial 24.3 per cent of the total FDI inflow in 2008. In actual terms, the FDI inflow to this sector has grown 32 times in last five years from a mere Rs. 1,074 crore in 2004 to a whopping Rs. 33,947 crore in 2008. Experts are of the opinion that the situation will improve by the end of 2009.

EPILOGUE

As we have experienced, no country across continents is immune to financial crisis in the present globalized era. It is important to try and make the system less vulnerable to crises in future. A number of reforms in the financial and banking system are required. The regulatory system must be reviewed in order to prevent such disasters in future. Our country has not been severely affected because of strong regulations, cautious approach to reforms, less exposure to global trade and a huge domestic market. These factors have acted as blessings in disguise. The overall economic situation across the globe has started to pickup gradually of late and economists are hopeful that things will improve by the end of 2009. Let's conclude the paper with a positive note with the hope that there will be light at the end of the tunnel.

References

Aiyer, S.S.A. (2009), "Services won't save us from recession", *The Economic Times*, Kolkata, 14th January.

Araghi, F. (2008), "Political Economy of the Financial Crisis: A World Histirical Perspective, *EPW*, Vol. XLIII, No. 45, November 8-14.

Babu, T (2008), "Six Characters in Search of a Crisis", *EPW*, Vol. XLIII, No. 45, November 8-14.

Bhaskar, P.V. and Mahapatra, B. (2008), Derivatives Simplified, Response Books, 1th Ed.

Brown, E. (2008), "Credit Default Swaps: Evolving Financial Meltdown and Derivative Disaster Du Jour", 11th April,

Chitala, R. (2008), "Seven Triggers of the Us Financial Crisis", *Economic and Political Weekly* (*EPW*), Vol XLIII, No. 44, November 1-07.

Duggle, A. (2008), "Global financial crisis: A slippery sloppy", *The Economic Times*, Kolkata, 1st October.

Kishore, R.M. (2005), Financial Management, Taxmann's, 6th Ed.

Krugman, P. (2008), "Fannie and Freddie", *International Herald Tribune*, 14th July.

Mahanti, T.K. (2009), "Seevice sector corners 24% of the total FDI inflows in 2008", *The Economic Times*, Kolkata, 6th April.

Pant, M. (2009), "Recession and real estate in India", *The Economic Times*, Kolkata, 13th February.

Rosen, R. (2007), "The Role of Securitisation in Mortgage Lending", Federal Reserve Bank of Chicago Essays on Issues, Number 244.

Roubini, N. (2008), "Rising Risk of a Systemic Financial Meltdown: The 12 Steps to Financial Disaster", 12th February, http://www.marketoracle.co.uk/Article3677.html

Ryan, S. (2008), "Fair Value Accounting: Understanding the Issues Raised by the Credit Crunch", Mimeo, Council of Institutional Investors

Sarkhel, J. (2009), "Global Financial Crisis of 2007-08", Lecture delivered in the Academic Staff College, The University of Burdwan.

13

Global Economic Crisis and India

R.S. BAWA AND MANJIT SINGH

Economic globalization, one of the dominant forces in the present-day world economy, a phenomenon whose consequences are widespread and continue emerging even today. In fact, the prospects of globalization, the dangers it can present to the viability of nation states, and the opportunities it offers for the process of economic development, are hotly debated themes. Globalization and the growing integration of economies and societies around the world is a complex process that affects many aspects of our lives. Rapid growth and poverty reduction in China, India, and other countries during the past 20 years is one aspect. The increasing poverty in Sub-Saharan Africa is another. The development of the internet and easier communication and transportation around the world represent one dimension and increased exposure to crisis in one major country is another. If America sneezes, whole world catches cold (Dunning and Hamdani, 1997).

Globalization has different implications at micro and macro-levels. At micro-level there is more pressure on business enterprises to continuously innovate and improve quality of products. The link between producers and consumers is quickly established through electronic media, Internet and E-commerce.

At macro-level, more and more countries have followed policies of liberalization, privatization, deregulation of markets, removing structural distortions and liberalizing FDI, etc. Thus rapid shift towards market-oriented policies has taken place, where profit motive and price mechanism determine the allocation of resources (Bawa, 2002). Globalization has created opportunities for developing countries. The experiences of China, India, Indonesia, Thailand, and some other countries have demonstrated that integration into the global economy is necessary for long-term growth and poverty reduction (World Bank, 2006).

As every coin has two sides, similarly, there are both positive and negative aspects of globalization. While globalization is a catalyst for and a consequence of economic development, it is also a messy process that creates significant challenges and problems. Small and low income countries may be exposed to new and new types of competition for which they may be unprepared.

It is now increasingly recognized that the process of globalization entails significant risks and potential large economic and social costs. Openness to global capital markets has brought greater volatility in domestic financial markets, particularly in countries whose financial systems were weak to begin with and economic policies lacked credibility. Large reversals in short-term capital flows (induced by the volatility of world capital markets) have led to severe financial crises and sharp increases in unemployment and poverty in the short-run. Similarly, trade liberalization has led in some countries to reduce demand for unskilled labour and lower real wages in the short-run; combined with a low degree of inter-sectoral labour mobility, job losses and income declines have often translated into higher poverty rates. As a result, there have been growing concerns about the negative effects of globalization, a burning debate on the plight of the world's poorest, whether many of the 1.2 billion people who still live on less than $1 a day are sharing the benefits of greater integration among economies or instead are disproportionately hit by short-run crises and economic downturns (Agenor, 2002).

More fundamentally, financial openness has limited the scope of developing countercyclical macroeconomic policy. The reason for this lies in the fact that with financial openness countries have to surrender autonomy over either exchange rate or monetary policy. Given open capital accounts, maintaining a fixed exchange rate implies forgoing the freedom to fix domestic interest rates, while control over the latter can only be regained by allowing the exchange rate to float. In addition, the scope for expansionary fiscal policies is often severely restricted by demands of foreign financiers (World Commission on the Social Dimension of Globalization, 2004).

The Asian Financial Crisis in 1997-98 was a period of financial crisis that gripped much of Asia beginning in 1997, and raised fears of a worldwide economic meltdown due to financial contagion. A significant determinant of the Asian financial crisis was financial market liberalization combined with poor institutional foundations for investor protection. However, as crisis gripped only relatively smaller economies of South Korea, Indonesia, Thailand and Malaysia, it did not turn into global crisis.

ORIGIN OF PRESENT GLOBAL FINANCIAL CRISIS

The present global meltdown is a result of the risks of globalization. It all began with the one and all American dream, that every American should have a home. Regardless of who you are and what you do, if you are an American, you should have something called a home. Real Estate business was in a boom, and financial agents thought that there wasn't a better time to give away loans. The household sector was given a boost with increased monetary supply by commercial financial companies, and people were given loans regardless of their credit rating. It was never expected that the boom in the Real Estate business would come to such an abrupt end, and the prices would reach all time low. The US economy, being a capitalist driven economy, didn't bother to indulge itself in the policies pursued by the prominent financial giants. Gradually these financial giants in this business started feeling the heat as "sub-prime" clients who defaulted in their repayment of loans. The properties which were mortgaged by the clients weren't even covering the principal amount of the loan, leave alone the principal and interest commitments. The credit offered to the people in indiscriminate fashion, achieving short-term goals and ignoring warnings from leading economists about long-term sustainability of the policy, backfired completely and companies like Lehmann Brothers, Merill Lynch and Freddie Mac's "bad assets" reached magnanimous proportions. An acute credit shortage was experienced in the economy, and simultaneous negative effects started occurring. The credit crunch meant that borrowing interest rates shot up in the market, companies slowed down their investment policies, production declined, lay offs increased, consumption decreased and the whole economy followed the downward spiral.

However, according to Reddy (2009), the reason for the present financial crisis was that some countries, notably the US, built large current account deficits. Some others, notably in Asia, built significant surpluses in current account and lent or invested in the US. Since these recurring imbalances persisted and increased over the years, correction was warranted by the markets. The much cherished sub-prime lending was only one of the symptoms of the lack of aggregate demand as the median wage was constant. The monetary policy, especially in US, was much accommodative. The money supply was in plenty and due to low interest rates, it found its way into speculative activities causing assets bubbles. There was no formal mandate to maintain financial stability. The result was a huge crash. The Central Banks ignored all these angularities occurring in the economy and failed to act timely. The multilateral institutions like the IMF did give warnings of the macroeconomic imbalances in big economies but no one would listen, as the IMF likes are dominated by the select economies.

What stands out glaringly in the crisis is episode was the regulatory failure. The regulatory failure was two-fold. First, some parts of the financial system were either loosely regulated or were not regulated at all, a factor which led to "regulatory arbitrage" with funds moving more towards the unregulated segments. The second failure lies in the imperfect understanding of the implications of various derivative products. In one sense, derivative products are a natural corollary of financial development. They meet a felt need. However, if the derivative products become too complex to discern where the risk lies, they become a major source of concern. Rating agencies in the present episode were irresponsible in creating a booming market in suspect derivative products. Quite clearly, there was a mismatch between financial innovation and the ability of the regulators to monitor them. It is ironic that such a regulatory failure should have occurred at a time when intense discussions were being held in Basle and elsewhere to put in place a sound regulatory framework. (Rangarajan, 2009)

IMPACT ON DEVELOPED COUNTRIES

The global financial crisis has triggered a serious slowdown in world economic growth including recession in the larger industrialized countries. Enterprises stopped hiring and many laid off workers in considerable numbers. The International Labour Organization (2009) explored the impact of the crisis on jobs and expected outcomes of several possible scenarios, the way it might evolve in the year ahead. In 2008, an estimated 6.0 per cent of the world's workers were not working but looking for a job, up from 5.7 per cent in 2007. Experience shows that the longer people stay out of work, the more their 'employability' deteriorates, making it progressively harder to get back into work. This is especially worrying for young workers who may get trapped into a lifetime of weak attachment to the labour market alternating between low paid insecure work and outright unemployment. In many developing countries well over half of the workforce is employed in conditions that fall short of decent work, and breaking out of such situations is at the core of the global development challenge set out in the Millennium Declaration and its poverty-reducing goals.

Thus, the year 2008, one of the worst years in the world's economic history, experienced a major global meltdown. A redeeming feature of the current crisis is that its magnitude is much lesser than that of the Great Depression of the 1930s when unemployment rate in the United States exceeded 25 per cent. In 2008, it stood at 6.5 per cent and has been predicted to remain around eight per cent in 2009. However, its magnitude has been more than expected—around 9 percent and in some states of U.S.A. reaching upto 12 percent.

IMPACT ON INDIA

Globalization has ensured that the Indian economy and its financial markets cannot stay insulated from the present financial crisis in the developed economies. The debate, therefore, can only be on the extent of impact and how resilient India is to withstand the storm with minimal damage.

The major factor in India's economic slowdown is the global financial meltdown and consequent economic recession in developed economies. Given the origin and dimension of the crisis in the developed countries, which have been called the worst since the Great Depression, every developing country has suffered to a varying degree. No country including India remained immune to the global economic shock.

Growth rate in India decelerated in 2008-09 to 6.7 percent which represented a decline of 2.1 percent from the average growth rate of 8.8 percent in the previous years, i.e. 2003-04 to 2007-08.

The rapid growth of Indian economy from 2003 04 to 2007 08 also made India an attractive destination for foreign capital inflows and net capital inflows that were 1.9 percent of GDP in 2000-01 increased to 9.2 percent in 2007-08. Foreign portfolio investment added buoyancy to the Indian capital markets and Indian corporates began aggressive acquisition sprees overseas, which was reflected in the high volume of outbound direct investment flows. (Govt. of India, 2009)

The relatively limited impact of the ongoing turmoil in financial markets of the advanced economies on the Indian financial markets, and the Indian economy as a whole, needs to be assessed in this context. Whereas the Indian current account has been opened up fully, though gradually, over the 1990s, a more calibrated approach has been followed to the opening of the capital account and to opening up of the financial sector. This approach is consistent with the weight of the available empirical evidence with regard to the benefits that may be gained from capital account liberalization for acceleration of economic growth, particularly in emerging market economies. The evidence suggests that the greatest gains are obtained from the opening to foreign direct investment, followed by portfolio equity investment. The benefits emanating from external debt flows have been found to be more questionable until greater domestic financial market development has taken place (Henry, 2007)

The Indian economy looked to be relatively insulated from the global financial crisis that started in 2008 when the 'sub-prime mortgage' crisis first surfaced in the US. In fact the RBI was raising interest rates until July 2008 with the view to cooling the growth rate and contain inflationary pressures. But as the financial meltdown, morphed into a global economic downturn with the collapse of Lehman Brothers on 23 September 2008, the impact on the Indian economy was almost immediate. Credit flows suddenly dried-up and, overnight, money market interest rate spiked to above 20 percent and remained high for the next month.

The effect on Indian economy was not significant in the beginning. The initial effect of the sub-prime crisis was, in fact, positive as the country received accelerated foreign institutional investment flows during September 2007 to January 2008. This contributed to the debate on 'decoupling', where it was believed that the emerging economies could remain largely insulated from the crisis and provide an alternative engine of growth to the world economy. The argument soon proved unfounded as the global crisis intensified and spread to the emerging economies through capital and current account of the balance of payments. The net portfolio flows to India soon turned negative as foreign institutional investors rushed to sell equity stakes in a bid to replenish overseas cash balances. This had a knock-on effect on the stock market and the exchange rates by creating the supply-demand imbalance in the foreign exchange market. The current account was affected mainly after September 2008 through slowdown in exports. Despite setbacks, however, the balance of payments situation of the country continued to remain resilient. (Govt. of India, 2009)

The financial market, IT/ITES, export and manufacturing sectors have been affected adversely. The IT/ITES sector is the major component of India's growth because the share in GDP given up by agriculture has been taken up by the services sector in recent past.

The global meltdown has not only affected the services sector, even the industrial sector has been affected adversely.

Major projects and expansion plans have been reviewed by the corporate sector and they started focusing on reducing costs and borrowings. The first half of the year 2009 is considered as the worst period. Despite all these problems, the biggest problem that still exists from the past is 'Information asymmetry'. It would be fine if our Government or the members of the major corporate sector don't know the problem or where to find the answer, but the truth is that they know both and are waiting for other countries to take steps. (Datt, 2009).

The Indian financial system is not directly exposed to the 'toxic' or 'distressed' assets of the developed world. This is not surprising since Indian banks have very few branches abroad. However, the indirect impact on the economy because of the recession abroad is very much there. The indirect impact is felt both through trade and capital flows. The fall in international commodity prices and more particularly crude oil reduced sharply the import bill from previous estimates. The recession abroad had an adverse effect on our exports of goods and services. There was a sharp deceleration in the rate of growth of exports in 2008-09. The decline in growth rate in exports adversely affected some sectors where exports constituted a significant proportion of the total production. Some such examples are textiles, automobile components and gem and jewellery. In contrast, to the strong inflow of over $100 billion in 2007-08, 2008-09 saw a net increase of only $10 billion in capital flows. The flow of portfolio capital turned negative. Indian firms have also experienced difficulties in raising money abroad. All this have an impact on the exchange rate. (Rangarajan, 2009)

IMPACT ON PRODUCTION AND EXPORTS

The industries most affected by weakening demand were airlines, hotels and real estate. Besides this, Indian exports suffered a setback and there was a setback in the production of export-oriented sectors. The government advised the sectors of weakening demand to reduce prices. It provided some relief by cutting down excise duties, but such simplistic solutions were doomed to fail. Weakening demand led to producers cutting production. To reduce the impact of the crisis, firms reduced their workforce to reduce costs. This led to increase in unemployment but the total impact on the economy was not very large. Industrial production and manufacturing output declined to five per cent in the last quarter of 2008-09. Consequently, a vicious cycle of weak demand and falling output developed in the Indian economy.

The adverse effect of the global financial crisis was also felt on the export sector, first, on account of the drying up of international financing and trade credit and then followed by a fall in global demand.

During the period (April-February) in 2008-09, the main drivers of exports growth were engineering goods and chemicals and related products. Petroleum products and textile exports witnessed a positive but low growth. However, handicrafts, primary products and gems and jewellery exports registered negative growth. The negative impact on the growth of India's exports becomes more evident from the fact that merchandise exports to the United States, which was the largest market, declined by 1.6 per cent during 2008-09 (April-February). On the other hand, merchandise exports to Asia (including ASEAN) grew by 6.9 percent and to Europe by 10.2 percent during this period. India's merchandise exports to South Asian countries also declined by 5.2 percent. (Govt. of India, 2009)

The impact of global recession was relatively less on India's services exports till December 2008, though the growth rate of services export moderated to 16.3 percent during April-December 2008-09. A negative growth in insurance and a sharp fall in the growth of travel services was registered during this period. Software services grew at 26 per cent, while financial services registered a robust growth of 45.7 percent despite the global financial crisis and fall in growth rate in world financial services exports. Business services growth was, however, at a lower rate of 3.9 percent. (Govt. of India, 2009)

EMPLOYMENT AND DEMAND

The global meltdown also led to job lay-offs across the world and also in India. Different Indian associates and CEOs of multinational companies started feeling the heat.

A weakening of demand in the US affected our IT and Business Process Outsourcing (BPO) sector and the loss of opportunities for young persons seeking employment at lucrative salaries abroad. India's famous IT sector, which earned about $ 50 billion as annual revenue was feared to fall by 50 per cent of its total revenues. This would reduce the cushion to set off the deficit in balance of trade and thus enlarge our balance of payments deficit. It has now been estimated that sluggish demand for exports would result in a loss of 10 million jobs in the export sector alone. (Datt, 2009)

According to International Labour Organization (2009), over 50 million could lose their jobs by 2009 worldwide. The worst thing is that as we live in an agrarian economy where the unemployment rate is already high and about 60% of the population is still dependent on agriculture, the rate of unemployment is rising further due to these worldwide lay-offs as most of the students of India go abroad for job purposes.

On the whole, the impact of the global crisis has been transmitted to the Indian economy through three distinct channels, viz., the financial sector, exports and exchange rates. The financial sector including the banking sector, equity markets, external commercial borrowings and remittances has not remained unscathed though fortunately, the Indian banking sector was not overly exposed to the sub-prime crisis. Only one of the larger banks, ICICI, was partly affected but managed to thwart a crisis because of its strong balance sheet and timely action by the Government, which virtually guaranteed its deposits. The equity markets have seen a near 60 percent decline in the index and a wiping off of about USD1.3 trillion in market capitalization since January 2008 when the Sensex had peaked at about 21,000. This is primarily due to the withdrawal of about USD12 billion from the market by foreign portfolio investors between September and December 2008 in order to strengthen the balance sheet of their parent companies. Commercial credit, both for trade finance and medium-term advances from foreign banks virtually dried-up. This had to be replaced with credit lines from domestic banks but at higher interest costs and caused the Rupee to depreciate, raising the cost of existing foreign loans. Finally, while the latest numbers are not yet available, remittances from overseas Indians have reportedly fallen as oil producing economies in the Gulf and West Asia suffered from decline in oil prices. The second transmission of the global downturn to the Indian economy has been through the steep decline in demand for India's exports in its major markets. The first sector to be hit was the gems and jewellery which felt the impact in November 2008 itself and where more than 300,000 workers have lost their jobs. The negative impact has since covered other export-oriented sectors like garments and textiles, leather, handicrafts, and auto-components. The 21 percent decline in exports in February 2009 was the steepest fall in exports for the last two decades. It is unlikely that exports will recover within this year. While exports of both goods and services account for about 22 percent of the Indian GDP, their multiplier effect for economic activity is quite large as the import content is not as high as for example in the case of Chinese exports. Therefore, an export slump would bring down GDP growth rate in 2009-10. The third transmission channel is the exchange rate as the rupee has come under pressure with the outflow of portfolio investments, higher foreign exchange demand by Indian entrepreneurs seeking to replace external commercial borrowing by domestic financing, and the consequent decline in foreign exchange reserves from US $ 299.2 billion in March 2008 to US $ 241.4 billion in March 2009. This is likely to continue because current account will remain in deficit and the capital account, which has been in deficit in the second and third quarters of 2008-09, will not generate the needed surplus to cover the current account deficit. This will imply further drawing down of foreign exchange reserves and continued downward pressure on the exchange rate. (Kumar, 2009)

MEASURES TAKEN AND THEIR IMPACT

To counter the negative fallout of the global slowdown on the Indian economy, the Government responded by providing a substantial fiscal expansion in the form of tax relief to boost demand and increased expenditure on public projects to create employment and public assets. The net result was an increase in fiscal deficit from 2.7 per cent in 2007-08 to 6.2 per cent of GDP in 2008-09. The difference between the actuals of 2007 08 and 2008-09 constituted the total fiscal stimulus, notwithstanding the fact that some expenditure was on account of the implementation of the Sixth Pay Commission award and the agriculture debt relief scheme (small farmers' debt waiver) announced in the Union Budget 2008 09. Together about 0.5 per cent of the GDP was committed prior to the dramatic deterioration of the international financial markets in September 2008. In implementing the fiscal stimulus, the Government increased its spending on the plan, both for Central sector as well as on Central assistance to State and Union Territories plans, by nearly 1 percent of the GDP. There was an increase of nearly 2.5 per cent of GDP on non-plan expenditure that included increased spending on fertilizers and food subsidies, agriculture debt waiver, defence, salaries and pensions. The Government renewed its efforts to increase infrastructure investments in telecommunications, power generation, airports, ports, roads and railways. (Govt. of India, 2009)

The RBI took a number of monetary easing and liquidity enhancing measures including reduction in cash reserve ratio, statutory liquidity ratio and key policy rates. The objective was to facilitate the flow of funds from the financial system to meet the needs of productive sectors. In the past, in well developed financial markets like the United States, monetary policy instruments and their effectiveness in meeting the objectives is well known. However, the financial crisis in the US market had the effect of fragmenting these markets, so that conventional instruments were no longer effective. This was only partly an issue of the Keynesian liquidity trap. In relatively less developed financial markets like India's, the effectiveness of instruments is constrained by missing and imperfect financial markets. The global crises accentuated the non-integrated nature of the markets, requiring more careful attention to the different channels, namely interest rate, money supply and credit and the instruments appropriate to each. Further, it became imperative to use both traditional (considered outdated by some) and unconventional instruments. The breadth and depth of the global crisis and the uncertainty and the fear surrounding it, required use of fiscal policy to supplement monetary policy. It was, therefore, necessary to ensure adequate coordination between the two, so that they did not work at cross-purposes. Though it would be far from the truth to claim perfection, by and large the conceptually sound approach was eventually implemented. (Govt. of India, 2009)

The Government also announced specific measures to address the impact of global slowdown on India's exports. These included extension of export credit for labour-intensive exports, improving the pre and post-shipment credit availability, additional allocations for refund of terminal excise duty/CST and export incentive schemes, and removal of export duty and export ban on certain items. Though it is not possible to substitute for the dramatic fall in foreign demand, these measures would be helpful in facilitating the adjustment of companies and workers to the new reality and to survive the temporary setbacks. (Govt. of India, 2009)

The policy stance of the Reserve Bank of India (RBI) in the first half of the year was oriented towards controlling monetary expansion, in view of the apparent link between monetary expansion and inflationary expectations partly due to the perceived liquidity overhang. In the first six months of 2008-09, year-on-year growth of broad money was lower than the growth of reserve money. The Government also took various fiscal and administrative measures during the first half of 2008-09 to rein in inflation. The key policy rates of RBI thus moved to signal a contractionary monetary stance. The repo rate (RR) was increased by 125 basis points in three tranches from 7.75 per cent at the beginning of April 2008 to 9.0 per cent with effect from August 30, 2008. The reverse-repo rate (R-RR) was however left unchanged at 6.0 per cent. The cash reserve ratio (CRR) was increased by 150 basis points in six tranches from 7.50 per cent at the beginning of April 2008 to 9.0 per cent with effect from August 30, 2008. (Govt. of India, 2009)

The credit policy measures by the RBI broadly aimed at providing adequate liquidity to compensate for the squeeze emanating from foreign financial markets and improving foreign exchange liquidity. At the same time, it was necessary to ensure that the financial contagion arising from the global financial crisis did not permeate the Indian banking system. These measures were, therefore, supplemented by sector-specific credit measures for exports, housing, micro and small enterprises and infrastructure. (Govt. of India, 2009)

The outflow of foreign exchange, as a fallout of crisis, also meant tightening of liquidity situation in the economy. To deal with the liquidity crunch and the virtual freezing of international credit, the monetary stance underwent an abrupt change in the second half of 2008-09. The RBI responded to the emergent situation by facilitating monetary expansion through decreases in the CRR, repo and reverse-repo rates, and the statutory liquidity ratio (SLR). The repo rate was reduced by 400 basis points in five tranches from 9.0 in August 2008 to 5.0 percent beginning March 5, 2009. The reverse-repo rate was lowered by 250 basis points in three tranches from 6.0 (as was prevalent in November 2008) to 3.5 per cent from March 5, 2009. The reverse-repo and repo rates were again reduced by 25 basis points each with effect from April 21, 2009. SLR was lowered by 100 basis points from 25 per cent of net demand and time liabilities (NDTL) to 24 per cent with effect from the fortnight beginning November 8, 2008. The CRR was lowered by 400 basis points in four tranches from 9.0 to 5.0 per cent with effect from January 17, 2009. (Govt. of India, 2009)

Apart from the measures taken to restore and revive the domestic economy, India continued to engage actively at various international fora like the G-20 group of countries (of which India is a member) and at the multilateral institutional mechanisms on the range of issues that arose from the global financial crisis. At the meeting in early April 2009, leaders of G-20 countries (including India), collectively committed themselves to take decisive, coordinated and comprehensive action to revive growth, restore stability of the financial system, restart the impaired credit markets and rebuild confidence in financial markets and institutions.

FUTURE SCENARIO AND CHALLENGES

India has the option of turning the crisis into an opportunity. The most binding constraints to growth and inclusion need to be addressed, which involve: improving infrastructure, developing the small and medium enterprises sector, building skills and targeting social spending at the poor. Systematic improvements in the design and governance of public programs are crucial to get results from public spending. Improving the effectiveness of these programs that account for about 9 10% of GDP will, therefore, be an important part of the challenge.

The most important challenge faced by our Government during this time is to ensure a balance between inflation and growth and also to stimulate ensured growth of demand and equality in income distribution. If our economy experiences high growth rates, it will lead to more exports from the country which will affect our domestic market and if economy experiences a decline in the inflation rate, it will lead to major imports to our country which will affect the government budget.

Indian economy has certain inherent strengths which would help in meeting the challenges ahead. We have still a large untapped market especially in rural areas which can sustain internal demand. A vast pool of science and technology graduates and millions of people who are familiar with English language and adapt better to the global situation are its strong limbs. India being the largest democracy of the world, existence of free media keeps the government in check and provides some insurance against excesses. Most importantly, India with half of its population being below 25 will remain the youngest country in the world. Given the appropriate skills, they will outwit challenges in any field. (Reddy, 2009)

Jobs must be protected even if it means some reduction in compensation at various levels. This is a useful tool to fight recession and it has also been tried in several countries. This suggestion should be implemented until such time that the economy gets revived. People cannot be thrown out of jobs without creating alternative avenues elsewhere in the economy. The unemployed have to be given unemployment allowance and financial assistance for self-employment under the schemes, which are commercially viable. There is need for labour market flexibility, but with safety nets. International institutions have to come to the rescue of the country in this gigantic task.

There is a need to orient the fiscal package towards inclusive growth so that the weaker sections benefit. This would require special emphasis, for instance, on rural infrastructure—rural roads and housing, instead of only highways and urban housing. Similarly, a much larger expenditure on primary and secondary education, health and sanitation can also result in a more inclusive growth process.

While there are indications that the economy may have weathered the worst of the downturn, in part, due to the resilience of the economy and also various monetary and fiscal measures initiated during 2008-09, nevertheless, the situation warrants close watch on various economic indicators, including the impact of the economic stimulus and developments taking place in the international economy. Taking policy measures that squarely address the short and long-term challenges would help achieve tangible progress and ensure that the outlook for the economy remains firmly positive.

References

Agenor, P.R. (2002), Does Globalization Hurt the Poor?, World Bank, Washington DC.

Balasubramanyam, V.N. (2001), Conversations with Indian Economists, Macmillan, Delhi

Basu, Kaushik (2000), "On the Goals of Development", in Meier, G.M. and J.E. Stiglitz (ed), Frontiers of Economic Development, Oxford University Press, New York.

Bawa, R.S. (2002), "Challenges and Opportunities of Globalization;:Implications for India", Presidential Address to 84th Annual Conference of Indian Economic Association, *The Indian Economic Journal*, Vol. 49(3).

Datt, Ruddar (2009), "Global Meltdown and its Impact on the Indian Economy", Mainstream, Vol. XLVII, No. 15.

Dhillon, S.S. and P.S. Raikhy (1999), "Social Choice, Growth and Income Distribution: Theory and Evidence" in IEA 82nd Annual Conference Volume, Amritsar.

Dunning, J.H. and Khalil A. Hamdani (1997), The New Globalism and Developing Countries, Bookwell, Delhi.

Govt. of India (2009), Economic Survey, 2008-09, Oxford University Press, New Delhi.

Henry, Peter Blair (2007), "Capital Account Liberalization: Theory, Evidence, and Speculation", *Journal of Economic Literature*, Vol. XLV, December.

International Labour Organization (2009), Global Employment Trends Report, International Labour Office, Geneva.

Kumar, Rajiv (2009), Global Financial and Economic Crisis: Impact on India and Policy Response, Indian Council for Research on International Economic Relations (ICRIER), New Delhi

Mohan, Rakesh (2008), "Global Financial Crisis and Key Risks: Impact on India and Asia", IMF-FSF High-Level Meeting on the Recent Financial Turmoil and Policy Responses at Washington D.C., October 9, 2008.

Rangarajan, C. (2009), The International Financial Crisis and Its Impact on India, Bureau of Parliamentary Studies and Training, Lok Sabha, Parliament House, New Delhi.

Reddy, Y.V. (2009), India and the Global Financial Crisis, Orient Blackswan, New Delhi.

Singh, Manjit (2008), Globalization and Economic Development: Experience of Developing Countries, Ph.D thesis submitted to Guru Nanak Dev University, Amritsar.

World Bank, World Development Indicators, Various Issues, Washington, D.C.

World Commission on the Social Dimension of Globalization (2004), A Fair Globalization: Creating Opportunities for All, New Delhi: Academic Foundation, their impact on policy evaluation", *Journal of Policy Modeling*, Vol. 4.

Reddy, Y.V. (2009a), Talks of several issues in the context of a new global financial architecture.

Reddy, Y.V. (2009a), India and the Global Financial Crisis: Managing Money and Finance, Orient Blackswan.

Reddy, Y.V. (2009b), "Global Financial Crisis and Asia", Justice Konda Madhava Reddy Memorial Lecture.

See, for example, Bernanke (2005).

See, Johansen (1960) and Rattso (1984), It is interesting to note here that Indian Plan models had relied heavily on Johansen macro-closure in the past in their approach to macroeconomic sub-model.

The Indian Government had already been undertaken at the beginning of 2008 a large expansionary fiscal package involving farmers' loan waiving, revision of salary of government employees, rural infrastructure, and primary education.

Total indirect tax revenue was 8% of GDP in the Base run

Von Arnim, Rudigor (2009): "Recession and rebalancing: How the housing and credit crisis will impact US real activity", *Journal of Policy Modeling*, 31, pp. 309-24.

Global Financial Turmoil: Impact on the Indian Economy

VIPLA CHOPRA AND BHARTI KAPUR

INTRODUCTION

The financial turmoil, which surfaced in August 2007 in the USA as a result of defaults of sub-prime mortgage loans, has blown into an unprecedented financial crisis. Though the epicenter of the crisis was the US sub-prime mortgage market, its shockwaves are being felt in financial markets of other emerging countries of the world, including Asia. The burgeoning crisis in the financial sector poses a threat to the real economy, as the financial sector is fully integrated to the real economy. Macroeconomic fundamentals like growth, employment, exports, imports and prices are bound to be affected. Banks and financial institutions all over the world are bound to face this challenge.

In the present paper an attempt has been made to study the impact of global financial crisis on Indian economy. The paper has been divided into three sections. Section I highlights the major factors responsible for the global financial crisis. Section II examines its impact on Indian economy to lift the economy out of the current economic recession. Measures undertaken by the government have been examined in section III.

Section I

Many varied and complex factors were responsible for this financial crisis. Factors pervasive in both the housing and credit markets, which developed over an extended period of time were responsible for this crisis. Some of these factors have been given below:

1. Former Chairman of the US Federal Reserve, Alan Greenspa followed loose monetary policy which resulted in the serious global financial crisis. In a bid to counter the financial crisis, the US Fed steadfastly decreased interest rates to 1% during the period till 2004 before increasing it to 5.25% in 2006. The combination of rising prosperity and low interest rates led to a sharp increase in demand for housing loans even as easy liquidity saw a run up in all asset values, including houses. This encouraged borrowers to assume expensive mortgages in the belief that they would be able to get refinance on more favourable terms. However, once interest rates began to rise and housing prices started to drop in many parts of the US in 2006-07, refinancing became more difficult. Defaults and foreclosures became commonplace once home prices stopped going up and then started falling.
2. When the banks and mortgage lenders that had securitized their loans by issuing mortgage backed securities, based on underlying mortgage payments, suddenly found the value of these securities falling rapidly as defaults rose, the situation worsened. Major banks and financial institutions, both in the US and in many other countries, that had borrowed and invested hugely in such securities had to bear huge losses. Credit default swaps that were meant to act as insurance against the risk that the borrowers will not pay back bank loans and make the financial system

less risky, failed to provide the expected comfort.

3. Speculation in residential real estate has also contributed to the crisis. A record level of nearly 40 per cent of home purchases were not intended as primary residencies rather for reinvestment purposes. Speculators left the market, as the market was not showing optimism, which led to a decline in investment sales much faster than the primary market.
4. Lenders had also offered more loans to higher-risk borrowers, including illegal immigrants. The sub-prime mortgages amounted to $35 billions in 1994, $ 160 billions in 1999, and $ 600 billion in 2006 (Table 1). Forty percent of all sub-prime loans were generated by automated underwriting in 2007. The mortgage brokers earned profits from a home loan

TABLE I

Year	*Value (in $ billions)*
1994	35 (5%)
1999	160 (13%)
2006	600 (20%)

Note: Figures in brackets are the share of sub-prime mortgage to total originations.

Source: US department. of the Treasury suspicious Activity Report.

boom but did not do enough to examine whether borrowers had ability to repay.

Sub-Prime Mortgages

5. Credit rating agencies are now under scrutiny for giving investment grade ratings to securitization transactions such as collateral debt obligations (CDOs) and mortgage backed securities (MBSs) based on sub-prime mortgage loans. Investors were encouraged to buy securities backed by sub-prime

mortgages because of high ratings, which helped to finance the housing boom. Many investors believed on agency ratings and the way ratings were used to justify investments and thus treated securitized products, some based on sub-prime mortgages as equivalent to higher quality securities.

6. Many financial institutions, particularly investment banks issued large amounts of debt during 2004-07 and invested that proceeds in mortgage backed securities (MBS), essentially believing that house prices would continue to rise, and that households would continue to make their mortgage payments. Borrowing at a lower interest rate and investing the proceeds at a higher interest rate is a form of financial leverage. This strategy proved profitable during the housing boom, but resulted in large losses when house prices began to decline and mortgages began to default. Beginning in 2007, financial institutions and individual investors holding MBS also suffered significant losses from the default of mortgage payments and the resulting reduced value of MBS.
7. The financial crisis was also the result of both government action and inaction. Lack of proper control by the regulatory authorities in the government also contributed to the crisis. The Securities and Exchange Commission (SEC) had admitted that the lack of self-regulation by investment banks was also responsible for the crisis. There is evidence that the Federal government depended on the mortgage industry to lower lending standards. The mortgage policies of Department of Housing and Urban Development encouraged the trend towards issuing risky loans. The capital requirements played an important role to stimulate mortgage securitization in the United States. After studying the major factors responsible for global meltdown, now we will study their impact on Indian economy.

SECTION II

IMPACT ON THE INDIAN ECONOMY

The current financial crisis which started in the west also affected Asia, including India. Some Indians were of the opinion that India was different and would not be affected because our financial system is quite robust. The US bankers once predicted that Indian banks would collapse because of their conservatism but the same thing now turned into a blessing. But still India has been facing major challenges like a large reduction in foreign reserves, a net outflow of foreign capital, plummeting stock prices and a sharp tightening of domestic liquidity. These factors led to rapid depreciation of the exchange rate and a surge in short-term interest rates. Further, it caused a decline in domestic demand and exports. Demand effects have been particularly severe in housing, construction, IT and consumer durables sector. As a result, production in the manufacturing sector has coursed downward and activities in the organized services sector (housing construction, IT) shrank sharply. The major social costs of the financial crisis relate to the enforcement of job-cuts, lay-offs and significant upheavals in the labour markets. Indian Economy, in one way or the other, is feeling the pinch of global economic turmoil which is evident from the following statistical records.

Impact on the GDP Growth Rate

The global financial crisis has adversely affected the GDP growth rate in India. The overall growth of GDP in 2008-09, at factor cost (at constant 1999-2000) prices was 6.7 percent which nose dived from high growth of 9.0 percent and 9.7 percent in 2007-08 and 2006-07 respectively (Table 2)

The deceleration of growth in 2008-09 was spread across all sectors except mining and quarrying and community, social and personal services. The growth in agriculture and allied activities slid down from 4.9 percent in 2007-08 to 1.6 percent in 2008-09, mainly on account of the high base effect of 2007-08 and due to a fall in the production of non-food crops including oilseeds, cotton, sugarcane and jute. The production of wheat was also lower than in 2007-08.

TABLE 2

Rate of Growth at Factor Cost at 1999-2000 Prices

(percent)

	2003-04	2004-05	2005-06	2006-07	2007-08	2008-09
Agriculture, forestry & fishing	10.0	0.0	5.8	4.0	4.9	1.6
Mining & quarrying	3.1	8.2	4.9	8.8	3.3	3.6
Manufacturing	6.6	8.7	9.1	11.8	8.2	2.4
Electricity, gas & water supply	4.8	7.9	5.1	5.3	5.3	3.4
Construction	12.0	16.1	16.2	11.8	10.1	7.2
Trade, hotels & restaurants	10.1	7.7	10.3	10.4	10.1	*
Transport, storage& communication	15.3	15.6	14.9	16.3	15.5	*
Financing, insurance, real estate & business services	5.6	8.7	11.4	13.8	11.7	7.8
Community, social & personal services	5.4	6.8	7.1	5.7	6.8	13.1
Total GDP at factor cost	8.5	7.5	9.5	9.7	9.0	6.7

*Trade, hotels and restaurants, transport and communication (together) grew at 9 percent, 2008-09.

Source: Central Statistical Organisation.

The manufacturing, electricity and construction sectors dropped to 2.4, 3.4 and 7.2 percent respectively in 2008-09 compared to 8.2, 5.3 and 10.1 percent respectively in 2007-08. Both decline in exports and as a result fall in domestic demand resulted in slowdown in manufacturing. The rise in the cost of inputs and the cost of credit dropped manufacturing margins and profitability during the year 2008-09. The impact of the global turmoil and associated factors also badly affected growth in manufacturing sector. The electricity sector continued to be hampered by capacity constraints and the availability of coal, particularly during the first half of the year.

The construction industry went through a boom phase with growth as high as 16.2 percent in 2005-06 and continued to grow thereafter moderately. The increase in the costs of construction due to a rise in the prices of inputs like steel and cement and interest costs had started impacting the industry.

The double squeeze on the costs, as well as the demand side, and the fall in the liquidity in mid-September 2008 precipitated a sharp downturn in this sector. Thereafter in the second half of the year 2008 the demand moderated, but costs remained high.

The higher growth in community, social and personal services during 2008-09 was mainly because of an expansionary fiscal policy that was reflected in the demand side of GDP as higher growth of Government consumption expenditure.

Impact on the Financial Sector

While the overall policy approach has been able to palliate the potential impact of the turmoil on domestic financial markets and the economy, with the increasing integration of the Indian economy and its financial markets with the rest of the world, there is recognition that the country does face some downside risks from these international developments. The risks arise mainly from the potential reversal of capital flows on a sustained medium-term basis from the projected slow down of the global economy particularly in advanced economies, and from some elements of potential financial contagion. In India, the adverse effects have so far been mainly in the equity markets because of reversal of portfolio equity flows, and the concomitant effects on the domestic forex market and liquidity conditions. The macro-effects have so far been muted due to the overall strength of domestic demand, the healthy balance sheets of the Indian corporate sectors, and the predominant domestic financing of investment.

The main impact of the global financial turmoil in India has spread out from the significant change experienced in the capital account in 2008-09 so far compared to 2007-08. Total net capital flows fell from US $ 17.3 billion in April-June 2007 to US $ 13.2 billion in April-June 2008. Nonetheless, capital flows are expected to be more than sufficient to cover the current account deficit this year as well. Foreign Direct Investment (FDI) inflows have jumped from US $8.5 billion during April-August 2007 to US $16.7 billion in the corresponding period of 2008. The portfolio investments by foreign institutional investors (FIIs) saw a net outflow of about US $ 6.4 billion in April-September 2008 as compared with a net inflow of US $15.5 billion in the corresponding period in 2007 (Table 3).

TABLE 3

Trend in Capital Flows

Component	*Period*	*2007-08*	*2008-09*
Foreign Direct Invt. to India	April-Aug.	8.5	16.7
FIIS (net) @	April-Sept.26	15.5	-6.4
Ext. Comm. Borrowings (net)	April-June	7.0	1.6
Short Term Trade Credits (net)	April-June	1.8	2.2
Memo			
ECB Approvals	April-Aug.	13.4	8.1
Foreign Exc. Reserves (Variation)	April-Sept. 26	48.5	-17.9
Foreign. Exc. Reserves (end period)	Sept. 26, 2008	247.8	291.8

Note: Data on FIIS presented in this table represent inflows into the country and, thus, may differ from data relating to net investment in stock exchange by FIIs.

Similarly, external commercial borrowings of the corporate sector declined from US $ 7.0 billion in April-June 2007 to US $ 1.6 billion in April-June 2008, partially in response to policy measures in the face of excess flows in 2007-08, but also due to the current turmoil in advanced economies. Recently, Indian exchange rate experienced significant pressure due to the existence of a merchandise trade deficit of 7.7 percent of GDP in 2007-08, and a current account deficit of 1.5 percent, and change in perceptions with respect to capital flows.

IMPACT OF CAPITAL OUTFLOWS ON DOMESTIC CURRENCY

Exchange rate volatility in India has increased in the year 2008-09 compared to 2007-08. The exchange rate of rupee vis-à-vis the dollar which stood at Rs. 39.9/$ on April 2008 has fallen steadily on account of net dollar outflows, led predominantly by portfolio investors pulling out of the country. It breached the Rs. 50 to the dollar mark, falling to Rs. 50.29 to the dollar on 27 October 2008 before recovering to Rs. 48-49 to the dollar in subsequent trading.

The higher volatility is reflected in the higher co-efficient

TABLE 4

Co-efficient of Variation (CV) of Daily Exchange Rate

Period	*Co-efficient of Variation (CV) of Daily Exchange Rate*
2004-05	2.3
2005-06	1.8
2006-07	1.9
2007-08	2.06
2008-09 (till Sept. 2008)	3.5

Source: Exchange rate data collected from RBI.

of variance of 3.5 percent in the period till September 2008, as compared to 2.06 percent and 1.9 percent in 2007-08 and 2006-07 respectively (Table 4).

Impact on the Indian Banking System

One of the key features of the current financial turmoil has been the lack of perceived contagion being felt by banking systems in Emerging Market Economies (EMEs), particularly in Asia. The Indian banking system has not experienced any contagion, similar to its peers in the rest of Asia. RBI undertook a detailed study in September 2007 on the impact of the sub-prime episode on the Indian banks. The study found that none of the Indian banks or the foreign banks, with whom the discussions had been held, had any direct exposure to the sub-prime markets in the USA or other markets. However, a few Indian banks had invested in the collateralized debt obligations (CDOs) bonds which had a few underlying entities with sub-prime exposures. Thus, no direct impact on account of direct exposure to the sub-prime market was felt. However, a few of these banks did suffer some losses due to the mark-to-market losses caused by the widening of the credit spreads arising from the sub-prime episode on term liquidity in the market, even though the overnight markets remained stable. Indian banks are well capitalized with a low level of non-performing assets (NPAs), though the level of NPAs is expected to go up as the slow down begins to bite. Thus the robust nature of our banks and financial institutions, alongwith the conservative and sound regulation by the Reserve Bank of India has made us better to face this challenge.

Impact on the Stock Market

The secondary market activity of the stock market began on a bullish note with BSE and NSE indices scaling new peaks, of 20,873 and 6,287 on January 8, 2008. However, this momentum could not be sustained and the indices showed significant downtrend in line with the fall in all the major international indices during the second half of January 2008. The highest recorded fall in the history of sensex was intraday fall of 1968 points in absolute terms in BSE sensex on January 21, 2008. The market remained bearish inspite of intermittent corrections in the stock market, due to the rising domestic inflation, rising oil prices and volatility in international financial markets and negative portfolio investment flows during February-March 2008. The indices improved during April 2008. However, the market sentiment turned cautious towards the end of May 2008 on account of rise in international equity markets, increasing concerns about domestic inflation, widening of trade deficit and depreciation of the rupee. The domestic stock markets showed an upward trend from mid-July to the first week of September 2008 but weakened thereafter and recorded losses till end December 2008. This was the result of slowdown in domestic activity, net outflow of funds from domestic capital market by foreign institutional investors, and volatility in international equity markets. During 2008, on a point to point basis, BSE sensex and Nifty indices dwindled by 51.8 percent and 52.4 percent respectively.

Impact on Export Sector

The impact of the crisis on India's export sector has been quite severe (Table 5). It depicts that India's exports have declined from $ 14.8 billion to $12.8 billion during October 2007 to October 2008, i.e. a fall 13.5 percent. There is 60 per cent trade deficit in 2008 compared to 2007 due to the reduction in exports. There is fall in exports due to the recessionary trends in the developed markets where the demand had shrunk. The growth in merchandise exports in India was 28.9 percent in US $ terms in 2007-08 compared to 3.6 in US $ terms in 2008-09. Among the sectors worst affected are gems, and jewellery, textiles (and within textiles the handloom sector), leather and leather products, cotton and man made yarn, tea, oil meals, marine products, carpets and handicrafts. The impact on employment is substantial as all these industries are highly labour-intensive. About 1.5 million jobs have already been lost or are in jeopardy in these sectors.

The trade impacts are, however, not confined to merchandise trade alone but have spilt over into the exports of invisibles. The impact of global recession was relatively less on India's services exports till December 2008, though the growth rate of services export moderated to 16.3 percent during April-Dec. 2008-09. A sharp decline in the growth of travel services

TABLE 5

Impact on Exports Sector in India

Date	*Value (in billion $)*
Oct-07	14.8
May-08	13.8
Jun-08	14.7
July-08	16.3
Aug-08	16
Sep-08	13.7
Oct-08	12.8
Nov-08	11.5
Dec. 08	12. 7
Jan-09	12.3

Source: *India Today*, Meltdown hits home, 23 March, 2009.

and a negative growth in insurance was recorded during this period. Despite the global financial turmoil and decline in growth rate in world financial services exports, Indian financial services registered a robust growth of 45.7 percent and software services went up at 26 percent. However, business services grew at lower rate of 3.9 percent.

Impact on Imports

Import growth began to fall from October 2008 and was

negative over the period, January to March 2009. For the year as a whole, i.e. 2008-09, the overall import growth was subdued at 14.4 percent in US terms. Growth in POL and non-POL imports was 16.9% and 13.2% respectively in US dollar terms. During 2008-09 (April-Feb.) fertilizers and edible oils registered high import growth to meet domestic demand. The growth in the imports of POL was high in the first half of the year due to the unusually high prices but moderated in the second half of the year. The trade deficit rose from US $ 88.5 billion to US $ 119.1 billion during 2007-08 to 2008-09.

Impact on Real Estate

The economic slowdown and tightening interest rates have resulted in slump in real estate industry. Due to the downturn, realty firms are now unable to raise money from the capital market through private equity. The banks have restricted their lending to this sector to avoid the risk, because of the global credit crunch. Property markets have depreciated substantially and lost the value of real estate. A slump in real estate is also having a negative effect on allied sectors like cement and steel.

Impact on Employment

Global recession also has a major impact on employment leading to job cuts, lay-offs and significant upheavals in the labour markets. The International Labour Organisation's (ILO) Global Employment Report for January 2009 gives a very dismal picture of employment. Considering three alternative scenarios, it projects an expansion in world unemployment ranging from 18 million to 51 million over the years end-2007 to end -2009. The corresponding figures for South Asia range from 4 million to 17 million. Even though separate figures are not presented for India, on the basis of the relative distribution of the workforce in South Asia, one could estimate job losses in India to be between 1.3 million and 6 million over this period.

The Indian government's official survey of the unemployment impact of the global crisis was conducted by the Labour Bureau, with a focus on eight sectors (handloom/ powerloom, textiles and garments, metals and metal products, gems and jewellery, automobiles, leather, transport and information technology/business process outsourcing). The

TABLE 6

Changes in Estimated Employment during April-June, Over March, 2009

(In lakhs)

S. No	*Industry Group*	*April, 2009*	*April-May 2009*	*April-June 2009*
1	Textiles	-0.09	-1.92	-1.54
2	Leather	0.05	0.28	0.07
3	Metals	0.01	-0.09	-0.01
4	Automobiles	0.01	0.07	0.23
5	Gems and jewellery	-0.28	-0.27	-0.20
6	Transport	-0.02	-0.03	-0.01
7	IT/BPO	-0.28	-0.34	-0.34
8	Handloom/Powerloom	0.23	0.34	0.49
	Overall (cumulative)	-0.38	-1.95	-1.31

Source: Labour Bureau's Quarterly Report on Effect of Economic Slowdown on Employment in India, during April-June 2009.

latest survey conducted in July 2009 revealed the employment trends during the period April-June 2009. Table 6 presents sector-wise changes in the estimated employment during April-June 2009 as compared to March, 2009.

Table 6 shows that the employment has fallen during the quarter April-June 2009. During the month of May, the estimated employment declined by 1.57 lakh whereas in the month of April the declined was 0.38 lakh. However there has been a slight improvement in the employment (0.64 lakh) during June, thus showing an overall decline of 1.31 lakh during this period. The maximum decline in employment is seen in textiles sector where it has declined by 1.54 lakh during April-June over March, 2009. Other sectors experiencing low/insignificant decline in employment are gems and jewellery, IT/BPO, metals and transport. In leather, automobiles and handloom/powerloom sectors there is a slight increase in employment during the quarter April-June over March, 2009.

Table 7 depicts average monthly percentage change in employment during April-June over March 2009 for these eight sectors. It shows that at overall level, the employment during the quarter April-June has declined by 0.29 percent. The results further indicated that in absolute terms the fall in employment in gems and jewellery sector during April-June over March 2009 is only 0.20 lakh whereas in percentage terms the average monthly fall in employment is maximum in this sector (1.65 percent). In textiles and IT/BPO sector the average monthly decline in employment during the period April-June over March, 2009 is at 0.63 percent and 0.34 percent respectively. The automobile sector shows an upward trend in average monthly employment over different periods under study. Decline in employment during the months of April and May period may be due to seasonality. Personal interaction of the officers associated with the textiles and gems and jewellery establishments revealed that shortage of workers during the period is experienced by them every year. According to them, the migrant workers prefer to visit their place of origin during this period, resulting in their decreased availability.

TABLE 7

Average Monthly Percentage Change in Employment during April-June Over March, 2009

(In percentage)

S. No.	*Industry Group*	*April, 2009*	*April-May, 2009*	*April-June, 2009*
1	Textile	-0.11	-1.18	-0.63
2	Leather	1.34	3.93	0.62
3	Metals	-0.07	-0.29	-0.03
4	Automobiles	0.10	0.59	1.24
5	Gems and Jewellery	-6.80	-3.26	-1.65
6	Transport	-0.65	-0.42	-0.09
7	IT/BPO	-0.86	-0.51	-0.34
8	Handloom/Powerloom	3.26	2.38	2.29
	Overall	-0.25	-0.64	-0.29

Source: Labour Bureau's Quarterly Report on Effect of Economic Slowdown on Employment in India, during April-June 2009.

SECTION III

To lift the economy out of the recession the Indian government took certain fiscal and monetary measures. On December 7, 2008 the government announced a fiscal package of

Rs. 35,000 crores. The major steps in terms of stimulus package announced by the government of India are:

1. A refinance facility of Rs. 4000 crores was provided to the National Housing Bank. Following this, public sector banks announced loans at reduced rates to small home loans seekers, in order to increase demand in retail housing sector. The housing package is the core of the government's new fiscal policy. It will give fillip to other sectors such as steel, cement, brick kilns, etc. Besides, the small and medium industries (SMEs) would too get an impetus by manufacturing all kinds of fittings and furnishings.
2. To boost the infrastructure, the India Infrastructure Finance Company Ltd. (IIFCL) has been authorized to raise Rs. 14,000 crores through tax free bonds. These funds will be used to finance infrastructure, more especially highways and ports. The IIFCL will be permitted to raise further resources by the issue of such bonds so that a public private partnership (PPP) programme of Rs. 1,00,000 crores in the highway sector is upgraded.
3. The RBI is providing Rs. 7000 crore to small Industries Development Bank of India (SIDBI) for direct lending to employment-intensive micro and small enterprises (MSE). There is a 4% reduction in excise duty on cars, steel, cement and a host of other products. The ad valorem tax on cement has been reduced from 12% to 8%.
4. The textile sector has been seriously affected due to declining orders from the world's largest market the United States. An allocation of Rs. 1400 crores has been made to clear the entire backlog in the Technology Upgradation Fund (TUF) scheme.
5. The government of India has provided Rs. 1450 crore to export sector. There has also been a 4% reduction in excise duty. The government has withdrawn export duty on iron ore fines. The levy on export of iron lumps has been reduced to 5% from 15%. The

RBI has extended the period of pre-shipment and post-shipment credit for export.

India's stimulus package of Rs. 35,000 crores which constituted 0.6% of GDP was too small to save the economy from financial meltdown so, the central government announced the second package of measures. The new package included the following measures:

1. The RBI has cut the repo rate from 6.5 percent to 5.5 percent and has also reduced cash reserve ratio (CRR) from 5.5 percent to 5 percent, to boost investment and spending and to revive growth.
2. The realty companies have been allowed to borrow from overseas to develop "integrated townships."
3. Drawback benefits have been enhanced for some exporters. Export-Import Bank has also got Rs. 5000 crores as credit from the RBI, to revive exports.
4. Public sector India Infrastructure Finance Company (IIFC) have been allowed to borrow Rs. 30,000 crores from the market by issuing tax-free bonds.
5. Depreciation benefit on commercial vehicles has been increased from 15 percent to 50 percent on purchases, in order to stimulate the commercial vehicles sector.
6. Ceiling on foreign institutional investments (FIIs) in corporate bonds has been increased to $ 15 billion from $ 6 billion, to seek much bigger FIIs.

There is no doubt that the government is motivated with good intentions and is thus aiming to spend a huge amount. But the success of the fiscal package will depend on the quality and speed of its implementation. There is a need to orient the fiscal package towards inclusive growth so that the weaker sections benefit. Expenditure on primary and secondary education, health and sanitation can result in a more inclusive growth process. The Indian economy should concentrate on developing the domestic market. Thus, inward looking policies should be preferred as against the outward looking approach of integrating the Indian economy to the world economy.

It is high time that the policy-makers in the Ministry of Finance, Commerce, Industry and Rural Development should get together to ensure that the planned expenditure-budgeted is quickly translated into productive capacities so as to create the much needed multiplier effect on private investment. It needs to be emphasized that implementation holds the key to bail out the Indian economy from the economic crisis.

References

Datt, Ruddar (2009): "Global Meltdown and Impact on the Indian Economy", *Mainstream*, April 2, 2009, 9-13.

Government of India (2009), "Report on Impact of Economic Slowdown on Employment in India", April-June 2009.

Government of India (2009), "Economic Survey, 2008-09".

Kumar, Raj, Sarika and Veeran Kochar (2009): "Global Economic Turmoil-Challenges for Indian Economy," *Political Economy Journal of India*, Vol. 18, Issues 1 and 2, 84-97.

Kandu, Sridhar: "Can the Indian economy emerge unscathed from the global financial crisis?", available at www.observer.india.com.

Mohan, Rakesh (2008): "Global Financial Crisis and Key Risks: Impact on India and Asia", available at http://rbi.org.in.

Nachane, Dilip M. (2009): "The Fate of India Unincorporated", *Economic and Political Weekly*, Vol. XLIV, No. 13, 115-22.

National Manufacturing Competitiveness Council (2008): "Current Global Financial Crisis and its impact on India, Measures for ensuring growth of the Real Sector of the Economy", available at http://nmcc.nic.in.

South Asia Region, The World Bank Group (2009): "Impact of Global Financial Crisis on South Asia", available at http://siteresources.worldbank.org.

Srinivasan, T.N: "Real and Financial Sector Linkages and Global Economic Crisis: India and China", available at www.isb.edu.

Impact of Financial Crisis on the Indian Economy

S.K. Dhage and B.G. Lobo

INTRODUCTION

The global economy is today facing unprecedented crisis with falling production and job losses. Most advanced countries are already in the grip of recession and the economic outlook for the developing countries is deteriorating rapidly. To prevent economic collapse the governments of the US and other developed countries are giving massive bailout packages to their failing banks and other institutions and virtually nationalizing them The state's direct intervention in the economy is in direct opposition to the ruling economic philosophy of the last three decades, characterised by an ideology of free markets, deregulation, liberalisation, privatisation and globalisation with the state exercising minimal interference in economic activities. The current global economic meltdown has exposed the hollowness of the philosophy of unfettered capitalism with its belief in free and unregulated markets.

The present crisis is the result of an unsustainable global growth pattern that had been emerging since 2000. The growth was driven to a large extent by strong consumer demand in the USA, stimulated by easy credit and supported by a booming housing market, coupled with a very high rate of investment demand and strong export growth in some developing countries, notably China. Growing US deficits were financed by increasing trade surpluses by China, Japan and other countries that had accumulated large foreign-exchange reserves and were willing to buy dollar denominated assets. At the same time increasing financial deregulation, along with a flurry of new financial instruments and risk management techniques such as mortgage backed securities, collateralized debt obligation, credit default swap, etc., encouraged massive accumulation of financial assets. The massive explosion of debt inevitably resulted in collapse of many established financial institutions, evaporating the liquidity and severely affecting the real economy. They were sustained by a growing level of debts in the household, corporate and public sectors.

The financial crisis has revealed major deficiencies in the regulatory and supervisory framework of financial markets. The US and other European countries have given huge stimulus package to revive the economy and restore confidence in financial markets in order to normalise credit flows. The leaders of the G-20 met in London on April 2 and have reiterated faith in an open world economy, with effective regulation and strong global institutions.

IMPACT OF THE CURRENT FINANCIAL CRISIS ON INDIAN ECONOMY

There is a very vast impact on various sectors of Indian economy by following selected economic sectors we can explain the impact of crises:

1. Economic Growth

Has the present global crisis affected India's domestic economy? To answer this it is necessary to look at our current macroeconomic fundamentals. Latest RBI estimates place India's growth rate during 2008-09 at 7.7 per cent. Most other estimates also place GDP growth for the year in the range of 7-8%. During the first quarter of 2008-09 (April-June) Indian economy grew at

7.9 per cent, though growth is expected to slow down in the subsequent quarters as the slowdown takes hold. The first indication has already come from the index of industrial production (IIP). According to latest data, the IIP grew 4.8% in September 2008 as against 7% in the corresponding period last year. The cumulative growth during April-September 2008 was only 4.9% as against 9.5% during the corresponding period in previous year. While the September figure is an improvement over the dismal growth of 1.3% recorded for August 2008, it is too early to see it as a recovery from the previous low.

2. Price Situation

The rate of inflation, as measured by the wholesale price index (WPI) has gone down during recent few weeks and more encouragingly declined sharply during the week ended 1 November to 8.98%, down from the previous week's 10.68% and the peak of 12.9 percent in first week of August. However, food inflation remains high. Moreover, inflation as measured by the consumer price index (CPI-IW) has not shown a decline. On the contrary, there is a steady rise in CPI-IW inflation from 7.7 per cent in June 2008 to 9.8 in September 2008. The combination of rising prices of consumer goods coupled and slowing growth does not bode well for the economy.

3. Banking Sector

The banking sector in India is largely (70%) dominated by the public sector. Partly as a result, India has not been witness to the kind of crisis of confidence seen in advanced countries. Additionally, strict regulation and conservative policies adopted by the Reserve Bank of India have ensured that banks in India are relatively insulated from the travails of their Western counterparts. However, this cannot be advanced as a reason either for continuance of public sector dominance or for resistance to further financial sector reform. The example of Canada where the private sector plays a major role in the banking sector and is, by and large, less affected by the present financial crisis is a case in point. Indian banks are well-capitalized with a low level of non-performing assets (NPAs), though the level of NPAs is expected to go up as the slowdown begins to bite. The Reserve Bank of India has initiated a series of steps to ease the liquidity problems being faced by banks. It has cut the cash reserve ratio to 5.5% and the repo rate at which the central bank pumps liquidity into the system to 7.5%. It has also reduced the SLR or statutory liquidity ratio to 24%, down from 25% earlier.

4. Capital Market

After the macroeconomic reforms in 1991, Indian economy has been increasingly integrated into the global economy. The financial institutions in India are exposed to the world financial market. Foreign institutional investment (FII) is largely open to the India's equity, debt market and market for mutual funds. The present crisis has significant impact on FII investment in India, as investors all over world lack confidence on the market. The crisis in confidence resulted in net outflow of $10.1 billion from both the equity and debt market in India in the year 2008, till 22nd Oct. This has significant impact on India's stock market and exchange rate. As higher FII outflows have a down pressure on the value of rupee at the same time a weaker rupee makes it costlier for FIIs and hedge funds to pull out of the market but decline in stock prices only adds to their woes. India's stock market index Sensex which touched above 21,000 mark in the month of January, 2008 has plunged below 10,000 during October. The movement of Sensex shows a positive and significant relation with the FII flows into the market. Data on Sensex at the weekend closing point and net FII in equity on the same day taken since 1st of August, 2008 till 17th Oct. figures a positive correlation of 0.66.

5. Impact of Capital Outflows on Domestic Currency

Exchange rate volatility in India has increased in the year 2008-09 compared to previous years. The exchange rate of rupee *vis-à-vis* the dollar which stood at Rs. 39.9/$ on 1 April 2008 has fallen steadily on account of net dollar outflows, driven predominantly by portfolio investors pulling out of the country. It breached the Rs. 50 to the dollar mark, falling to Rs. 50.29 to the dollar on 27 October 2008 before recovering to Rs. 48-49 to the dollar in subsequent trading. The higher volatility is reflected in the higher co-efficient of variance of 3.58 per cent in the period up to September 2008, as against 2 per cent in 2007-08 and 1.9 per cent in 2006-07.

6. Exchange Rate Volatility and India's External Trade

After registering an export growth of 29.02 per cent and import growth of 35.4 per cent during 2007-08, growth merchandise export growth fell 15% in dollar terms in October 2008. This is the first time in five years that exports have actually shown a dip, reflecting the growing adverse impact of the global slowdown. If the present trend continues there is a danger that India will not achieve the export target of $ 200 bn for the current fiscal.

The tumultuous development in the past one year had a negative impact on the pace of economic activity in India as well. The economy, which was growing at eight to nine per cent, has slowed down. The tentative estimates expect the economy to have grown at around five per cent, though official estimates place it at more optimistic seven per cent. The stock market has lost 50 per cent of its value. The rupee has lost some 20 per cent of its value in terms of the dollar. There have been huge job losses in sectors of the economy with large export dependence, such as textiles and diamond cutting and polishing. No fresh recruitment and job creation is taking place even in the high-profile IT sector. The government has come out with several stimulus packages with additional spending on infrastructure and tax concessions.

It must, however, be said that due to adoption of a pragmatic economic policy, India has not been as adversely effected by the global meltdown as other countries which had

TABLE I

Indicator	*Period*	*2007-08*	*2008-09*
(Growth in Per Cent)			
Real GDP Growth	April-December	9.0	6.9
Industrial production	April-February	8.8	2.8
Services	April-December	10.5	9.7
Exports	April-March	28.4	6.4
Imports	April-March	40.2	17.9
Stock Market (BSE Sensex)	April-March	16,569	12,366
Rs. per US$	April-March	40.24	45.92

Source: Current State of Indian Economy, FICCI, February 2009.

fully embraced market capitalism. India adopted a policy of economic liberalisation in 1991, discarding the model of a socialist and closed economy. There was deregulation of the economy, most controls on setting up of new industrial units were removed, import tariffs were reduced and a policy of encouraging foreign investment was initiated. This helped India becoming a part of the global economic network and the industrial sector becoming globally competitive. The country achieved economic growth of 6.5 per cent during 1992- 2002, which jumped to eight-nine per cent from 2003 onwards, as compared to four per cent during four decades prior to 1991. While the economy was deregulated, key industries in oil, steel, mining and other sectors remained in the public sector. India also took the saner path of not going for capital account convertibility on the foreign-exchange front.

Impact of Economic Crises on India's Economic Indicators

Table 1 shows the impact of financial crises on Indian economy real GDP growth was 9 per cent in 2007-08 which has decreased to 6.9 percent in 2008-09. Industrial production, service, export and import decreased from 8.8, 10.5, 28.4, 40.1 percent respectively to 2.8, 9.7, 6.4 and 17.9 percent. BSE Sensex also decreased from 16,569 to 12,366. Value of rupee also decreased 40.24 to 45.92 per US $.

POLICY SUGGESTIONS IN DEVELOPING COUNTRIES LIKE INDIA FOR CRISES

Many developing countries enter this crisis with advantages that they lacked during the shocks of the 1980s or 1990s. The strengthening of macroeconomic policies—including fiscal and external positions, in many cases—leaves them less vulnerable. Sovereign debt is better managed in most countries than at the time of the Asian crisis, and the move to flexible exchange rate arrangements makes it easier for countries to partially absorb the shock through exchange-rate adjustment. And the number of people worldwide living in extreme poverty has dropped by more than 300 million since the East Asian crisis, expanding ever so slightly the narrow margin for survival at the bottom of the income scale. Finally, the onset of the crisis itself has diminished inflation pressures, dramatically changed expectations, and (for net importers) reduced commodity prices, which should reduce strains on some developing economies.

Developing countries will need all these advantages as they move to limit the damage from this crisis. The first priority is to prevent financial contagion from crippling domestic banking and non-banking financial sectors. Because of the high level of inter linkages among the world's financial firms and sectors, these effects have begun to arrive before the real economy effects in some countries. Stock markets have declined sharply, some currencies have depreciated substantially, and sovereign interest-rate spreads have risen with the "flight to safety" in world markets. At a more micro level, some developing-country exporters are already finding it hard to obtain the trade credits that are their lifeblood, which could cripple export sectors that will soon be hit by the fall in foreign demand.

So just like in the developed countries, it is important that the developing countries take quick, decisive, and systematic measures to ensure that credit crunches and bank collapses are avoided locally. And in extending deposit guarantees, governments need to set adequate floors and coordinate policies to avoid "beggar-thy-neighbour" policies, while guarding against the long-run moral hazard effects that will make the regulators' job harder in the future.

Developing countries that enter the crisis with large balance-of-payments and fiscal deficits will be the most vulnerable to these effects. Such countries will have larger financing and adjustment needs, if the current account swings sharply from deficit to balance as capital dries up, as occurred in the Asian financial crisis. This will put a deep strain on the balance sheets of domestic firms and banks, potentially leading to a cascade of bankruptcies and bank failures. If their fiscal resources are already strained to the limit, then it may be impossible to mount domestically financed rescues of their financial sectors. These countries will likely have to seek financing for the international financial institutions (discussed below), especially at a time when bilateral donors are already straining to meet domestic crisis needs.

More generally, developing-country governments have

two main macroeconomic tools for responding to the negative shock that is coming their way: monetary policy and fiscal policy. One great risk is that if the credit crisis is not effectively resolved, the global economy could enter a period of deflation like the one that Japan suffered through in the 1990s. In that environment, standard monetary policy will not likely be effective in the developed economies. Firms in these countries are already on or near the global technological frontier, so there is limited room for industrial upgrading, meaning that any credit-financed expansion would primarily be in terms of production capacity. But in the face of low demand and excess capacity, developed country firms are not likely to want or be able to borrow to finance expansion.

In the developing world, by contrast, there is more room for credit-financed industrial upgrading, which may give more room for monetary policy to work in those countries that can afford to use it. Not all countries will be able to; some may find themselves forced to tighten monetary policy and increase interest rates to prevent excessive currency depreciation or capital outflows. But some governments may be able to provide some monetary stimulus by lowering interest rates and encouraging investment in sectors where industrial upgrading is most likely to have payoffs.

On the fiscal-policy side, developing-country governments have a variety of tools that they could use to cushion the blow of the shock. Governments with some fiscal space can respond by injecting some well-designed fiscal stimulus into their economies, to generate domestic demand that can offset the expected decline in foreign demand. Developing countries have pressing needs that can be met through public investments. One such need is building of infrastructure, especially after a period when private-sector growth has sometimes outstripped the ability of the public sector to provide the infrastructure needed to sustain that growth and rural infrastructure where the infrastructural gap exists between urban and rural areas.

A second area for investment is social protection and human development, to ensure that a temporary shock is not converted into severe permanent declines in welfare of poorer households. There are many programs that have been shown in evaluations to be worth investing in; governments should prioritize protection and expansion of those that most effectively buffer the impact of crises on the poorest households. Examples of the types of programs to consider could include conditional cash transfer programs to keep disadvantaged children in school, like Indonesia's program during the 1997-98 crisis (Cameron 2002), public-works employment (or workfare) programs like India's Employment Guarantee Scheme (Gaiha, 2004), and subsidies on the consumption of inferior goods (those that are not consumed by the non-poor). Such programs will be appropriate responses for countries with healthy reserves, current-account surpluses or small deficits, and solid fiscal policies. An obvious example is China, where higher domestic demand could also help cushion the crisis' effects on trading partners. In other countries with less fiscal room for maneuver, programs like these should be a priority for donor support.

In sum, policy-makers in developing countries are likely to be facing dilemmas whose solution will be highly dependent on how they behaved during the boom period (e.g., allowing more lax or tighter macro-policies, or building buffers against shocks or not), as well as how the global shocks affect their individual economies. Their ability to respond to the crisis depends on whether emerging markets have room to act in a prudent countercyclical way by increasing domestic demand without sacrificing excessively their fundamentals. These fundamentals include the countries' fiscal positions, debt levels, domestic inflation rates, and the health of their domestic banking sector. Some developing countries have scope to do this, while others have less room for fiscal maneuver and still others are already experiencing credibility shocks and capital flight out for higher quality.

One danger is that countries which are affected, cannot or do not want to recognise they are affected. Developing countries are now in a better fiscal position to react and smoothen the impact than a decade ago. However, while many have built up external assets, there are concerns for those countries whose current account deficits have recently ballooned due to the food and fuel crisis. Moreover there will also be questions marks about the flexibility of the fiscal and monetary institutions in some countries. Yet countries need to be prepared as they will be hit—e.g. Cambodia's growth will decline from more than 10% in 2007 to less than 5% in 2009.

Few poor countries have such leveraged financial systems as in developed countries, and many do not have a short-term foreign debt which needs financing (such as Pakistan, Iceland and Hungary). But some might. Further, trade finance has become a particular challenge as 90% of trade is financed on short-term credit.

The social effects are already visible in developing countries. The key export for Zambia is mining and the industry has seen the copper price reduce by 40% in a few months due to slower demand (even China is now entering a period of "low" growth rates not seen for decades, e.g. 7.5% projected growth in 2009). A result has been a lay-off of workers. How would the social consequences be addressed by economic and social policies, e.g. by promoting short-term productive activities or investing in tailored social protection?

An obvious response would be to accelerate reforms and introduce policies to attract investment and promote growth. We know a lot about what policies and factors promote growth (see the Growth Commission report), but less so on what are the most binding constraints in a given country setting. Growth diagnostics aim to examine binding constraints and are underway in several countries. Now that international capital flows and the recession bites, binding constraints to growth over the medium-term may shift. For instance, it is likely that the binding constraints in Zambia in a situation of high copper prices and mining investment differ from those in a situation of low copper prices, weak investment and falling exports.

The current macroeconomic and social challenges posed by the global financial crisis require a much better understanding of appropriate policy responses:

1. There needs to be a better understanding of what can provide financial stability, how cross-border cooperation can help to provide the public good of international financial rules and systems, and what the most appropriate rules are with respect to development;
2. There needs to be an understanding of whether and how developing countries can minimise financial contagion;

3. Developing countries will also need to manage the implications of the current economic slowdown—after a period of strong and continued growth in developing countries, which has promoted interest in structural factors of growth, international macroeconomic management will now move up the policy agenda. Do countries have room to use fiscal and monetary polices?
4. Developing countries need to understand the social outcomes and provide appropriate social protection schemes;
5. There will also be implications for development policy:

There will be limits to financial solutions if the problems lie in the real economy, but develop-ment finance institutions may be able to take some risks and support investment flows to developing countries, counteracting reductions in other financial flows. Whether Development Financial Institutions (DFI) can take higher risks might be informed by past experience, for example by looking at what happened during the Asian financial crisis of the late 1990s. During this period DFI portfolios were riskier, loan losses higher and returns lower than they are at present. And yet this poorer financial performance has not had an adverse affect on institutional credit ratings.

CONCLUSION

The Indian economy has shown considerable resilience in the face of the present global financial crisis. The financial sector has emerged without much damage thanks in part to our strong regulatory framework and in part on account of state ownership of most of the banking sector. However, it would be naïve to expect the real economy to be completely unaffected by the global slowdown. The immediate impact of the crisis is the drying up of dollar liquidity as FIIs pull out their money from the stock market and sources of overseas credit and trade credit dry up. While large corporate will no doubt be affected, the worst affected are likely to be the exports and SMEs (small and marginal enterprises) that contribute significantly to employment generation.

While some evidence is beginning to emerge, individual developing countries need urgent access to updated research on country-specific economic, social and political impacts of the financial crisis. This is needed to inform appropriate policy responses which address the current downturn but which will not sacrifice long-term objectives. We suggest that each developing country needs to set-up a crisis task force to consider the best possible and urgent policy responses at country level. In addition, developing countries will have an interest in stable global financial rules which allow for new rules to reduce pro-cyclicality in international capital flows, transparency, and a greater voice for developing countries. Developed countries should not worsen the financial mess they pass on to developing countries, and improve their commitments on aid and development finance as the case for aid is stronger now than it was before. They could suggest new investment targets for countries; better incentives for investment officers inside DFIs and the need for new aid funded crisis funds that could be linked to DFI operations in a transparent and open way, similar to the global partnership of output based aid.

REFERENCES

Akyuz, Yilmaz (2008), "The global financial crisis and developing countries", Resurgence, December, Penang: Third World Network.

Bernanke, B.S. (1983). "Non-Monetary Effects of the Financial Crisis in the Propagation of the Great Depression", *American Economic Review*, Vol. 73, pp. 257-76.

Berner, Richard. 2008, "A Deeper US Recession Goes Global." Morgan Stanley Global Economic Forum (online publication), October 7 ed.

Chandrasekhar, C.P. (2008a), "Global liquidity and financial flows to developing countries: new trends in emerging markets and their implications", G-24.

Ghosh, Jayati and C.P. Chandrasekhar, eds. (2008), A Decade After: Financial crisis and recovery in East Asia, New Delhi: Tulika Books, forthcoming.

International Monetary Fund. 2008, World Economic Outlook: Financial Stress, Downturns, and Recoveries, Washington, DC: IMF.

Mishkin, F.S. (1994), "Preventing Financial Crises: An International Perspective," Manchester School, 62, (1994): 1-40.

Impact of the Global Financial Crisis on the Indian Economy

M. Sundara Rao and P. Ramu

Globalization has ensured that the Indian economy and financial markets cannot stay insulated from the present financial crisis in the developed economies. The turmoil in the international financial markets of advanced economies that started around mid-2007, has exacerbated substantially since August 2008. The financial market crisis has led to the collapse of major financial institutions and is now beginning to impact the real economy in the advanced economies. As this crisis is unfolding, credit markets appear to be drying up in the developed world. With the substantive increase in financial globalization, how much will these developments affect India. The debate, therefore, can only be on the extent of impact and how resilient India is to withstand the storm with minimal damage! In the light of the fact that the Indian economy is linked to global markets through a full float in current account and partial float in capital account.

There is need to analyze the impact of this crisis based on three critical factors, availability of global liquidity; demand for India investment and cost thereof and decreased consumer demand to Indian exports. The concerted intervention by central banks of developed countries in injecting liquidity is expected to reduce the unwinding of India investments held by foreign entities, but fresh investment flows into India are in doubt. India, like most other emerging market economies, has so far, not been seriously affected by the recent financial turmoil in developed economies. The reasons for the relative resilience shown by the Indian economy o the ongoing international financial markets' crisis has to be identified first to know the actual extent of the impact of global financial crisis on Indian economy and to search for the needed approach to the management of the exposures of the Indian financial sector entities to the collapse of major financial institutions in the global economy.

INITIAL IMPACT OF GLOBALIZATION ON INDIAN ECONOMY

During the post-reform period Indian economy emerged as relatively open economy, though the capital account not being fully opens. Due to the gradual open up process the current account transactions amounted to about 53 per cent of GDP in 2007-08, up from about 19 per cent of GDP in 1991. On the front of capital account, the total transactions increased from 12 per cent of GDP in 1990-91 to around 64 per cent in 2007-08. However, the current global financial crisis has shown liquidity risks and it can rise manifold during a crisis and can pose serious downside risks to macroeconomic and financial stability. The R BI is able to put in place steps to mitigate liquidity risks at the very short-end. Some of the important measures by the Reserve Bank in this regard include, first, restricting the overnight unsecured market for funds to banks and primary dealers as well as limits on the borrowing and lending operations of these entities in the overnight inter-bank call money market. Similarly, large reliance by banks on borrowed funds can exacerbate vulnerability to external shocks. This has been brought out quite strikingly in the ongoing financial crisis in the global financial markets.

The Indian economy has started experiencing for some time the impact of the deepening recession in the U. S., the U.K., Europe and elsewhere. Reduced forex earnings were due mainly to the sharp depreciation of the rupee against the dollar and other major currencies. Rupee exports were actually higher by 4.3 per cent. But this was not adequate to offset the effect of the drop in value of the rupee. The rupee cost of imports got exaggerated by 24 per cent. This would have accentuated inflationary pressures but for the sharp fall in global oil and other commodity prices. The export target of $200 billion for 2008-09 cannot be realised. It is now expected to be reached in 2009-10 as the rupee is expected to firm up once the new government is sworn in and there may be a reversal of forex outflows after some time.

Reflecting the severe impact of the global meltdown, India's economic growth slumped to 6.5 per cent during 2008-09. Evidently, the two stimulus packages put in place earlier during the fiscal year 2008-09, as also the measures announced in the interim budget to spur the economy, would take some more time to show effect and, therefore, the onus is now on the RBI to provide the necessary impetus by cutting its key policy rates. The other big challenge for the new government is going to be on the external account. The larger issue here is to shore up the balance of payments at a time capital flows have reversed and when both invisible earnings (software exports and income from other services) and remittances from overseas Indians have come under pressure. The sharp fall in overseas trade comprising both exports and imports in January 2009 is a cause for worry. A fall in imports is due to low domestic demand.

IMPACT OF GLOBAL FINANCIAL CRISIS ON INDIAN FINANCIAL SECTOR

One of the key features of the current financial turmoil has been the lack of perceived contagion being felt by banking systems in Emerging Market Economies (EMEs). The Indian banking system also has not experienced any contagion, similar to its peers in the rest of Asia. A detailed study undertaken by the RBI in September 2007 on the impact of the sub-prime episode on the Indian banks had revealed that none of the Indian banks or the foreign banks, with whom the discussions had been held, had any direct exposure to the sub-prime markets in the USA or other markets. However, a few Indian banks had invested in the collateralized debt obligations (CDOs)/bonds which had a few underlying entities with sub-prime exposures. Thus, no direct impact on account of *direct exposure* to the sub-prime market was in evidence. However, a few of these banks did suffer some losses on account of the mark-to-market losses caused by the widening of the credit spreads arising from the sub-prime episode on term liquidity in the market, even though the overnight markets remained stable. The Reserve Bank has announced a series of measures to facilitate orderly operation of financial markets and to ensure financial stability which predominantly includes extension of additional liquidity support to banks.

Along with the inbuilt precautionary measures the banks were advised to formulate specific policies covering exposure limits, collaterals to be considered, margins to be kept, sanctioning authority. In view of the rapid increase in loans to the real estate sector raising concerns about asset quality and the potential systemic risks posed by such exposure, the risk weight on banks' exposure to commercial real estate was increased. The impact of the global financial crisis on the Indian financial system will be three-fold: The element of GDP growth driven by off-shore flows will be diluted; correction in the asset prices which were hitherto pushed by foreign investors and demand for domestic liquidity putting pressure on interest rates. While the global financial system takes time to recover leading to low demand for investments in emerging markets, the impact will be on the cost and related risk premium.

The impact will be felt both in the trade and capital account. Indian companies which had access to cheap foreign currency funds for financing their import and export will be the worst hit. The impact of which, again, will be three-fold: Reduced capacity expansion leading to supply side pressure; increased interest expenses to affect corporate profitability and increased demand for domestic liquidity putting pressure on the interest rates. Consumer demand in developed economies is certain to be hurt by the present crisis. The impact of which, once again, will be three-fold: Export-oriented units will be the worst hit impacting employment; reduced exports will further widen the trade gap to put pressure on rupee exchange rate and intervention leading to sucking out liquidity and pressure on interest rates.

The impact on the financial markets will be, equity market will continue to remain in bearish mood with reduced off-shore flows, limited domestic requirement due to liquidity pressure and pressure on corporate earnings; while the inflation would stay under control. Increased demand for domestic liquidity will push interest rates higher and we are likely to witness gradual rupee depreciation. Overall, while RBI would inject liquidity through CRR/SLR cuts, maintaining growth beyond 7% will be a struggle. The banking sector will have the least impact as high interest rates, increased demand for rupee loans and reduced statutory reserves will lead to improved NIM while, on the other hand, other income from cross-border business flows and distribution of investment products will take a hit. Given the dependence on foreign funds and off-shore consumer demand for the Indian economic growth.

India cannot wish away from the negative impact of the present global financial crisis but should quickly focus on alternative remedial measures to limit damage. As the overall policy approach has been able to mitigate the potential impact of the turmoil on domestic financial markets, there is recognition that the country does face some downside risks from the international developments. The risks arise mainly from the potential reversal of capital flows on a sustained medium-term basis from the projected slow down of the global economy, particularly in advanced economies. In India, the adverse effects have so far been mainly in the equity markets because of reversal of portfolio equity flows, and the concomitant effects on the domestic forex market and liquidity conditions. The macro-effects have so far been muted due to the overall strength of domestic demand. The FDI inflows have continued to exhibit accelerated growth during 2007-08.

The corporate sector has, in recent years, mobilized significant resources from global financial markets for funding, both debt and non-debt, their ambitious investment plans. The demand for bank credit and non-food credit growth has indeed accelerated in 2008-09. The financial crisis in the advanced economies and the likely slowdown in these economies could have some impact on the IT sector. According to the latest assessment by the NASSCOM, the software trade association, the current developments with respect to the US financial markets are very eventful, and may have a direct impact on the IT industry and likely to create a downstream impact on other sectors of the US economy and worldwide markets. As a whole, the combined impact of the reversal of portfolio equity flows, the reduced availability of international capital both debt and equity, the perceived increase in the price of equity with lower equity valuations, and pressure on the exchange rate, growth in the Indian corporate sector is likely to feel some impact of the global financial crisis.

Large swings in capital flows—as has been experienced between 2007-08 and 2008-09 so far—in response to the global financial market turmoil have made the conduct of monetary policy and liquidity management more complicated. The recent innovation with respect to SLR for combating temporary systemic illiquidity is particularly noteworthy. The relative stability in domestic financial markets, despite extreme turmoil in the global financial markets, is reflective of prudent practices, strengthened reserves and the strong growth performance in recent years in an environment of flexibility in the conduct of policies. Active liquidity management is a key element of the current monetary policy stance. Liquidity modulation through a flexible use of a combination of instruments has, to a significant extent, cushioned the impact of the international financial turbulence on domestic financial markets by absorbing excessive market pressures and ensuring orderly conditions. In view of the evolving environment of heightened uncertainty, volatility in global markets and the dangers of potential spillovers to domestic equity and currency markets, liquidity management will continue to receive priority in the hierarchy of policy objectives over the period ahead. The Reserve Bank will continue with its policy of active demand management of liquidity through appropriate use of the CRR stipulations and open market operations (OMO) including the MSS and the LAF, using all the policy instruments at its disposal flexibly, as and when the situation warrants.

RECENT MONETARY AND FISCAL MEASURES ADOPTED

To counteract the impact of global financial crisis on the different sectors of the country the Indian Government' announced the first stimulus package on December 7, 2008. Along with tax revenue foregone, the December package was estimated to cost Rs. 30,000 crore. The Government's latest stimulus package announced on January 2, 2009 has not met the high expectations it had raised. In the second package there is no provision for direct plan expenditure. Nor is there a reduction in indirect taxes. The absence of 'direct' fiscal measures is one of the main reasons why the recent package suffers even in comparison with the first. But there are other reasons why both the stimulus packages have disappointed.

The government has been constrained by its fiscal position. The supplementary budget of October and December pre-empted the space for more liberal spending to stimulate the economy. Bulk of the large appropriations made then were for non-productive expenditure such as for meeting salary hikes and petroleum and other subsidies. Taking the off-budget items (oil, fertilizer bonds and so on) the size of the fiscal deficit of the Centre and the States is estimated to rise to 10 per cent of the GDP. The government claimed that such a large expenditure would have the same contra cyclical effects as the measures outlined in the two packages. However, the fact remains that fiscal management over the recent past — when the economy was growing fast—did not proactively provide for the lean years. Fiscal responses to the economic slowdown, out of necessity, have been muted.

That has also meant that the government will lean even more heavily on the RBI. One of the invidious consequences has been that for all practical purposes the Union Finance Ministry seems to have usurped the central bank's role in monetary management. In the event, since mid-September the RBI has effected sweeping cuts in the policy as well as statutory rates, with some of these announcements coinciding with the stimulus packages. Recently the RBI has initiated exceptional measures like reducing repo rate from 9 per cent to 5.5 per cent and the reverse repo from 6 per cent to 4 per cent. The CRR has been brought down from 9 per cent to 5 per cent to increase the extent of public spending. On 4th March 2009, the RBI cut its repo and reverses rates by 0.50 percentage point. The move is clearly intended to lower the cost of bank borrowing.

There are far too many factors at work, global and

domestic, that will keep the economy down. Two areas of serious concern are worth noting: the unsustainable fiscal situation and falling exports. Both are linked to the global economic crisis. The government's inability to spend much more than it did in each of the three stimulus packages to reverse the rapid slowdown in the domestic economy is well documented. Governments around the world needed to come out with such stimulus packages to boost demand, whose shrinkage is a cause as well as a manifestation of the global economic crisis. For whatever reason, India may claim to have escaped the full brunt of the economic crisis, but there is no doubt that it will remain affected for a long time to come. As has been the case with most other countries, urgent monetary and fiscal measures are being taken to revive the economy. The interim budget stayed clear of significant stimulus measures, concentrating its spending proposals on the present government's flagship social sector schemes. Barely a week later, however, the Government announced cuts in excise duties and service tax. The package is estimated to cost over Rs. 29,000 crore which will push the fiscal deficit higher.

The Planning Commission, Government of India constituted a Committee on Financial Sector reforms which is popularly known as the Raghuram Rajan Committee. The report given by the Committee is the latest addition to several landmark documents that have set visions of hope for India to live up to its potential. The report calls for a new paradigm in the financial sector. The report states that there are some advantages, so to say, of remaining a low flyer. To start with, when the global economy goes on a downward spiral, the relatively lower levels of exposure act as a natural insulator against immediate shocks. But such approaches are fatalistic. If India is destined to play a major role in the world's polity, it has to get its economy onto a higher growth orbit. For this, the country's financial sector needs to be shipshape.

The report dwells on aspects of the Indian economy where the reforms can go deep, and perhaps could be less controversial. For instance, few can differ on the importance of addressing problems relating to financial exclusion. The chapter "Broadening Access to Finance", which deals with the important issue of financial inclusion, is an example of a much-required, but less controversial area of reform. The eight chapters cover the range of reforms that are required in the financial services. Finally the committee focused on the three important reasons for financial sector reforms, which are inclusiveness, growth, and stability. This adds to the existing body of knowledge on the state of play of the nation's economy in a very important sector, and its 28 proposals would help in creating a better and more inclusive financial system, which will enable India to rise to higher levels of sustained economic growth.

CONCLUSION

The current global financial crisis has shown liquidity risks in India and it can rise manifold during a crisis and can pose serious downside risks to macroeconomic and financial stability. The RBI is able to put in place steps to mitigate liquidity risks at the very short-end. Some of the important measures by the Reserve Bank in this regard include, first, restricting the overnight unsecured market for funds to banks and primary dealers as well as limits on the borrowing and lending operations of these entities in the overnight inter-bank call money market. Similarly large reliance by banks on borrowed funds can exacerbate vulnerability to external shocks. This has been brought out quite strikingly in the ongoing financial crisis in the global financial markets. India may claim to have escaped the full brunt of the economic crisis, but there is no doubt that it will remain affected for a long time to come

There is guarded optimism about the coming year in some quarters. The industrial and financial climate is expected to benefit from the huge tax concessions and high government spending. The analysis about the impact of global financial crisis on India's financial sector ultimately reveal that the problem in India is not availability of money with the banks but persuading them to lend. The RBI has admitted that that risk management, difficult even in normal times, is even more difficult in an environment of uncertainty and downturn. Risk aversion is something that is not alien to public sector banking. Peculiar constraints faced by government owned banks have prevented their officers from taking commercial risks. It is difficult to see how in these recessionary conditions they can be persuaded to lend aggressively. India has by-and-large been spared of global financial contagion l for a variety of reasons. India's growth process has been largely domestic demand driven and its reliance on foreign savings has remained around 1.5 per cent in recent period. It also has a very comfortable level of forex reserves. Financial stability in India has been achieved through perseverance of prudential policies which prevent institutions from excessive risk taking, and financial markets from becoming extremely volatile and turbulent. Towards this end this study suggests for the effective implementation of the recommendations made by the Raghuram Rajan Committee recommendations for further strengthening the Indian financial sector to meet the global challenges.

References

Baldev Raj Nayar (2001), Globalisation and Nationalism.

Henry, Peter Blair (2007), "Capital Account Liberalization: Theory, Evidence, and Speculation", *Journal of Economic Literature*, Vol. XLV, December.

International Monetary Fund (2008): "Global Financial Stability Report", October.

Kavalijit Singh (2000), Taming Global Financial Flows.

Mohan, Rakesh (Oct. 9, 2008), "Global Financial Crisis and Key Risks: Impact on India and Asia", (IMF FSF High Level Meeting, Washington D.C.).

Prasad, Eswar S., Raghuram G. Rajan and Arvind Subramanian (2007), "Foreign Capital and Economic Growth", Brookings Papers on Economic Activity.

Reserve Bank of India (2008), Annual Policy Statement for the Year 2008-09, April,

Reserve Bank of India Bulletin, April (2007), "Development of Financial Markets in India".

Reserve Bank of India Bulletin, June (2007), "India's Financial Sector Reforms: ostering Growth While Containing Risk", December.

Romesh Sobti (Sept. 21, 2008), The Global Crisis and its Impact on India.

World Bank (2003), The Little Data book.

World Bank (2008), "Global Development Finance 2008", June.

17

Global Economic Meltdown and its Impact on the Indian Economy

Asim K. Karmakar

INTRODUCTION

The global financial meltdown and consequent economic recession in developed economies have clearly been major factor in India's economic slowdown. Given the origin and dimension of the crisis in the advanced countries, which some have called the worst since the Great Depression of the 1929, every developing country has suffered to a varying degrees, depending on their exposure to sub-prime and the related assets. No country, including India, remained immune to the global economic shock.

The crisis surfaced around August 2007 with the bursting of the bubble in the sub-prime mortgages in the US as reflected in the credit markets. Eventually, the sub-prime crisis had affected financial institutions in the US, Europe and elsewhere including the shadow banking system comprising *inter alia* investment banks, hedge funds, private equity and structured investment vehicles, and in the process, had caused, within a few months, a huge financial meltdown, a string bankruptcies and a sharp global imbalances and slowdown in practically all industrialized countries. The collapse of the Lehman Brothers in Mid-September 2008 further aggravated the situation leading to the crisis of confidence in the financial markets and, as the Reserve Bank of India (RBI) Governor D. Subbarao (2009) had rightly pointed out that from three channels: the trade channel affecting the capital and current account of balance of payments, the financial channel and the confidence channel, it arose. The resulting uncertainty cascaded into a full-blown financial crisis of global dimensions.

The gradual softening of international interest rates during the last few years, coupled with relatively easy liquidity conditions across the world, forced investors who take risks leading to expansion in the sub-prime market. The word 'sub-prime' refers to borrowers (who are not related as 'prime') and who do not have a sound track record of repayment of loans. The risks inherent in sub-prime loans were sliced into different components and packaged into host of securities and structured investment instruments like Collateralized Debt Obligations, synthetic CDOs. Credit rating agencies has assigned risk ranks to them to facilitate marketability. Intermediaries such as hedge funds, pension funds and banks, who held in their portfolios, were not fully aware of the risks involved. Moreover, the securitization process was not backed by due diligence and led to large-scale default. When interest rate rose leading to defaults in the housing sector, the value of the underlying loans declined along the price of the products. Institutions were saddled with illiquid and value-eroded instruments, leading to liquidity crunch; the crisis in the credit market subsequently spread to the money market as well. Households and corporate accustomed to high asset values in the present globalized economies were adversely affected by the bursting of the asset bubbles, and contributed to sudden and severe contradiction in demand and loss of confidence. The reason for bursting of the asset bubbles is not far to seek. Actually, the asset bubbles was on the process of creation out of excess liquidity growth due to the excessive accommodative monetary policy of the advanced industrialized countries, especially of the US, i.e., allowing the supply of money to be plentiful and interest rate low relative to appropriate level, which in turn, caused investors on the look out for yield as well as to take either under-priced risks or excessive risks. Such excess liquidity at last found its way into speculative activities, causing asset bubbles. Investors were under the impression that the prices of such assets like real estate or equity will keep increasing in future. These developments resulted in drastic reductions in activity in the real sectors. Thus the initial problems in the financial sector were transmitted to the real sector with adverse feedback effects.

India could not insulate itself from the adverse developments in the international financial markets, despite having a banking and financial system that had little to do with investments in structured financial instruments carved out of sub-prime mortgages, whose failure had set-off the chain of events culminating in global crisis. The feedback effect of the crisis on the Indian economy was not significant in the beginning. The initial effect of the sub-prime crisis was, in fact, positive, as the country received accelerated Foreign Institutional Investment (FII) flows during September 2007 to January 2008. This contributed to the debate on "decoupling hypothesis," where it was believed that the emerging Asian economies, especially the larger ones like China and India could remain insulated from the crisis and provide an alternative engine of growth to the world economy in moderating the global downturn and paving the way for a worldwide recovery in a year or so. The argument soon proved unfounded as the global crisis intensified and spread to the emerging economies through different channels.

In the above backdrop the present paper expresses some facets of the global crisis, including its impact on some sectors of the Indian economy. In Section II, we examine at how through trade channel the effects of global crisis and economic slowdown fall on the Indian economy. Section III analyses the impact of the crisis on the Indian cultivators. Section IV discusses the impact of the crisis on the employment situation in India. Section V concludes.

EFFECTS OF GLOBAL CRISIS AND ECONOMIC SLOWDOWN ON INDIA THROUGH TRADE CHANNEL

Government of India's Economic Survey, 2006-07

vociferously articulated that "the sub-mortgage loan crisis is the major financial crisis of the new millennium whose origin is in the United States (US) housing market. Subsequently, this spread to Europe and some other parts of the World. The sub-prime crisis has also impacted the emerging economies. India has remained insulated from this crisis. The banks and institutions in India do not have marked exposure to the sub-prime and related assets in matured markets. Further, India's gradual approach to the financial sector reforms process has played positive role in keeping India immune from such international shocks." But this presumption made by the Economic Survey that India would in no way be affected by the crisis was wrong. The recent Indian growth story was analogous to the story of speculative bubble-led expansion that was the characteristics of the several other developed and developing countries during the same period. This is so because recent economic growth in India is dependent upon greater global integration, related to financial deregulation that spurred consumption as well as credit boom and combined with fiscal concessions to spur consumption among the richest population of the country. This led to rapid increase in aggregate GDP growth at the cost of greater employment generation and agrarian improvement. The proliferation of financial activities thus became combined with rising asset values to enable credit-finance consumption surge among the rich and the middle classes in our country. In the 1990s and beyond we find as a result a rise in debt-financed housing investment and private consumption among the elite and the middle class. These developments in the financial sector resulted in drastic reductions of activity in the real sector and those were transmitted quickly to the real sector with adverse effects.

By the middle of 2008, things began to turn worse. The credit-financed consumption spark, which is turn, generated higher rates of investment, did not match with the growth of the domestic market. This mismatch was reflected in the Indian economy. Besides, the deepening of the global crisis and subsequent deleveraging and risk aversion however affected the Indian economy leading to slowing of growth momentum. The growth of GDP at factor cost (at constant 1999-2000 prices) at 6.7% representing deceleration from high growth rate of 9% and

9.7% in 2007-08 and 2006-07 respectively (*Economic Survey, 2008-09*). The year 2008-09 closed with industrial growth at only 2.4% as per the Index of Industrial Production. However, industrial production picked in December 2007, fell by 6.5% in April 2008 as a consequence of successive shocks, the most being the knock-on effects of the global financial crisis. The manufacturing, electricity and construction sectors decelerated to 2.4, 3.4 and 7.2% respectively in 2008-09 from 8.2, 5.3 and 10.1% respectively in 2007-08. The growth in production sectors was adversely affected by the impact of global recession. The crisis became intensified by causing sharp decline in exports of manufacturers and reversal of capital flows. With the onset of the crisis, mainly after September 2008 we find that the Indian economy was seriously affected by the trade channel through drastic reduction in earnings from exports of goods and services, first, on account of the drying up of international financing and trade credit, followed by a fall in global demand. There was significant decline in merchandise exports, reflecting fall in exports of all commodity groups. The biggest falls were recorded in the export of rice, raw cotton, ready-made garments, sugar and molasses, iron ore, iron and steel, gems and jewellery. More generally, small and medium industries were adversely affected whenever there was such type of stress in the financial and real sectors. There also had been spillover effects on invisibles through lower remittances from non-residents and earnings from tourism. Thus the fallout of the crisis has also permeated onto the services sector. Despite that, imports continued to grow. So the trade deficits as well as the current account deficit had increased. The current account was mainly affected after September 2008 mainly through slowdown in exports and it had increased three-fold by the last quarter of 2008-09. What made things worse was that capital was also leaving India, causing the capital account to turn negative during the third quarter of 2008-09, which altogether indicating a net outflow of US $3.7 billion, as against an inflow of US $ 31.0 billion in Q3 of 2007-08 attributable to net outflow under portfolio investment, banking capital and short-term trade credit. Net external commercial borrowings(ECBs) remained lower at US $ 3.9 billion in Q3 of 2008-09 (US $ 6.2 billion in Q3 of 2007-08), as the liquidity conditions tightened in the international financial markets and ECBs became more difficult and expensive. The net portfolio flows to India turned negative (the extent of reverse of capital flows in case of India was US $ 15.8 billion during February-June, 2008) as Foreign Institutional Investors (FIIs) rushed to sell equity stakes in bid to replenish overseas cash balances. This had a knock-on-effect on the stock market and the exchange rates through creating the supply-demand imbalances in the foreign exchange market.

Bond, money and credit markets had been affected indirectly through the dynamic linkages. The domestic bond markets were affected, since the government securities market and the corporate bond market were opened up. They were affected indirectly, since the drying up of bond and credit markets globally made corporate substitutes overseas funds with domestic funds. Cumulatively, these impacted the forex markets, warranting the use of forex reserves and the management of liquidity in money markets. The drying up of liquidity, a fallout of repatriation of portfolio investments by FIIs, affected credit markets in the second half of 2008-09. This was compounded by the risk aversion of the banks to lend and the reluctance of the borrowers to borrow, because of the considerable uncertainties in the level of economic activity. Paul Krugman's remark in early January 2009 in this connection is worth remembering, 'This looks an awful lot like the beginning of a second Great Depression... recent economic numbers have been terrifying, not just in the United States but around the world. Manufacturing, in particular, is plunging everywhere. Banks aren't lending; businesses and consumers aren't spending." However, the extent of the external financial and monetary shock on the Indian monetary-financial system is found to be in contraction in reserve money by more than 15% between August 2008 and November 2008. Reserve money growth collapsed from 26.9% in August 2008 to 10.3% in November 2008 and further to 6.4% in March 2009. Despite these, M1 growth and M2 growth decelerated. Subsequently, credit growth decelerated sharply to 17.1% in March 2009, partly because of transmission of OECD recession effects to Indian exporters and organized manufacturing. From October 2008, there were also falls in FDI. All was associated with significant depreciation of the currency, with the rupee filling by more than 30% against the dollar from around January, 2008 through a positive shock of the global turmoil. The decline in rupee became more pronounced after the collapse of the Lehman Brothers in mid-September 2008. The cumulative effect of the above is on real-sector activity. It is now possible to argue that the global forces have dampened the domestic activity.

The policy-makers' stress on acquiring excessive capital flows, before the onset of the global financial crisis, led to increase in forex reserve as well as contributed to monetary expansion, which fuelled liquidity growth. WPI inflation reached a trough of 3.1% in October 2007, month before global commodity price inflation zoomed to double digits from low single digits. The rising oil and commodity prices, contributed to significant rise in prices, with annual WPI peaking at 12.9% in August 2008.

It is now obvious also that such global crisis will adversely affect upon workers of India through falling employment, lower wages and more adverse working conditions, and indirectly through reduced access to public goods and services. The global crisis also meant that the economy has had been experiencing extreme volatility in terms of fluctuation in inflation level.

IMPACT OF GLOBAL RECESSION ON THE INDIAN CULTIVATORS

The impact of the crisis on Indian agriculture has even more severe than has been apprehended. The farmers in our country face problems like frequent droughts or floods, volatile monsoons, soil degeneration, lack of institutional credit and insurances leading to excessive dependence on private money-lenders, difficulties in marketing and high volatility of crop prices. Further in liberalized world the Indian farmers have to work in highly uncertain and volatile international environment. Volatile crop prices often leads the farmers to respond to the wrong signal and they finding no other alternatives have to adjust themselves by changing their cropping pattern. This requires for them new varieties of seeds and other inputs supplied by MNCs. Small and marginal farmers find themselves in real difficulty if crops fail or output prices remain low. Further, they have to face continuous rising prices of inputs. Financial liberalizations measures caused significant slowdown in the growth of bank credit, particularly from commercial banks to rural areas and a relative fall in proportion to bank credit flowing to the priority sectors, especially agriculture. Bank credit growth fell from 22.3% in 2007-08 to 17.3% in 2008-09 (*Economic Survey*, 2008-09). Thus the impact of the slowdown in rural banking fell disproportionately on poor and small borrowers. The agrarian crisis in most part of the country is often substantially related to the decline in the access of peasant farmers to institutional finance, which is the direct result of financial liberalization. Measures taken by the government, which have reduced credit towards farmers and small producers have contributed to rising costs, greater difficulty of accessing necessary working capital for cultivation and other activities, and reduced the economic viability of cultivations, thereby adding directly to rural distress. There is ample evidence here in India that the deep crisis of the cultivable community, which has been associated with to a proliferation of farmers' suicides and other evidence of distress such as migration and even hunger deaths in different parts of rural India, has been related to the decline of institutional credits (*Ghosh*, 2009).

The global meltdown in commodity prices particularly in energy, metals and agricultural intermediates across the world, most of which are tradeables, has led to corresponding decline in domestic prices (*Economic Survey*, 2008-09). The fall in international prices of several commodities (both agricultural and non-agricultural) has impinged on small produces and farmers' income via import competition as well as low prices in sectors such as cotton and oilseeds production. Farmers now face lower prices of their output even as food prices have continued to increase.

EFFECT OF GLOBAL FINANCIAL CRISIS AND ECONOMIC SLOWDOWN ON EMPLOYMENT IN INDIA

Major markets in India have been seriously affected by the global financial crisis and economic slowdown with a dearth of employment opportunities in the financial year 2008-09. Some sample survey data in this connection will help us to indicate employment losses in the wake of the global financial crisis and economic slowdown.

According to the report on "Effect of Economic Slowdown on Employment in India", which is based on a sample survey of 2581 units conducted by the Labour Bureau, Ministry of Labour and Employment, during October-December 2008, covering eight sectors like mining, textiles and garments, metal and metal products, gems and jewellery, automobiles, construction, transport, and information technology (IT)/business process outsourcing (BPO) industry, there was decrease in employment of about half a million workers during the period. The most affected sectors were gems and jewellery, transport and automobiles where employment has declined by 8.58% , 4.03%, and 2.42% respectively during the period . In textile sector, 0.91% of workers have lost their jobs. Another thin sample survey conducted to asses the employment situation in January 2009 over December 2008 indicated a loss of about 1 lakh jobs in the month of January 2009. The employment decline was more rapid in case of export units (1.13% per month) compared to non-export oriented units (0.81% per month), pointing to the direct role of global meltdown. A sample survey conducted by the Department of Commerce for 402 exporting units revealed job loss (direct and indirect) to the tune of 1,09,513 persons during August 2008 to mid-January 2009. Another survey in a single state (Gujarat) has found that more than 400 thousand jobs have been lost due to recession in the diamond industry by February 2009 (*Task Force for Diamond Sector, 2009*). The Confederation of India Textiles Industry has estimated that at least 1.2 million jobs in textile and garment production had been lost by March 2009, not to speak on the substantial declines in money wages for daily contracts and piece rate work for the usual workers and migrant workers, the latter coming from the far-off backward and most distressed regions of the country. What emerges, in fact, is that the employment squeeze in the organized sector in the recent years has a tremendous impact on the unorganized sectors via the backward linkages with the former. Even the National Commission for Enterprises in the Unorganised Sector (NCEUS) is of the view that the recent global crisis has impacted serious repercussions on the Indian economy and especially the poor who are the unorganized workers working in sectors like construction, handlooms, textiles, apparel, leather products, gems and jewellery, metal products, carpets, oil mills, marine products, and handicrafts. The situation urgently calls for a revival from the part of the government in the form of a major fiscal stimulus comprising of (i) Programmes to boast pro-poor public investment in physical and social infrastructure, (ii) Expansion in scope and coverage of social security schemes for the unorganized workers so that they are immediately assured of a minimum level of social protection, (iii) Schemes/ Programmes which protect and promote incomes of the poor.

CONCLUSION

The current global financial crisis is first and foremost a crisis of neoliberalism reflecting the failure of unfettered market functioning, most especially in financial markets. It is also a product of the hegemony of global finance and is a structural one as well as of cyclical nature that cannot be easily resolved only through the self-regulating character of capitalism. There is one view that the failure of governance at all levels is truly indicative of the failure of the whole economic system, or what some have described this financial tsunami as a failure of capitalism. A suitable redesign of international and domestic institutions may aid the process of recovery.

There is now increasing recognition that where recession or depression, the nature of the current crisis, is altogether profoundly different from those of east Asian currency crisis that happened more than a decade ago or the crisis occurred during the Great Depression of the 1930s. The root causes of the current crisis and economic slowdown, according to the IMF (February 2009) lie in "market failure... bred by a long period of high growth, low interest rates and volatility and policy failures in financial regulation—which was not equipped to see the risk concentration and flawed incentives behind the financial innovation boom; macroeconomic policies—which did not take into account building systematic risks in the financial system and in housing markets." Such crisis of world-wide magnitude where the economic system of any country is more or less integrated with the world economic system in this globalized era is bound to be reflected. India as one of the emerging market economies cannot be remained immune from this crisis and now simply is suffering the after-effects of this financial tsunami unleashed in the US.

References

Ghosh, Jayati (2009): "The Global Financial Crisis and the Working Class in India," Prabhat Kar Memorial Lecture delivered at Jadavpur University on 13 June, Kolkata.

Government of India (2008-09): Economic Survey, Ministry of Finance, OUP.

Karmakar, Asim K. (2008): "India's External Debt—An Evaluation of its Status during the Reform Period", *Rabindra Bharati Journal of Economics*, Vol II, March.

Nachane, D.M. (2009): "The Fate of India Unincorporated," in Global Economic and Financial Crisis, Essays from *Economic and Political Weekly*, Orient Blackswan Pvt. Ltd

Rakshit, M. (2008): The Sub-prime Crisis: A Primer, Money and Finance, 3(3), 75-124

———, (2009): "India Amidst the Global Crisis," in Global Economic and Financial.

Ram Mohan, T.T. (2008): "From the Sub-prime to the Ridiculous," *EPW*, November 8.

———, (2009): "The Impact of the Crisis on the Indian Economy," in Global Economic and Financial Crisis, Essays from *Economic and Political Weekly*, Orient Blackswan Pvt. Ltd.

Reddy, Y.V. (2009): India and the Global Financial Crisis: Managing Money and Finance, Orient Blackswan Private Limited, Hyderabad.

Subbarao, D. (2009): "Impact of the Global Financial Crisis on India: Collateral Damage and Response," Speech delivered in Tokyo, 18 February.

Implications of Global Recession for the Indian Economy

P.S. KAMBLE

INTRODUCTION

Economic stability is a must for rapid and all round economic development of the economy. It is rapid and all round development facilitates rapid social development of the economy necessary for social welfare maximisation of the society. In absence of stability it is rather difficult both the economic as well as social development so as to material social welfare maximisation of the society. Hence, economic stability is a must. Trade cycle and its different phases such as recession, depression creates economic instability and works as a hindarable in socio-economic development of the economy. These restrict socio-economic development of a country, which can have several evil consequences on the economy as well as society. The financial crisis arised in August 2007 in USA converted into global financial crisis and thereby global slow down or recession. India being one of the countries of the world emphasing on globalisation can not stay away from global financial crisis as well as slow down. This demands to study global recession in the context of Indian economy, the nature and extent of recession in India and more importantly, its impact on Indian economy. It against this overall backdrop, the present research paper examines the implications of global recession/ meltdown for an Indian economy.

OBJECTIVES OF THE STUDY

The important objectives of the present study are as follows:

1. To study concept of recession or economic slow-down;
2. To examine nature and extent of recession/economic meltdown in India;
3. To assess impact of recession on Indian economy;
4. To derive implications of global recession for an Indian economy.

HYPOTHESIS OF THE STUDY

A hypothesis of the present research study is as mentioned below:

> "India is not away from the phenomenon of global recession. But Indian economy has been considerably affected by the global slowdown."

DATA BASE AND RECESSION METHODOLOGY

The present research paper endeavours to study the phenomenon of global recession with emphasis on nature, extent and impact. For this, this study has selected the latest period of five years from 2004-05 to 2008-09. The study solely relies on the secondary data published by the Government of India, RBI, CSO and others such as Economic Survey, Annual Report and others. The present study makes use of the parameters like GDP, sectoral distribution of GDP, Growth in Foreign Trade, Trends in Foreign Currency Reserves, Foreign Direct Investment (FDI), Inflation, Credit Supply, and Employment. The processing of data has been undertaken by employing statistical techniques, namely, Compound Growth Rate, Percentage Share, Variation, Coefficient of Variation, etc. For this, the study also makes use of computer softwares such as Excel and SPSS.

A BACKDROP OF GLOBAL RECESSION

Recession is a macroeconomic problem. It is one of the phases of trade or business cycle. The term trade cycle in economics refers to the wave like fluctuations in the aggregate economic activity, particularly employment, output and income. Business cycles are ups and downs in economic activity.[1] According to Haberer, "The business cycle in the general sense may be defined as an alteration of periods of prosperity and depression of good and bad trade." J.M. Keynes has defined a trade cycle in a comprehensively manner as "A trade cycle is composed of periods of good trade characterised by rising prices and low unemployment percentages, alternating with periods of bad trade characterised by falling prices and high unemployment percentages." When prosperity ends, recession begins. It is a turning point rather than a phase. It is relatively for a shorter period of time. The noteworthy features of recession as a phase of business cycle are[2]: fall in employment, decreasing industrial output, wage rates fall but lag behind prices, fall in prices, bank loans cut sharply, bank reserves rise, bank clearings fall, high discount rates, falling cost of production, profits disappear, rise in business failures, little speculations, falling business, inventories, building construction stop, feeing of hesitation.

The financial crisis began with the bursting of the housing bubble in the US and high incidence of defaults on sub-prime mortgages early last year has its origins in the loose monetary policy followed under former chairman of the US Federal Reserve, Allan Greenspan.[3] In a bid to counter the economic slowdown brought on by the dotcom bust of 2000, the US Federal stead fastly lowered interest rates to 1% during the period till 2004 before raising it to 5.25% in 2006. The combination of rising prosperity and low interest rates led to a sharp increase in demand for housing loans even as easy liquidity saw a run up in all asset values, including houses. This encouraged borrowers to assume expensive mortgages in the belief that they would be able to get refinance on more favourable terms. However, once interest rates began to rise and housing prices started to drop in many parts of the US in 2006-07 refinancing became more difficult. Defaults and foreclosures became common place once home prices stopped going up and then started falling. What made matters worse was that banks and mortgage payment, suddenly found the value of these securities falling rapidly as defaults rose. Major banks and financial institutions both in the US and in many other developed countries that had borrowed and invested hugely in such securities lost heavily. The first hint of trouble came from the collapse of two Bear Stearns hedge funds early last. Subsequently a number of other banks and financial institutions also began to show signs of distress. However, matters really came to a head with the bankruptcy of Lehman Brothers an economic investment bank in September 2008.[4] This financial crisis spread all over the world, especially in developed countries, which has been converted into global meltdown or recession.

The IDBI Gilts in a report 2007 titled 'Decoupling or Recoupling has analysed whether crisis in US economy would impact other economies or not. The latest report 2008 explains how the channels have impacted other economies. There are three channels, namely, Trade Channels, Financial Channels and Trade and Finance Integrated Channels.[5] The Indian policy-makers need to be vigilant and proactive to minimise the impact of the crisis that is expected to be worsen in 2009.[6]

GLOBAL RECESSION AND INDIAN ECONOMY: AN ANALYSIS

The present section of this research paper is important one.

It endeavours to examine the phenomenon of global recession in the context of Indian economy with the help of some parameters mentioned in research methodology so as to identify the nature, extent and impact on the economy.

Conventional wisdom holds that the Great depression helped produce a more equal income distribution. But Margo finds that the data do not support it.[7] Wheelock maintains that the Great depression caused lasting changes in monetary institutions that ultimately gave monetary policy an inflationary bias.[8]

Gross domestic product (GDP) is an indicator of economic development of the economy. It is also a major constituent of aggregate economic activity in the economy. The trends in GDP of India have been presented in Table 1.

TABLE 1

Trends in GDP of India (GDP at Factor Cost at Current Prices)

(in Rs. crore)

Year	*GDP at factor cost*
2004-05	2877701
2005-06	3282385
2006-07	3779384
2007-08	4320892
2008-09	4933183
CGR 2004-05 to 2006-07	14.60%
CGR 2007-08 to 2008-09	14.17%

Note: CGR = Annual Compound Growth Rate.
Source: Central Statistical Organisation.

The period taken into account by the present study is of latest five years from 2004-05 to 2008-09. It is divided into two phases

or period into 2004-05 to 2006-07 as pre-recession and 2007-08 to 2008-09 as during recession in the context of India. From the data results in Table 1, it is adequately clear that global recession has not affected adversely economic growth of India. The rate of economic growth of India was higher and more or less similar for both the periods, i.e. pre-recession and during recession. It was more than 14 percent and a fall is meagre during the recession period.

Recession can prevail in the different productive sectors and their economic activities in the economy. Hence, changes in sectoral distribution of GDP of India have been examined. The necessary information is presented in Table 2 below.

TABLE 2

Growth in Sectoral Distribution of GDP of India (GDP at Factor Cost at 1999-2000 Prices)

Productivity Activity	*2004-05*	*2005-06*	*2006-07*	*2007-08*	*2008-09*	*Variance*	
						I	*II*
Agriculture, Forestry & Fishing	10%	5.8%	4%	4.9%	1.6%	9.48%	5.44%
Mining & Quarrying	8.2%	4.9%	8.8%	3.3%	3.6%	4.41%	0.04%
Manufacturing	8.7%	9.1%	11.8%	8.2%	2.4%	2.84%	16.82%
Electricity, Gas & Water Supply	7.9%	5.1%	5.3%	5.3%	3.4%	2.44%	1.80%
Construction	16.1%	16.2%	11.8%	10.1%	7.2%	6.31%	4.20%
Trade, Hotels & Restaurants	7.7%	10.3%	10.4%	10.1%	8%	2.34%	0.65%
Transport, Storage & Communication	15.6%	14.9%	16.3%	15.5%	9%	0.49%	21.12%
Financing, Insurance, Real Estate & Business Services	8.7%	11.4%	13.8%	11.7%	7.8%	6.51%	7.60%
Community, Social & personal Services	6.8%	7.1%	5.7%	6.8%	13.1%	0.54%	19.84%
GDP at factor cost	7.5%	9.5%	9.7%	9%	6.7%	1.48%	2.64%

Note: I = 2004-05 to 2006-07 period, II = 2007-08 to 2008-09 period.
Source: Central Statistical Organisation.

It is observed that agriculture and allied activities in India had fluctuations in pre as well as during recession period. The pre-recession period had greater and negative variations than the during recession period. But its growth rate was dismal especially in 2008-09. It is revealed that the growth of manufacturing sector has been greatly and negatively varied especially during 2007-08 to 2008-09, which is a during recession period. The activities like electricity, gas and water supply, construction have shown negative variations during recession period, but they are lower than the pre-recession period. Trade, hotels and restaurants have shown mild negative variations during recession. Transport, storage and communication, financing, insurance and business services have been varied significantly and negatively during recession. But, community, social and personal services have shown positive variations during recession. Thus, manufacturing, transport, storage and communication, finance, insurance and business have been adversely affected by the recession.

Recession also can adversely affect demand in the economy as an aggregate variable. Hence, demand side growth contribution to GDP in India has been taken into consideration.

TABLE 3

Demand Side Growth Contribution and Relative Shares to GDP

Contribution to growth	*2004-05*	*2005-06*	*2006-07*	*2007-08*	*2008-09*	*Variance*	
						I	*II*
Consumption (Private)	38.8%	46.3%	38.7%	53.8%	27.%	19%	359.12%
Consumption (Government)	4.8%	7.1%	5.8%	8%	32.5%	1.33%	300.12%
Gross Capital Formation	71.3%	63.8%	45.6%	55.7%	NA	174.66%	55.7%
Net Exports	10.1%	- 41.1%	-13.2%	-14%	-29.5%	65.7.12%	120.12%
Relative Shares							
Consumption (Private)	65.5%	59.3%	57.5%	57.2%	55.5%	2.28%	1.44%
Consumption (Government)	10.6%	10.3%	9.9%	9.8%	11.1%	1.44%	120.12%
Gross Capital Formation	30.5%	33.3%	34.4%	36.2%	NA	4.04%	1.62%

Source: Central Statistical Organisation.

From the above table, it is revealed that private consumption growth has been significantly but negatively varied during recession. But government consumption has increased significantly and positively during recession. Export growth was rapidly negative during recession in India. The relative contribution to GDP reveals that private consumption has played a prominent role in the determination of our GDP than the government consumption during recession. But government consumption has varied positively and significantly during recession. Capital formation has also shown a positive variation.

Foreign trade is an important parameter concerned with

international transactions and consequently with global recession. Here it is examined with reference to India during recession. The necessary data is presented in Table 4 below.

TABLE 4

Growth in Foreign Trade of India

Year	*Foreign Currency Reserves*
2004-05	593121
2005-06	647327
2006-07	836597
2007-08	1196023
2008-09	1230066
CGR 2004-05 to 2006-07	18.76%
CGR 2007-08 to 2008-09	2.84%

Source: Economic Survey of Government of India, 2008-09.

The data results in Table 4 reveal that during recession exports growth have been declined significantly. But the decline in imports growth was very meagre and marginal. Consequently, the gaps between exports and imports have been widened tremendously resulting in rapid growth in trade deficit. Thus, exports have been affected adversely by the recession.

Along with exports, imports and trade balance, it is also necessary to consider other indicators of external sector. Table 5 below gives the necessary information about that.

It is revealed that imports have been grown rapidly than exports, which have increased deficit in trade balance rapidly. Invisibles balance have been shown a meagre growth during recession period. Likewise, External Commercial Borrowings (ECBs), Foreign Direct Investment (FDI) have shown an insignificant growth. But, external debt has shown a significant growth during recession than the pre-recession period.

Foreign currency reserves is an important parameter of trends in international economic transactions. Table 6 presents the data concerning trends in foreign currency reserves of India.

It is observed that growth in foreign currency reserves of India during pre-recession period was rapid and significant. But

TABLE 5

Selected Indicators of the External Sector

(As % of GDP)

	2004-05	*2005-06*	*2006-07*	*2007-08*	*2008-09*	*Variance*	
						I	*II*
Exports	12.2%	13%	14.1%	14.1%	15.2%	.91%	0.6%
Imports	16.9%	19.4%	20.9%	21.9%	27.1%	4.8%	13.52%
Trade Balance	– 4.8%	- 6.4%	- 6.8%	- 7.8%	- 12%	1.12%	8.82%
Invisibles Balance	4.5%	5.2%	5.7%	6.3%	7.8%	0.36%	1.12%
Current Account Balance	- 0.4%	- 1.2%	- 1.1%	- 1.5%	- 4.1%	.19%	3.38%
ECBs	0.7%	0.3%	1.8%	1.9%	0.8%	.60%	.60%
FDI	0.5%	0.4%	0.8%	1.3%	1.7%	.04%	.08%
Portfolio Investment	1.3%	1.5%	0.8%	2.5%	-1.3%	.13%	7.22%
External Debt	18.5%	17.2%	17.9%	18.9%	26.2%	.42%	26.64%

Source: Reserve Bank of India.

TABLE 6

Year	*Foreign Currency Reserves*
2004-05	593121
2005-06	647327
2006-07	836597
2007-08	1196023
2008-09	1230066
CGR 2004-05 to 2006-07	18.76%
CGR 2007-08 to 2008-09	2.84%

Source: Economic Survey of Government of India, 2008-09.

during recession growth in foreign currency reserves was marginal only.

This can be an indicator of adverse impact of recession.

Foreign investment can be affected by the phenomenon like recession. Hence, growth and composition of foreign investment in Indian economy was observed during pre as well as during recession period.

TABLE 7

Growth in Foreign Investment of India

Year	*Foreign Investment*	*FDI*	*Portfolio Investment*
2004-05	13000	3713	9287
2005-06	15528	3034	12494
2006-07	14753	7693	7060
2007-08	44957	15401	29556
2008-09	4032	15373	-11341
CGR 2004-05 to 2006-07	6.52%	43.94%	8.71%
CGR 2007-08 to 2008-09	-10.31%	- 0.18%	- 3.83%

Source: Reserve Bank of India.

The data in Table 7 reveals that FDI have been decreased during recession than pre-recession period. Besides this, portfolio investment has registered a negative growth during

TABLE 8

Credit Supply by Banks

(Rs. in crore)

Credit Flow from	*2008*	*2009*	*Coefficient of Variance*
Public Sector Banks	307310	341442	7%
Foreign Banks	36116	6483	98%
Private Banks	78301	51559	29%
All Scheduled Commercial Banks	430724	408099	4%

Source: Reserve Bank of India.

recession. Thus, FDI and foreign investment and portfolio investment have been affected adversely by the recession. Credit supply in the economy can be adversely affected by the effects of recession. Hence, trends in supply of credit by different types of banks is examined.

The statistical information in Table 8 shows that except public sector banks, credit supply by all other types of banks have been declined significantly. Especially, credit supply by foreign banks has been decreased rapidly during the state of recession.

Along with the trends in credit supply by banks, its utilisation/deployment pattern also is useful in assessing impact of recession on Indian economy. The deployment pattern of bank credit is shown in Table 9.

TABLE 9

Development of Gross Credit by Major Sectors

(Rs. in crore)

Sector	*2007-08*	*2008-09*	*Coefficient of Variance*
Agriculture & Allied	44966	63313	24%
Industry	169536	187515	0.71%
Personal Loans	54730	54991	0.33%
Services	132419	93580	24%
Total	401650	399400	0.39%

Source: Reserve Bank of India.

It is revealed that except agriculture, credit supply to different productive sectors has either shown a negative growth or a meagre positive growth. Credit supply to Industry and Personal Loans and Total has increased marginally during the recession period. Besides, credit supply to service sector has been declined significantly.

Inflation is also an important indicator of fluctuations in aggregate economic activity and thereby different phases of trade cycle. The data about trends in inflation in Indian economy is displayed in Table 10.

TABLE 10

Trends in Inflation in India

Year	*Wholesale Price Index*	*Consumer Price Index for Industrial Worker*
2004-05	187.3	520
2005-06	195.6	542
2006-07	206.2	125
2007-08	215.8	133
2008-09	234	145
CGR 2004-05 to 2006-07	4.92%	4.90%
CGR 2007-08 to 2008-09	8.43%	9%

Source: Economic Survey, Government of India, 2008-09.

The data results of Table 10 reveal that inflation rate was significant based on wholesale price index as well as consumer price index. It is expected to fall in inflation rate so far as impact of recession is concerned.

TABLE 11

Average Inflation WPI

(%)

Commodities	*2004-05*	*2005-06*	*2006-07*	*2007-08*	*2008-09*	*Variance*	
						I	*II*
All Commodities	6.5	4.4	5.4	4.7	8.4	1.10%	6.84%
Primary Articles	3.7	2.9	7.9	7.6	10.1	7.21%	3.12%
Food	2.7	4.8	7.8	5.5	8	6.57%	3.12%
Non-food	0.7	- 4.5	5.1	12.6	11.2	23.09%	0.98%
Fuel, Power, Lubricants	10.1	9.5	5.6	0.9	7.5	5.97%	21.87%
Manufactured Goods	6.3	3.1	4.4	5	8.1	2.59%	4.80%

Source: Department of Industry, Policy and Promotion, Government of India.

Further enquiry into the trends in commoditywise inflation rates also is useful in assessing impact of recession on Indian economy.

It is observed that inflation rate related to fuel, power and lubricants, and all commodities has shown a higher level and growth during recession also. Inflation rate of primary articles, food, and manufactured goods has shown a considerable growth. Only inflation rate of non-food items has shown a fall, which was marginal only.

According to the report on "Effect of Economic Slowdown on Employment in India" by Ministry of Labour in October-December 2008, there was decrease in employment of about half a million workers during the period.[9] The most affected sectors were gems and jewellery, transport and automobiles, where employment has declined by 8.58%, 4.03% and 2.42% respectively. In textile sector, 0.91% of workers have lost their jobs. It was also found a loss of about one lakh jobs in the month of January 2009.[10] The survey in January-March 2009 by Ministry of Labour, Government of India indicated improvement in the selected sector with employment rising by a quarter million.[11]

Sectors registering increased employment were gems and jewellery (3.08%), textiles (0.96%), IT-BPO (0.82%), handloom, powerloom (0.56%) and automobile (0.10%).

IMPLICATIONS OF GLOBAL RECESSION FOR AN INDIAN ECONOMY

The thorough study of the phenomenon of global recession by taking into consideration some economic parameters during the period of five years from 2004-05 to 2008-09, which is divided into pre-recession and during recession reveals that global slow down is a mixed phenomenon so far as Indian economy is concerned. No doubt, economic meltdown is in existence in Indian economy to some extent. Hence consequently, it has adversely affected some sectors of the Indian economy. But it is a fact that majority of productive sectors and economic activities in Indian economy has not been touched and affected by the global recession.

Economic development as shown by GDP trends adequately shows that recession has not been affected on development of the Indian economy. It was a significant growth rate of development even during the recession period. But the sectoral distribution of India's economic development highlights that manufacturing, construction, transport, storage and communication, finance, insurance, real estate and business services have been adversely affected by recession considerably. Exports have been badly affected by the meltdown, but no adverse effects on imports of India. Trade balance is negative as usual but it has been widened significantly. External debt of India has been increased considerably even during recession. But India's foreign currency reserves coupled with foreign investment, FDI and portfolio investment have been declined significantly during recession. Except public sector banks, the credit supply by all other types of banks have been declined considerably during recession. Likewise, excluding agriculture sector, total credit supply as well as credit to industry and service sectors has been declined significantly due to recession. Inflation has not been adversely affected by the recession. On the contrary, it has been increased considerably. Likewise, except inflation relating to non-food items, all other goods inflation has shown a substantial increase during recession. But growth in private consumption was negative significantly during the recession.

The noteworthy thing is that total employment as well as employment by some productive activities have been declined significantly during recession.

Hence, policy implications so as to revive Indian economy from the recession and to eliminate its adverse effects should be rigorous and honest efforts to promote development of both the industry as well as service sectors with due attention towards the development of agriculture sector in the economy through increased credit supply by the banks other than public sector. The policies are necessary to implement so as to promote exports though incentives and employments coupled with control of imports. It is necessary to provide incentives to attract foreign investment in general, and FDI in particular. The special emphasis should be given on generating employment, which will also promote private consumption growth. Thus, we cannot neglect the phenomenon of global slowdown, even it is mixed so far as its nature, extent and adverse impacts in the context of India are considered.

CONCLUDING REMARKS

Economic meltdown is a global problem, hence its appearance in Indian economy is not natural. The study of global recession in the context of Indian economy adequately proves that, it has been in existence in our economy. Likewise, we are also getting some evidences of revival of Indian economy. The present research paper is an attempt to analyse the phenomenon of global recession in the context of Indian economy. No doubt, it has been adversely affected some sectors of Indian economy. The Government of India coupled with the RBI have been endeavouring for reviving of our economy from the recession. But future government interference and measures implementation is necessary. A hypothesis of the present paper has been tested and proved through the necessary analysis and interpretation. The need of the hour is to undertake a micro level study mainly relied on primary data, is essential.

NOTES AND REFERENCES

1. Agarwal, Amol (2008), Impact of the crisis on Indian economy: Exploring channels and policy option, a Research Report, IDBI, p. 1.
2. Dr. Kamble, P.S. (2005), Business (Macro) Economics, Arth Publishers, Karad, pp. 162-63.
3. Government of India (2009), Economic Survey, 2008-09, Government of India, New Delhi, p. 265.
4. *Ibid.*, p. 14.
5. *Ibid.*, p. 166.
6. *Ibid.*, p. 2.
7. *Ibid.*, p. 267.
8. *Ibid.*, p. 3.
9. *Ibid.*, p. 268.
10. Kundu, Sridhar (2008), Can the Indian economy emerge unscathed from the global financial crisis?, A Research Paper, Internet, p. 1.
11. Mark, Wheeler (1998), The Economics of the Great Depression, Institute for Employment Research, Western Michigan University, p. 1.

Impact of Global Financial Crisis on India: An Analysis

CHANNABASAVAN GOUDAP AND K.A. RASURE

INTRODUCTION

The Indian economy looked to be relatively insulated from the global financial crisis that started in August 2007 when the 'sub-prime mortgage' crisis first surfaced in the US. In fact the RBI was raising interest rates until July 2008 with the view to cooling the growth rate and contains inflationary pressures. But as the financial meltdown, morphed into a global economic downturn with the collapse of Lehman Brothers on 23 September 2008, the impact on the Indian economy was almost immediate. Credit flows suddenly dried-up and, overnight, money market interest rate spiked to above 20 percent and remained high for the next month. It is, perhaps, judicious to assume that the impacts of the global economic downturn, the first in the center of global capitalism since the Great Depression, on the Indian economy are still unfolding.

The severity and suddenness of the crisis can be judged from the IMF's forecast for the global economy. For the first time in 60 years, the IMF is now forecasting a global recession with negative growth for world GDP in 2009-10. The IMF has revised its forecasts downwards thrice since July 2008, and it is not yet certain that this will be the last revision. The WTO has predicted that world trade, which has virtually collapsed in the second half of 2008 is likely to decline by as much as nine percent in 2009-10. We have already seen exports from world's major exporters, like Germany, Japan and China, plummeting by more than 35 percent in the last quarter of 2008. The sharp decline in economic activity is despite the large stimulus, estimated at more than USD 3 trillion, those OECD economies have put in place. The worst downside scenario could be for the US economy being trapped in a Japan like "L" shaped recovery for the next few years. This will imply a further decline in world exports and softening of global commodity prices. In turn, it will result in sharp slowdown in world exports and result in widespread unemployment and social stress in major exporting economies. This could well generate irresistible protectionist sentiments and if governments do succumb to these, it will unleash the dreaded downward cycle which could see the global economy plunging over the precipice into a prolonged recession. It is, therefore, prudent not to underestimate the severity of the present crisis. Thus, the present study is seeking to anlyse the impact of global crisis on Indian economy.

ORIGIN OF GLOBAL FINANCIAL CRISIS

The proximate cause of the current financial turbulence is attributed to the sub-prime mortgage sector in the USA. At a fundamental level, however, the crisis could be ascribed to the persistence of large global imbalances, which, in turn, were the outcome of long periods of excessively loose monetary policy in the major advanced economies during the early part of this decade (Mohan, 2007 and Taylor, 2008).

Global imbalances have been manifested through a substantial increase in the current account deficit of the US mirrored by the substantial surplus in Asia, particularly in China, and in oil exporting countries in the Middle East and Russia (Lane, 2009). These imbalances in the current account are often seen as the consequence of the relative inflexibility of the currency regimes in China and some other EMEs. According to

Portes (2009), global macroeconomic imbalances were the major underlying cause of the crisis. These saving-investment imbalances and consequent huge cross-border financial flows put great stress on the financial intermediation process. The global imbalances interacted with the flaws in financial markets and instruments to generate the specific features of the crisis. Such a view, however, offers only a partial analysis of the recent global economic environment.

Excessively loose monetary policy in the post-dot com period boosted consumption and investment in the US and, as Taylor argues, it was made with purposeful and careful consideration by monetary policy-makers. As might be expected, with such low nominal and real interest rates, asset prices also recorded strong gains, particularly in housing and real estate, providing further impetus to consumption and investment through wealth effects. Thus, aggregate demand consistently exceeded domestic output in the US and, given the macroeconomic identity, this was mirrored in large and growing current account deficits in the US over the period (Table 1). The large domestic demand of the US was met by the rest of the world, especially China and other East Asian economies, which provided goods and services at relatively low costs leading to growing surpluses in these countries. Sustained current account surpluses in some of these EMEs also reflected the lessons learnt from the Asian financial crisis. Furthermore, the availability of relatively cheaper goods and services from China and other EMEs also helped to maintain price stability in the US and elsewhere, which might have not been possible otherwise. Thus measured inflation in the advanced economies remained low, contributing to the persistence of accommodative monetary policy.

The emergence of dysfunctional global imbalances is essentially a post-2000 phenomenon and which got accentuated from 2004 onwards. In fact, Taylor (2008) argues that the sharp hike in oil and other commodity prices in early 2008 were indeed related to the very sharp policy rate cut in late 2007 after the sub-prime crisis emerged. It would be interesting to explore the outcome had the exchange rate policies in China and other EMEs been more flexible. The availability of low priced consumer goods and services from EMEs was worldwide. Yet, it can be

TABLE I

Current Account Balance

(Per cent to GDP)

Country	*1990-94*	*1995-99*	*2000-04*	*2005*	*2006*	*2007*	*2008*
China	1.4	1.9	2.4	7.2	9.5	11.0	10.0
France	0.0	2.0	1.3	-0.6	-0.6	-1.0	-1.6
Germany	-0.4	-0.8	1.4	5.1	6.1	7.5	6.4
India	**-1.3**	**-1.3**	**0.5**	**-1.3**	**-1.1**	**-1.0**	**-2.8**
Japan	2.4	2.3	2.9	3.6	3.9	4.8	3.2
Korea	-1.0	1.9	2.1	1.8	0.6	0.6	-0.7
Malaysia	-5.2	1.8	9.8	15.0	16.7	15.4	17.4
Philippines	-4.0	-2.8	-0.7	2.0	4.5	4.9	2.5
Russia	0.9	3.5	11.2	11.0	9.5	5.9	6.1
United Arab Emirates	8.3	4.6	9.9	18.0	22.6	16.1	15.8
United Kingdom	-2.1	-1.0	-2.0	-2.6	-3.4	-2.9	-1.7
United States	-1.0	-2.1	-4.5	-5.9	-6.0	-5.3	-4.7
Memo:							
Euro area	n.a.	0.9@	0.4	0.4	0.3	0.2	-0.7
Middle East	-5.1	1.0	8.4	19.7	21.0	18.2	18.8

@:1997-99.

Note: (-) indicates deficit.

Source: World Economic Outlook Database, April 2009, International Monetary Fund (2009c).

observed that the Euro area as a whole did not exhibit large current account deficits throughout the current decade. In fact, it exhibited a surplus except for a minor deficit in 2008. The stable macroeconomic environment encouraged underpricing of risks. Financial innovations, regulatory arbitrage, lending malpractices, excessive use of the originate and distribute model, securitisation of sub-prime loans and their bundling into AAA tranches on the back of ratings, all combined to result in the observed excessive leverage of financial market entities.

COMPONENTS OF THE CRISIS

Most of the crises over the past few decades have had their roots in developing and emerging countries, often resulting from abrupt reversals in capital flows, and from loose domestic monetary and fiscal policies. In contrast, the current ongoing global financial crisis has had its roots in the US. The sustained rise in asset prices, particularly house prices, on the back of excessively accommodative monetary policy and lax lending standards during 2002-06 coupled with financial innovations resulted in a large rise in mortgage credit to households, particularly low credit quality households. Most of these loans were with low margin money and with initial low teaser payments. Due to the 'originate and distribute' model, most of these mortgages had been securitized. In combination with strong growth in complex credit derivatives and the use of credit ratings, the mortgages, inherently sub-prime, were bundled into a variety of tranches, including AAA tranches, and sold to a range of financial investors.

The deep and lingering crisis in global financial markets, the extreme level of risk aversion, the mounting losses of banks and financial institutions, the elevated level of commodity prices (until the third quarter of 2008) and their subsequent collapse, and the sharp correction in a range of asset prices, all combined, have suddenly led to a sharp slowdown in growth momentum in the major advanced economies, especially since the Lehman failure. Global growth for 2009, which was seen at a healthy 3.8 per cent in April 2008, is now projected to contract by 1.3 per cent (IMF, 2009c) (Table 2). Major advanced economies are in recession and the EMEs— which in the earlier part of 2008 were widely viewed as being decoupled from the major advanced economies—have also been engulfed by the financial crisis-led slowdown. Global trade volume (goods and services) is also expected to contract by 11 per cent during 2009 as against the robust growth of 8.2 per cent during 2006-07. Private capital inflows (net) to the EMEs fell from the peak of US $ 617 billion in 2007 to US $ 109 billion in 2008 and are projected to record net outflows of US $ 190 billion in 2009. The sharp decline in capital flows in 2009 will be mainly on account of outflows under bank lending and portfolio flows. Thus, both the slowdown in external demand and the lack of external financing have dampened growth prospects for the EMEs much more than that was anticipated a year ago.

TABLE 2

Global Economic Outlook for 2009 (per cent) Month of Forecast

Indicator	*July*		*October*		*November*		*January*		*April*	
	2008	*2009*	*2008*	*2009*	*2008*	*2009*	*2008*	*2009*	*2008*	*2009*
1. Global Growth	4.1	3.9	3.9	3.0	3.4	0.5	3.4	0.5	3.8	- 1.3
(a) Advanced Economics	1.7	1.4	1.5	0.5	1.0	-2.0	1.0	-2.0	0.9	- 3.8
(b) EMEs	6.9	6.7	6.9	6.1	6.3	3.3	6.3	3.3	6.1	1.6
2. World Trade Volume	4.1	3.9	3.9	3.0	4.1	-2.8	4.1	-2.8	3.3	- 11
3. Consumer Price Inflation										
(a) Advanced Economics	3.4	2.3	3.6	2.0	3.5	0.3	3.5	0.3	3.4	- 0.2
(b) EMEs	9.1	7.4	9.4	7.8	9.2	5.8	9.2	5.8	9.3	5.7

@: Volume growth in goods and services.

Source: World Economic Outlook, various issues, International Monetary Fund.

INITIAL IMPACT OF THE SUB-PRIME CRISIS ON INDIA

The initial impact of the sub-prime crisis on the Indian economy was rather muted. Indeed, following the cuts in the US Fed Funds rate in August 2007, there was a massive jump in net capital inflows into the country. The Reserve Bank had to sterilise the liquidity impact of large foreign exchange purchases through a series of increases in the cash-reserve ratio and issuances under the Market Stabilisation Scheme (MSS). With persistent inflationary pressures emanating both from strong domestic demand and elevated global commodity prices, policy rates were also raised. Monetary policy continued with pre-emptive tightening measures up to August 2008.

The direct effect of the sub-prime crisis on Indian banks/ financial sector was almost negligible because of limited exposure to complex derivatives and other prudential policies put in place by the Reserve Bank. The relatively lower presence of foreign banks in the Indian banking sector also minimized the direct impact on the domestic economy (Table 3). The larger presence of foreign banks can increase the vulnerability of the domestic economy to foreign shocks, as happened in Eastern European and Baltic countries. In view of significant liquidity

TABLE 3

Share of Banking Assets Held by Foreign Banks with Majority Ownership, 2006

(in %)

Country	*0-10*	*Country*	*10-30*	*Country*	*30-50*	*Country*	*0-10*	*Country*	*10-30*
Algeria	9	Moldova	30	Senegal	48	Algeria	9	Moldova	30
Nepal	9	Honduras	29	Congo	47	Nepal	9	Honduras	29
Guatemala	8	Ukraine	28	Uruguay	44	Guatemala	8	Ukraine	28
Thailand	5	Indonesia	28	Panama	42	Thailand	5	Indonesia	28
India	5	Cambodia	27	Kenya	41	India	5	Cambodia	27
Ecuador	5	Argentina	25	Benin	40	Ecuador	5	Argentina	25
Azerbaijan	5	Brazil	25	Bolivia	38	Azerbaijan	5	Brazil	25
Mauritania	5	Kazakhstan	24	Mauritius	37	Mauritania	5	Kazakhstan	24
Nigeria	5	Pakistan	23	Burundi	36	Nigeria	5	Pakistan	23
Turkey	4	Costa Rica	22	Seychelles	36	Turkey	4	Costa Rica	22
Uzbekistan	1	Malawi	22	Lebanon	34	Uzbekistan	1	Malawi	22
Philippines	1	Tunisia	22	Nicaragua	34	Philippines	1	Tunisia	22
South Africa	0	Mongolia	22	Chile	32	South Africa	0	Mongolia	22
China	0	Sudan	20	Venezuela	32	China	0	Sudan	20
Vietnam	0	Morocco	18	Georgia	32	Vietnam	0	Morocco	18
Iran	0	Colombia	18	Armenia	31	Iran	0	Colombia	18
Yemen	0	Malaysia	16			Yemen	0	Malaysia	16
Bangladesh	0	Jordan	14			Bangladesh	0	Jordan	14
Sri Lanka	0	Russia	13			Sri Lanka	0	Russia	13
Ethiopia	0	Egypt	12			Ethiopia	0	Egypt	12
Togo	0					Togo	0		

Notes: 1. A bank is defined as foreign owned only if 50 percent or more of its shares in a given year are held directly by foreign nationals. Once foreign ownership is determined, the source country is identified as the country of nationality of the largest foreign shareholder(s). The table does not capture the assets of the foreign banks with minority foreign ownership.

2. World Bank staff estimates based on Bankscope data.

Source: World Bank (2008).

and capital shocks to the parent foreign bank, it can be forced to scale down its operations in the domestic economy, even as the fundamentals of the domestic economy remain robust. Thus, domestic bank credit supply can shrink during crisis episodes. For instance, in response to the stock and real estate market collapse of early 1990s, Japanese banks pulled back from foreign markets—including the United States—in order to reduce liabilities on their balance sheets and thereby meet capital adequacy ratio requirements. Econometric evidence shows a statistically significant relationship between international bank lending to developing countries and changes in global liquidity conditions, as measured by spreads of interbank interest rates over Overnight Index Swap (OIS) rates and U.S. Treasury bill rates. A 10 basic-point increase in the spread between the London Interbank Offered Rate (LIBOR) and the OIS sustained for a quarter, for example, is predicted to lead to a decline of up to 3 percent in international bank lending to developing countries (World Bank, 2008).

IMPACT OF LEHMAN FAILURE: CAPITAL OUTFLOWS

There was also no direct impact of the Lehman failure on the domestic financial sector in view of the limited exposure of the Indian banks. However, following the Lehman failure, there was a sudden change in the external environment. As in the case of other major EMEs, there was a sell-off in domestic equity markets by portfolio investors reflecting deleveraging. Consequently, there were large capital outflows by portfolio investors during September-October 2008, with concomitant pressures in the foreign exchange market. While foreign direct investment flows exhibited resilience, access to external commercial borrowings and trade credits was rendered somewhat difficult. On the whole, net capital inflows during 2008-09 were substantially lower than in 2007-08 and there was a depletion of reserves (Table 4). However, a large part of the reserve loss (US $ 33 billion out of US $ 54 billion) during April-December 2008 reflected valuation losses.

The contraction of capital flows and the sell-off in the domestic market adversely affected both external and domestic financing for the corporate sector. The sharp slowdown in demand in the major advanced economies is also having an adverse impact on our exports and industrial performance. On the positive side, the significant correction in international oil and other commodity prices has alleviated inflationary pressures as measured by wholesale price index. However, various measures of consumer prices remain at elevated levels on the back of continuing high inflation in food prices.

TABLE 4

Trends in Capital Flows

(US $ billion)

Component	*Period*	*2007-08*	*2008-09*
Foreign Direct Investment to India	April-February	27.6	31.7
FIIs (net)	April-March	20.3	-15.0
External Commercial Borrowings (net)	April-December	17.5	6.0
Short-term Trade Credits (net)	April-December	10.7	0.5
Total capital flows (net)	April-December	82.0	15.3
Memo:			
Current Account Balance	April-December	-15.5	-36.5
Valuation Gains (+)/Losses (-) on Foreign Exchange Reserves	April-December	+9.0	-33.4
Foreign Exchange Reserves (variation)	April-December	76.1	-53.8
Foreign Exchange Reserves (variation)	April-March	110.5	-57.7

FISCAL IMPACT

Government finances, which had exhibited a noteworthy correction starting 2002-03, came under renewed pressure in 2008-09 on account of higher expenditure outgoes due to: (i) higher international crude oil prices (up to September 2008) and the incomplete pass-through to domestic prices, (ii) higher fertilizer prices and associated increase in fertilizer prices, (iii) the Sixth Pay Commission award, and (iv) debt waiver scheme. The fiscal stimulus packages involving additional expenditures and tax cuts have put further stress on the fisc. Reflecting these factors, the Central Government's fiscal deficit more than doubled from 2.7 per cent of GDP in 2007-08 to 6.0 per cent in 2008-09, reaching again the levels seen around the end of the 1990s. The revenue deficit at 4.4 per cent of GDP will be at its previous peak touched during 2001-02 and 2002-03. Primary balance again turned into deficit in 2008-09, after recording surpluses during the preceding two years (Table 5). Net market borrowings during 2008-09 almost trebled from the budgeted Rs. 1,13,000 crore to Rs. 3,29,649 in the revised estimates (actual borrowings were Rs. 2,98,536 crore as per Reserve Bank records) and are budgeted at Rs. 3,08,647 crore (gross borrowings at Rs. 3,98,552 crore) in 2009-10.

In view of the renewed fiscal deterioration, the credit rating agency Standard and Poor's has changed its outlook on long-term sovereign credit rating from stable to negative, while reaffirming the 'BBB-'rating. If bonds issued to oil and fertilizer companies are taken into account, the various deficit indicators will be even higher. Moreover, in order to boost domestic demand, the Government has announced additional tax sops subsequent to the interim vote-on-account budget putting further pressure on fiscal position. Thus, while the slowdown in the domestic economy may call for fiscal stimulus, fiscal manoeuvrability is limited.

According to the IMF, based on measures already taken and current plans, it is estimated that government debt ratios and fiscal deficits, particularly in advanced economies, will increase significantly. For the G-20 as a whole, the general government balance is expected to deteriorate by 3½ percent of GDP, on average, in 2009. While the fiscal cost for some countries will be large in the short-run, the alternative of providing no fiscal stimulus or financial sector support would be extremely costly in terms of the lost output (IMF, 2009b).

TABLE 5

Key Fiscal Indicators of the Central Government

(Per cent to GDP)

Year	*Gross fiscal deficit*	*Gross primary deficit*	*Revenue deficit*
1990-91	7.8	4.1	3.3
1995-96	5.1	0.9	2.5
2000-01	5.7	0.9	4.1
2001-02	6.2	1.5	4.4
2004-05	4.0	0.0	2.5
2005-06	4.1	0.4	2.6
2006-07	3.5	-0.2	1.9
2007-08	2.7	-0.9	1.1
2008-09 RE	6.0	2.5	4.4
2009-10 BE	5.5	1.8	4.0

RE: Revised Estimates. BE: Budget Estimates.

Note: 1. Negative (-) sign indicates surplus. 2. Oil and fertilizer bonds issued during 2008-09 were 1.8 per cent of GDP.

IMPACT ON THE REAL ECONOMY

Reflecting the slowdown in external demand, and the consequences of reversal of capital flows, growth in industrial production decelerated to 2.8 per cent in 2008-09 (April-February) from 8.8 per cent in the corresponding period of 2007-08. On the other hand, services sector activity has held up relatively well in 2008-09 so far (April-December) with growth of 9.7 per cent (10.5 per cent in the corresponding period of 2007-08). Services sector activity was buoyed up by acceleration in "community, social and personal services" on the back of higher government expenditure. Overall, real GDP growth has slowed to 6.9 per cent in the first three quarters of 2008-09 from 9.0 per cent in the corresponding period of 2007-08. On the expenditure side, growth of private final consumption expenditure decelerated to 6.6 per cent from 8.3 per cent. On the other hand, reflecting the fiscal stimuli and other expenditure measures, growth in government final consumption expenditure accelerated to 13.3 per cent from 2.7 per cent.

CREDIT GROWTH IN INDIA

In view of the changed environment due to capital outflows and risk aversion, there was a substantial shrinking of non-bank sources of funding in India—such as domestic capital markets, funding from NBFCS and mutual funds and external funding in the form of commercial borrowings and ADRs/GDRs (Table 6). Accordingly, there was a sudden rush for bank credit from the various sectors of the economy and there were perceptions of credit crunch. Moreover, in view of incomplete pass-through to domestic petroleum prices in the first half of 2008-09 (before the sharp correction in international crude oil prices), there was a large demand from petroleum companies for bank credit. For almost similar reasons, fertilizer companies also had a large resort to bank credit. Reflecting these factors, growth in non-food bank credit (y-o-y) accelerated to around 30 per cent by October 2008. Nonetheless, there was a perception that there was credit crunch during this period, which could be attributed to a large decline in non-bank sources of funding. The slowdown of the manufacturing sector and a temporary build-up in inventories as well as liquidity problems faced by mutual funds and NBFCs during this period added to an increased demand for bank credit. At the same time, there might have been an increase in precautionary demand for bank credit in the last quarter of 2008 in view of the heightened uncertainties. The cumulative impact of all these demand pressures was reflected in acceleration of non-food bank credit from around 25-26 per cent in the quarter July-September 2008 to around 30 per cent in October 2008. Accordingly, a number of steps were taken by the Reserve Bank to make available adequate rupee and forex liquidity and to ensure adequate flow of credit.

TABLE 6

Flow of Resources to the Commercial Sector

(Rupees crore)

Item	*2007-08*	*2008-09*
(A) Adjusted nonfood Bank Credit by Commercial Banks (1+2) @	4,44,807	4,14,902
1. Non-Food Credit	4,32,846	4,06,287
2. Non-SLR Investments	11,961	8,615
(B) Flow from OtherMajor Sources (3+4)	3,35,698	2,64,138
3. Domestic Sources	1,72,338	1,50,604
4. Foreign Sources	1,63,360	1,13,534
Total Credit (A+B)	**7,80,505**	**6,79,040**

Note: Data are provisional.
Source: Reserve Bank of India (2009b).

Non-food bank credit growth has, however, moderated from the peak of around 30 per cent in October 2008 to around 18 per cent by end-March 2009. This could be attributed to both demand and supply factors. The demand-side factors include the significant moderation in industrial activity over the past few months, the substantial correction in international commodity and raw material prices and the still elevated bank lending rates. On the supply side, some risk-aversion on the part of the banks could have reduced the availability of bank credit. The cumulative impact of deceleration in bank credit, relatively strong deposit growth and various measures by the Reserve Bank to increase liquidity is mirrored in the Reserve Bank's LAF operations—switch from an average net repo (injection) of around Rs. 45,600 crore in September 2008 to an average net reverse repo (absorption) of around Rs. 43,000 crore during January-March 2008.

POLICY RESPONCES

As noted earlier, the main impact over the past few months, especially following the collapse of Lehman Brothers in September 2008, has been the outcome of the reduction in net capital inflows and the significant correction in the domestic stock markets on the back of sell-off in the equity market by FIIs. The reduced foreign funding and the lacklustre domestic capital market had put pressures on some segments of the financial system, such as NBFCs and mutual funds. A substantial proportion of collections of mutual funds reflected bulk funds from the corporate sector under the money market schemes, partly reflecting tax and other regulatory arbitrage. As alternative sources of funding dried up and also due to the substantial correction in stock prices, there were large redemption pressures on mutual funds. While the mutual funds promised immediate redemption, there assets were relatively illiquid. Maturity mismatches between assets and liabilities of mutual funds further aggravated the problems. Drying up of funds with mutual funds, which in turn were provider of funds to other sectors, further accentuated the flow of funds. Consequently, all the pressure for fund availability came to rest on banks: from the corporate sector unable to get external funds or equity, from NBFCs and from mutual funds; and the perception of a credit crunch emerged.

In view of the lower level of capital inflows, there were some pressures in the foreign exchange market. Consistent with its policy objective of maintaining orderly conditions in the foreign exchange market, the Reserve Bank sold foreign exchange in the market. While foreign exchange sales attenuated the mismatch in the foreign exchange market, these operations drained liquidity from the rupee market and accentuated pressures on the rupee liquidity. Accordingly, the Reserve Bank has been pro-actively managing liquidity since mid-September 2008 to assuage the liquidity pressures through a variety of measures. The cash-reserve ratio (CRR) was reduced from 9 per cent (September 2008) to 5 per cent by early January 2009 injecting nearly Rs. 1,60,000 crore of primary liquidity in the system. Fresh issuances under MSS were stopped and buyback of existing MSS securities was also resorted to to inject liquidity into the system. Buybacks were timed with government market borrowing programme. Following the amendment to the Memorandum of Agreement on the MSS, Rs. 12,000 crore was transferred to the Government cash account from the MSS cash account. Reflecting the various operations, MSS balances declined from Rs. 1,75,362 crore at end-May 2008 to around Rs. 88,000 crore by end-March 2009. Other measures taken by the Reserve Bank in response to the global financial crisis include cut in the statutory liquidity ratio (SLR), opening of new refinancing windows, refinance to SIDBI and EXIM Banks, and clawing back of prudential norms in regard to provisioning and risk weights. The measures to improve forex liquidity included increase in interest rate ceilings on non-resident deposits, and easing of restrictions on external commercial borrowings and on short-term trade credits.

Simultaneously, in view of the adverse impact of the global slowdown on the domestic economy, policy rates were also cut—the reverse repo rate by 425 basis points from 9.00 per cent to 4.75 per cent and the reverse repo rate by 275 basis points from 6.00 per cent to 3.25 per cent. However, it may be noted that, at present, the reverse repo rate (the lower band of the LAF corridor) is the operational policy rate, whereas, in the period prior to mid-September 2008, the repo rate (the upper band of the LAF corridor) was the operational policy rate. The effective policy rate has, thus, seen a larger cut of 575 basis points from 9.00 per cent in mid-September 2008 to 3.25 per cent now. This is mirrored in the money market interest rates (weighted average of call, market repo and CBLO) falling from 9.3 per cent in September 2008 to 3.8 per cent in March 2009 (2.8 per cent as on April 22, 2009).

Furthermore, in view of the large government market borrowing programme, the Reserve Bank has been conducting purchases of government securities under its open market operations (OMO) as warranted by the evolving monetary and financial market conditions. On March 26, 2009, the Reserve Bank announced a calendar for OMOs for the first half (April-

September 2009) of the fiscal year. Taking into account the expected unwinding of MSS securities of Rs. 42,000 crore during April-September 2009 and other factors in view, the Reserve Bank announced that it intended to purchase government securities of Rs. 80,000 crore under OMOs during the first half. The OMO calendar and amounts are indicative and the Reserve Bank will have the flexibility to make changes in the amount of OMO depending on the evolving liquidity conditions and its other operations. These actions reflect the need for close co-ordination between government debt management and monetary policy operations. This can be done smoothly in our case since the Reserve Bank also acts as the debt manager for the government.

CONCLUSION

The ongoing global financial crisis can be largely attributed to extended periods of excessively loose monetary policy in the US over the period 2002-04. Very low interest rates during this period encouraged an aggressive search for yield and a substantial compression of risk-premia globally. Abundant liquidity in the advanced economies generated by the loose monetary policy found its way in the form of large capital flows to the emerging market economies. All these factors boosted asset and commodity prices, including oil, across the spectrum providing a boost to consumption and investment. Global imbalances were a manifestation of such an accommodative monetary policy and the concomitant boost in aggregate demand in the US outstripping domestic aggregate supply in the US. This period coincided with lax lending standards, inappropriate use of derivatives, credit ratings and financial engineering, and excessive leverage. As inflation began to edge up reaching the highest levels since the 1970s, this necessitated monetary policy tightening. The housing prices started to witness some correction. Lax lending standards, excessive leverage and weaknesses of banks' risk models/stress testing were exposed and bank losses mounted wiping off capital of major financial institutions. The ongoing deleveraging in the advanced economies and the plunging consumer and business confidence have led to recession in the major advanced economies and large outflows of capital from the EMEs; both of these channels are now slowing down growth in the EMEs.

REFERENCES

International Monetary Fund (2009a), "Group of Twenty: Note by the Staff of International Monetary Fund", January.

Lane, Philip (2009), "Global Imbalances and Global Governance", Paper presented at the `Global Economic Governance: Systemic Challenges, Institutional Responses and the Role of the New Actors', Brussels, February.

Mohan, Rakesh (2006a), "Coping With Liquidity Management in India: A Practitioner's View", *Reserve Bank of India Bulletin*, April.

Portes, Richard (2009), "Global Imbalances" in Mathias Dewatripont, Xavier Freixas and Richard Portes (Ed.), "Macroeconomic Stability and Financial Regulation: Key Issues for the G20", Centre for Economic Policy Research, London.

Taylor, John (2009), "The Financial Crisis and the Policy Responses: An Empirical Analysis of What Went Wrong", Working Paper 14631, January, National Bureau of Economic Research.

World Bank (2008), Global Development Finance, 2008: The Role of International Banking, World Bank.

The Global Financial Crisis and the Indian Economy

MANDAKINI MAHORE AND SAMIT MAHORE

The global financial crisis which began with the bursting of the housing bubble in the United States and aggravated by the collapse of several international financial institutions beginning with Lehman Brothers swiftly had an impact on the real sectors and has caused a recessionary environment in the US, Japan and European countries. Although, initially, the emerging market economies including India felt that they could decouple themselves from global financial meltdown, it was soon recognized that this was simply not possible. Thus the adverse impact of the recession in the countries of the OECD on India was much more than that was initially envisaged. Reviving the economy required strong stimuli from both fiscal and monetary policy measures, but it was soon realised that the scope for providing fiscal stimulus side was very limited.

These gave rise to trade surpluses in the rest of the world, distributing the sub-prime holdings globally. The trade surpluses persisted as the Asian countries pursued export-led growth and they blocked appreciation of their currencies against the dollar to maintain their competitiveness. A great portion of the surpluses were re-invested in dollars. Therefore, long-term interest rates did not rise even when the Federal Reserve raised short-term rates in 2004. Artificially low interest rates prompted investors to increase risky lending at diminished risk premiums. In this conceptualisation, the failure to address problems in the area of trade deficits can trigger policy responses in the area of monetary policy that can ultimately create even bigger problems. More important for India, large trade deficits cause real distortions, the consequences of which are costly, though they may be slow to emerge. Most importantly, citizens have been encouraged to view their appreciated (bubble?) assets as a substitute for cash in the bank.

On the consequences for the global economy, there have been statements from responsible analysts and even the Federal Reserve that the United States' economy is likely to face a contraction in the second and third quarters of 2008, annualising about one percent. The Treasury Secretary has promised slower growth rather than a contraction through a slew of measures and it remains to be seen whether the worrying United States unemployment data of November 2007 is part of a monthly trend, or just a blip. Against this backdrop, it is possible to look at likely consequences for the Indian economy and impact, if any, on gross domestic product (GDP) growth.

The other side of the coin is that contraction in the United States would lead to less demand for imported goods, impacting imports. There is the argument that the Indian economy is sufficiently decoupled from the rest of the world and that there is robust domestic demand and employment creation – this would cushion the economy from external shocks. But this may not be quite true. In 2002, trade was only 17 percent of GDP but it is now close to 40 percent. Thus, the trade dependency of the Indian economy has doubled in the last five years. The United States is the top trading partner for India (though China is catching up) and there would be the concern that exports to the United States may fall. The current monetary policy in India is battling with the need to control inflation, keep interest rates at level that promotes growth while simultaneously attempting to prevent undue appreciation of the rupee—a task considered to be very difficult to accomplish altogether. Already, export orders for the textile sector have fallen significantly, and large job losses are being reported. The appreciation of the rupee is largely due to accentuated capital flows, and free and flexible financial markets and, hence, the concern of the RBI Governor that this is likely to be exacerbated by the contraction in demand in the United States.

The policy response in India is likely to be to ensure that that the rupee does not appreciate 'too much', a task that will entail active sterilisation operations by the RBI. These sterilisation operations, through issue of market stabilisation bonds, entail an additional fiscal burden on the government for the interest costs of these bonds. Energy costs have risen but adjustment of consumer prices has not been possible due to political compulsions of the coalition. It is likely that fiscal stresses on the government may increase. It is this total picture of rupee appreciation, lower exports and fiscal stress that is causing worries in the Indian Finance Ministry and the Planning Commission.

There have been several promises at reducing processes and procedures that have not been implemented. The reforms in agriculture, much needed and much announced, remain only on paper. There is, thus, the need to find a peg to hang the lower GDP growth rate anticipated in 2008. It is politic to blame it on global factors than on delays in infrastructure development, poor reforms in education, health and insurance, and flip flops on monetary policy. The sub-prime crisis offers such an opportunity and, in the forthcoming months, one is likely to see enhanced explanations of how the Indian economy has been affected.

Growth performances vary substantially among developed and developing countries. African growth exceeds OECD growth by margins not seen for 25 years; East Asia's growth is diverging as much as it did during the last significant global economic downturn in the early 1990s. The magnitude of the crisis will depend on the response of the USA and EU. Trillion dollar rescue packages are launched around the world, but while the markets may eventually respond, the UK is already in a recession. Its magnitude will depend, in part, on how accommodative monetary policy can be, with the recent interest rate cut a sure sign the authorities are concerned more about the financial crisis than recent inflationary pressures. There is less scope for expansionary fiscal policy—in fact these rescue measures have increased public debt.

Effects of Global Financial Crisis on Indian Economy

The economic impacts could include:

1. Weaker export revenues;
2. Further pressures on current accounts and balance of payment;
3. Lower investment and growth rates; and
4. Lower employment.

Social impacts include:

1. Lower growth translating into higher poverty; and
2. More crime, weaker health systems and even more difficulties meeting the Millennium Development Goals.

Finance must serve the real sector. The three key functions of financial sector are to protect property rights, reduce transaction costs and have high transparency. But Asians do have the advantage of being pragmatic and have deep historical and cultural wisdom to accept the facts of life and to adjust accordingly. Asians have to recognize that we live in an inter-dependent world, we need to cooperate to live in an increasingly small and fragile planet. We have national rights, as well as global responsibilities. How we move forward will depend on all our fountains of patience and understanding to listen to other views and hopefully find the right way forward.

This economic crisis in the US has also affected the Indian markets. The value of Rupee has fallen further. This will result in critical imports, like Crude Oil, becoming more expensive, which will add to the inflation that is already above 12%. Floods in many parts of India have further added to the high cost of basic necessities with prices of vegetables doubling in a week.

Global economic meltdown has affected almost all countries. Strongest of American, European and Japanese companies are facing severe crisis of liquidity and credit. India is not insulated, either. However, India's cautious approach towards reforms has saved it from possibly disastrous implications. The truth is, Indian economy is also facing a kind of slowdown. The prime reason being, world trade does not functions in isolation. All the economies are interlinked to each other and any major fluctuation in trade balance and economic conditions causes numerous problems for all other economies.

Global economic meltdown has affected almost all countries. Strongest of American, European and Japanese companies are facing severe crisis of liquidity and credit. India is not insulated, either. However, India's cautious approach towards reforms has saved it from possibly disastrous implications. The truth is, Indian economy is also facing a kind of slowdown. The prime reason being, world trade does not functions in isolation. All the economies are interlinked to each other and any major fluctuation in trade balance and economic conditions causes numerous problems for all other economies.

Textile employers claim 700,000 jobs were eliminated in their industry in 2008. Since October, thousands of diamond-polishing workshops have shut down and more than 200,000 people in the gem and jewelry industry have reportedly lost their jobs just in the Surat region of Gujarat. In a February 26 article titled "Indian towns that fuelled the boom hit hard," the *London Financial Times* reported that tens of thousands of workers who recently migrated to Coimbatore, a center of textile and auto production in southern India, have been forced to return home after their jobs were cut.

The United Nations' World Food Programme (WFP) has warned that the migration of newly jobless workers back to their rural family homes risks exacerbating a longstanding crisis in rural India. The WFP's "Report on the State of Food Insecurity in Rural India" found rising levels of "food and nutrition insecurity." 230 million people—one fifth of India's total population are undernourished—and a total of 350 million are considered food insecure, which is defined as "consuming less than 80 percent of minimum energy requirements." Hundreds of millions more eke out an impoverished existence and are at risk of being pushed into the abyss by unemployment or illness. 70 percent of India's population survives on less than $2 per day.

Especially troubling for the government was the recent report that India's economic growth slowed in the last three months of 2008 to an annualized rate of 5.3 percent. This was far below government forecasts and belied its claims, confidently repeated in the preceding weeks, that economic growth in India in the 2008-9 fiscal year, which ended on March 31, was more than 7 percent. Manufacturing output actually contracted by 0.2 percent in the last quarter of 2008, while agriculture, which continues to provide over half of India's population with its livelihood, suffered a 2.2 percent decline.

India's economic development strategy is predicated on the country registering an annual growth in exports of 20 percent or more. The government had set an export target of $200 billion for this year—less than one-sixth of the value of China's exports in 2007—but it is now expected that the figure will be around $170 billion.

The economic crisis has led to a rapid swelling of India's budget deficit. Whereas the government had projected a deficit in 2008-9 equal to 2.5 percent of GDP, in last month's interim budget it conceded the figure would be 6 percent and predicted a deficit equal to 5.5 percent of GDP in the coming fiscal year, which starts in April. The latter projection, the rapid deterioration of India's fiscal position has led the world's is highly optimistic given the bleak outlook facing the Indian economy. Major bond-rating agencies to warn that they may soon slash India's credit rating. Following the presentation of India's budget, Standard and Poor said India's debt position is unsustainable, switched its outlook for Indian debt to "negative," and said it may soon downgrade India's debt rating to junk bond status from the current level of BBB, the lowest investment grade rating. The world economic crisis, however, precludes any return to rapid economic growth. The next government, whatever its political coloration, will come under intense pressure from domestic and foreign capital to dramatically curb public spending with devastating consequences for India's impoverished toilers

The Indian Government believes the recent economic meltdown that has devastated the robust American banking sector, will have no direct impact on India thanks to the overflowing foreign cash reserves, the regulatory nature of our banking sector and the carefully calibrated, cautious and gradual liberalization policy designed by architects of the economy. The Deputy Chairman of the Planning Commission, Montek Singh Ahluwalia, told reporters: "Our banking system is not directly exposed to any significant extent to what are now called toxic acids." Singh, who is accompanying the Prime Minister, Dr. Manmohan Singh, to the United States further said: "I have seen the numbers of the estimated exposure, it is very small". However, he admitted that if this uncertainty continues for long then it will have an indirect fall out on the Indian economy. Analysts feel that despite the frantic efforts by the Bush Administration to bail the country out of this crisis, the Wall Street meltdown will be protracted and might spillover into the next calendar year. While the United States and other Western economies continue to plunge into their respective economic crises, Asian giant India feels that emerging economies can play a vital role in the stabilization of the world economic system. "BRIC (Brazil, Russia, India and China) can play a vital role in future to shape up the world economy," Ahluwalia said. He emphasized the need for adopting a cautious approach in the liberalization process, but added that there is no need for slowing down on this count. If Ahluwalia"s assessment on inflation comes true, it would be good news for the middle and lower income groups which are facing back breaking steep pricing for the last few months. Ahluwalia believes the government is taking various measures to curb inflation and that it will come down to a single digit figure over the next calendar year.

The crisis has been accompanied by changes in employment and relative prices that have adversely impacted especially upon three sections of the population that were already very vulnerable: cultivators, migrant workers and home-based women workers. In addition, it has sharply affected food insecurity which was already a problem in the country. The impact of the crisis on agriculture is much more severe than has been recognized. Cultivators in India have already been through more than a decade of agrarian crisis, which persisted even through the period of rising international crop prices. The problems of farming in India are both deep and varied. They include weather problems such as less reliable monsoons, more frequent droughts or floods, soil degeneration, lack of institutional credit and insurance leading to excessive reliance on private moneylenders, problems in accessing reliable and reasonably priced input, difficulties in marketing and high volatility of crop prices.

Very recent evidence suggests that as export-based industries such as garments face heightened competitive pressure, they pass this pressure on to home-based women workers by reducing the effective rates for piece-rate work. Thus, even nominal piece rate wages have fallen in many such activities, even as prices of necessities such as food have continued to increase. *"Recession has hit the entire world. Wherever we go everybody is talking about it and each and every trade is affected by it."Recession is like a disease, how then can these workers remain unaffected by it?"—Manali Shah, Self-Employed Women's Association, India* The global economic recession is negatively affecting workers everywhere. Media and policy-makers have focused on the rising unemployment of formal salaried workers. Little attention, however, has been paid to the impact of the crisis on informal firms and workers, nor the consequences of new entrants into the informal economy.

In reality, economic downturns often affect the informal economy in the same ways they affect the formal economy. Like formal firms, informal firms are affected by decreased demand, falling prices, and fluctuations in exchange rates associated with economic crises. Like formal wage workers, informal wage workers face loss of jobs or greater informalization of their employment contracts. Indeed, during down-turns, informal wage workers are often the first to lose their jobs. The economic crisis has resulted in a significant downturn in trade. Decreasing incomes and increasing uncertainty in the global North correlate with trends of decreased consumption and demand for imports. Exports from developing countries and countries with economies in transition are estimated to decline, in 2009, in the range of 7 to 9 per cent in volume.

Factory and other wage workers are losing jobs or having their contracts restructured (fewer hours and benefits, fixed terms). Industrial outworkers are receiving fewer or smaller work orders: some have had existing orders cancelled or simply have not been paid. Those who supply raw materials or accessories for export manufacturing also face declining work orders or cancellation of existing orders.

The impact of the global crisis has been transmitted to the Indian economy through three distinct channels, viz., the financial sector, exports and exchange rates. The financial sector including the banking sector, equity markets, external commercial borrowings and remittances has not remained unscathed though fortunately, the Indian banking sector was not overly exposed to the sub-prime crisis. Only one of the larger banks, ICICI, was partly affected but managed to thwart a crisis because of its strong balance sheet and timely action by the government, which virtually guaranteed its deposits.

The equity markets have seen a near 60 percent decline in the index and a wiping off of about USD 1.3 trillion in market capitalization since January 2008 when the Sensex had peaked at about 21,000. This is primarily due to the withdrawal of about USD12 billion from the market by foreign portfolio investors between September and December 2008. The foreign investors withdrew these funds in order to strengthen the balance sheet of their parent companies. Commercial credit, both for trade finance and medium-term advances from foreign banks has virtually dried-up. This has had to be replaced with credit lines from domestic banks but at higher interest costs and has caused the Rupee to depreciate raising the cost of existing foreign loans. Finally, while the latest numbers are not yet available, remittances from overseas Impact on India and Policy Response The second transmission of the global downturn to the Indian economy has been through the steep decline in demand for India's exports in its major markets. The first sector to be hit was the gems and jewellery which felt the impact in November itself and where more than 300,000 workers have lost their jobs. The negative impact has since covered other export-oriented sectors garments and textiles, leather, handicrafts, and auto components.

The 21 percent decline in exports in February 2009 is the steepest fall in exports for the last two decades. It is unlikely that exports will recover within this year. While exports of both goods and services, still account for only about 22 percent of the Indian GDP, their multiplier effect for economic activity is quite large as the import content is not as high as for example in the case of Chinese exports. Therefore, an export slump will bring down GDP growth rate in this year. The third transmission channel is the exchange rate as the Rupee has come under pressure with the outflow of pc folio investments, higher foreign exchange demand by Indian entrepreneurs seeking to replace external commercial borrowing by domestic financing, and the consequent decline in foreign exchange reserves.

AGRICULTURE AND ALLIED ACTIVITIES

In the year 2007-08 the farm sector comprising of agriculture, forestry and fishing, registered a growth rate of 4.5 percent. Economic Advisory Council to the Prime Minister estimated it to be around 3 percent in the year 2008-09. But in the third quarter of 2008-09 it has contracted to 2.2%. In the past, crisis in agrarian economy had hit hard the economic growth; as a result India witnessed some of its bad years. However, as share of agriculture in GDP dropped over time, bad impact in this sector did not affect the overall GDP growth that much. For last couple of years the rate of growth averaged 4 percent. Its share in GDP has been falling over the years and this is due to relatively higher expansion in other sectors.

Industry

GDP in the industrial sector averaged 8 percent in the year 2007-08 and declined to 5 percent in the first quarter of the year 2008-09. The Index of Industrial Production (IIP) registered a negative index in the month of October 2008. The global economic crisis had its adverse effect on industrial sector especially in manufacturing, mining and electricity. In fact in the third quarter of 2008-09, manufacturing growth rate contracted to –0.2%.

Services

This is the most important sector for Indian economy as its share in the GDP has been rising significantly since 1950-51 and currently its share in the GDP is averaged 63 percent. This sector comprises of trade, hotels, transport, storage, communication, financing, insurance, business services, real estate, community, social and personal services and construction. In the fiscal year 2007-08 this sector has registered a growth rate of 10.7 percent, which has come down to 9.3% in the third quarter of 2008-09 and the relative difference is very small. This decline is due to falling growth rate of construction, trade and hotels. But there is a rapid increase in the growth rate of community, social services and personal services, which has posted a robust growth rate of 17.3 percent against 5.3 percent in the same period a year ago. Financing, insurance, real estate and business services also grew at a high rate of 9.5 percent.

Effects on Banking Sector

In India, with an effective regulatory system based on international best standards I place and greater involvement and coordination of both the government and central bank in macroeconomic management through sound public finance policy and a forward looking monetary policy such a situation could be warded-off. Although India did not have direct exposure to troubled financial institutions and dubious financial instruments the country is facing the indirect impact of a financial crisis. This, in sum, is the official position that has been put forth in the Reserve Bank of India's Report on Trend and Progress of Banking in India 2007-08.

The report makes a clear distinction between rules based and principle based supervision. The Principle-based Regulation (PBR), of which the Bank of England is the originator, has about 11 principles of business such as integrity, skills, care an diligence, management and control, market conduct, etc. the regulated entities are given the responsibility to bring their business objectives in alignment with the objectivities of the regulator. The rules-based regulation involves dictating through detailed prescriptive rules and supervisory actions. In India, the RBI report notes that there has been a move away from structured regulation to prudential regulation which are applicable to big and small banks. The idea is to evolve a PBR, after ensuring that all banking entities are able to absorb and faithfully adhere to fundamental obligations enjoined upon them to ensure financial stability.

The slow down of economic growth always means a slow down in new job openings. The crisis brings a psychological impact, a rising unemployment and poverty, uncertainty for the future, a fall in consumption; the economy goes into a downward spiral where governmental intervention becomes a necessity. Governments and International institutions have concluded that they need to use various instruments of fiscal and monetary policies to reduce the size of crisis and her endurance.

The effect on the Indian economy was not significant in the beginning. The initial effect of the sub-prime crisis was, in fact, positive, as the country received accelerated Foreign Institutional Investment (FII) flows during September 2007 to January 2008. This contributed to the debate on "decoupling," where it was believed that the emerging economies could remain largely insulated from the crisis and provide an alternative engine of growth to the world economy. The argument soon proved unfounded as the global crisis intensified and spread to the emerging economies through capital and current account of the balance of payments (BoP). The net portfolio flows to India soon turned negative as Foreign Institutional Investors (FIIs) rushed to sell equity stakes in a bid to replenish overseas cash balances. This had a knock-on effect on the stock market and the exchange rates through creating the supply demand imbalance in the foreign exchange market.

GLOBAL DOWNTURN AND THE THIRTEENTH FINANCE COMMISSION

The Thirteenth Finance Commission (THFC) was appointed in November, 2007 against the backdrop of considerable progress on the fiscal responsibility and budget management (FRBM) legislations by the centre and the states.

At the time the THFC was constituted, there was no hint that the sub-prime crisis in the United States would turn successively into a global banking crisis, global financial crisis and a global economic crisis. At the time of presenting the union budget for 2008-09, the ramifications of the evolving global crisis on the Indian economy were not known. The then finance minister, while presenting the budget, had indicated that after the obligations on account of the Sixth Central Pay Commission became clearer, the THFC would be requested to revisit the road map of fiscal adjustment and suggest a suitably revised road map taking into account these liabilities and the need to bring the liabilities on account of oil, food and fertilizer subsidies into fiscal accounting. Accordingly, in July 2008, the Finance Commission was asked to review the road map of fiscal adjustment and suggest a suitably revised road map with a view to maintaining the gains of fiscal consolidation through 2010 to

2015. Thus, even the additional term of reference did not mention the global downturn and its impact on the fiscal situation.

With a view to minimizing the impact of the global downturn on the Indian economy, the union government came out with three fiscal stimulus packages in quick succession (December 2008, January 2009 and March 2009). The important policy measures announced in these packages included cuts in tax rates, increase in plan expenditure, lowering of interest rates on export and housing finance, authorization to India Infrastructure Finance Company (IIFICL) to raise tax-free bonds to finance infrastructure projects and increasing the market borrowing limits of the states by Rs. 30,000 crore.

Currently, there is total uncertainly regarding the duration and depth of the present crisis and the kind of further stimulus that is needed in future. The expectation that the adverse impact of the global financial crisis will be minimal on the Indian economy has been belied. It now looks that the crisis is much deeper and recovery will take much longer than Indian economy has been belied. It now looks that the crisis is much deeper and recovery will take much longer than expected. Even the milder Asian financial crisis, which was followed by the implementation of the Fifth Pay Commission recommendations, had its impact on the Indian economy. GDP growth averaged 5.2% between 1997-98 and 2002-03, as compared with the average growth of 6.6% in the preceding five years. What we are now facing is a global crisis accompanied by the implementation of the recommendations of the Sixth Central Pay Commission. Obviously, one can expect the adverse impact to be much more severe and to last much longer. Finance Minister Pranab Kumar Mukherjee in his reply to the interim budget debate has indicated that the medium-term objective is to revert to the path of fiscal consolidation as early as 2010-11, provided the US and the organization of Economic Cooperation and Development (OECD) economies come out of their contractionary phase by the year end.

Appropriate Policy Responses

The current macroeconomic and social challenges posed by the global financial crisis require a much better understanding of appropriate policy responses:

1. There needs to be a better understanding of what can provide financial stability, how cross-border cooperation can help to provide the public good of international financial rules and systems, and what the most appropriate rules are with respect to development;
2. There needs to be an understanding of whether and how developing countries can minimise financial contagion;
3. Developing countries will also need to manage the implications of the current economic slowdown—after a period of strong and continued growth in developing countries, which has promoted interest in structural factors of growth, international macroeconomic management will now move up the policy agenda. Do countries have room to use fiscal and monetary polices?
4. Developing countries need to understand the social outcomes and provide appropriate social protection schemes;
5. There will also be implications for development policy: and
6. There will be limits to financial solutions if the problems lie in the real economy, but development finance institutions may be able to take some risks and support investment flows to developing countries, counteracting reductions in other financial flows.

References

Bhaduri, A. (2009), "Understanding the Financial Crisis", *Economic and Political Weekly*, Vol., XLIV, Nos. 13, 28, March.

Bhattacharya, S. (2009), "The Lending Puzzle", *The Financial Express*, 6 March.

Bose, A. (1989), "Short Period Equilibrium in a Less Developed Economy", in M. Rakshit (ed.), Studies in the Macroeconomics of Developing Countries (New Delhi: Oxford University Press).

Pat, K.A. (2009), "Why Indian Banks Are Healthy in This Global Crisis", *Economic and Political Weekly*, Vol., XLIV Nos. 17, 25, April.

Patnaik, P. (2009), "Speculation and Growth under Contemporary Capitalism", Kale Memorial Lecture, Gokhle Institute of Politics and Economics, January.

Reddy, G.R. (2009), "Global Downturn and the Thirteenth Finance Commission", *Economic and Political Weekly*, Vol. XLIV, Nos. 17, 25, April.

Sen, S. (2008), "US Financial Crisis: A Classic Ponzi Affair?", *Mainstream*, 27 October.

The Economist (2008), "The Decoupling Debate", 6, March.

Vaidyanathan, A. (2009), "Reviving the Economy: Problems and Prospects", *Economic and Political Weekly*, Vol. XLIV, No. 6, February 7-13.

21

The Sub-prime Crisis and its Impact on the Indian Economy

R.Y. Mahore

The objective of this paper is to analyse the background and consequences of global financial crisis on the Indian economy. The 2008 Great Global Credit Crisis will be seen in history as a major turning point, just as the 1930s Great Depression set in motion the Second World War and changed the financial landscape for nearly 80 years. The hallmark of the current crisis is Complexity, so that we would have look at it from the perspective of history, macro and micro-details. In essence, four historical mega-trends paved the conditions for crisis. The first was the appearance in 1989 of 3 billion labour force into the market economies following the end of the Cold War that gave rise to a global flood of cheap goods and low inflation for nearly two decades.

The second was the monetary policy responses to the Japanese bubble/deflation since 1990, which gave rise to over two decades of almost interest free yen loans globally, creating the famous Yen carry trade. We could trace the Japanese bubble to the Plaza Accord of 1985, when Japan allowed its exchange rate to overshoot. The supply of almost interest free funding to combat Japanese domestic deflation was effectively to subsidize the rise of financial engineering, and created bubbles elsewhere, most prominently in the East Asian crisis economies between 1990 and 1996.

The third force was the emergence of financial engineers, basically scientists and physicists, who applied their technical and statistical skills to financial markets. Underlying their sophisticated models was one fatal flaw, that the world of risk was a bell shaped statistical curve that ignored the long-tailed black swan risk. It was the underestimation of once in 400-year risks that proved their undoing.

The fourth was the phase of global deregulation, from the reduction of tariffs under WTO, the removal of capital controls under IMF and the philosophy that minimal intervention and letting markets determine prices and competition would create global efficiency. Such philosophy permeated the basic textbooks and the international bureaucracy. Essentially, these mega-trends were four arbitrages that created converging globalization—wage arbitrage, financial arbitrage, knowledge arbitrage and regulatory arbitrage. Unfortunately, the four arbitrages also led to four excesses that were the hallmark of the present crisis—excess liquidity, excess leverage, excess complexity and excess greed. Note that complexity creates opacity and therefore grand opportunities for fraud

History will record that the failure of Lehman Brothers on 15 September 2008 was a major mistake, causing massive shocks to the world's banking system, with stock markets seeing almost meltdown. Banks in the US and Europe were partly nationalized and investment banks disappeared as a separate unit in the US. In 2008, it is estimated that global stock markets lost roughly US $27 trillion or over 40 percent whilst major real estate markets dropped by about 20 percent. In October 2008, the Bank of England has estimated that the mark-to-market losses in bond and credit securities would be in the region of US $2.8 trillion, double what the IMF predicted at US $1.4 trillion. This was equivalent to 85% of global bank's tier 1 capital of US $3.4 trillion. Nouriel Roubini, however, has predicted that the US total losses in credit and securities could total as much as US $3.6 trillion, which would wipe out the capital of the banking system of US $1.5 trillion.

Firstly, the global nature of the present US crisis can be seen in the following context. At the end of 2007, the US had GDP of US $13.8 trillion, compared with Japan (US $4.4 trillion) and China (US $3.2 trillion). By 2007, gross savings in the US had fallen to 14% of GDP, net savings to 1.7% of GDP and current account deficit (funded from abroad) had risen to US $720 billion or 5.2% of GDP. As a result of years of cumulative deficits, the US had gross and net international liabilities of US $16.3 trillion and US $2.5 trillion6 respectively (data at end 2006). On the other hand, Japan and China together held half of the total US government treasury securities at the end of July 20077. As at the end of June 2007, foreigners owned 56.9 percent of marketable US Treasury securities, 24 percent of corporate and other debt, 21.4 percent of US government agency paper and 11.3 percent of total US stock market capitalization8. So, the losses in the US will be felt badly by the rest of the world, both directly and indirectly.

Secondly, the comparative balance sheets are even more illuminating. Based on IMF data, global GDP at the end of 2007 was US $54.5 trillion, of which the largest bloc was EU (US $15.7 trillion), North America (US $15.2 trillion), Asia (US $11.8 trillion, but only US $7.5 trillion excluding Japan). Global total financial assets, namely bank assets, bonds and stock market capitalization) amounted to US $229.7 trillion or 421 percent of GDP, with the EU largest at 549 percent, North America at 442 percent and Asia roughly at global average of 419 percent, but only 370 percent excluding Japan. In other words, financial sector leverage, which was only 108 percent of GDP in 1980 according to McKinsey data has risen to four times GDP by 2007. The notional value of financial derivatives amounted to US $596 trillion at the end of 2007, which was 10.9 times GDP. About two-thirds of this was relatively simple interest-rate derivatives, but nearly US $58 trillion was the rapidly growing CDS market. The exchange traded derivatives were US $95 trillion in size. Together, these financial derivatives were 14 times global GDP. In a nutshell, the world has become significantly more leveraged in the last two decades.

The Prime Minister of India, the Finance Minister as well as the Deputy Chairman of the Planning Commission, Mr Montek Singh Ahluwalia, have expressed anxiety over the impact of the sub-prime crisis in the United States on the growth in India. In fact, Mr Ahluwalia has said that this is more worrying than the rise in energy prices. It is only the Governor of the Reserve Bank of India (RBI) who has not expressed similar views, focusing his concern more on growing capital flows and the impact on the currency.

Two articles in the Financial Times offer an interesting overview of the debate, the causes, effects and consequences of the United States sub-prime crisis. There is the argument that over the past several years, the United States' trade deficit has persistently drained spending from the United States' economy. As a result, much of manufacturing failed to recover after 2001 which then prompted the Federal Reserve to push interest rates to all times low. This staved off recession but gave rise to the housing bubble—a house price inflation, a construction boom, explosive growth of non-traditional sub-prime mortgages, a debt financed consumer spending scenario and, yet, larger trade deficits.

The fiscal situation of the central government is worrisome. The problem is largely structural and not cyclical. The slowdown of the economy has only partly contributed to the deterioration in 2008-09. The government has to institute a restructuring programme towards achieving fiscal consolidation. The finance minister in his 2008-09 budget speech had stated ,"It is widely acknowledged that the fiscal position of the country has improved tremendously." Indeed while presenting the interim budget 2009-10, he claimed that breaching of the fiscal deficit targets was mainly due to the global economic slowdown when he stated, "...extraordinary economic circumstances merit extraordinary measures. Our government has decided to relax the FRBM targets."

The Indian economy looked to be relatively insulated from the global financial crisis that started in August 2007 when the 'sub-prime mortgage' crisis first surfaced in the US. In fact the RBI was raising interest rates until July 2008 with the view to cooling the growth rate and containing inflationary pressures. But as the financial meltdown, morphed in to a global economic downturn with the collapse of Lehman Brothers on 23 September 2008, the impact on the Indian economy was almost immediate. Credit flows suddenly dried-up and, overnight, money market interest rate spiked to above 20 percent and remained high for the next month. It is, perhaps, judicious to assume that the impacts of the global economic downturn, the first in the center of global capitalism since the Great Depression, on the Indian economy are still unfolding. The severity and suddenness of the crisis can be judged from the IMF's forecast for the global economy. For the first time in 60 years, the IMF is now forecasting a global recession with negative growth for world GDP in 2009-10. The IMF has revised its forecasts downwards thrice since July 2008, and it is not yet certain that this will be the last revision. The WTO has predicted that world trade, which has virtually collapsed in the second half of 2008 is likely to decline by as much as nine percent in 2009-10. We have already seen exports from world's major exporters, like Germany, Japan and China, plummeting by more than 35 percent in the last quarter of 2008. The sharp decline in economic activity is despite the large stimulus, estimated at more than USD3 trillion, that OECD economies have put in place. Yet the bad news does not stop. The worst downside scenario could be for the US economy being trapped in a Japan like "L" shaped recovery for the next few years. This will imply a further decline in world exports and softening of global commodity prices. In turn, it will result in sharp slowdown in world exports and result in widespread unemployment and social stress in major exporting economies. This could well generate irresistible protectionist sentiments and if governments do succumb to these, it will unleash the dreaded downward cycle which could see the global economy plunging over the precipice into a prolonged recession. It is, therefore, prudent not to underestimate the severity of the present crisis.

At the top are concerns of a direct impact on financial institutions in India. The RBI has clarified that the exposure of Indian banks and institutions to the crisis is 'marginal'. There is a story in *Business Standard* that claims that State Bank of India, ICICI Bank, Bank of Baroda and Bank of India are set to book mark to market losses on their foreign offices to credit derivatives. The *Business Standard* has estimated the total of these losses to be around US $3 billion for the four banks put together, and has commented that the provisioning made by these banks so far has been quite small. Given the size of the banks and their balance sheets, even if these figures were accurate, there would be little impact on the overall performance of the banks. In short, the direct fall-out effect of the collapse of the sub-prime mortgages to institutions in India is likely to be quite insignificant.

Second, it is clear that there would be weak or no growth in the United States, and estimates by the World Bank suggest that high-income countries would grow at just 2.2 percent this year, as against 7.1 percent for developing countries (estimates put China at 10.8 percent, India at 8.4 percent and South Asia at 7.9 percent). Given low inflation expectations in the United States, the World Bank suggests that emerging countries would pull high-income countries behind them. The benign part of the projection is that low growth in the developed countries would keep commodity price increases under control, lessening risks of inflation in the developing countries, and adding to stimulus for growth.

The policy response in India is likely to be to ensure that that the rupee does not appreciate 'too much', a task that will entail active sterilisation operations by the RBI. These sterilisation operations, through issue of market stabilisation bonds, entail an additional fiscal burden on the government for the interest costs of these bonds. Energy costs have risen but adjustment of consumer prices has not been possible due to political compulsions of the coalition. It is likely that fiscal stresses on the government may increase. It is this total picture of rupee appreciation, lower exports and fiscal stress that is causing worries in the Indian Finance Ministry and the Planning Commission.

On the positive side, data reveals that the quarter ending December 2007 has been quite good for Indian manufacturing as well as the services sector, asset prices in terms of equities and real estate remain firm, and revenue collections have been extremely buoyant. The Indian industry seems less than concerned about domestic demand growth. The measures by the RBI to curb liquidity have yielded positive results and inflation appears to be a lesser worry than in China.

The worry lies in two areas. The first is that, capital formation, in terms of investments in plant and machinery, after reaching a peak in the middle of last year, appears to be stagnant and likely to be going down. The effects of this slow down started in 2008 and also continued in 2009. This may be balanced by capital spending for infrastructure. The government will come out with some initiatives, especially in the power, aviation and shipping sectors. The second is that trade deficit continues to be very high and is increasing, signaling the lack of competitiveness in the economy. The Finance Minister has already promised that he would consider sops to exporters in the forthcoming budget. He is, therefore, wary of controls on capital flows and has been encouraging banks to reduce lending rates to spur consumption and growth. This is at variance with the task given to the RBI—that of controlling inflation and excess liquidity. Policy alternatives appear to be at cross purposes.

EFFECT OF THE US FINANCIAL CRISIS ON INDIA

It is often said that when the US sneezes the rest of the world catches a cold. This three-part series looks at how India, China, and Russia have been affected by the US financial crisis. Before we get into detail about how much this US problem is spreading globally, we should understand the severity of it and the possible consequences in the US. How sick is the US?

Some have compared the situation in the US with the Great Depression of 1929, but this situation is far from a depression—in fact it's not even a recession. In the Great Depression there was no work and there was widespread poverty. People struggled through the winter with no heating and no food. We are not seeing such extensive suffering in the US. In the US, August 2008 unemployment figures were at 6.1%, according to the US Bureau of Labour Statistics. In the Great Depression unemployment was higher than 25%. The Commerce Department reported that GDP growth was at 2.8%, hardly indicative of a recession, although this was revised down from the 3.3% figure it projected a month ago. Even before this controversial rescue plan was shot down, Indian markets took a dive of their own on Monday 29 September. The stock market sank to an 18-month low and the rupee a 5-year low. The stock market dropped 5.3% to 12,595.75.

According to *Business Standard*, vice-president of Karvy Stockbroking Ambareesh Baliga, said, "We are advising our clients to stay away from trading till selling by Foreign Institutional Investors (FIIs) stops. Also, there is no support to the markets from any domestic institution. While markets are below their fundamental levels, fear has gripped investors and there is panic selling." While US investors and consumers are concerned about who will foot the bill for this $700 billion plan, to Indian and non-US markets that doesn't matter. They just want it to happen so as to restore confidence and of course liquidity.

Crowds gathered outside the Bombay Stock Exchange to watch the markets drop, with many investors angry. Why should failure of the world's most advanced financial system hurt individual Indian investors? But the fact remains that the "Bush administration's failed economic policies" as speaker of the House Nancy Pelosi described it, is everybody's business. The US Senate has rejected the $700 billion bailout package proposed by the Secretary of Treasury. This has led to a global panic and resulted in fall in markets world wide.

All the political parties are supportive of the existing subsidies in place for Petrol, Diesel and other fuels. This populist act coupled with a week Rupee will adversely affect the Indian economy by increasing the budget deficit which currently stands at around Rs. 1.15 trillion. The prospect of high prices and increasing inflation is not good news for the UPA government, specially as election nears..

According to official data, industrial growth in August has plummeted to mere 1.3% compared to the same month in 2007. That definitely is cause of concern for policy-makers and industries. This data also raised fear of low GDP growth of India. It is being suspected that, our country will face huge problems in achieving even 7.5% growth rate in this fiscal. April-August industrial growth rate is 4.9% which is also the lowest for the first five months of a financial year in 14-year period except 1998 and 2001. To make matters worst, a member of the PM's economic advisory council and director of the National Institute of Public Finance and Policy have confessed that India is going through industrial recession.

Several crucial sectors of Indian economy are likely to face serious problems in coming months. Foremost among them is real estate sector. The demand for houses have reduced significantly and property prices across India has registered 15-20% fall. Things are likely to get worst as another 20 percent drop in prices is quite possible in coming six months. The woes of real estate have spread to construction industry as well. Because of less demand for houses, construction companies are going to suffer big time. Financial services segment is also likely to be a major victim of economic slowdown because of less demand for credit and reduced liquidity in market.

These three segments account for almost one third of services GDP and because of their current and impending plight, attaining 7.5% GDP growth in this current year is quite improbable. Industrial slowdown will also affect transport services. Transport companies are likely to witness drastic fall in their business and profits. Global recession will also lead to less tourists coming to India. That will negatively affect tours and travels industry. Author—Mritunjai Kumar, expert economist and prolific writer.

Global economic meltdown has affected almost all countries. Strongest of American, European and Japanese companies are facing severe crisis of liquidity and credit. India is not insulated, either. However, India's cautious approach towards reforms has saved it from possibly disastrous implications. The truth is, Indian economy is also facing a kind of slowdown. The prime reason being, world trade does not functions in isolation. All the economies are interlinked to each other and any major fluctuation in trade balance and economic conditions causes numerous problems for all other economies.

THE CRISIS AS A LOST OPPORTUNITY FOR THE INDIAN FINANCIAL SECTOR

Conservative mind and repressive financial legislations are not good often. The merchant banking industry of the country remains backward to handle the opportunities provided by the vibrant domestic corporate sector. The financial crisis is often compared to many geological and climatic catastrophe like tsunamis and tornadoes. Taken on that line, the crisis like a cyclone in a tropical island has uprooted many big institutions. One among them is the investment bank group.

The US investment bankers performed critical role in

facilitating the expansion of corporate activities. The American deregulated financial set-up has helped the investment bankers to flourish and expand their business to all corners of the world. The US banker's financial advisory sophistication is well recognized in the corporate world. In India, when the largest company-the government owned Oil and Natural Gas Corporation of India (ONGC) decided for IPO few years back, the government has appointed Morgan Stanley and DSP Merrill Lynch as the lead managers. When many of these unique species of financial institutions collapsed during the crisis, it became a golden opportunity for many countries and institutions to acquire these investment bankers at throw away prices. The US administration has done its best to keep the control of the failed investment bankers in US hands. The bail-out-*cum*-rehabilitation strategy was to merge the fallen banks with other US banks.

But still, some of the failed banks were taken by the foreign institutions especially financial institutions from Japan and a few strategic invertors from the Middle East. Japanese Nomura Bank has taken majority share in Lehman Brother's Asian operations. Few other Japanese banks also have gone for the acquisition opportunity. Sumitomo Mitsumi has taken significant share of the Goldman and Sachs and Mitsubishi UFJ has acquired Morgan Stanley.

The financial services of the merchant bankers will certainly have high demand in India given the market oriented economy and a vibrant domestic corporate sector. Unlike in China, the private sector character of the corporate sector and the competitive overseas ambitions of the firms make India a good market for financial services provided by the investment bankers. Hence, developing credible investment bankers is a priority for India than for China.

Recently, the Nomura bank has started investment operations in India. With the disappearance of the former established players like the Morgan Stanley, the field is open for new players. The existing Indian merchant bankers like SBI Capital and ICICI Securities remains infants in the industry. They indeed failed to take the crisis as an opportunity by not going for the fallen but experienced institutions like the Morgan Stanley. The government recently has appointed the Jeffries as the lead manager for the proposed disinvestment of the Cochin

Refineries Limited indicating the continuing underdeveloped status of our merchant bankers. When investment bankers from Japan are coming into India with added competence, our financial service industry remains backward is a matter of concern.

With many of the top IT companies save HCL having half their revenues from financial and banking segments, no doubt they are going to take a harsh beating, with Infosys already losing $2 bn. the past week(Sept end 2008)) out of an approximate $10 bn. lost by Indian IT companies listed on the US market. Banks may suffer as Lehman Brothers and Merrill Lynch had invested substantially in the formers's stocks.

The government does not systematically gather employment data—a national employment survey is conducted only once every five years—and more than 90 percent of workers are in the so-called "informal" sector, meaning that have no statutory benefits and that their jobs can be cut by their employers at will. Textile employers claim 700,000 jobs were eliminated in their industry in 2008. Since October, thousands of diamond-polishing workshops have shut down and more than 200,000 people in the gem and jewelry industry have reportedly lost their jobs just in the Surat region of Gujarat. In a February 26 article titled "Indian towns that fuelled the boom hit hard," the *London Financial Times* reported that tens of thousands of workers who recently migrated to Coimbatore, a center of textile and auto production in southern India, have been forced to return home after their jobs were cut.

The United Nations' World Food Programme (WFP) has warned that the migration of newly jobless workers back to their rural family homes risks exacerbating a longstanding crisis in rural India. The WFP's "Report on the State of Food Insecurity in Rural India" found rising levels of "food and nutrition insecurity." 230 million people—one-fifth of India's total population are undernourished—and a total of 350 million are considered food insecure, which is defined as "consuming less than 80 percent of minimum energy requirements." Hundreds of millions more eke out an impoverished existence and are at risk of being pushed into the abyss by unemployment or illness. 70 percent of India's population survives on less than $2 per day.

Especially troubling for the government was the recent

report that India's economic growth slowed in the last three months of 2008 to an annualized rate of 5.3 percent. This was far below government forecasts and belied its claims, confidently repeated in the preceding weeks, that economic growth in India in the 2008-9 fiscal year, which ended on March 31, was more than 7 percent. Manufacturing output actually contracted by 0.2 percent in the last quarter of 2008, while agriculture, which continues to provide over half of India's population with its livelihood, suffered a 2.2 percent decline.

India's economic development strategy is predicated on the country registering an annual growth in exports of 20 percent or more. The government had set an export target of $200 billion for this year—less than one-sixth of the value of China's exports in 2007—but it is now expected that the figure will be around $170 billion. While India's economic outlook may appear cheery when compared with the advanced capitalist economies, whose economies are rapidly contracting, the dramatic slowing of India's growth constitutes a body blow to the Indian bourgeoisie's ambitions to transform India into a world power and will undoubtedly lead to explosive class conflict. Indian Prime Minister Manmohan Singh has repeatedly said that India needs economic growth of 8 percent if it is to keep pace with China and the ASEAN countries, let alone catch up with the major imperialist powers. And just as importantly, he has argued that the only way to maintain a "popular constituency" in favour of "reform"—that is support for the bourgeoisie's drive to transform India into a cheap-labour producer of world capitalism—is by maintaining very high growth. Otherwise it will be impossible to absorb the tens of millions who will be joining the labour force in the coming years as a result of population growth and the bourgeoisie's drive to supplant petty producers in agriculture and handicrafts and the large number of family-owned shops with production and commercial firms organized along advanced capitalist lines.

Several years ago, India's Planning Commission warned that if India grew at only 6.5 percent a year, its jobless rate would still jump, resulting in another 70 million unemployed by 2012. The economic crisis has led to a rapid swelling of India's budget deficit. Whereas the government had projected a deficit in 2008-9 equal to 2.5 percent of GDP, in last month's interim budget it conceded the figure would be 6 percent and predicted a deficit equal to 5.5 percent of GDP in the coming fiscal year, which starts in April. The latter projection is highly optimistic given the bleak outlook facing the Indian economy. The combined deficit for Centre and state governments has almost doubled as a proportion of GDP, rising from 5.7 in the 2007-8 fiscal year to 11.1 percent in 2008-9.

The rapid deterioration of India's fiscal position has led the world's major bond-rating agencies to warn that they may soon slash India's credit rating. Following the presentation of India's budget, standard and poor said India's debt position is unsustainable, switched its outlook for Indian debt to "negative," and said it may soon downgrade India's debt rating to junk bond status from the current level of BBB, the lowest investment grade rating.

THE GLOBAL FINANCIAL CRISIS AND THE INDIAN CORPORATE SECTOR

How the present wave of global financial crisis is going to affect our economy is a critical question. There are of course many channels for the financial crisis to have its influence on our economy. The depreciation of the rupee, decline in exports, set back to employment expansion in the IT sector are few of them. But an important impact is that on the corporate sector. The foreign source of funds for the domestic corporate is going to dry up. Corporate investment is going to decline during the next few quarters and perhaps sometimes for few years depending upon the speed in which global financial sector recovers. This is perhaps the most important way in which the present global financial crisis is going to affect our macro-economy.

The domestic corporate sector has emerged as the major force in investment expansion, employment generation, and infrastructure creation, etc. over the last one decade. The corporate income tax emerged as the single largest tax revenue for the government. Besides, expansion of corporate sector has resulted in highly paid jobs and as result of this, the personal income tax revenue also expanded significantly. These two taxes contribute to 51% of the government's total tax revenue. The share of direct taxes was just 18% in 1990. All these indicate the corporatisation of our economy after reforms.

Indian corporate over the last five years is living in an environment where there is easy exposure to sizable foreign funds. The corporate purchase of foreign funds in different forms—ECBs (External Commercial Borrowings), FCCBs, Depository Receipts and Exchangeable Bonds have facilitated the expansion activities of our corporate in organic as well as inorganic mode.

The global economic recession is negatively affecting workers everywhere. Media and policy-makers have focused on the rising unemployment of formal salaried workers. Little attention, however, has been paid to the impact of the crisis on informal firms and workers, nor the consequences of new entrants into the informal economy.

In reality, economic downturns often affect the informal economy in the same ways they affect the formal economy. Like formal firms, informal firms are affected by decreased demand, falling prices, and fluctuations in exchange rates associated with economic crises. Like formal wage workers, informal wage workers face loss of jobs or greater informalization of their employment contracts. Indeed, during down-turns, informal wage workers are often the first to lose their jobs.

POLICY MEASURES

In our view, it is more important to focus policy attention on removing some of the many remaining structural bottlenecks on raising the potential GDP growth rate. Essentially, this will imply efforts at improving the investment climate both for domestic and foreign investors; removing the entry barriers for the entry of corporate investment in education and vocational training; improving the delivery of public goods and services and expanding physical infrastructure capacities including a major effort at improving connectivity in the rural regions. These measures will constitute the package of second generation of structural reforms and will enable the Indian economy to climb out of the downward cyclical phase and then to extend the upward phase for a longer period than was achieved in the last cycle.

What started off as US sub-prime lending crisis in the US housing market turned into a global financial crisis and then to a global economic crisis. Though the developed countries like Japan, US and UK, due to this global financial crisis are witnessing recession in their economies, India is witnessing a positive and significant growth rate although lower than 9%. Rate of growth of GDP in 2007-08 was around 9% and it was around 7.8% in first half of the year 2008-09. But the third quarter of 2008-09 has registered a growth rate of 5.3% as unveiled by the Central Statistical Organisation (CSO). Agricultural sector has registered a negative growth rate of –2.2% and manufacturing growth rate contracted to –0.2% in the third quarter. But agriculture has done well in last two years.

The effect on the Indian economy was not significant in the beginning. The initial effect of the sub-prime crisis was, in fact, positive, as the country received accelerated Foreign Institutional Investment (FII) flows during September 2007 to January 2008. This contributed to the debate on "decoupling," where it was believed that the emerging economies could remain largely insulated from the crisis and provide an alternative engine of growth to the world economy. The argument soon proved unfounded as the global crisis intensified and spread to the emerging economies through capital and current account of the balance of payments (BoP). The net portfolio flows to India soon turned negative as Foreign Institutional Investors (FIIs) rushed to sell equity stakes in a bid to replenish overseas cash balances. This had a knock-on effect on the stock market and the exchange rates through creating the supply demand imbalance in the foreign exchange market. The current account was affected mainly after September 2008 through slowdown in exports. Despite setbacks, however, the BoP situation of the country continues to remain resilient.

Before the onset of the financial crisis, the main concern of the policy-makers was excessive capital inflows, which increased from 3.1 per cent of GDP in 2005-06 to 9.3 per cent in 2007-08. While this led to increase in foreign exchange reserves from US $ 151.6 billion at end-March 2006 to US $ 309.7 billion at end-March 2008, it also contributed to monetary expansion, which fuelled liquidity growth. WPI inflation reached a trough of 3.1 per cent in October 2007, a month before global commodity price inflation zoomed to double digits from low single digits. The rising oil and commodity prices, contributed to a significant rise in prices, with annual WPI peaking at 12.8 per cent in August 2008. The monetary policy stance during the first half of 2008- 09 was therefore directed at containing the prices rise. Surely, the economic slowdown in 2008-09 has adversely affected state finances significantly. Available information on the revised estimates for 14 states for 2008-09 shows that the position has deteriorated since due to the slowdown in the economy and declining tax devolution and the revenue surplus is likely to be reduced by about 0.2% of GDP and the fiscal deficit may increase by about 0.7 percentage point.

With the recessionary climate in the OECD countries and the slowdown in the Indian economy, it would be unrealistic to expect any significant adjustment in the deficit and 2008-09 level of deficit would continue. Nevertheless, there will be a lot of expectations that the budget will provide yet another stimulus package. Furthermore, form the viewpoint of reviving the economy speedily; the government will have to increase allocations to infrastructure and some of the asset creating flagship schemes such as rural roads. Equally important is the need to provide clear signals to the private sector and this would require initiating a number of reforms.

The finances of state governments are likely to be under considerable stress on several counts. First, given the slowdown in the economy, revenue accrual from taxes may come down. Second, battling the recession requires considerable demand injection into the economy through public investment in social services and other related sectors. Therefore, states may be required to undertake increased expenditure on essential services which will require larger resource mobilization. Third, owing to the decline in revenue resources of the central government, both tax devolution and non-plan grants by the centre have declined significantly for the year 2008-09 (RE). fourth, there has been an increase in the proportion of high cost debt within the total outstanding market loans till 2007-08, which entails a larger interest payment by the states, thereby pushing committed expenditure of the states are likely to be under pressure for implementation of the recommendation of SCPC which will inordinately increase their salary and pension bill.

In India lobbying for lower interest on such loans is most

vociferous from producers of durables and from real estate and housing companies. Reducing the cost of consumer credit is unlikely to make a significant difference to aggregate dement because they constitute a relatively small proportion of total spending. A general reduction in interest rates could improve their current profit and loss accounts (and also of enterprises in general). But it will not by itself make a significant difference to the returns to fresh investment even in these sectors, much less in others.

There is a strong case for asking the THFC to make recommendations covering the two years of 2010-11 and 2011-12. It would be difficult for the finance commission to make an assessment of the resources and needs of the centre and the states in view of the prevailing uncertainty emanating from the global downturn. Cutting short the period covered by the finance commission and plan period co-terminous thereby addressing the vexatious issue of non-plan and plan revenue expenditure dichotomy. Finally, it would help address uncertainty arising from the proposed introduction of GST from April 2010.

UPA ministers have vowed that the deterioration of India's fiscal position is only temporary. "Conditions in the years ahead are not likely to be normal," said Mukherjee in his budget speech, "and, therefore, the high fiscal deficit is inevitable. We will return to the [tighter fiscal] targets once the economy is restored to its recent trend growth path."

References

Business Standard (2008), Sub-prime Crisis to hit 4 big banks' profits, 7 January.

Dirk Willem te Velde (2008), "The Global Fianacial Crisis and Developing Countries", Background Note, Overseas Development Institute, UK, October.

Ghosh Jayati (2009), "Global Crisis and the Indian Economy", Chapter 3, UNDP India.

Guillen Mauro (2009), "The Global Economic and Financial Crisis: A Timeline", the Lauder Institute, Wharton Arts and Sciences, University of Pennsylvania.

Justin Yifu Lin, (2008), "The Impact of the Financial Crisis on Developing Countries", Korea Development Institute, Seoul, 31 October.

Marjit Sugata, (2009), "Global Crisis and the Indian Economy—On a Few Unconventional Assertions", Centre for Studies in Social Sciences, Calcutta.

Narayan S. (2008), "The Sub-Prime Crisis—Likely Consequences for the Indian Economy", Institute of South Asian Studies, National University of Singapore.

Narayan, S. (2009), "Inflationary Pressures in Indian Economy", Institute of South Asian Studies, National University of Singapore.

Rajiv Kumar (2009), "Global Financial and Economic Crisis: Impact on India and Policy Response", (UNDP, India report) ICRIER, New Delhi.

Sheng Andrew (2009), "From Asian to Global Financial Crisis", Third KB Lall Memorial Lecture of the ICRIER, New Delhi, February 7.

Subbarao Duvvuri, (2009), "Impact of the Global Financial Crisis on India—Collateral Damage and Response" Governor of the Reserve Bank of India.

Tharoor Shashi (2009), "Indian Economy Bright Spot in Global Crisis", *The Epoch Times*, March 19-25.

Thorat, Usha (2009), "Impact of Global Financial Crisis on Reserve Bank of India (RBI) as a regulator", Deputy Governor of the Reserve Bank of India.

World Bank (2007), Global Economic Prospects.

World Economic Outlook, "Crisis and Recovery", International Monetary Fund, April 2009.

22

The Global Financial Integration, Innovations, Damages and the Indian Economy: A Perspective

MOHAMMAD ASIF AND HENA NISAR

INTRODUCTION

We are the survivor of a century which marks its identity with the concepts of globalization, post-modernization, innovation, diversification and global integration. Now the whole world is like a global village, boundaries, languages, disparity, regulations are the talks of the past. From all these we just mean that in recent times we all are the dwellers of only one nation and that is the globe. What happens in the one part of the globe immediately reflects its impact on the other parts.

Proponents of economic globalization point to many significant benefits of it. Better communication mechanism and lower transportation costs have provided consumers with access to lower priced goods and a much broader range of products. International capital flows have financed production facilities in countries where labour is relatively abundant and ready to be profitably employed in more productive and remunerative activities. The spread of technological and marketing know how and other ideas across national borders have also contributed to the more productive employment of local labour force, enabling them to raise their standard of living.

Nevertheless, this global integration has also disrupted the economic circumstances of many people and by-passed the economies of many others. Accordingly, critics of economic globalization have strong reasons for concern.

They recognized that the benefits of economic integration have come with some very high costs, most international economists regard it as a process that cannot be stopped or substantially reversed without very damaging consequences. And one of the examples of the kind is the recent financial crisis.

THE ARCHITECTURAL FRAMEWORK OF THE GLOBAL FINANCIAL CRISES

We are now in the midst of the worst financial crises since the great depression. The crises are the latest phase of the evolution of the financial market under the radical financial deregulation process that began in the late 1970's. This evolution has taken the form of cycles in which deregulation accompanied by rapid financial innovation stimulates powerful financial booms that end in crises. Governments respond to crises with bailouts that allow new expansions to begin. As a result, financial markets have become ever larger and financial crises have become more threatening to society. (Crotty, 2008)

While the US sub-prime mortgage market triggered the current financial crises, its deep cause on the financial side is to be found in the flawed institutions and practices of what is often referred to as the New Financial Architecture (NFA). The term NFA refers to the integration of modern day financial markets with their associated regime of light government regulation. The construction of NFA began with the long process of radical financial deregulation that originated in the US and UK in the late 1970's and accelerated after 1980. Since then a gravitational shift of Economic activity from the production of goods and non-financial services to finance has been underway. One indicator of this process has been the rapid growth since then of the share of financial profits in total corporate profits. Also reflective of this process of "financialisation" is the explosive growth of private debt-household, non-financial and financial business—as a proportion of gross domestic product, and the pilling of layers upon layers of claims with existence of instruments like options, futures, swaps and the like, and financial entities like hedge funds and structural investment vehicle. With financialisation, the employment of money capital in the financial markets and in speculation, more generally, to make more money, by-passing the route of commodity production increasingly became the name of the game.

The flood of private debt to finance such activity has been sustained by successive booms on asset prices, indeed, such booms have, in turn been fed by the explosion of debt. As long as the asset price bubble grows, consumers and businesses get access to more credit to buy more home or financial assets because their creditworthiness is determined by the market values of the assets they hold, which act as collateral. The rise of asset values and the intensification of the speculative mania contribute to the growth of borrowing which, in turn, flames the fires of speculation and further rise of asset values. On the supply side of the financial markets in the competitive race to grab the hindmost of the profits in store, a whole array of players get into the act of frenzied "financial innovation", leading to the multiplication of financial assets of all kinds, for instance, the securitization of mortgage loans through the collateralized debt obligation, or the credit default swap to speculate on the quantity of credit instrument. It is only when the asset price bubble pops and underlying collateral thus vanishes in thin air that all hell breaks loose across financial institutions and markets, and across countries in this world of globalized finance.

In short, the main flaws of the NFA which spiraled the credit crises around the globe can be jortted down as follows:

(i) The NFA is built on a very weak theoretical foundation;

(ii) It has widespread perverse incentives that create excessive risk;

(iii) Innovation created important financial products so complex that they could not be priced correctly and therefore lost liquidity when the boom ended;

(iv) The claim that commercial banks distributed almost all risky assets to capital markets and hedged whatever risk remained was false;

(v) Regulators allowed banks to hold assets off-balance sheet with no capital requirement;

(vi) It allowed giant bakns to measure their own risk and set their own capital requirements which naturally led to excessive risk-taking;

(vii) The NFA facilitated to growth of dangerously high system-wide leverage; and

(viii) Heavy reliance on complex financial products in a tightly integrated global financial system created channels of contagion that raised systematic risk. (Crotty 2008)

THE PRESENT CRISIS

The latest International Monetary Fund (IMF) analysis (February 2009), for example, considers that the root causes of the current crisis lay in market failure.........bred by a long period of high growth, low real interest rates and volatility and policy failures in financial regulation—which was not equipped to see the risk concentrations and flawed incentives behind the financial innovation boom; macroeconomic policies—which did not take into account building systematic risk in the financial system and in housing markets; and global architecture—where a fragmented surveillance system compounded the inability to see growing vulnerabilities and links.

The speed of disintegration and deregulation of global financial system, especially in U.S., led it to the epicentre of the current crisis. The first possible bubble that was seen as likely to collapse was the "hard landing", even crash, of the dollar as the U.S. increasingly became the largest debter country in the world with a continous current account deficit running for long.

The roots of this meltdown started strengthening with the failure of two Bear Stearns hedge funds and consequent freezing of the high risk collateralized debt obligation markets in June 2007 and deepened in September 2008 when one of the lynchpins of the financial system, Lehman Brothers, gave signs that it was facing insolvency and collapse.

Prof. Amit Bhaduri (2009) advocates that the nature of the crisis can only be understand by recognizing the main characteristics of the financial system that become so vulnerable to collapse due to falling asset prices. He finds three sets of inter-related facts which seem to capture the nature of this financial vulnerability. First, there emerged a set of financial institutions and companies that were in the lending business almost like usual commercial banks, but had no "lender of last resort". They resembled instead a shadow banking system which lacked the explicit banking of a monetary authority on the one hand, and escaped largely its regulation on other. In the true spirit of free market enterprise, finance could go on innovating new credit instruments with little regulation.

Second, without a lender of last resort at the top, innovative shadow banking resulted in what may aptly be described as a circular rather than a vertical network of credit interdependence. It happened basically through a system in which these shadow bankers, especially large investment banks, through mutual underwriting, insured each other's debt with derivatives as the most prominent debt instrument, and then went into "Securitisation" of these debts by mixing them in different ways. These debts in different combination of financial packages were then sold to private parties, including institutional investors, as securities or asets the world over according to their supposed degree of risk ascertained again by private credit rating agencies within the shadow financial system. Thus the whole game could be played within the private financial system virtually without regulation.

Finally, by treating each other's debt as asset in the capital base for lending the volume of lending could be expanded enormously. "Low margin, high volume" by pushing loans to more risky borrowers became the name of the game. This was symbolized by sub-prime lending. However, this circular credit structure was subject to two opposing magnifying effects from the beginning. On the one hand, with the supposed increase in the capital base, easy expansion in credit through many layers of leverage became possible. On the other, the capital base itself became increasingly vulnerable due to the magnifying effect of each defaulted loan, as each loan was linked or correlated with the asset base of several other shadow bankers in whose asset structure those securitized loans had entered. This "double magnification" largely accounts for the fragile circular credit structure on the supply side. To put it differently, continuous innovations in credit instruments rapidly raised leverage while increasing the number of layers on the capital base, whereas the increase in the number of layers raised both the proportion of non-performing loans and reduced the capital base in a magnified way in case of each default through its "Correlation effect" on the shadow banking system as a whole.

THE CRISIS CONTAGION IN THE INDIAN ECONOMY

It is often said that when the US sneezes the rest of world catches a cold and hence India did. India, like other emerging markets, has suffered a more severe impact than supposed earlier. India's Gross Domestic Product (GDP) growth, it need to be emphasized, had started decelerating in the first quarter of the 2007-08, nearly in months before the outbreak of the US financial turbulence and considerably ahead of the surge of recessionary tendencies in all developed countries from August-September 2008.

After clocking an average of 9.4 percent during three successive years from 2005-06 to 2007-08, the growth rate of real GDP slowed down to 6.7 percent (revised estimates) in 2008-09. Industrial production grew by 2.6 percent as compared to 7.4 percent in the previous year. In March 2009, imports fell by 12.2 percent and exports fell by 20.0 percent. The trade deficit widened from $ 88.5 billion in 2007-08 to $ 119.1 billion in 2008-09. Current account deficit increased from $ 17.0 billion in 2007-08 to $ 29.8 billion in 2008-09. Net capital inflows at US $ 9.1 billion (0.8 percent of GDP) were much lower in 2008-09 as compared with US $ 108.0 billion (9.2 percent of GDP) during the previous year mainly due to net outflows under portfolio investment, banking capital and short-term trade credit.

However, the Indian financial Institutions had only a low exposure to sub-prime crisis as majority are public sector enterprises. But the largest private financial institution, ICICI banks, has indeed exposure to this crisis but it is the domestic regulatory environment prevent such institution to indulge neck deep in to shady financial transactions like this. Therefore, it is the strong regulatory environment that really saved the India economy from a full-fledged crisis.

Despite these implications India is hit by the crisis due to India's growing integrations into the world economy as pointed out by D. Subbarao the present governor of RBI, India's integration into the world economy over the last decade has been remarkably rapid. Going by the common measure of globalization, India's two-way trade (merchandize exports plus imports), as a proportion of GDP, grew from 21.2 percent in 1997-98, the year of the Asian crisis, to 34.7 percent in 2007-08.

India's financial integration with the world is very deep. Importantly, the Indian corporate sector's access to external funding has markedly increased in the last five years. During this period 2003-08, the share of investment in India's GDP rose by 11 percentage points. While funds were available domestically, they were expensive relative to foreign funding. In a global market awash with liquidity and on the promise of India's growth potential, foreign investors were willing to take risks, and provide funds at a lower cost. Last year, for example, India received capital inflows amounting to over 9 percent of GDP as against a current account deficit in the balance of payments of just 1.5 percent of GDP. These capital flows, in excess of the current account deficit, evidence the importance of external financing and the depth of India's financial integration.

Subbarao explain that the contagion of crisis has spread to India through three channels-the financial channel, the real channel, and the confidence channel.

As a consequence of the global liquidity crisis, Indian banks and corporate faced hardship to access overseas finance and left with no option but to depend upon domestic banking sector. This also led the corporate sector to withdrew their investment from domestic money market mutual funds which put redemption pressure on mutual funds and further pressure on non-banking financial companies (NBFC's). This switchover from overseas finance to domestic finance created pressure both in the money markets and credit markets. On the other hand, the economy foreign exchange market got disturbed due to reversal of capital flows as part of the global deleveraging process. At the same time the corporates were demanding foreign currency to meet their external obligations. Both these factors caused the rupee to depreciate.

Now looking at the real channel the picture is quiet clearer. The United States, European Union and the middle East, which account for three quarters of India's goods and services trade, are in a synchronized down turn. Hence, the crisis follows direct effect on the economy through a downfall in demand for exports. For example, service export growth is showing a slowdown as the recession is strengthening its roots.

As explained above that the crisis also spread through confidence channel. Whenever a global crisis enters the market it creates havoc over consumers and investors regarding their spending practices because of the general setback to confidence. Increasing unemployment further enhance the impact on consumer spending. Nevertheless the tightened global liquidity situation in the period immediately after the Lehman failure in September 2008, increased the risk aversion of the financial system. Banks, in such a situation, would like to hoard capital or will lend at a steep price.

When the crisis broke, there was a general perception that the Indian economy is less likely to be affected. But the above discussion makes it clear that despite very low exposure, of the Indian financial institutions, to the crisis, India has been affected through the external shocks and domestic vulnerabilities from all the channels. And this necessitated our government and central authorities to get into action with their competing policies to prevent the economy from indulging deep into this recession contagion.

INDIAN'S POLICY RESPONSE FOR CURBING DOWN THE CRISIS

The global financial crisis combined with the looming risk of recession have led to calls for dramatic policy interventions, including coordinated interest rate cuts, bailouts for the banking sector, and large fiscal stimulus packages. The global financial crisis in the second half of the financial year changed the focus of Indian fiscal policy from achieving the targets under the Fiscal Responsibility and Budget Management (FRBM) Act to providing a growth stimulus. However, recognizing the depth and extra ordinary impact of this crisis, the central government launched two fiscal stimulus packages in December 2008 and January 2009. These stimulus packages, together amounting to about 3 percent of GDP, included additional public spendings, particularly capital expenditure, government guaranteed funds for infrastructure spending, cuts in indirect taxes, expanded guarantee cover for credit to micro and small enterprises and additional support to exporters. These packages came on top of an already announced expanded safety-net for rural poor, a farm loan waiver package and salary increase for government staff, all of which too should stimulate demand.

The country is facing difficult economic situation, the cause of which is not emanating from within its boundaries. However, our government had two policy options before it. In view of falling buoyancy in tax receipts, the government could have taken a decision to cut expenditure and thereby live within the estimated deficit for the year. The second option was to increase public expenditure, even with reduced receipts, to stimulate economy by creating demand and maintain the growth trajectory which the country was witnessing in the recent past. The government took the second option of increasing public expenditure to boost demand and increase investment in infrastructure sector.

Now looking at the other side of the coin, the monetary measures. For competing the situation major monetary policies have been came into action primarily after Lehman collapse in September 2008. Prior to that, the RBI had focused on fighting inflation and had adopted measures that contributed to tightening rather than relaxation. The flight of capital from India as well as the drying up of dollar credit abroad meant that both rupee and dollar liquidity were tightly squeezed. The sharp depreciation of the rupee with respect to the dollar required the RBI to intervene with dollar sales and this also impacted negatively on rupee liquidity.

The principal monetary responses since October 2008 include:

(i) reduction in the repo rate from 9% to 5.5% and in the reserve repo rate from 6% to 4%;
(ii) reduction in the cash reserve ratio from 9% to 5%; and
(iii) reduction in the statuary liquidity ratio from 25% to 24%.

This was supplemented by a wide variety of measures to support liquidity, including to distressed segments of the financial system such as non-banking financial companies (NBFCs) and mutual funds.

The Reserve Bank policy response was aimed to containing the contagion from outside to keep the domestic money and credit markets functioning normally and see the liquidity stress did not trigger solvency cascade. This marked reversal of Reserve Bank's policy stance from monetary tightening to monetary easing in response to easing inflationary pressures and moderation in growth.

RBI's policy packages included both conventional and unconventional measures. The conventional side is already mentioned above in the principal monetary measures. Among the unconventional measures an important one is rupee-dollar swap facility for Indian banks, to give them comfort in managing their short-term foreign funding requirements. Others are an exclusive refinance window as also a special purpose vehicle for supporting non-banking financial companies, and expending the lendable resources available to apex finance institutions for refinancing credit extended to small industries, housing and exports.

POLICY EVALUATION

"India will be affected by the global financial meltdown, but strong fundamentals and a pro-active monetary policy management will possibly allow it to ride the crisis." World Bank.

One of the most important issues in this phase of crisis was the domestic liquidity problem and monetary conditions that has been effectively managed by RBI with the help of variety of its monetary instrument like, CRR, SLR, Reporate, refinance, Market Stabilization Scheme (MSS), and Liquidity Adjustment Facility (LAF), etc. Both, macro-prudential and micro prudential policies adopted by the RBI have ensured financial stability and resilience of the banking system. While credit expansion by private sector and foreign banks was significantly lower during 2008-09 especially to retail and small and medium enterprise (SME) borrowers, public sector banks (covering nearly 70 percent of banking assets) maintained their credit growth to employment impacting sectors such as SME, agriculture, real estate, and infrastructure. These monetary responses has been accompanied *vis-à-vis* complemented by the fiscal stimulus provided by the government of India although it appeared some what limited due to India's fiscal position.

CONCLUSION

Strong fundamentals of the Indian financial system and less exposure of its financial institutions to the outside world more or less stopped crisis contagion to corrupt the system deeply. It allowed the Indian authorities a significant play of actions for curbing down the adverse impacts of this meltdown. Although there are some direct impacts on few very important macroeconomic variables viz. rupee depreciation, decline in forex reserves, etc. and also it is well known that impact of all this was slowing down of output and employment; so the reality is that the Indian economy has already been hit quite severely, but despite these facts Indian is still the second fastest growing economy in the world. Indian policy response to the recent situation was commendable. The economy is improving at a good speed as policy packages and increased public spending have been providing new opportunities for output and employment growth. Since the crisis is not grown and advanced within the economy, but an imported one, we hope that India will soon come out of it as the globe has already been showing the signs of recovery.

REFERENCES

Bhaduri, A. (2009) 'Understanding the Financial Crisis', *Economic and Political Weekly*, March 28, 2009, Vol. XLIV, No. 13, pp. 123-25.

Crotty, James (2008) 'Structural causes of the Global Financial Crisis. A Critical Assesment of the New Financial Architecture, Political Economy Research Institute (PERI), Working Paper No. 180, Available at www.peri.umass.edu

Crotty James (2009) 'Profound Structural Flaws in the US Fianancial System that helped cause the Financial Crisis, *EPW*, March 28, 2009, Vol. XLIV, No. 13, pp. 127-35.

Chandrashekhar, C.P., and Ghosh, Jayati (2008) 'India and Global Financial

Crisis, *Business Line,* business daily from the Hindu group of publications, Tuesday October 21, 2008, available at www.hindubusinesslive.com.

'Fiscal Policy Strategy Statement,' available at http;//indiabuget.nic.in, accessed on August 20th, 2009.

Gopinath, Shyamala (2009) 'Some Reflections of the Recent Global Financial Turmoil Indian Perspective, Speech delivered by Deputy Governor, RBI, at the Annual Conference of FEDAI (Foreign Exchange Dealers, Association of India) on January 10, 2009.

Ghosh, Jayati 'The Global Financial Crisis, Developing Countries and India; 'Indian Economy can overcome Financial Crisis', World Bank, available at http;//news.in msn.com/business, accessed on March 20th, 2009.

Isard, Peter (2005) 'Globalisation and the International Financial System, whats wrong and what can be done, Cambridge University Press, 2005.

Jhun Jhunwala, Bharat (2007), 'Globalisation and Indian Economy', Kalpaz Publications, 2007.

Kapadiya, A., Jayadev, A. (2008), 'The credit crisis; where it came from, what happened, How it might end, *EPW*, December 6, 2008, pp. 33-41.

Kumar, Rajiv 'Global Financial and Economic Crisis: Impact on India and Policy Response, by Director and Chief Executive, Indian Council for Research on International Economic Relations (ICRIER), New Delhi.

Mohan, R.T.T., 'The Impact of the crisis on the Indian Economy', *EPW*, March 28, 2009, Vol. XLIV, No. 13, pp. 107-14

Mello, D.B. (2009) 'Financialisation and Tendency to stagnation, Review Article, *Economic and Political Weekly*, May 9, 2009, Vol. XLIV, No. 19, pp. 27-30.

Rakshit, M. (2009) 'India Amidst the Global Crisis', *Economic and Political Weekly*, March 28, 2009, Vol. XLIV, No. 13, pp. 94-106

Shri Yogesh Agarwal (2008), 'The Present Economic Crisis and its impact on India', speech delivered by CMD, IDBI Bank Ltd. at the Haryana Institute of public Administration, December 20, 2008.

Shang, A. (2009) 'The first Network Crisis of the 21st Century, A Regulatory Post-Mortem, *EPW*, March 28, 2009, Vol. XLN, No. 13, pp. 73-79.

Straw, Will (2008) 'The Global Meltdown', center for American Progress, December, 2008.

Subbarao D. (2009) 'Impact of the Global Financial Crisis on India. Collateral Damage and Response speech delivered in Tokyo on Feb. 18, 2009.

Thorat, Usha 'Impact of Global Financial Crisis on Reserve Bank of India (RBI) as a National Regulator.

Varghese, T., Santhosh 'Innovations for Crisis and Economic Meltdown. Implication for Growth and Economic Policy.'

Index